CW01263852

'This is a very important work which, with the usual eye for detail and ear for "silent" voices Michael Snape has, uncovers and tells a story that needs to be told widely. Sadly, as Michael himself says, much of what he has discovered has been kept quiet for all manner of reasons. It means that the life of Major General Merton Beckwith-Smith has been ignored or simply unknown by far too many for far too long.

One thread in his life was his Christian faith, which clearly shaped many of his decisions and behaviours. It is remarkable to read *Forgotten Warrior* and I commend it highly. It has enabled me to consider again some of the values and confusions that dominate in war. It has also given me a far greater insight into one particular general who, as Michael says, was a fine example of a Christian leader who navigated his way through very complex times and sadly has not been given the credit or even the simple space and time his life deserves.'

Tim Thornton, former Bishop at Lambeth and Bishop to His Majesty's Forces

'Major General Merton Beckwith-Smith was the most senior British officer to die in captivity in the Second World War. Yet, as Michael Snape eloquently reveals in this new biography, Beckwith-Smith's life (and untimely death) was more than just a tragic footnote to that global conflict.

Using the particulars of Beckwith-Smith's life and times, Snape sheds new light on the realities of combat, defeat and captivity in the age of total war. Beautifully written and deeply researched, this book is a poignant and powerful testament to the enduring importance of faith, courage and compassion to the profession of arms.'

Dr Aimée Fox, King's College London, and author of *Learning to Fight: Military Innovation and Change in the British Army, 1914–1918*

Michael Snape is the inaugural Michael Ramsey Professor of Anglican Studies at Durham University. He is an ecumenical lay canon of Durham Cathedral and the official historian of the Royal Army Chaplains' Department. His research focuses on the interplay of war and religion in the English-speaking world, and his recent books include *A Church Militant: Anglicans and the armed forces from Queen Victoria to the Vietnam War* (OUP, 2022), and *God and Uncle Sam: Religion and America's armed forces in World War II* (Boydell, 2015). He is married, has two grown-up daughters and lives in County Durham.

The Farmington Trust

This biography was commissioned by the Farmington Trust, as many of the Christian values exemplified in the life of Major-General Merton Beckwith-Smith are espoused and promoted by the Farmington Trust today. The Farmington Trust awards scholarships to teachers of religious education; to headteachers in values and standards; to senior members of the UK's armed forces in moral and ethical leadership; and to military chaplains, chaplains to young offender institutions, and to clergy engaged in pastoral ministries. The Farmington Trust also organises forums for headteachers, in which they meet and discuss educational issues of common interest; promote good practice; share useful ideas; and enable participants to benefit from a supporting and encouraging environment. The Trust also holds meetings for bishops and deans to discuss areas of mutual concern.

The Farmington Trust would like to thank Canon Professor Michael Snape, of Durham University, for writing such an interesting and well-researched biography, and Sam Richardson, CEO of SPCK, for so readily agreeing to publish this book.

Sir Ralph Waller KBE
Director of the Farmington Institute

FORGOTTEN WARRIOR

The life and times of Major-General
Merton Beckwith-Smith
1890–1942

Michael Snape

First published in Great Britain in 2023

Society for Promoting Christian Knowledge
36 Causton Street
London SW1P 4ST
www.spck.org.uk

British Library Cataloguing-in-Publication Data
A catalogue record for this book is available from the British Library

Front cover image courtesy of the Imperial War Museum, H 2827.
Back cover image courtesy of Harry Henderson.

Hardback ISBN 978–0–281–08691–7
eBook ISBN 978–0–281–08692–4

1 3 5 7 9 10 8 6 4 2

Typeset by Manila Typesetting Company
First printed in Great Britain by TJ International
Subsequently digitally printed in Great Britain

eBook by Manila Typesetting Company

Produced on paper from sustainable forests

Contents

For the officers, men and families of the 18th Division, 1939–45

Foreword

Many fine soldiers have served in the Coldstream and Welsh Guards, and both regiments have seen scores of Guardsmen earn gallantry awards. Their stories stand as eloquent testimonials to the quality of the Household Division. Less well known, however, is the unique story of Major-General Merton Beckwith-Smith, whose professionalism and powers of leadership shaped the Welsh Guards in its formative years, and served to comfort and inspire thousands of British prisoners of war after the fall of Singapore in 1942.

Very few of Britain's leaders – military or civilian – emerged with credit from the greatest defeat in British military history. Beckwith-Smith, however, who had risen to command the 18th Infantry Division, committed himself to the welfare of his 16,000 soldiers. Amidst hunger, disease and despair, he founded a divisional university and a divisional theatre, improved the care of the sick and wounded, and sought to ensure that his 'family', as he always called them, were adequately fed.

As a committed Christian, he also led in matters of the spirit by promoting religious life and supporting the work of his chaplains. His devotion to the needs of his soldiers – whether of mind, body or spirit – meant that his forcible separation from them in August 1942 was a cause of genuine sorrow and regret; emotions that turned into anger and grief on the news of his premature death in Formosa the following November.

It is rare indeed for generals to win honour in defeat, let alone admiration in captivity. Yet Beckwith-Smith – whose decisive leadership was marked by charm, humanity and compassion, and was rooted in his strong Christian faith – earned both distinctions. That his story has been obscured and forgotten is a longstanding injustice, and in commending this book I hope that Merton Beckwith-Smith will inspire future generations as a man of faith, courage and action.

Charles Guthrie
Field Marshal Lord Guthrie

Preface

Major-General Merton Beckwith-Smith DSO, MC (or, to use his full name, Merton Beckwith Beckwith-Smith) is unfamiliar even to historians of the British Army in the Second World War. Though he was among the most senior British officers to be captured at the fall of Singapore in February 1942 – the biggest capitulation in the history of the British Empire – students of this singular catastrophe have struggled to grasp his particulars and, more strangely, even his name. Sir John Smyth VC (a close contemporary who, like Merton, commanded a brigade in France in 1940 and a division, unsuccessfully, against the Japanese in 1942) referred to him after the war as 'Major-General N. Beckwith Smith'.[1] More recently, Merton has been dubbed 'Mark Beckwith-Smith',[2] and even 'Major-General Beckworth-Smith'.[3] His DSO, earned in France in 1914, has been misattributed to his actions at Dunkirk in 1940, while his contribution to 'the 18th Division's university' in Changi, very much his brainchild, has been overlooked.[4] He was not even mentioned in a 1991 biography of Lieutenant-Colonel (later Brigadier) Philip Toosey, who distinguished himself on the Burma Railway – though Toosey was, as we shall see, something of a protégé.[5] More understandably, given the confusion over his whereabouts in the last few months of his life, it has often been claimed that Merton died in Japan, or on the voyage there.[6] In fact, he died more than a thousand miles away, in Formosa, in November 1942, where he had been for two months. He was not present, as has been wrongly surmised, at the infamous Selarang Incident on Singapore Island in September 1942, nor did he perish much later in the war, in 1944.[7]

A paucity of biographers has not helped this regnant confusion. There is currently no entry for Merton in the *Oxford Dictionary of National Biography*, while Richard Mead's *Churchill's Lions*, a compendious 'biographical guide to the key British generals of World War II', tabulates his wartime career (among dozens of 'other significant generals') in the space of just five lines, where he is vaguely noted as having 'died in captivity'.[8] Perhaps echoing Napoleon's apocryphal aphorism 'Give me lucky generals', the very few commentators who have sought to appraise Merton's career have seen it solely through the prism of luck. That this narrative is rooted in the stoicism and reticence of the war years is suggested by a letter written by his eldest son, Peter, in late November 1942, in which he remarked that 'It seems an absolute tragedy that someone who had devoted his entire life to soldiering should have the misfortune he had in the end.'[9] An identical note was struck in Merton's post-war obituary in the *Household Brigade Magazine*, in which Merton's old friend Lieutenant-General Charles ('Budget') Loyd wrote: 'In war, some are lucky and some are unlucky in varying degrees; none can have been less favoured by fortune than "Becky".'[10] Likewise, Sir John Smyth opined that Merton 'was a fine soldier who deserved better fortune than he was to experience in his few brief days of the battle for Singapore'.[11] Certainly, unlike 'Bill' Slim, Merton was never given the opportunity to redeem failure and turn 'Defeat into Victory' against the Japanese, as Slim famously styled it. And yet, as this book will show, he did enjoy a very different kind of success, albeit off the battlefield, and his merits have been widely recognized – even by those for whom the details of his life are otherwise hazy. In the verdict of Colin Smith, for example, Merton was a 'popular and efficient' commander while, according to Julie Summers, he was 'one of the best loved and respected of all the senior officers' captured at Singapore.[12]

Eighty years after his death, this book seeks to redress the apparent mismatch between Merton's acknowledged virtues and historical reputation, and to demonstrate his significance as a professional soldier and, in the direst of circumstances, as a remarkable leader. It also foregrounds the Christian faith that underpinned his personal life as well as his military career, a faith that helped him to rally the spirits of his 16,000 soldiers despite acute privation, unfathomable adversity and his own (albeit well-concealed) dismay, doubts and confusion.

Maps

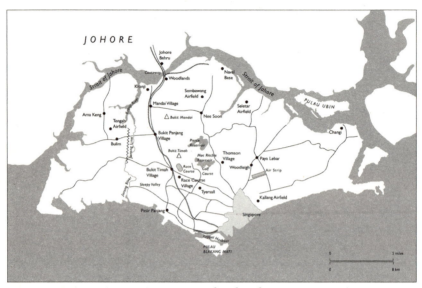

Figure 1 Singapore Island, February 1942

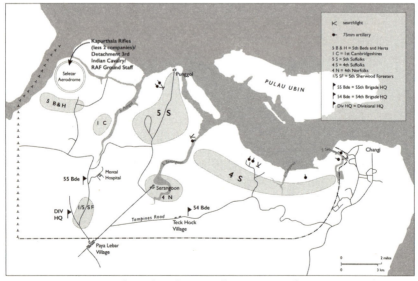

Figure 2 54th and 55th Brigade sectors, February 1942

x

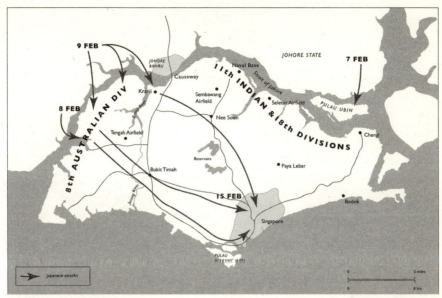

Figure 3 The Japanese invasion of Singapore, 8–15 February 1942

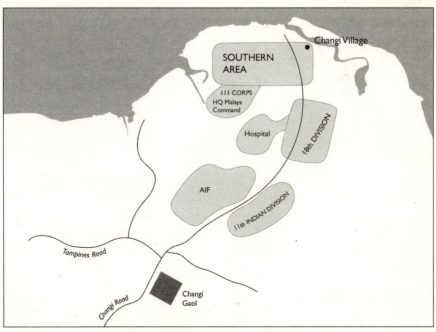

Figure 4 POW areas, Changi, March 1942

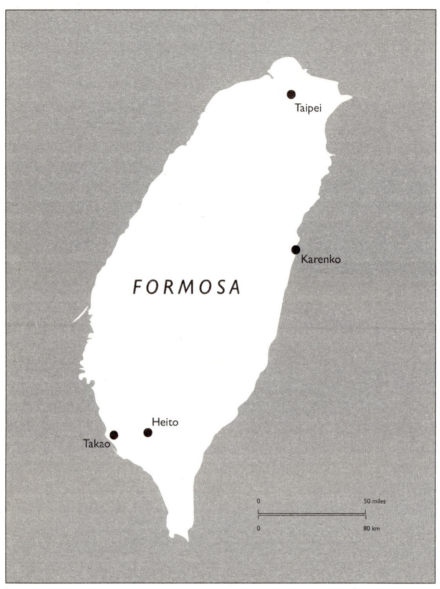

Figure 5 Formosa in 1942

List of illustrations

List of abbreviations

AA and QMG	Assistant Adjutant and Quartermaster General
ABCA	Army Bureau of Current Affairs
ADC	aide-de-camp
AIF	Australian Imperial Force
ATS	Auxiliary Territorial Service
BEF	British Expeditionary Force
CAB	Cabinet Office
CB	Companion of the Order of the Bath
CIGS	Chief of the Imperial General Staff
CO	commanding officer
CRA	Commander Royal Artillery
CRE	Commander Royal Engineers
DSO	Distinguished Service Order
GHQ	General Headquarters
GOC	General Officer Commanding
GSO	General Staff Officer
IJA	Imperial Japanese Army
INA	Indian National Army
IWM	Imperial War Museum
KCB	Knight Commander of the Order of the Bath
KG	Knight of the Order of the Garter
MC	Military Cross
MO	medical officer
NAAFI	Navy, Army and Air Force Institutes
NCO	non-commissioned officer
OBE	Officer of the Order of the British Empire
ODNB	*Oxford Dictionary of National Biography*

OTC	Officers' Training Corps
POW	prisoner of war
PT	Physical Training
RA	Royal Artillery
RAChD	Royal Army Chaplains' Department
RAMC	Royal Army Medical Corps
RAOC	Royal Army Ordnance Corps
RASC	Royal Army Service Corps
RE	Royal Engineers
RMP	Royal Military Police
RSM	Regimental Sergeant Major
TA	Territorial Army
TEWT	Tactical Exercise Without Troops
TNA	The National Archives
VC	Victoria Cross
WO	War Office
WVS	Women's Voluntary Services

Author's note

With respect to sources, this book relies primarily on the papers of Merton Beckwith-Smith, now held by different members of his extended family. Amidst the Covid pandemic, the main series (listed as MBS/1 in the bibliography) was provided in digital form by John Beckwith-Smith, and the numbers refer to PDFs in that collection. The second series (MBS/2) is a much smaller body of digitized material later supplied by Harry Henderson, who also provided transcriptions of the letters that comprise MBS/3. Finally, Lucy Woodd kindly contributed electronic copies of the material which comprises MBS/4. In terms of style, and in the interests of clarity, I have amended the punctuation in some private correspondence and have expanded abbreviations and acronyms where appropriate. In my use of quotations, and to underline the racial character of the Second World War in the Far East, an aspect of the conflict perceived and rehearsed by the Allies and the Japanese alike, I have retained the racialized language of the era. Finally, with respect to terminology, I have refrained from referring to the subject of this biography as 'Becky', preferring instead to call him Merton.

In keeping with documents from the time, military ranks have been rendered both as 'Major General' and 'Major-General', 'Lieutenant Colonel' and 'Lieutenant-Colonel', 'Second Lieutenant' and 'Second-Lieutenant'.

1

'Second to none' – the Coldstream Guards

On 30 April 1889 Mr Beckwith Beckwith-Smith married Mrs Burton R. P. Persse (née Georgina Butler Moore) at St Paul's, Knightsbridge. It was a suitably impressive and fashionable affair, the church having 'a most pleasing appearance', being 'beautifully decorated with the choicest white blooming plants'. In terms of the ceremony, 'the bride was given away by her brother-in-law, Colonel Webber-Smith', the best man was Captain the Honourable George Bryan of the 10th Hussars, and the marriage was solemnized by the groom's brother, the Revd Oswald Smith, assisted by the bride's brother-in-law, Canon Aldridge, and the Revd E. Ker Gray, of St George's Chapel in Albemarle Street. After the reception, at the Alexandra Hotel, Hyde Park, the couple departed 'for a lengthened tour on the Continent amid the congratulations of their many friends and relatives'.[1] It seemed, as was no doubt intended, to be a quintessential society wedding.

However, this appearance was somewhat deceptive. For, on the bride's side, Canon Aldridge was vicar of the obscure Church of Ireland parish of Eyrecourt, County Galway, while Webber-Smith was a lieutenant-colonel in the South Staffordshire Regiment (which, as a run-of-the-mill county regiment, could not compare in social terms with the swanky 10th Hussars).[2] Georgina, in other words, had (re-)married well. First married, aged 23, in February 1885 to Burton R. P. Persse of Moyode Castle, County Galway, her much older husband (a Justice of the Peace, former High Sheriff of the county, renowned huntsman, and father of 11 children) died 'from rheumatic fever', apparently brought on by a hunting accident, the following May.[3] How the widowed Georgina came to meet her second husband, with whom she enjoyed an affectionate and enduring marriage, is not known, but that she rather 'married up' when they tied the knot at St Paul's, Knightsbridge,

1

seems clear enough. Beckwith Beckwith-Smith, a bachelor aged 39, came from minor gentry stock and was a highly successful stockbroker.[4] With an affability that seems to have matched his acumen in the City, and while keeping a comfortable home in London, Beckwith rose from being the tenant of Glynde Place, an impressive Tudor pile in East Sussex, to being owner and laird of Aberarder in Inverness-shire. Having purchased this property in 1900 for £19,875 from the Standard Life Assurance Company (in a sale that was later, unsuccessfully, contested by its previous owner), on his death in 1926 Beckwith left an estate valued at just over £127,000.[5]

Merton Beckwith-Smith was born just over a year into their marriage, on 11 July 1890, and he was followed by a sister, Muriel (or Cissy), in 1891. They were the couple's only children. Besides their mutual love of hunting, shooting and horses, Merton inherited other traits from each of his parents. From his father, with whom he appears to have had an affectionate if somewhat distant relationship, he acquired a geniality and charm that marked him out throughout his adult life, for (even allowing for the generosity of posthumous encomiums) Beckwith was mourned on his Aberarder estate as 'a most kindly and courteous gentleman, most generous, and ever ready to help any cause that was for the good or improvement of the strath'.[6] From Georgina, who outlived him by six weeks, dying on Christmas Day 1942, Merton imbibed a personal piety and strong ambition that she encouraged, as we shall see, throughout his life. Like many of the Protestant, Anglo-Irish gentry, she was sprung from military stock (Georgina's antecedents, the Eyres of Eyrecourt, had fought against Napoleon, under Simón Bolívar in South America, and in the Crimea), and, in manner reminiscent of Douglas Haig's moral and religious formation at the hands of a devoutly Presbyterian mother,[7] it was Georgina's simple Protestant piety that set the tone for Merton's personal faith, at least until his capture by the Japanese in 1942. Indeed, besides their love of field sports, Georgina had this in common with her first husband, Burton R. P. Persse, who was described in one obituary as 'a most religious man':

A profane word was never heard from his lips, and his name was never mentioned in connection with an unlawful deed. On the contrary, he was most attentive to his religious duties, and, as far as the human eye could see no man could be more just and upright.[8]

2

Furthermore, through her eldest child and only son, Georgina strove assiduously to promote her family's standing in the world, overcoming the parvenu image which came (inevitably if implicitly) with the social handicaps of their Irish gentry background – an impediment even for the Duke of Wellington, and famously caricatured in Thackeray's rumbustious novel *The Luck of Barry Lyndon* – and newly made money.

In 1896, Merton penned his first surviving correspondence. Addressed to 'Grannie Moore' in Ireland, and written on behalf of himself and Cissy, his first epistolary effort read: 'DARLING GRANNIE i AM writing to you it is my first attempt at a letter cissy hopes you are very well and so do I Both send our Best love.'[9] His formal schooling, however, began at Warren Hill School, a preparatory and boarding school in Eastbourne, Sussex, where he was resident by 1901.[10] Only a few miles from his childhood home at Glynde Place, here Merton was prepared for life at Eton College, one of England's oldest and most prestigious public schools. Founded by King Henry VI in 1440, by the outbreak of war in 1914 Eton had the distinction of having Prince Henry, the third son of King George V, among its pupils – the first son of a reigning British monarch to be schooled rather than tutored.[11] Nevertheless, Etonians of Merton's earlier, Edwardian generation were typically 'the sons of clergymen, bankers, peers and businessmen',[12] and, as John Lewis-Stempel has indicated, most of Merton's peers were no doubt very like himself:

> In truth, British public schools were not congregations of boys of good breeding. Outside of Eton, Harrow and Winchester, few of the 150 or so Edwardian schools in the Headmasters' Conference – membership of which constituted the definition of public school status – drew their intake from the aristocracy, or even the cream of the landed gentry. The prospective parents clamouring at the wrought iron gates or oaken door were the professional classes – doctors, army and navy officers – and successful businessmen ... All one needed was money.[13]

If 'many an Edwardian gent in a country house was only a generation or two away from the counting house via Charterhouse',[14] as the distinguished military historian Sir Michael Howard (a Wellingtonian) remarked, 'the English upper classes traditionally made up for the comfort of their background and the privileges of their station by ten years of misery at boarding-school.'[15]

However, and if nothing else, the austere, all-male culture of England's public schools was for generations an ideal preparation for military leadership. Advertised by the many training corps established from the mid-Victorian period, their Classical curriculum and emphasis on physical fitness, courage, team spirit and public service all helped to underpin their military culture. Eton, though, had a more accentuated military tradition than most. Perhaps the most famous Old Etonian of the nineteenth century was the Duke of Wellington and, by the turn of the twentieth century, 'dense populations of Old Etonians' filled the officers' messes of the most fashionable (or 'smartest') regiments of the British Army, namely the Guards, the cavalry and the Rifles.[16] In 1882, Lady Elizabeth Butler, the foremost British military artist of her day, underlined the vigour of Eton's military tradition in her painting *Floreat Etona!*, which depicted the death of Lieutenant Robert Elwes, of the Grenadier Guards, at the Battle of Laing's Nek the previous year. More than a decade before the outbreak of the First World War, almost 1,500 Old Etonians had served in the South African War, where one in ten of them had died.[17] However, and after the reforms initiated by Thomas Arnold at Rugby School, the moving and overarching spirit in England's public schools was a vigorous and eminently practical Christianity. Typically 'light on doctrine and ritual, heavy on ethics', it buttressed their military character by exalting courage, self-sacrifice and self-restraint, together with a strong sense of *noblesse oblige*.[18] With Anglican clergymen dominating the Headmasters' Conference and community life centred on daily (sometimes twice-daily) chapel attendance,[19] the pervasive spirit of the public schools was that of 'Christian manliness' (or 'muscular Christianity'), and their characteristic product was generations of paternalistic 'Christian Gentlemen' – physically, intellectually and morally equipped to serve monarch, nation and Empire.[20]

Merton (a tough but diminutive figure, notable for his red hair) was an archetypal product of this system and, on 6 December 1909, shortly after matriculating at Oxford, he had a very public opportunity to show what Eton had done for him. For, while out hunting with the Southdown Foxhounds:

4

Mrs. Reginald Parker, of Ryders Wells, Ringmer, got into difficulties in crossing the flooded river [Uck] and was in imminent danger of being drowned when she was rescued in an exhausted condition by young Mr. Merton Beckwith-Smith (son of the gentleman now residing at Glynde Place), and [William] Wood, the second whip.[21]

The following February, as reported in the *Morning Post*, it was 'the pleasing duty of the lady – who was more grateful to her rescuers than words could express – to present them with the Royal Humane Society's vellum certificate', termed by her husband 'the V.C.'s of the hunting field'. In a faltering speech, Mr Reginald Parker expressed his relief that 'England still breeds sons with courage to dare and presence of mind to act in sudden emergencies of great peril'.[22] In response:

> In a short, but manly speech, Mr. Merton Beckwith-Smith thanked Mrs. Parker with all his heart for that which he should value throughout his life. He thanked Mr. Parker for his kind words and assured Mrs. Parker that he was glad to have rendered the assistance he did, and he felt any other member of the Hunt would have done as he did. He only hoped Mrs. Parker would soon be in the hunting field again.[23]

However, in a telling indication of the social dynamics of this presentation, 'the Master [of hounds] stepped up and returned thanks on behalf of Wood, who was also presented with a gold scarf-pin – in the shape of a horseshoe with a solid gold fox on it'.[24]

Letters of congratulation flowed in from all quarters. One Alice Brand, of Little Dene near Lewes, for example, wrote to say that 'It was quite wonderful how Merton held Mrs Parker up with one arm, holding himself up with a branch',[25] while Lonsdale Duncan, hitherto unknown to Georgina, wrote to her from the Union Club in Brighton:

> I am a stranger [but] I must however write to congratulate you on your boy. He was perfectly splendid today in the appalling accident to Mrs. Parker. For a young boy his presence of mind, and promptitude were wonderful, and Mrs. Parker certainly owes her life, as much to him as to any one. You have every reason to be proud of him.

I hope he himself will not have any bad effects upon his great ducking and the terrible strain on him. *My daughter is looking forward with great pleasure to her visit to you on Friday* [my italics]. Apologising for writing.[26]

From Merton's former housemaster at Eton, R. S. De Havilland, came an encomium addressed to Merton himself:

My dear Merton, I hear that you performed a very gallant action out hunting the other day with the South Down [*sic*]. It was a very great pleasure to hear of, and we send you our best congratulations. It is a good omen for the future and I assure you I was very glad indeed and very proud to hear of it. I am sure your people were too. I was very sorry not to see you at the end of the term, though you did make up for the Old Boy by coming down. We were knocked out of the House and Lower Boy Cup . . . it is a sad result after all these years . . .[27]

However, four days later, on 12 December, De Havilland also wrote to Georgina:

Very many thanks for your letter. I read extracts from it to the boys after prayers last night. I thought the occasion demanded it. Please thank Merton very much for his letter and also Becky (I must call him that to you) for his . . . Also very many thanks for the invitation . . . It would be very nice to come to Glynde and I hope sincerely an opportunity will come, with very kind regards and congratulations to you all again.[28]

Though Merton matriculated in 1909, he appears to have spent little time at Christ Church and did not take his degree. When the decennial census was taken in 1911, he was listed as a second lieutenant in the Coldstream Guards at Victoria Barracks, Windsor.[29] That same year, he took a riding class with the Royal Horse Guards.[30] According to his regimental record of service, Merton entered the Army direct from university and did not attend the Royal Military College at Sandhurst, which by this time had become 'the main route' to a commission in the infantry and cavalry regiments of the British (and Indian) armies.[31] Still, there were several ways in which a commission could be obtained, and from 1905 to the outbreak of war in 1914 the Guards ran 'their own probationary officer scheme', ostensibly because the expense of serving in the Guards acted as a deterrent for Sandhurst cadets.[32] Probationers were nominated by senior Guards officers and, if they passed their military apprenticeship, which included two exams in military subjects, they would receive a regular commission.[33] Evidently, the chance of a commission in the Coldstream Guards was too good for Merton (or his parents – and these were often family decisions, given the costs involved) to let slip.[34] As Gary Sheffield has remarked: 'For a son to be commissioned into a smart regiment was tangible evidence of the social arrival of a family, and the son would be keen to conform and to be accepted as an officer and a gentleman.'[35] Whatever else, the decision to leave Oxford and eschew Sandhurst was not dictated by cost. Such were their modest rates of pay that *all* Army officers required a private income of some kind, while the fees of a Sandhurst cadet whose father was classed as a 'private gentleman' were £150 per annum, a minor sum in comparison to the costs of 'uniforms, mess bills, servants' wages, horses and personal weapons' for an officer in the Brigade of Guards.[36]

Clearly, Merton was deemed just the sort of young gentleman the Coldstream Guards were looking for, his credentials helped by his family's wealth, a public school education ('an almost essential rite of passage' for any officer),[37] his status as an Old Etonian and his recent award from the Royal Humane Society. The fact that he had also been initiated as a Freemason into Apollo University Lodge while at Oxford in February 1910 was also to his advantage (the Craft was so strong in the Foot Guards that a Household Brigade Lodge had been formed in 1896 and the Guards Division went on to adopt the masonic symbol of the 'All Seeing Eye' as its insignia in 1916).[38] And Merton did not disappoint. Commissioned a second lieutenant on probation on 3 August 1910, his regular commission was dated 1 August 1912 and he was subsequently posted to the regiment's 1st Battalion.[39]

In joining the Coldstream Guards, Merton was joining more than a picturesque ensemble of Household troops. Immensely jealous of their regiment's prestige and pedigree (the regimental motto was *Nulli Secundus*, or 'Second to None'), as late as 1944 its officers were solemnly warned that the regiment's proper name was 'His Majesty's Coldstream Regiment of Foot Guards'; that it had never been commonly known as the '2nd Guards' (whereas the Grenadiers were widely known as the '1st Guards', and the Scots as '3rd Guards'); and that:

> It should be noted that the expression COLDSTREAMS is never used either in reference to the Regiment or to a number of members of the Regiment. The Regiment should always be referred to either as 'The Coldstream Guards' or merely 'The Coldstream' and individual members as the 'Coldstreamers'.[40]

A self-consciously English regiment, it had large charitable funds at its disposal for the benefit of Coldstreamers and their families past and present, and its officers were eligible to be married in the venerable Guards Chapel, admission to which was tightly regulated.[41] However, underneath this carapace of custom and tradition, the Coldstream remained an elite fighting regiment. The health of the monarch was never drunk in a Coldstream mess – such gestures of loyalty being superfluous – and, as Michael Howard remembered of typical Coldstream officers:

> Their function was to fight, and when not fighting to hunt, shoot, gamble, drink and generally engage in traditional warrior pastimes as their forbears had done for generations . . . Most had been to Eton, and many were interrelated over many generations. Cowardice or misbehaviour – 'putting up a black' – would thus taint them for life, so it simply did not happen.[42]

Happy in this milieu, Second Lieutenant Beckwith-Smith greeted Britain's declaration of war on Germany on 4 August 1914 with enthusiasm. The family steward at Glynde Place wrote to Beckwith, now at Aberarder, three days later:

> I had a very nice letter from Mr Merton this morning. He seems anxious to get to the front. I do hope he will come home safely. We both think of you and Mrs Beckwith in this anxious time and trust to God all will be well.[43]

Five days later, a family friend, 'Bobby' White, reported that he had been part of a party that had motored out to Aldershot to see Merton, whom he found 'looking so nice and fresh, well, cheery and hearty, and working away like mad'. Furthermore, he enthused, 'The whole Division at Aldershot is most magnificent, and starts for the war ready and equipped in every sense, as fine a body of men as there are in Europe.'[44] Britain's official historian of the war on the Western Front, Sir James Edmonds, agreed, writing that 'in every respect the Expeditionary Force of 1914 was incomparably the best trained, best organized, and best equipped British Army which ever went forth to war'.[45]

On 13 August, at Southampton, the 1st Coldstream embarked for France on the SS *Dunvegan Castle* as part of the 1st (Guards) Brigade of the 1st Division, the senior battalion in an elite brigade that also comprised the 1st Battalion of the Scots Guards, the 1st Battalion of the Black Watch and, until it was overwhelmed in a valiant rearguard action at Étreux on 27 August, the 2nd Battalion of the Royal Munster Fusiliers.[46] As a friend, Blanche Gibbs, the mother of a fellow officer, reassured Georgina on 12 August, the tight-knit world of the pre-war regiment would help see their sons through their coming ordeal: 'The 1st Battalion goes off at break of dawn tomorrow (Thursday) . . . Merton has gone abroad with a Battalion full of friends.'[47]

This was not to last long, however. Disembarking at Le Havre on 14 August, the battalion proceeded to the Belgian border, which it crossed on 23 August, by train and by hard marching. By the following day it was caught up in the long and storied retreat from Mons, fighting at Étreux on 27 August and retreating southward, towards Paris, until it reached Coulommiers, in the Île-de-France, on 5 September.[48] The following day, as part of Marshal Joffre's vast counteroffensive on the Marne, the battalion (together with the rest of the British Expeditionary Force (BEF)) began its advance to the north-east, pursuing the retreating Germans until it reached the River Aisne a week later. With the Germans now dug in on the high ground behind the river, and possessing a much greater weight of artillery, there the BEF ground to a halt, its momentum sapped by 'the utter exhaustion of men and horses [and] the impact of cold, wet weather on tired men'.[49] Amidst the stalemate on the Aisne, trench warfare began in earnest, the dominance of German artillery resulting in nearly 20,000 British casualties between 12 September and 3 October.[50]

Inevitably, given the nature of the hard but mobile fighting of these first weeks of the war, and the postal chaos that ensued, Merton remained uncommunicative, a situation that caused a fretful Georgina (who wrote a series of letters at this time)[51] to seek information about her son wherever it could be found. On 13 September, for example, a correspondent wrote from Norwich informing her that she had spoken to a wounded officer of the 12th Lancers, which had been close to the Guards, and that another officer had told her that 'a great many packages sent out to our boys never come to hand. Everybody is so continually on the move.'[52] A fortnight later, a Nigel Law of the Foreign Office wrote to say that:

My mother saw Mrs Bertie Studd today and she had just heard from her husband Major Studd [second in command of the 1st Coldstream] to say that Merton was quite well and that 'he had done extremely well'. She asked me to write and tell you to say, at the same time, that such praise from her husband means a good deal.[53]

It was, no doubt, scant consolation at the time that Law, together with other friends and contemporaries of Merton (civilian, naval and military), were prone to say how jealous they were of him being at the Front.[54] However, amidst trying rumours of severe Coldstream casualties,[55] fears and worries over Merton's safety and whereabouts were dispelled in spectacular fashion by news of his exploits on the Aisne. According to the war diary of the 1st Coldstream:

During this period [28 September – 14 October] the 1st Battalion Coldstream Guards held a front with 2 Companies remaining [and] 2 Companies in Support (in dug-outs). Reliefs were carried out every night. The daily bombardment was not usually directed at the trenches which suffered only slightly – the bulk of the German shells being directed against our Artillery or Communications in rear.

The weather being invariably good:

On October 4th 1914 one platoon of No. 2 Company led by 2/lt. M.B. Smith rushed with the bayonet and cleared an advanced German trench within 100 [yards] of our line. This was extremely well carried out and completely successful.[56]

Significantly, the trigger for this action was a change of command for 1st (Guards) Brigade. At the end of September, Brigadier-General Ivor Maxse, a Coldstreamer, was recalled to England to take command of a New Army (or 'Kitchener') Division and was replaced by Brigadier-General Charles FitzClarence of the Irish Guards. A supremely combative officer who had been awarded the Victoria Cross (VC) for his role in the defence of Mafeking, there FitzClarence had distinguished himself leading trench raids against the Boer positions and, in the siege-like conditions he found on the Aisne, he deduced that similar measures were now required, especially with regard to a series of forward entrenchments covered by 'one long trench shaped like a fish hook'.[57] As FitzClarence stated the rationale for the raid: 'These [German] trenches are very close to our main line of trenches and are probably observation posts for the enemy's Artillery. I considered it a necessary duty to attack them.'[58]

It was no doubt significant that Merton's platoon was chosen for the early evening raid, a selection that would seem to bear out reports that he had already attracted the favourable attention of his superiors. He had, furthermore, reconnoitred the position on the night of 3 October, apparently crawling out 'twice towards the German lines to find out what he could, which was not very much'.[59] According to the orders for the raid, the attacking platoon of 50 men was to form up at 7.30 p.m. on 4 October and advance at 8.00, the Guardsmen (lightly equipped with only 'bandoliers, rifle and bayonet') keeping low in the darkness and making for the centre of Fish Hook Trench. This was to be 'taken with the bayonet' and, once carried, the platoon would advance to take the second trench. A further party comprising 30 men (including some Royal Engineers and equipped with shovels and rifles) would, if Merton thought it 'practicable', then advance to 'fill in the nearest trench'. All the attackers would return to their trenches with a 'blast on the whistle' and the password to be used would be 'Coldstream'. Careful preparation was essential:

The Plan of attack will be explained carefully to all ranks and the whole operation will be carried out in absolute silence and

the position of the moon at the time of the advance and any land
mark likely to help men in keeping their direction both in advancing
and returning will be pointed out to them.[60]

Widely recognized as 'the first British trench raid of the war',[61] it was to
set a costly pattern of trench-raiding that would endure throughout the
war (and, moreover, would be a key feature of R. C. Sherriff's celebrated
1928 play *Journey's End*). Despite the undoubted courage of the attackers,
and the spirit of aggression on display, it did not go entirely according to
plan. As the commanding officer of the 1st Coldstream, now Major Leslie
Hamilton, put it in his report:

> The first trench was occupied without any opposition and was found to
> be empty. About 15 Germans were lying dead in this trench probably
> killed by shell fire and our snipers on the 4th. After a short pause the
> advance was continued towards the second trench about 70 yards distant
> from the first, when about half-way to this trench a few shots were fired
> and Second Lieutenant M. Beckwith Smith gave the order to charge.
>
> The officer led the charge and reached the trench first, closely
> followed by his platoon.
>
> They jumped into the trench and bayonetted and shot all the
> Germans in it, about 20 in all.
>
> Second Lieutenant M. B. Smith was knocked down in the struggle and
> shot through the Arm [but] Lance-Corporal Russell bayonetted the two
> Germans who were attacking the officer, thereby saving the officer's life.
>
> Fire was then opened by the Germans from a third trench and
> strong reinforcements were seen coming up.
>
> Having complied with the first part of the orders issued to him, i.e.
> to take the first two trenches, it became evident that it would now be
> impossible to fill in the first trench; Second Lieutenant Smith, therefore,
> gave the order to withdraw to our trenches, in accordance with the
> orders he had received.
>
> This withdrawal was successfully accomplished.[62]

The Coldstream's casualties amounted to eight wounded (including
Merton) and two missing, presumed killed. Given that the mission was

undertaken at night, with the attackers unpractised and denied even the benefit of hand grenades, it was not an exorbitant price to pay for a defiant display of offensive spirit.

Although it failed to eliminate the threat posed by 'Fish Hook Trench', the indomitable FitzClarence pronounced the affair, which he had originated, 'entirely successful'.[63] Though this was disingenuous, FitzClarence was clearly more concerned with the morale than with the tactical value of the raid, and awards (with their attendant publicity) duly followed. Widely rumoured before its confirmation,[64] Merton's appointment as a companion of the Distinguished Service Order (DSO) was approved on 9 November 1914 and gazetted four days later, his citation reading:

> On the night of October the 4th, near Vendresse, with a party of 50 men, he attacked and carried with the bayonet the advanced German trenches, disabling 20 of the enemy, and displayed great enterprise and coolness in this operation, in which he was wounded.[65]

Although the creation of the Military Cross (MC) (for officers) and the Military Medal (for other ranks) in December 1914 begs the question of whether Merton would have been awarded the MC for this action had it occurred later in the conflict,[66] his was the first DSO to be awarded to the Coldstream Guards since the outbreak of war,[67] it led to an inundation of messages of congratulation to Georgina ('You must be the happiest woman in England', as Katharine Fitzroy wrote on 10 November),[68] and it provided good copy for a British public hungry for good news, particularly as casualties mounted and the prospects of a lengthy war grew. Indeed, news of Merton's award (and, on occasion, Lance-Corporal Russell's Distinguished Conduct Medal) was published in organs ranging from the *Aberdeen Daily Journal* to the *Times of India* (and, of course, by the *Daily Mail*).[69]

Merton was fortunate in other respects, too. Badly wounded on the Aisne in October 1914, he would not return to France until March the following year, by which time he had been mentioned in despatches (in December) and had escaped the catastrophic bloodletting that was the First Battle of Ypres, which raged from mid-October to mid-November. Such was the ferocity of the fighting involved in halting the German push against this gateway to the Channel ports – and the last Belgian city in Allied hands – that Ypres became the graveyard of the original BEF. By mid-November, despite a flow of replacements, the 1st Division had been reduced to fewer than 3,000 men, and the 1st (Guards) Brigade, now incorporating the 1st Cameron Highlanders, to fewer than 300. Notable casualties included FitzClarence himself, who was killed leading a trench raid on 12 November.[70] On 29 October, Merton's battalion lost *all* its remaining frontline officers in the fighting around Gheluvelt, its 80 survivors being commanded by its quartermaster, Lieutenant Jock Boyd. The two replacement officers it then received had become casualties by 2 November.[71] Faced with this ghastly toll, Merton's correspondents in France were full of foreboding. On 3 November, Lancelot Merivale Gibbs (or 'Lags'), the transport officer of the 2nd Coldstream Guards, described conditions as 'awful',[72] while Fiennes Cornwallis of the 17th Lancers, another friend from Eton on his way to the front with Indian Expeditionary Force A,[73] wrote towards the end of that month:

Almost everybody we know seems to have been either killed or wounded. One feels almost ashamed of having not got there yet, but I expect we shall soon have had enough of it, once we get there. I am no fire-eater for one, and feel very little desire at present to face a German bullet.[74]

Friends of Georgina's wrote of their relief, even envy, that Merton was a convalescent in England. On 10 November, one wrote that Merton was well out of the 'hell out there' and hoped 'that his convalescence will be a very long one'.[75] Another remarked, far too optimistically as it turned out, 'What a fortunate mother you are – your son home and his soldiering days done and finished and his laurels gained.'[76] In the 1st Coldstream Guards, what 'friends' survived were unequivocal. When his former soldier servant wrote to Georgina on 19 January 1915, thanking her for a Christmas box of cigars, he emphasized that 'I hope for his sake he doesn't come out here just yet.'[77] 'Lags' was more practical, writing on 16 November: 'Get well quickly and I should go on the staff of [Kitchener's] army, it is safer.'[78]

On 11 March 1915, his convalescence complete, Merton (who had been promoted to lieutenant in December) returned to France. There he became adjutant of the 1st Coldstream four days later, a role in which he developed his nascent talent for staff work. In view of the loss of so many pre-war officers, and with the preparation of a celebrated raid to his credit, Merton was an obvious choice for this key administrative role, which he discharged until the end of August. Among the many duties associated with this notoriously 'demanding job', which involved a litany of personnel and administrative matters, was keeping the battalion's war diary, which he diligently wrote in his distinctive, rather spidery hand.[79] And, at this point, competent staff officers, whose fundamental function was the complex and critical business of 'orders and plans',[80] were in chronically short supply. In the first weeks of the war, the number of staff officers in the BEF stood at just over 40; by the end of 1915, and with the vast growth in the size and complexity of the Army, this had risen to more than 300.[81] For those with an aptitude for staff work, a battalion adjutancy was natural preparation for the assumption of a formal staff role at brigade level and above, a role often learned through an apprentice-type system.[82]

By the end of August 1915, and by now a captain, Merton was deemed sufficiently competent and intelligent (unsurprisingly, university men often found themselves 'earmarked for the staff')[83] to assume the role of Staff Captain with the 2nd (Guards) Brigade. The business of the Staff Captain was essentially that of logistics, involving (in the words of one contemporary) 'an enormous amount of work . . . with no excitement to enlighten it'. From this position Merton progressed in July 1916 to become brigade major of the 1st (Guards) Brigade. Judged by Bernard Montgomery (a brigade major at the same time) to be 'the most interesting of all Staff jobs', this was focused on operations, intelligence and personnel, with the crafting of clear and comprehensive orders a crucially important skill. In August 1917, Merton was promoted to General Staff Officer Grade 2 (GSO 2) of the Guards Division, which had formed in France two years earlier and comprised the 1st, 2nd and 3rd Guards Brigades. Here, and now raised to the temporary rank of major, Merton performed the tasks of the brigade major in the much larger world of the division, sharing his duties with a General Staff Officer Grade 1 (GSO 1).[84]

The dates of these progressions were in themselves telling: July 1916 was the opening month of the Battle of the Somme, whereas August 1917 was the initial month of the Third Battle of Ypres (or Passchendaele) – major offensives in which the Guards Division played a conspicuous (and costly) part. Mentioned in despatches for a second and a third time in November 1915 and November 1916, Merton's talents as a staff officer were further acknowledged in December 1917, when he was transferred to the General Headquarters (GHQ) of the BEF at Montreuil-sur-Mer, where he remained throughout 1918.[85] With GHQ having expanded tenfold since August 1914,[86] by the end of the war Merton was a GSO 2, and part of a staff of 21, to another Coldstreamer, Sir Ivor Maxse, now the BEF's Inspector General of Training.[87] Here, on occasion, Merton felt under-occupied, writing to Georgina on 30 June 1918: 'There is nothing much doing here for the moment yet one's days seem to be pretty full up. It takes me a long time getting about but you know I don't mind the air and the country.'[88] However, although a staff officer for most of the war, Merton's career at brigade and divisional level from 1915 to 1917 belied the wartime myth of the comfortable, chateau-based 'red tab'. As Richard Holmes put it: 'Being on the staff of a fighting formation was certainly no sinecure', and staff officers were 'by and large honest, brave and hardworking'.[89] Although staff officers laboured under the suspicion of ill-deserved decorations (the Prince of Wales' MC being a case in point),[90] Merton was awarded the MC in June 1917, a decoration usually granted for gallantry in the field and one that could be readily acquired by diligent staff officers, who were expected 'to move freely around the front lines'.[91] In September 1917, a (French) *Croix de Guerre* followed, though the reason for this award (which, like other foreign decorations, could be awarded by 'set quota') is unclear.[92]

Otherwise marked by a bout of German measles in 1917, an attack of the Spanish flu the following year, and a mysterious fall from an aeroplane,[93] Merton's war was notable for his marriage to Miss Honor Dorothy Leigh at St Margaret's, Westminster, on 14 March 1918 – exactly a week before the great German spring offensive of 1918 broke on the Western Front. His bride was the only daughter of John Blundell Leigh, of Stratton Audley, Bicester, and her maternal grandfather was the First Marquess of Abergavenny. Widely covered in the press, among the large and 'very smart' congregation were Her Highness Princess Marie-Louise of Schleswig-Holstein, a granddaughter of Queen Victoria, who signed the register, and Winston Churchill, then Lloyd George's Minister of Munitions. The marriage was solemnized by Canon Edgar Sheppard, Sub-Dean of the Chapel Royal, and by Guy Rogers, a former chaplain to the Guards on the Western Front and now the Vicar of West Ham.[94] It was, however, a source of regret that the Prince of Wales, though expected, could not attend, thus 'disappointing the pretty girls he has been dancing with on leave', as the *Daily Mirror* put it in 'To-Day's Gossip'.[95]

How Honor and Merton met is unclear, though they had common equestrian interests and (according to the *Sunday Pictorial*) she had been previously engaged to 'her cousin, Lord Alington's heir',[96] namely Captain the Honourable Gerard Philip Montagu Napier Sturt, another Old Etonian and one of Merton's contemporaries in the 1st Coldstream Guards. (Badly wounded in September 1914, the unfortunate Sturt died of his wounds on 11 November 1918.)[97] If there was a certain air of tragedy around the bride (her mother, Lady Rose Nevill, had died in 1913, which helps to account for her close relationship with Georgina),[98] their partnership was to prove a very close and happy one. Furthermore, the marriage itself (into the aristocracy, conducted in a major London church, and attended by royalty) was a major marker in the onward (and upward) march of the Beckwith-Smith family, a march that had largely relied on the character and capacities of Merton.

The experience of war, and the coming of peace, clearly had a profound effect on Merton's view of the world and of his place within it. As we shall see, it coloured his response to the foreign policy crises of the late 1930s and left him with a growing sense of being especially – and undeservedly – blessed by Providence. In July 1932, on his forty-second birthday and amidst various financial worries, he wrote to Georgina:

> Yes – indeed what blessings have been poured upon me and I can't see why – nor I daresay can a good many others! But that doesn't matter. I mean to stick to it all and to go on trying to be worthy of it.[99]

Three months later, on the anniversary of his raid on the Aisne, and his only wound of the war, he went on to reflect:

> Well, here I am with my Battalion. I must say I didn't expect to be this day 18 years ago. It seemed a pretty near shave then but just think of the thousands who went as close and a good deal closer in the four years that followed.[100]

This strong, if understated sense of the workings of Providence, together with an implicit recognition of an underlying message in the parable of the talents (Matt. 25.14–30) – to whom much is given, much is expected – framed Merton's faith and underpinned his sense of duty. Indeed, and for a devout and quietly conventional Christian, it could scarcely have been otherwise. As Anthony Seldon and David Walsh have pointed out:

> Public schoolboys were to die at almost twice the average for all those who served. Whereas some 11 per cent of those who fought overall were to die as a direct result of the fighting, the figure for public schoolboys was over 18 per cent.[101]

For Eton, with its particularly strong links with the Army, the rate of loss was higher still: of the 5,650 old boys who served, 1,157 (more than 20 per cent) were killed.[102] As for Merton's regiment, the Coldstream Guards lost 180 officers and 3,680 other ranks, killed in action or died of wounds, and the officers of the 1st Battalion suffered more than any of its other three wartime battalions, with 66 losing their lives.[103] Of these 180 Coldstream officers, no fewer than 86 were Old Etonians.[104] In retrospect, and faced with the shattering losses incurred by his generation, his class and his peers, to have emerged almost unscathed after more than four years of war – happily married, with a growing family and financially secure – seemed, to Merton, if not a miracle, then at least a very singular act of divine Providence. Indeed, Sir John Ross's three-volume regimental history of the Coldstream Guards in the war, published in 1928, underlined this fact by listing Merton as one of only six surviving Coldstream officers who had 'served continuously at the front except for short periods of service at home'.[105]

The decade following the war, though, was a quiet period in which Merton's post-war reflections crystallized and his convictions deepened – aided, no doubt, by the responsibilities of fatherhood and by a happy marriage to a strong churchwoman who had, as we shall see, presented him with a copy of the 1662 Book of Common Prayer on their engagement. Merton's eldest son, Peter Merton, was born in June 1919, three days before the signing of the Treaty of Versailles, and he was followed by Rosemary Honor in November 1920; by Sarah (as her family knew her) in January

1925; and by John Moore in June 1929.[106] In professional terms (and spared the immediate demands of the Anglo-Irish War, the occupation duties of the British Army of the Rhine, and post-war interventions in Russia, the Black Sea and the Baltic) Merton served as brigade major of the 2nd Guards Brigade from April 1919 to August 1920, following its return from Germany. Finally relinquishing his temporary rank of major, he then studied at the Staff College at Camberley from January 1921 to January 1923 and returned to the 1st Coldstream for nine months thereafter. Posted to the War Office for a year as a GSO 3 in October 1923, he returned to the battalion in 1924. Such was the undemanding rhythm of regimental life that he even had time to study at the London School of Economics for five months. Promoted to major in November 1925, Merton had to bring his London-bound existence to an end in October 1926 when he was sent to take charge of Oxford University Officers' Training Corps (OTC), with the local rank of lieutenant-colonel. Here, and based in Oxfordshire, Merton spent four years training and recruiting in a milieu that was now feeling the effects of a growing anti-war mood of internationalism and even outright pacifism (in February 1933, the Oxford Union went on to pass the hugely controversial motion that 'This house will in no circumstances fight for King and Country').[107] Nevertheless, Merton's style and personal charm appear to have won out. Subsequently, it was reported that he had been 'chosen for the highly responsible and very difficult task of commanding the Oxford University O.T.C.', where he proved successful 'because his mind is not of the rigid military type, and even the pacifist sections at Oxford regarded him as a man deserving his popularity'.[108] On his appointment to India in 1937, it was also noted that he had done 'a great deal to bring the corps up to full strength and encourage undergraduates to take Regular commissions'.[109] Evidently, these years at Oxford were viewed with approval at the War Office, and in July 1930 he was promoted to lieutenant-colonel.[110] His future in the Coldstream Guards seemed assured. However, through the intervention of a royal patron, his career was about to take a very different course.

2

The Welsh Guards and Lahore

The next major development in Merton's career occurred just weeks later, when Edward, Prince of Wales (or 'David' to his family and inner circle), wrote to the Under Secretary of State at the War Office requesting Merton's transfer from the Coldstream to the Welsh Guards. The Prince's letter also proposed that Merton be appointed the 1st Battalion's second-in-command, to replace Major P. L. M. Battye, who was due to retire that October, and that Merton 'should, if the above transfer be approved', retain his current rank of lieutenant-colonel.[1] A new regiment, having been authorized by Royal Warrant in February 1915, the Welsh Guards had been raised through direct enlistment in Wales and by the transfer of Welshmen serving in other regiments of the British Army, especially the Brigade of Guards.[2] Part of the Guards Division from its formation in August 1915 to November 1918,[3] in June 1919 this single-battalion regiment acquired its first Colonel of the Regiment (as opposed to Colonel-in-Chief, who was King George V) in the form of the popular and glamorous Prince. However, not even the regiment's patronage and status could save it from the threat of disbandment in 1920, when swingeing cuts were being made to the size and budget of the Army. In addition to the Welsh Guards, the Irish Guards were also threatened with redundancy on the grounds of expense and recruitment, but the case was weak: quickly perceived as a plot contrived by the three senior regiments of Foot Guards, and faced with vocal opposition in Wales and in Ireland (despite the ongoing Anglo-Irish War),[4] the shadow passed – 'but it was to be a long and exacting task for the young regiment to establish itself as the equal to the best of the Brigade of Guards'.[5]

On its return to Britain in 1919, and to soldiering at various stations in London District (namely Warley, Windsor, London and Aldershot), the regiment's foremost duties were ceremonial, and here the Welsh Guards (particularly after the bloodletting of 1915–18) were at a distinct disadvantage, for such duties were a relative novelty. The problem of being *in* but not yet *of* the Brigade of Guards was betrayed by telling deficiencies in turnout and drill, and even by the tendency of Guardsmen to loiter around the speakers at Hyde Park Corner.[6] The interwar years, therefore, were a period of adjustment, in which the Welsh Guards could grow into their allotted role as an elite regiment, initially (at least) with the active interest and support of star royalty. In developing this culture, a strong emphasis was placed on drill (the Welsh Guards first trooped their colours in 1928); on competitive team sports (especially rugby, football and cricket); on the regimental choir (inevitably, for a Welsh regiment); and, among the officers, on equestrian pursuits such as hunting, polo and point-to-point racing.[7]

Clearly, Merton's professional background, sporting interests and equestrian expertise made him invaluable to this long-term project of shaping the regimental life and ethos of the Welsh Guards, but his own relationship with the Prince of Wales also played a part. The origins of their unequal friendship remain obscure, but it seems likely that they met when the Prince was serving on the staff of the Guards Division in the latter months of 1915, an experience which made a deep impression on the heir to the throne. Though he basically trailed its first commander, the Earl of Cavan, and duly moved with 'Fatty' Cavan to XIV Corps in January 1916, Edward always held that: 'The Guards Division was a great club; and, if tinged with snobbishness, it was the snobbishness of tradition, discipline, perfection and sacrifice. They were the shock troops of the British Army; their prestige was purchased in blood.'[8] A disappointing 'no-show' at Merton's wedding in March 1918, the Prince attended a house party with the Beckwith-Smiths at Longleat in July 1923 and Honor proved a useful supporter of the Prince's charitable causes, notably the Prince of Wales Sea Training Hostel for Boys for the Merchant Navy, which was opened in Limehouse at a cost of £10,000.[9] The couple remained close to him during Merton's years of regimental soldiering with the Welsh Guards, with Edward's handwritten Christmas cards being addressed to 'Honor and Becky'.[10]

After his abdication in 1936, it was reported that Merton was 'a great friend of the Duke of Windsor [and] was his A.D.C. on many occasions, including that memorable day of his reign when an attempt was made on his life' – a reference to an apparent attempt to shoot Edward in

Hyde Park in July 1936, purportedly at the behest of the Italian embassy, or so the would-be assassin claimed.[11] Furthermore, and besides their mutual equestrian interests (Merton beat the Prince in 'the Brigade of Guards inter-regimental steeplechase' in March 1921),[12] they shared the same informal, patrician style. If this had disarmed Merton's potential critics at Oxford, it was very much on display at Victoria Barracks, Windsor, on St David's Day 1933 – a date which, since 1915, had been the regimental day of the Welsh Guards.[13] In addition to the customary parade and presentation of leeks, this was a showcase for the Prince's widely touted common touch. As the *Daily Telegraph* reported:

> The Prince of Wales attended the annual St. David's Day ball of the Welsh Guards at Victoria Barracks, Windsor, last night.
>
> When he entered the ballroom with the commanding officer, Lt.-Col. M.B. Beckwith-Smith and Mrs. Beckwith-Smith, he was greeted with loud cheering.
>
> A 'Paul Jones' [i.e. a mixer dance] was announced, and the Prince immediately entered into the spirit of the dance, which was repeatedly encored. Before it finally closed his Royal Highness had danced with no fewer than ten different partners, the wives and daughters of officers and non-commissioned officers . . .
>
> His Royal Highness visited the canteen during the interval, and had a long chat with some of the non-commissioned officers.
>
> When dancing was resumed he amused the company by conducting the band when they played music for a fox-trot. This was encored so many times that the Prince got tired, and declared that conducting the band was much more strenuous than dancing.
>
> At a later period in the proceedings his Royal Highness officiated as master of ceremonies and requested the band to play such tunes as 'Pack up your troubles' and 'Tipperary.' This resulted in the whole company joining with the Prince in singing these favourite war-time songs as they were dancing.
>
> Before leaving the Prince suggested that all present should form in a community dance. There was an enthusiastic response, and the Prince, with Mrs. Beckwith-Smith as partner, led off what proved to be one of the most successful numbers.[14]

Though commissioned into the Grenadier Guards in June 1914 (after a spell as a midshipman in the Royal Navy, followed by several terms at Oxford, where he did not take a degree), the popular if dilettante prince took a genuine interest in the Welsh Guards throughout his life. Indeed, he wore its uniform during the Second World War and was to claim that the colonelcy of the Welsh Guards was an office 'which meant more to him than any other'.[15] (Rather poignantly, among his prized possessions throughout his aimless, post-abdication exile were retired drums from both the Welsh and the Grenadier Guards.)[16] According to a half-centenary history of the Welsh Guards, 'From 1920 until he became King, His Royal Highness the Prince of Wales was our Colonel. He showed the keenest concern in the welfare of the Regiment and always displayed a lively interest in our activities.'[17] What Merton felt at the time about Edward's relationship with the twice-married Wallis Simpson, or about his abdication in December 1936, is unclear, but (together with Honor) he sent his congratulations on their marriage in June 1937, and a personal loyalty to his friend and patron seems to have endured.[18] Highly instrumental in Edward's abdication was the Archbishop of Canterbury, the Scottish-born Cosmo Gordon Lang, who afterwards made an ill-advised radio broadcast in which he chastised Edward for having 'sought his happiness in a manner inconsistent with the Christian principles of marriage, and within a social circle whose standards and ways of life are alien to all the best instincts and traditions of his people'.[19] In this regard it seems significant that Honor kept some doggerel 'Lines to the Archbishop of Canterbury' in her scrapbook, which ran:

My Lord Archbishop
What a scold you are
And when your man is down
How bold you are
In Christian charity how cruel you are
Oh Auld Lang Swine
How full of Cant. U-A.[20]

For his part, correspondence in the Royal Archives shows how, in the early summer of 1937, Merton organized a wedding gift of silver salvers for the now Duke and Duchess of Windsor, courtesy of the members of the Welsh Guards Club,[21] and how he also deplored the Duke's loss of his colonelcy. Although the Duke was keen to retain this cherished link with the Welsh Guards from his de facto exile in France, an aspiration which met with the approval of his brother, King George VI, this did not sit well with its officers, and the idea was quickly dropped – a development which the former king thought especially hurtful. Nonetheless, Merton wrote to Edward 'to assure him how much every Welsh Guardsman, past or present, regretted that he could not continue as their Colonel'.[22] He also subsequently wrote to his fallen patron with various regimental news and, in November 1937, to report that he had been offered command of the Lahore Brigade in India. With the Duke clearly touched by his continuing attention, it seems reasonable to surmise that Merton's obvious loyalty to the former monarch, and his distant posting to India, were not wholly unconnected.[23]

Nevertheless, there was far more to Merton's career with the Welsh Guards than cultivating the wilful and wayward Prince of Wales. Owing to the Prince's lobbying, and retaining his present rank, Merton was posted to the Welsh Guards on 14 October 1930.[24] In a departure from established norms, whereby the Foot Guards had only served at home in peacetime, the Welsh Guards had deployed to Egypt in April 1929 as part of the British Army's largest overseas garrison after India.[25] Merton joined its single battalion as second-in-command (and at his own expense) just before the end of its tour, returning from Cairo with the battalion in December 1930.[26] In October 1932, he was duly appointed its commanding officer, a role which he had essentially performed for several months. Billed as something of a catch by the regiment's half-centenary history, it recalled that: 'His mental and physical energy were boundless, his imagination vivid and his enthusiasm infectious. He was a first class shot and an accomplished horseman.'[27] More specifically, a later regimental history identified Merton's prime contribution as lying in the realm of battlefield training, complementing the emphasis on drill embodied by Regimental Sergeant Major William Stevenson: 'He took in hand the Battalion's field training, and with quiet insistence instilled the realism and skills which were to pay off so well only a few years later.'[28] This was borne out in Merton's routine annual report of 1932, in which it was stated that:

He has every reason to be proud of the strides the Battalion has made during the past year – especially in regard to its work in the field. Colonel Beckwith-Smith has determination and great personal charm of manner. I feel sure he has only one standard in view – the very highest and that he will attain that standard. I am more than satisfied with the way the Battalion has been commanded and consider that Colonel Beckwith-Smith's abilities are above the average of his rank.[29]

The only disappointment was that it rated Merton's vaunted horsemanship as 'only average'.[30]

Still, Merton's readjustment to regimental life was far from trouble-free, as his letters to Georgina disclosed. As a new regiment keen to prove its mettle amidst the notorious inter-regimental rivalry of the British Army, even the 1st Battalion's sporting fixtures were a source of stress, with Merton admitting that its football and rugby matches caused him 'agonies of anxiety'.[31] In April 1932 he was obliged to leave Oxfordshire for Aldershot, and then to face a further relocation to Windsor owing to the battalion's annual change of station. As he put it in a letter to Georgina in May 1932, it was fortunate that they had the financial means 'to keep so many houses going'.[32] In June, he reported that:

We start our Battalion Training next Monday and it lasts for 3 weeks and I am entirely responsible. At Oxford one was out of touch with these things, and anyhow I've never had to do the job before, so I'm naturally a bit conscious as to how it will go and, like you, I like to have things just right.[33]

A few days earlier, the sundry vexations of command had led him to confess to his mother:

I am deep in the troubles of regimental life again. I must say I've never felt more like telling them all to go to hell and let me return to heaven [i.e. Aberarder] and then on the top of these business worries (not really so bad) are little ones like a burst boiler at Stratton . . .[34]

Evidently, under the impact of the worldwide Depression which had begun in 1929, even Merton and Honor were feeling the squeeze, in relative terms at least. Amidst a weakened economy and mass unemployment, the cost of maintaining a stable of 'dud racehorses' was beginning to tell – and Honor was, as Merton noted, inclined to be a worrier.[35] At the end of 1932, and five years before Honor inherited Lingfield Park racecourse from an uncle, Richard Cecil Leigh of Lyburn Park, Salisbury, some financial support from Georgina proved especially welcome.[36] Lastly, there were concerns about Peter, their eldest son, his lack of academic ability and his prospects of passing his entrance exam for Eton.[37]

Still, despite these professional and personal travails, Merton made a success of more than seven years with the Welsh Guards. One of his more pragmatic (if prosaic) innovations, very much in keeping with his acknowledged flexibility, was to ditch the tradition of marching the battalion to its new station every year. Newly arrived in Windsor, he confided to Georgina in October 1932:

Theoretically we were supposed to march the whole way [from Aldershot]. We started off all together and marched past the generals but after a bit we put one company into charabancs and sent them a certain way – then another company and so on so that none marched more than about 10 miles and everyone except the Transport was in barracks here by 1.30 pm instead of 5.30 pm. The *Morning Post* photographer dogged us for a good long way but I hope he did not see.[38]

Though this stratagem remained undetected in 1932, in 1933, and with a move to the capital in prospect, Merton was compelled to go public, although without admitting what had happened the previous year. As a *Daily Mirror* journalist reported on 25 September:

The Army has taken to the road – not in the old foot-slogging way, but by luxury motor-coaches, and the innovators are the Welsh Guards, one of the senior regiments.

Four hundred officers and men of the 1st Battalion are returning to Wellington Barracks, London, from Windsor to-day in twelve luxurious vehicles equipped with ash-trays and looking glasses.

As the War Office allows travelling charges only by the cheapest route, the unit will pay the extra cost of the coach journey.

'I think we are the first regiment to change barracks by motor-coach', Lieutenant-Colonel Beckwith-Smith, the commanding officer, told me yesterday.

'It avoids the awkward marches from barracks to station at Windsor and the inconvenience to traffic if we march from Paddington to Wellington Barracks.

'For economy, we marched to Windsor from Aldershot, a distance of twenty miles. The distance from Windsor to London is twenty-five miles – too far to march in a day.'[39]

In October 1934, Merton was promoted to colonel, and left the 1st Battalion to assume the role of Regimental Lieutenant-Colonel, thereby taking command of the regiment and its regimental district, as well as overseeing the Welsh Guards Comrades' Association.[40] Amidst a chorus of congratulation,[41] his role with the Welsh Guards was now essentially administrative, with a strong focus on recruitment and maintaining the fabric of the regiment. As Major-General Charles Grant, commander of the Brigade of Guards and of the London District, put it:

What you want is subalterns . . . Of course there are good fellows in the line who don't want to go to India but these are usually married. You know I will do anything I can to help you. You must be sorry to leave your Battalion – it is a chapter closed in life – but you have every reason to congratulate yourself on all you have done for it.[42]

Besides the regiment's part in King George V's jubilee celebrations of May 1935, which took him to Cardiff to participate in a jubilee procession, what also came within Merton's purview at the regimental headquarters of the Welsh Guards was a whole brigade of London Territorials, namely the 142nd (8th London) Infantry Brigade. With none of the four battalions of the London Regiment capable of fielding more than 320 men, at its annual summer camp Merton was obliged to form 'composite platoons, companies and battalions' so that temporary units of 'reasonable strength' could be fielded and put through their paces.[43] Although this expedient was open to the charge of compromising unit cohesion, Merton's annual report of September 1935, written by Major-General C. G. Liddell, General Officer Commanding (GOC) of the Territorial Army's 47th (2nd London) Division, was glowing in its approval of Merton's approach and methods:

Col. B. Smith is a very able and intelligent officer, with a thorough knowledge of his profession [and] a pleasing personality which makes him popular with all ranks and enables him to get the best out of his subordinates. His tactical knowledge is sound and his judgment good. He understands the Territorial and has gained the confidence and respect of his Brigade. He [has] commanded his Brigade particularly well and has brought them to a high state of efficiency. Keeps himself physically fit by hunting, point to point, shooting etc. In my opinion he is considerably above the average of his rank in ability and professional knowledge.[44]

In 1937, with Merton now acknowledged as 'one of the most popular C.O.'s the Welsh Guards have ever had', his role with London's Territorials was adjusted. He was given command of its premier 'Officer Producing Units', a role well-suited to his experience with the OTC at Oxford, though not without its frustrations given the relaxed mores of the Territorial Army.[45] His task (in the event cut short by his move to India) was to produce future officers from the ranks of the famously smart Artists' Rifles, Inns of Court Regiment, Westminster Dragoons, and Honourable Artillery Company.[46]

Although possibly influenced by his relationship with the Duke of Windsor, Merton's appointment to the command of a brigade in India (of which he was notified by Lord Gort, then Military Secretary at the War Office, on 7 October 1937)[47] was a natural progression for a soldier of his rank, experience and prospects. As Brian Holden Reid has written of Harold Alexander, Merton's close contemporary (and, to Merton at least, his rival), who commanded the Nowshera Brigade from 1934 to 1938:

Command of a brigade [in India] underscored publicly a recognition that Alexander was one of the Army's future commanders. Imperial policing was the traditional function of the Army, and was the main school of its generals; all the principal commanders of the First World War had been nursed on 'small wars'.[48]

As commander of the Lahore Brigade and Brigade Area, which comprised both British and Indian units (which, in aggregate, formed 'the Army in India'), over his prospective term of four years Merton could anticipate action on the North-West Frontier, with all its tactical and logistical challenges; he could acquire invaluable knowledge of the Indian Army, a vital asset for a future imperial commander; and he could hone his skills in civil–military relations, working with the civil powers and with Indian dignitaries and politicians.[49] His brigade area in the Punjab, a religiously mixed and politically volatile province in the 1930s, included the city of Amritsar, scene of the notorious Jallianwala Bagh massacre of April 1919, in which hundreds of civilians had been shot on the orders of Brigadier-General Reginald Dyer. In April 1938, Merton appeared in the Indian Army List as one of 34 temporary brigadiers commanding India's brigades and brigade areas. Most were Staff College graduates and all except one had earned the MC or DSO, with 15 holding both awards. The majority, 25, were officers of the Indian Army, Merton being one of only nine from the British.[50]

Another mark of Merton's progress in professional terms, Merton and Honor embarked for this potentially fruitful command in January 1938, sailing at their own expense on the P&O liner RMS *Strathmore*.[51] The couple were now better placed financially due to Honor's Lingfield inheritance, and their departure was also eased by the knowledge that Peter (who was 'not good on paper' and had struggled academically at Eton) had been accepted for Sandhurst on Christmas Eve 1937 – though it was 'his last shot', and he subsequently found it challenging to meet the exacting standards of the Royal Military College.[52] Travelling in the company of Princess Patricia of Connaught, another grand dame and grandchild of Queen Victoria,[53] the Beckwith-Smiths had a pleasant voyage on the plush new *Strathmore*, acclaimed as a 'splendid ship' by Merton. As he reported to Georgina on 9 February, the night before they docked at Bombay, 'we have been so happy on board here', and his spirits had been raised still further by winning 'over £10 in various sweepstakes'.[54]

Honor did not stay long in India, however, returning to Britain the following month. As Merton wrote to Georgina from Brigade House, Lahore, on 25 March, they had nonetheless been able to enjoy 'a sort of second honeymoon', a fact that induced a characteristic reflection: 'God is indeed good to us having given us so much of this world's goods – and so much happiness with it.'[55] Indeed, after 20 years of a happy marriage, the pull of home proved irresistible. By early July, and as the situation in Lahore and on the Frontier seemed 'quiet', Merton had already applied for a month's home leave, paraphrasing Scripture by claiming: 'It is easier for a camel to pass through the eye of a needle than for a rich man to resist the temptation of such a loving home.'[56] Permission granted, and with the means to afford a return flight with Imperial Airways, he flew home by stages, taking off on 18 July and arriving in England on the evening of the following day.[57] Returning to India in mid-August, he wrote to assure Georgina that 'the proof one can get home in three days will make us all feel very much closer – and I think probably by next spring it will be a matter of 36 hours only'.[58] By this stage, Honor was preparing to return to India with their daughters, but the international situation was deteriorating markedly, as we shall shortly see.

Merton formally took command at Lahore on 12 February 1938,[59] and he quickly adjusted to his multifaceted role, partly by learning Urdu and by reading up on the imperial hero, Sir Henry Lawrence (1806–57), a distinguished soldier and the celebrated architect of British administration in the Punjab.[60] As the principal recruiting ground for the Indian Army, Merton was struck by how strong an impress the army made on the province, and (as he saw it, in typically paternalistic terms) the benefits which flowed from that fact. In April 1938 he wrote to Georgina that:

To learn something of our wonderful Indian soldiers and the organisation of the army is alone absorbing. I think it is not unfair to say that the Indian army does more for the welfare of the people of India than all the education and civil and social work done by the politicians, missionaries and other well-meaning folk. I mean that the thousands who pass through the ranks of the army each year are taught how to take care of themselves physically – they get education – fairly sanitary houses – and their wives too are taught something of hygiene and infant welfare.[61]

While a welcome perk was the cheap hire of polo ponies from the Indian cavalry regiment of the Lahore Brigade, namely the 6th Duke of Connaught's Own Lancers,[62] Merton's admiration for the Indian Army was wholly professional. He wrote in October how he had inspected the 6th Lancers before they redeployed to Delhi:

[W]ent to see the train taking the families of my Cavalry Regiment to Delhi. They only had 104 wives and 500 odd children which I am told is small for an Indian Regiment but it amused me as of course an English Regiment only has about 30 or so wives – officially anyhow! The Cavalry Regiment itself is marching to Delhi – 300 miles. They get there about the 24th and the Regiment from there comes here, arriving about the 30th. I went out this evening to say goodbye to them in their camp 20 miles out on the Amritsar Road – rather an inspiring sight – 500 horses all looking hard and fit – 400 men and 4 British officers. It all looked very business-like . . .[63]

Significantly, and perhaps because he was more attuned to their wiles, it was the British element of his command (which mainly comprised the 1st Duke of Cornwall's Light Infantry)[64] that caused Merton most concern. In May 1938, he wrote that:

I am also amusing myself by chasing my British Infantry Regiment who are very pleased with themselves but who I have found still feed their men like dogs. My visiting the men's suppers in the evenings has created quite a stir.[65]

Likewise, he was appalled by the treatment of patients in the British military hospital, in May 1938 recounting 'a visit to my British Hospital to see what sort of meal the poor devils get in the evening'. His findings were alarming:

I can't say I was very impressed – battered eggs . . . custard and sago pudding dished out as far as I could see into the fingers – and of course no bed tables or trays for any bed patients – a disgrace really but then there are so many things that are a disgrace about the Army in India that one does not know quite where to begin kicking up a fuss.[66]

In terms of civil affairs, Merton mixed with the governor of the Punjab, Sir Sikandar Hayat Khan, its chief of police, and the chief of the Federal

High Court.[67] He also rubbed shoulders with the Anglican Bishop of Lahore, George Barne, who had a shared interest in Henry Lawrence;[68] hosted dozens of military, civil and ecclesiastical guests at his residence (namely Brigade House, Lahore);[69] visited schools; and was much impressed by a new initiative in dairy farming, writing in August 1938:

> [T]here is usually something of interest to be seen somewhere on my estate. For instance, they are building a new Dairy Farm to be equipped with all the latest pasteurising machinery and a refrigerating plant – and it is always interesting to go down in the evening and see the 120 odd cows and buffaloes being milked – all done by Indians.[70]

Though there was some frustration over his 'very parochial work', such as arbitrating a dispute between a Hindu official and a Muslim landowner 'over some building plans' ('typical of course in a small way of what is going on all over India'),[71] there can be no doubt that Merton found India fulfilling. Noting in May 1938 that his friend 'Budget' Loyd was now commanding officer of the 1st Guards Brigade at Aldershot, he averred that his own command at Lahore was very much the 'better job', and his satisfaction was evident from a brief article he wrote for the Welsh Guards Comrades' Association's 1938 annual report.[72] The dramatic landscape of northern India, and extended visits to Himalayan hill stations,[73] added to his enjoyment and furnished plenty of news for Georgina, and in October 1938 he reported how:

> I had to make two speeches at public tea parties and attend two dinners with Indians – the last of which [was] followed by a visit to an Indian Cinema which I quite enjoyed – a simple love story with lots of blood and thunder . . . They are trying to develop the film industry in this country – a marvellous country of course for photography.[74]

In terms of dramatic love stories, Merton's months in India also saw a cooling of his enthusiasm for the Duke of Windsor. In August 1938, he rather ruefully compared Edward to Bonnie Prince Charlie: 'I don't however think that Windsor will attempt a landing in Wales, though those of us who knew him could never fail to fall to his charm conscious though we are of his faults.'[75] The following month, he voiced his sympathy for an accidental monarch who was now faced with the cataclysmic prospect of war with Germany:

> I can't help feeling sorry for the King at the present time and wondering how he feels about it all. You know of course that the one thing the Duke of Windsor told his ministers was that there was to be no war in his time. Pity he didn't last a bit longer! I see a photo of him and Mrs. S. at Naples in my paper today. She looks too awful.[76]

Another feature of Merton's time in India was his growing involvement in ecclesiastical matters. In part a function of his seniority, and the expectation that commanding officers should lead in religious as in other matters, it was also an extension of his involvement in church affairs at Stratton Audley, and of his previous role as secretary of St Paul's Episcopal Church, Aberarder.[77] Given the sheer size of its jurisdiction, and problems posed by climate and disease, the capacity of the chaplains of the small, state-funded Indian Ecclesiastical Establishment to minister to British soldiers and government officials in India had always been limited,[78] and by April 1938 Merton had found himself acting as a stand-in for services in Lahore cantonment, informing Georgina that:

> The organ here rather reminds me of the one at Aberarder. I'm sure that Honor would play it better than the woman who does play it on occasions when there is no band. The morning I took the service here I had to sit where the minister usually sits.[79]

However, the more routine duty of reading the lesson at the weekly (Anglican) parade service occasioned a further reflection:

> I read the lesson this morning St John XX 1–23 and someone said I did it well. Anyhow, one takes the trouble to read it as if one understood what was meant. I must say I sometimes long to alter one or two of the words to make the meaning a bit clearer.[80]

Though improving the text of the King James Bible was beyond Merton's remit, he was able to dictate the arrangement of Anglican public worship in the cantonment. As he put the situation to Georgina on 1 May:

> We had our parade services at 7.30 am this morning. They used to have no parade services after 1st May but the padre used to go round to a unit and hold a service somewhere in the lines. I have put my foot down and said that as we have a really rather beautiful and cool church a parade service is to be held in it every other Sunday, as in the winter but at an earlier hour. The troops coming in any clothes and a shortened service. The Padre started by saying it would interfere with his 8 am communion service so I said the troops came first. Then he said there would be no band – so I said get an organist! Then I said cut out the sermon (as he can't preach).[81]

With the chaplain clearly perturbed by this intervention, the battle of wills dragged on:

> [H]e submitted a programme [wrote Merton] in which the sermon still figured. He said he wished to say a few words about the Guards and the [centenary of the] Guards Chapel . . . I told him I didn't wish the Guards forced down the throats of people here and again suggested the erosion of the sermon – to which I thought we had agreed. Not a bit of it. We had a most weird arrangement wherein I read the lesson just as everyone was clearing their throats to sing the Venite – the lesson followed by a hymn – followed by creed, prayers, another hymn, sermon, another hymn all rushed and cut about. I told him what I thought as soon as I came out – but, oh dear, they are the limit when you think of the chances they have and the importance, if one is starting a new series, of starting well. However . . . he is being sent off somewhere else in a month's time and if necessary I shall take the services myself.[82]

Clearly disposed to make best use of the cantonment church, Merton added:

> The Bishop told me that the reason why the churches in cantonments generally in India were rather beautiful is that the Engineer officers

who were detailed to build them were given a year's leave and sent off to Europe to study church architecture! I can't see that being done in these days.[83]

Still, conflict of another kind increasingly dominated Merton's horizons during his months in India, especially given the assertiveness of Hitler's Germany in the last 18 months of general European peace. Though the 1919 treaties of Versailles and St Germain prohibited the unification of Germany and Austria, the *Anschluss* of 1938 left Merton disinclined to fight. Profoundly affected by the ordeal of 1914–18, immersed in happy family life and fearful of the likely fate of Peter, by 25 March 1938 Merton had taken the view that 'The fewer potty little states the better.'[84] A fortnight later, and having devoured a book on 'Czecho-Slovakia' which Georgina had sent, he went on to say that he was in favour of 'a big and strong Germany in central and S.E. Europe' rather than a mosaic of 'squabbling' statelets, partly because Germany 'would have less time and cause for bothering about getting back her colonies elsewhere'.[85] However, the question of the Sudetenland grew ever more acute, with Merton's aversion to war intensified by Honor's plans to bring their daughters out to India. Hoping that peace sentiment in Germany might prevail,[86] on 5 September he wrote how 'these are anxious days for even those of us who are far removed from the apparent storm centre – especially when all those we love are so much closer to the centre than we ourselves are'. Consequently, he prayed that 'the European situation' would be settled in 'the one sensible and Christian way'.[87] By mid-September, with war looking likely, and Honor about to sail for India on the troopship *Dorchester*, Merton had grown distinctly agitated, especially given the potential threat of German and Italian submarines. On 12 September he confessed to Georgina that:

I am in a terrible state of anxiety for fear that on one side anything would stop Honor starting while on the other that something may happen when she is in the Mediterranean. I haven't known whether to wire and stop her starting – or what – for one feels that by the time the wire got to her everything may have altered. In the end one has had to rely on an all-seeing Providence and one hopes on an

Embarkation Staff that will not allow the ship to sail if there is any danger.[88]

Given these worries, his response to Chamberlain's efforts and to the Munich Agreement of 30 September was one of inexpressible relief. Writing to Georgina late that evening, Merton confided that:

> I went along at our 7 pm to listen to my Staff Captain's wireless and there I heard confirmed the rumour that had been current all day that complete agreement had been reached at Munich – and not only that but the thing that one had always hoped for – a resolution for Germany and ourselves not to resort to war again. Even now I hardly dare believe that it is true . . . I know you will be going to the wee Kirk to offer up your thanks for this miracle, the work of a humble and contrite-hearted man . . .[89]

With a new chaplain in place, Merton was gratified that the news was received appropriately in Lahore, writing ten days later, and after a day of thanksgiving for the Munich settlement had been held at home on Sunday 2 October, that:

> Even our temporary Padre here gave us a suitable address – and then what I liked and had hoped – made us go down on our knees after his sermon and say the General Thanksgiving. He is a young man who was under me in the O.T.C. at Oxford. I had him and his wife and another Padre . . . to dine one night last week.[90]

And, though the illusion of peace with Nazi Germany faded quickly over subsequent months, as the rump of Czechoslovakia was invaded in March and pressure placed on Poland over the Danzig Corridor, Merton continued to view the prospect of war with great reluctance. On 24 August he confided to Georgina that 'What I long for above all things is the peace and opportunity to enjoy all the good things which God and my wife and my parents have bestowed on me.'[91] On Saturday 2 September, he wrote again:

I personally think we were rather unwise to give Poland a more or less unconditional guarantee. I would anyhow have gingered them to get Danzig and the Corridor settled. Budget and I said when we were at the Staff College in 1921 that these were the two things most likely to lead to another European war . . . One wonders what is going on inside Germany. It is no good hoping for too much but the Czechs and Austrians may give trouble.[92]

Nevertheless, despite Merton's reluctance to face the horrors of war again, in professional terms this was inevitable. Consequently, after eight months in India (during which Honor and Rosemary were hosted by the Viceroy in New Delhi)[93] the Beckwith-Smiths were en route back to England – once again by air, but with Honor and the children leaving first, to be met by Georgina at Croydon aerodrome.[94] As the British Army expanded in anticipation of war, an officer with Merton's experience was in great demand, and in June 1939 the *Times of India* reported that he was 'under orders of transfer to England' and was scheduled to leave on the 8th.[95] However, this was clearly a typo, for, in an article published in India's *Civil and Military Gazette* on 24 June, it was reported that Merton was due to leave Lahore four days later (the 28th) to take command of the 1st Guards Brigade at Aldershot. Conscious that his four-year term at Lahore had been heavily curtailed, in an interview Merton stated that: 'I am taking away with me an excellent impression of the efficiency of the Indian Army. Though I have been here only a few months, I would not have missed this experience for anything.'[96]

Nor could Merton ignore the significance of his appointment or wonder about his place in an expanding army. On 11 June he wrote to Georgina:

I begin to feel that at a time like this in England they ought to send for people like myself . . . I can assure you I watch very closely to see who has been promoted. One feels with all this increase of numbers of men they must soon want an increase of staff and commanders – but if they don't promote someone like Budget how can I hope – and I am no one's pet boy like some of these younger men are![97]

In fact, 'Budget' Loyd was promoted that very month, but Merton's transfer from Lahore (once deemed 'a better job') and appointment to the 1st Guards Brigade left him puzzled about his own position and prospects, especially as he worried that he had been deskilled and even sidelined by his 16 months in India. As he confided to Georgina before leaving Lahore:

> I suppose by this time you have heard THE news and I hope it has given you pleasure and that we shall be granted peace in which we may all enjoy the appointment together. It is a quarter of a century ago since I served as a Second Lieutenant in the 1st Guards Brigade and went to the war with it. I was Brigade Major of it in the war for 18 months and since the war I have commanded a company and a Battalion in it. But I shall come back a stranger to its movements after less than 18 months in this country – so perhaps they were right to send for me and bring me up to date.[98]

Arriving in England early in July, by mid-August, after a few days in Aberarder, Merton was in training with his old brigade. Writing from Alton in Hampshire, he reported a routine which would become bleakly familiar over the coming months of the 'Phoney War':

> I had my first day's training of my new Brigade here yesterday – and we were out all night – a lovely night and it all went quite fairly well. But I was as busily employed with distinguished guests – such as Duff Cooper, a Trans Jordanian sheikh, an Indian Brigadier and a French officer – as with training my Brigade.[99]

And there was a nagging frustration, too, about his new role. On 24 August, he told Georgina:

> No need to be proud – or, anyhow, too so, as what I have done has been done only by steady plodding. I must say I sometimes feel I am capable of even a bigger job than I have now but perhaps the call or the opportunity will come one day soon.[100]

This was understandable, for longstanding mobilization plans were simply being implemented. Merton could write on 2 September: 'I personally have very little to do as plans made some time ago are being put into force and one can only sit and criticize the poor devils who are doing all the work.'[101] Britain's declaration of war the following day would change this completely.

3

1st Guards Brigade

In September 1939, the 1st Guards (or 1st Infantry) Brigade was composed
of regular soldiers and recalled reservists, its component units being the
3rd Battalion of the Grenadier Guards, the 2nd Battalion of the Coldstream
Guards and (despite the brigade's 'Guards' designation) the 2nd Battalion
of the Hampshire Regiment. There was, in addition, a single company of
light anti-tank guns.[1] As commander of one of the three brigades (numbered 1st–3rd) of the 1st Infantry Division, Merton's immediate superior
was a slightly younger and more glamorous contemporary, Major-General
Harold Alexander. Born in 1891, schooled at Harrow, trained at Sandhurst
and commissioned into the Irish Guards in 1911, 'Alex' had served with
distinction on the Western Front, where he had earned the MC and the
DSO. As one of the Army's rising stars in the interwar years, Alex had
commanded the Nowshera Brigade on the North-West Frontier and had
distinguished himself in the Loe Agra and Mohmand campaigns of 1935.
A hugely capable soldier, skilled diplomat, and always impeccably turned
out, Alexander would have a glittering wartime career, ending the war
in Europe as a Knight Commander of the Order of the Bath (KCB) and
Supreme Allied Commander in the Mediterranean. In 1946, he was raised
to the peerage as Viscount Alexander of Tunis and became a Knight of the
Order of the Garter (KG).[2] However, all this lay ahead. Alex, previously an
aide-de-camp (ADC) to the King, was put in command of the 1st Division
in 1939 as a 'safe pair of hands, the cool Guardsman always in control'.[3]

For Viscount Gort, commander of the recreated BEF, Alex was a natural
choice to command the 1st Division, one of the first four divisions of the
British Army to deploy to France that autumn. Yet another Guardsman,
Gort was a product of Harrow and Sandhurst and had been commissioned
into the Grenadier Guards in 1905. A much-wounded survivor of the
Western Front, he had outshone even his peers in terms of grit and sheer

luck, being awarded the VC, the MC, and the DSO (three times), and he was mentioned in despatches on eight separate occasions. Though he had previously served as Chief of the Imperial General Staff (CIGS), Gort was no more suited to that role than he was to command the BEF. Owing both appointments to the patronage of the Secretary of State for War, Leslie Hore-Belisha, with whom he had a chequered relationship, Gort was a simple fighting soldier, his rise driven by the fact that the publicity-savvy Hore-Belisha 'sensed that the Army needed a hero figure at its head, particularly a young one'.[4] Gort, in other words, was an excellent *divisional* commander, for which role his 'integrity, experience, shrewd common sense and that most worthy of all qualities, true simplicity' were best suited.[5] As Montgomery put it after the war:

> Gort was a most delightful person, a warm-hearted friend, sincere in his dealings, and incapable of anything mean or underhand. He was the perfect example of the best type of regimental officer; he knew everything there was to know about the soldier, his clothing and boots, and the minor tactics of his battlefield. The highest command he had ever held before had been an infantry brigade. He was not clever and he did not bother about administration; his whole soul was in the battle and especially in the actions of fighting patrols in no man's land.[6]

Given the trajectories of Gort, Alexander and others, there was some justification for Merton's initial concern that he was being passed over, an anxiety fuelled by the fact that, while he was Secretary of State for War, Hore-Belisha pushed strongly 'to reduce the age of senior officers'.[7] When Gort was appointed CIGS in 1937, with the substantive rank of general, he was the youngest holder of that office. Furthermore, at the outbreak of the Dunkirk campaign the average age of the BEF's divisional commanders was only 53 (the same age, in fact, as Gort himself).[8] Aged 49 on the outbreak of war, Merton was understandably perplexed about his position in the new military hierarchy, especially as the Army was growing exponentially, with a force of 50 British and Commonwealth divisions planned from September 1939.[9] Besides the possibility of not being promoted as the Army expanded, as the 'Phoney War' went on there was even the risk of being replaced by a younger man before he had had the opportunity to prove himself as a brigade commander. As autumn passed into winter, Merton's fears that his career might well have stalled were brought to a head by the remarkable circumstances of one exceptional appointment. In this case, Adrian Carton de Wiart, a Belgian-born swashbuckler who had lived in retirement in Poland from 1924 to 1939, was appointed to command the newly formed 61st Infantry Division. A colourful figure who had earned the VC and DSO during the First World War, Carton de Wiart had lost an eye in Somalia before arriving on the Western Front in 1915, where he also lost a hand but earned renown as a battalion and brigade commander. (Indeed, so colourful a figure was Carton de Wiart that he proved to be the model for the Boche-biffing Brigadier Ben Ritchie-Hook in Evelyn Waugh's famous *Sword of Honour* trilogy of 1952–61.) However, such claims to fame wore on Merton, a much steadier professional. As he complained to Georgina on 29 November:

> I hear Carton de Wiart has been given a Division – as one of my superiors said, it would have been very nice if more of us had left 20 years ago and spent our time in hunting and shooting with the knowledge that we shall be promoted as soon as war broke out.[10]

These tidings had not been made any more palatable by Peter's observation that 'It looks as if you are being left behind!'[11] Nevertheless, reassured by a second opinion that his current position would provide 'useful experience' and that he had the consolations of his family as well as his faith, Merton claimed to be unworried. This, however, was belied in his next letter to his mother, in which he once again enquired: 'Have you heard that Carton de Wiart has got a Division? A wonderful fighting soldier of course but one would have thought a little out of touch with modern military thought.'[12]

Besides these sensitivities around precedent and promotion, Merton found the outbreak of war hard to come to terms with after 20 years of peace and flourishing family life. While still hungry for promotion, he relished neither the prospect of further bloodletting nor his renewed separation from home. On 6 September, he wrote to Georgina on the 'folly and madness' of war and, at the end of the month, from his new billet in France, he wrote wistfully to Honor: 'It was almost more than I could bear when I walked down to the bridge over the mill stream that runs through our village with the moon shining full on a scene of absolute peace.'[13] And for those who led the BEF, the professional soldiers who had served as relatively junior officers in the First World War, these were poignant times. Stationed in north-eastern France, often on the very battlefields of the old Western Front, the pristine cemeteries and memorials of the Imperial War Graves Commission seemed ubiquitous, while the devastation wrought by the previous war was still very much in evidence. As Alan Allport has put it:

This was countryside long familiar to British troops, the 'blood-stained cockpit' of Europe over which their predecessors had fought so many times. Evidence of the most recent episode of violence, the war of 1914 to 1918, was everywhere. In many places only saplings stood . . . Weathered trench lines remained visibly etched into the wet clay soil. As the troops arrived and dug in, so the ground surrendered the detritus of the past; steel helmets, shell cases, spent cartridges, gas masks.[14]

Writing his routine 'Sunday school letter' to Georgina on 3 October, Merton described his visit to 'Happy Valley' cemetery in Fampoux, near Arras, then home to the headquarters and principal railhead of the BEF.[15] While its name and situation triggered much happier memories of Aberarder, the experience was a stark reminder of mortality:

Then in a 10 minute lull I had when I got back here this evening I took a short stroll – where do you think to – to a cemetery called Happy Valley. The cemetery alone would have made me think of home but the name doubly so – and well named it is too for a more peaceful spot in this delightful little valley it would be impossible to imagine – and there the first names I came across were those of Guardsmen including two officers of the Welsh Guards, Ballard and Byrne, of whom I had never even heard.[16]

Likewise, a return to life in French billets stirred vivid memories of the old days, not all of which were reassuring. Writing to Georgina later in October, Merton mused:

It is all just as it was in the winter of 25 years ago except for the immediate presence of the enemy and death . . . It brought a very big lump to my throat last night when I went to a concert given by one of my battalions here and we had all the old songs – and the men on the stage dressed up as women – and the same jokes and laughter and smoky atmosphere with the draft whistling up one's legs. I wondered whether I was not looking at the ghosts of my generation.[17]

And there was much time for reflection in the so-called *Sitzkrieg* that marked the 'Phoney War' on the Western Front. According to instructions issued to Gort by Hore-Belisha on 3 September, the BEF (or 'British Field Force', as it was also known) was under the command of General Alphonse Georges, 'the French Commander-in-Chief "North-East Theatre of Operations"'. Though under French command, Gort was 'at liberty to appeal to the British Government' if he felt the BEF to be endangered, and it was expected that his troops would remain in their specified 'Theatre of Operations'.[18] In other words, as in 1914, the BEF would supplement the efforts of the French Army which, with its 80 divisions, would bear the brunt of the ground war. Four British divisions, among them the 1st, had arrived in France by mid-October, with another following in December. Eight Territorial divisions arrived between January and the end of April 1940.[19] Of these, the five regular divisions were 'reasonably well-equipped and trained' but the Territorials much less so, with three being treated as large labour units. At least that corresponded with the assumed nature of the coming campaign, for the BEF was not prepared to fight a mobile war. Instead, 'it was heavily dependent on the French High Command and its strategy, and on fighting a static, defensive war not so very different from that of 1914–18'.[20] Sandwiched between the French Seventh Army (to its left) and the French First Army (on its right), the BEF had the job of bolstering Allied defences along the Franco-Belgian border in anticipation of another German thrust through neutral Belgium, a task made more urgent still by the fact that France's vaunted Maginot Line did not cover that section of the frontier. Still, even this mundane task proved controversial, with his criticisms of the speed with which defences were being constructed in the British sector culminating in Hore-Belisha's resignation in January 1940.[21]

Apart from some aerial combat, there was scant military action in the British sector: 'The main activities were marching, digging trenches and constructing pill-boxes.'[22] However, and in common with other British brigades,[23] Merton's 1st Guards Brigade spent some time on the Maginot Line in February,[24] the rationale being to oil inter-Allied co-operation at all levels and attune British units to frontline conditions. However, even in the Saar the situation was quiet in the early weeks of 1940, with nothing like the perilous raiding and counter-raiding of the previous war. Writing to Georgina from near Arras on 6 March, Merton reflected that:

> The dangers down there aren't very great – anyhow nothing compared to most places as I knew them last time. They were just enough to make people feel they were doing something, and I think we were lucky not to suffer more than we did . . . I felt rather like FitzClarence urging my fellows on as he urged me on in October 1914 and I fancy I had the same difficulty as he had – i.e. to overcome the unwillingness of my commanding officers to risk the lives of any of their officers or men. One doesn't want to take foolish risks but nothing venture – nothing have . . . All the same it was most interesting and useful experience for the young officers and men, though they'll be lucky if they get away with anything so light again before this is over.[25]

In personal terms, Merton's *Sitzkrieg* was marked by sundry vexations and frustrations. Inevitably, and as in 1914, postal arrangements took time to settle, with post from Scotland (and Aberarder) being especially prone to delay, a situation eased by Georgina's annual return to London for the winter.[26] Given Merton's fondness for grouse, this had culinary implications as attempts were made to post birds to Merton's mess from Aberarder. These were valiant efforts, but not always successful: in mid-November, Merton wrote to Georgina admitting to having 'had to get up during the night' after a brace of grouse had arrived in deceptively 'perfect condition'.[27] Matters were not helped by attempts to obtain a Parisian chef for the mess. In the event, despairing of their facilities, two successive chefs walked out before a 'Grenadier corporal' was discovered who liked cooking and showed 'some proficiency at it'.[28] Home leave was also problematic, and it was not until the end of November that it was 'freely talked of' in France.[29] Consequently, it was not until January that Merton was able to return to London for a 'week of peace', at the end of which he 'walked away with a heavy heart from Honor in the gloom of Victoria Station'.[30] Some additional leave was obtained that April, for on 11 May (the day after the German invasion of Holland, Belgium and Luxembourg) Merton wrote a hurried note to Georgina:

> It seems a month at least since I saw you [in London]. I wish I thought it could be only that till I see you again – but who knows that all this excitement may not bring the end sooner than one thinks possible . . . Meanwhile I'm glad I took my leave when I did and the memory of those glorious and happy days . . . that little walk in the park with you, after a big lunch and a service at the Guards Chapel, will keep me going for a long time.[31]

Although Merton felt the sharp pangs of separation from his wider family, his eldest son, Peter, who had been commissioned into the Welsh Guards in July 1939,[32] came to France with its 1st Battalion in mid-November. Travelling via Marseille and Paris, this was attached to GHQ in Arras, and finding him did not prove difficult.[33] As Merton reported to Georgina, Peter had been spotted at 'the base' and he tracked him down the following day, in high spirits and 'delighted to be in this country'.[34] However, personal factors did not blind Merton to his son's shortcomings – nor those of his old battalion. As he wrote to Georgina the following week, after an extended visit from Peter:

> The things he really likes to talk about are Aberarder and the Hunting – and he, like I, wonders what will happen about both when this is over . . . He is interested too in his Battalion and likes too to talk about the men and officers. I don't know that he thinks much of some of the latter and I think they are rather a mixed lot. The battalion has certainly had a pretty rough time of it all this year for they haven't been anyone's children and naturally I should like to have them as mine.[35]

As for Peter, who was now a 20-year-old subaltern:

> I think it is quite on the cards that Peter may be sent home. He, like a real man, doesn't want to be and I, of course, refuse to interfere . . .

Don [Gurney] said that he was terribly slow in understanding but that, given a job to do, you could always rely on Peter to do it . . . I could see that he found it terribly hard to take in all that is going on here, so I sent him to stay one night with his friend Robert Windsor Clive to get some sort of picture from his own level. He came back here yesterday afternoon and we had a good chat far into the night . . .[36]

But even Merton had difficulty in adjusting to his circumstances. Under active service conditions his horizon was dominated by brigade affairs and his social life restricted to the claustrophobic circle of his own (usually much younger) staff officers. As he lamented in November: 'The weeks go by and I hardly ever go outside my own estate and I become mentally more and more like the sugar beet by which I am surrounded.'[37] In February, after a busy fortnight, he wrote that 'at times I have felt I could scream to be left alone'.[38] By the end of March, the unrelenting drabness of his inert military existence was starting to vex Merton, who took up gardening as a source of constructive recreation. On 31 March he wrote to Georgina:

I found a nice old 18th century chateau quite close [to] here the other day in a wood full of anemones and violets with not a soldier near the place. I'd like to move my mess there as here we have our office in the same house as we live and this means we are never away from the soldiery and they really have very few ideas of how to behave when they get together in a body.[39]

A week earlier, after dining with 'Budget' Loyd, now a major-general and GOC of the 2nd Division,[40] Merton had aired his frustration with the constant earwigging of his staff officers, and its vast potential for mischief:

I had a great tête a tête dinner with Budget the other night and we both let ourselves go. One never gets a chance under these conditions to say what one really feels, for the younger ones all listen all the time.[41]

But despite his dreary, goldfish bowl existence, there was plenty to do – whether in the brigade itself, receiving visiting dignitaries or liaising with the neighbouring French. Anxious to be visible to his troops, for whom a brigadier could seem a remote and extraneous figure, Merton tried to be an immediate presence. For example, though beset by a cold just before Christmas, he refused to renege even on minor commitments. As he told Georgina on 17 December:

> I had to go to a company concert last night. I had been to a pantomime the night before held in a station goods shed but there was a brazier between me and the stage at which I could thaw my feet . . . this time it was in a barn – no brazier, not much roof and an enormous number of doors – so I more or less had to be carried out . . . [However] I was determined not to disappoint anyone by chucking – for I believe the troops like to see one, though they haven't the faintest idea of one's name or what a Brigadier does except possibly to authorise an issue of rum very occasionally and almost always to find fault with any work done or begun![42]

Christmas Day also saw him very much out and about. As he recounted to Georgina:

> I went to two different Church parades today and spent all the morning here going round looking at billets and preparations for Christmas dinner and chatting with men here and there. I only had to say something to one lot for having had too much before midday – I need hardly say they were nothing really to do with my own Brigade.[43]

Visitors, too, had to be received and entertained, with Hore-Belisha, the King, Neville Chamberlain and Winston Churchill (now, once again, First Lord of the Admiralty) among those received between November 1939 and March 1940.[44] Though Churchill's dreadful French was a cause of embarrassment when he visited with a French general, Merton's contact with his allies began almost immediately, being hosted at a French mess as early as 2 October. Although it proved to be 'a most interesting morning', and his French stood up to the cross-questioning of his hosts over lunch, Merton could not help noticing the absence of grace in the army of the secular Third Republic, a short silence before the meal being merely a prelude to 'the mess president rising to announce the menu'.[45] Further exchanges ensued. In February, Merton was present at an awards ceremony for three French generals, his comments betraying a typical Guardsman's instinctive disdain for the turnout of his allies:

> I attended an attractive little ceremony in a nice old square the other day. Two or three high French generals being invested with a high order of the Legion of Honour. Three French battalions on parade – much smarter than I expected and all fit and hard and keen looking. I have dined and lunched with French generals and was received here yesterday with a little guard of honour as there is a French H.Q. next door to me.[46]

There was, however, much less decorum in evidence at a French football match on Easter Sunday, which 'ended with only about 18 players on the field and a free fight between them in which one lady from the crowd joined! So, it was well worth seeing.'[47] Differences were also apparent in their approaches to the Germans. At the end of March, in an argument with his French liaison officers over war aims (the French being 'determined to have the Rhine as their frontier' and 'to occupy Germany for 50 years' if needs be), Merton felt obliged to produce Cuthbert Headlam's *History of the Guards Division in the Great War* and a page which showed 'the casualties of this Brigade in 10 days on the Somme'.[48]

Besides its general dreariness, the winter of 1939–40 was also 'the coldest winter in living memory'. Amidst freezing conditions, periodic thaws and heavy falls of snow and rain, the miseries of endless digging-in became ever more acute.[49] For Merton, who was quartered in a 'semi-inhabited chateau' from late September, even chateau life was far from idyllic: 'here they have never known such a winter.'[50] Although there was electric light, the winter witnessed a losing battle with its central heating system. In scenes perennially familiar to the British householder, the Royal Engineers failed to provide a competent plumber,[51] and even the fuel supply proved insufficient for his 'enormous' habitation, despite being close to the rich coalfields of Artois.[52] Nevertheless, Merton's chief concern was for his men. In his very first letter of the war to Georgina, and despite his own anguish, he observed their stoicism with admiration, noting that 'The troops take it all very philosophically.'[53] And, though the thermometer plummeted in December,[54] by late October Merton was already complaining about their living conditions:

[T]hey are marvellous. Never a grumble and you should see some of their billets – lofts with many of the tiles missing and no felt or anything under the tiles and the wind whistling through. And what is more only one blanket apiece. This last mentioned is monstrous and I said so at a conference Alex had on Friday. *He did not know* [my italics]. I bet all the men at the base have two if not more apiece.[55]

By mid-December, Merton's concern had become general:

Heaven knows how many degrees of frost last night and bitter cold again today but lovely and dry – but, oh, I feel so sorry for some of the troops in their billets this weather. Few of them ever complain and I'm lucky, of course, in that most of my officers know how to and do look after their men. But there are some units round about me here who don't – and yet, as they aren't under my command, I can't say much.[56]

If the background of the rank-and-file regulars under Merton's command helped inure them to the discomforts of the winter of 1939–40 (the inter-war army followed the age-old peacetime pattern of enlisting 'usually the young, the poor and the desperate'),[57] Merton modelled his accustomed resilience and buoyancy: 'I can usually manage a smiling exterior if my heart is often heavy within me,' as he put it in January 1940.[58] Evidently, one of the pillars of this approach was his deep if undemonstrative Christian faith. If army officers were expected to set an example in churchgoing as in other moral and professional matters, for Merton, a good churchman, this was a heartfelt experience and not just an onerous inconvenience. On the weekend before his departure for France, he had left the 'pig sty and pandemonium' of Aldershot to spend Sunday at Stratton Audley.[59] There, possibly betraying his Low Church sympathies, and some underlying tensions with the incumbent, he and Honor eschewed St Mary and St Edburga's in favour of worship elsewhere:

> We went to church at Poundon this morning as it was choral communion at Stratton and Honor and I did not fancy that though we have buried the hatchet with Fox. They have a very nice service at Poundon with part of the Communion Service in the Morning Service and then a break . . . Honor and Rosemary and I stayed for the second half of the service.[60]

The following week, having departed for France on Wednesday 20 September,[61] Merton attended an open-air service for the Protestants of one of his battalions, a service led by a Methodist chaplain. While this reflected the pan-Protestant character of the interwar Royal Army Chaplains' Department (RAChD), it also exposed the confessional cleavages of a largely pre-ecumenical age, for the Roman Catholics remained conspicuous by their absence, as 'not even war will induce [them] to join in with the remainder'.[62] Although these divisions also dictated that the use of French Catholic churches was denied to the Protestant and Jewish chaplains of the BEF (which resulted in Merton attending services in his mess, an agricultural laboratory and even a local cinema),[63] these secular surroundings did not diminish the comfort which Merton derived from his Sunday observance. While there was an element of leading by example (Merton was particularly fond of reading the lesson, which he did in France as he had in Lahore),[64] his identity as a solid, Prayer Book Anglican went much deeper. If things could get too 'High' at Stratton Audley, his exposure to Methodism was hardly more palatable, Merton confiding to Georgina at the end of October that his Methodist padre had turned out to be 'a bit of a tub thumper'.[65]

However, for Merton, faith and churchgoing was also a profoundly familial experience. It was a mainstay of his regular correspondence with Georgina, he insisted on Peter's attendance at 'Early Service in our mess here' during his son's brief visit to his headquarters,[66] and it was also a vital ingredient in the cement that bound his marriage to Honor. Indeed, in a letter written to her at the end of September 1939, Merton mentioned a detail that does much to explain his deep attachment to the 1662 Book of Common Prayer, an attachment not simply born of habit or conditioning:

I was very close to you this morning when we had a little morning service followed by a communion in the laboratory of this big farm. It was almost more than I could stand for with your prayer book which you gave me when we were engaged. I just felt that the last 20 years had been a dream and that I was back where we had started life together. Yet I thank God for that dream as I know you do – and nothing and no one can take the memory of it away from us or the certainty of more to come.[67]

Over and above all this sat the question of the war and its developments. Despite the *Sitzkrieg* on the Western Front, the nature and direction of the conflict as it unfolded elsewhere furnished ample food for thought. In that regard, the sinking of the battleship *Royal Oak* in Scapa Flow in October 1939; the Battle of the River Plate in December; the mood of India; Stalin's invasion of Finland; the position of neutrals such as Italy; and the future of the Nazi–Soviet Pact all elicited keen comment and speculation in Merton's correspondence.[68] Frustrated with the strategic lethargy he witnessed all around him, Merton even wondered whether France was turning into a second India – territory which the British Army garrisoned but which might, in time, become a base from which to sally forth to mount its campaigns, thus 'conducting the war as we did in the days of Marlborough'.[69] However, on 9 April, the German invasion of Denmark and Norway put the Allies firmly on notice. As Merton wrote to Georgina 12 days later, the prospects of leave had now evaporated and 'The last fortnight has been rather a trial for our nerves here and seems to have dragged a bit in consequence.'[70] Mounting tension at the growing prospect of action also occasioned an uncharacteristically mean-spirited reflection. Always a little jealous of Alexander, in a letter to Georgina he contrasted their very different marriages, noting: 'My movements are a little dependent on Alex's . . . He says now he doesn't know where his wife is! I don't fancy either of them are very good correspondents. Separation must be very much easier for the likes of them.'[71] Everything changed, however, with the German invasion of Holland, Belgium and Luxembourg on 10 May. From this point, excepting a pencilled note dashed off to Georgina the next day, in which he noted 'all this excitement' and Churchill's appointment as Prime Minister,[72] Merton's correspondence dried up. He was now faced with the problems of command amidst a chaotic campaign that would end as the largest military defeat – and the greatest moral triumph – in modern British history.

In accordance with plans devised in November 1939, the German invasion of the Low Countries triggered an Allied advance into Belgium in support of the Belgian Army. Emblematic of a determination to keep the ground war off French soil, and to utilize Belgium's river systems for defensive purposes, under the terms of 'Plan D', the BEF and its French allies rolled forward to take up positions along the River Dyle, which runs north to south, roughly ten miles east of Brussels.[73] Advancing in two columns, with Merton commanding its vehicles while its infantry marched in parallel, the 1st Guards Brigade moved into Belgium on 11 May. Two days later, it was digging in along the Dyle, with Merton's headquarters established in a convent in Ijzer.[74] By this point, the Dutch were already surrendering to the north but a much more dangerous situation was unfolding to the south-east. As Daniel Todman has stated: 'The Franco-British advance into Belgium had all the success of a hedgehog sticking its head into a food can.'[75] Even before the 1st Guards Brigade had entrenched, at the northern end of the Maginot Line German armoured columns had traversed the Ardennes (a manoeuvre deemed impossible by the French high command) and had shattered the shaky French defences on the River Meuse around Sedan. Closely supported by a dominant Luftwaffe and its fearsomely ubiquitous Ju 87 (Stuka) dive-bombers, German tank columns sped across the plains of northern France and, by 19 May, had reached the Channel coast near Abbeville. In stupefying contrast to the tempo of the First World War and the malaise of the *Sitzkrieg*, German forces had rampaged 200 miles in just ten days. For the Allies, however, the strategic implications were cataclysmic. There were few reserves to call upon and, pressed by the advancing Germans from the north and from the south, 'the élite of the French and British forces were now trapped in a vast pocket, with their backs to the sea', their disarray compounded by the death of their overall commander, General Gaston Billotte, in a road accident.[76]

The role of the 1st Guards Brigade in the Franco-Belgian campaign of May–June 1940 must be seen in the context of the vast conflict that swirled around it. One of roughly 40 British brigades in an army dwarfed by that of its allies (the French Army had more than 100 divisions on the Western

Front by 1940),[77] its contribution – and that of its commander – was necessarily limited. However, its fighting retreat showed Merton's mettle as a leader, much as Gort's character and example steadied the BEF as a whole.[78] According to the regimental history of the Coldstream Guards in the Second World War, Merton, whose headquarters had moved to 'some convenient cellars under a school', issued orders to pull back to Brussels, and the line of the Brussels–Charleroi Canal, on 16 May. (The code word that triggered this tricky 17-mile withdrawal was a biblical one: 'Goliath'.)[79] And, amidst a growing torrent of refugees, the retreats continued. Having reached the canal on 17 May, an order to fall back to the line of the River Dendre was then given. Arriving at the Dendre the following day, orders were promptly issued at a brigade conference to withdraw to the River Scheldt. This began on 19 May, amid grisly signs of German air superiority. As Lionel Bootle-Wilbraham, commanding officer (CO) of the 2nd Coldstream and the future Lord Skelmersdale, remembered: 'There were unpleasant sights on the way. Refugee columns had been strafed, leaving a debris of carts, dead horses and human bodies strewn across the road.'[80] Once behind the Scheldt – 'a substantial anti-tank obstacle', as Bootle-Wilbraham noted – the brigade took up position in and around the village of Pecq, its defences closely supervised by 'Brigadier Becky'.[81] On 20 May, its bridge over the Scheldt was blown. However, a German attack was mounted the next day and, in a manoeuvre characteristic of their aggressive reconnaissance and probing tactics,[82] the Germans infiltrated across the Scheldt – but then proved unable to dislodge the defenders of Pecq. Despite the tenacious stand of the brigade, on 22 May another order came through to retreat a further six miles, this time across the Franco-Belgian border 'to the line of posts and block-houses which the BEF had been working on through the winter'.[83]

However, on arrival it transpired that these defences were largely notional – merely shallow anti-tank ditches and a thin belt of barbed wire. Still, 23 May was fairly quiet, as was the 24th. On that day, as Bootle-Wilbraham recounted:

Brigadier Becky came up to walk around the line. He told me that when he had been visiting a neighbouring battalion a German [despatch rider] had come up the road and run straight at their party but had been able to turn around again and make good his escape without having been shot at. He brought good news in that my line was to be shortened, so I was able to withdraw No. 4 Company from the right of the line and put it in support of No. 2 Company on the left.[84]

While similar preparations were made, 25 May proved to be 'another ominously quiet day',[85] as did the 26th, a Sunday. With a deceptive calm descending, and the brigade improving new positions, Wilbraham-Bootle recalled that 'A routine based on the old Guards Divisional Trench Standing Orders, of which Brigadier Becky had given me a copy, was put into force.'[86] There were, Wilbraham-Bootle went on, signs of unaccustomed comfort at brigade headquarters:

I visited Brigade Headquarters in a princely château belonging to an industrial magnate of Roubaix. There was Louis XV furniture in the rooms and Lancret and Watteau paintings on the walls [and] I revelled in the unexpected luxury of bath salts and scented soap. At an excellent luncheon Brigadier Becky warned me of the possibility of a further withdrawal; and in fact, later in the day we got orders to hold the line of the River Lys between Le Touquet and Pont Rouge.[87]

On 27 May, the prolonged retreat of the 1st Guards Brigade entered a still more hazardous phase. Though the situation to its front remained quiet, its supporting artillery was now short of ammunition, logistics having collapsed in the mayhem of recent days. Rumours of a withdrawal to Dunkirk were now in the air, and the evacuation – Operation DYNAMO – had in fact already started. A conference was once again held at brigade headquarters and, as Bootle-Wilbraham remembered:

Brigadier Becky looked very serious as he came into the conference. His opening remark showed how bad the situation was. We were told 'to arrive as a fighting formation in the area around Hondschoote, Killem, Warhem, about ten miles from Dunkirk'. A look at the map showed that it involved a march of at least sixty miles. The withdrawal was to begin at 10 p.m., covered by rearguards; the line was finally to be abandoned at midnight. We were to march to a staging area in the neighbourhood of Locre, Neuve Eglise, Mariebourg – names familiar to anyone who had been in the Ypres Salient in World War I.[88]

Crossing the River Deûle, this long retreat would be accomplished by hard marching, a minimum of transport, and with the constant danger that 'what had hitherto been a comparatively orderly withdrawal might well become a rout'.[89] Still, the brigade pulled back as arranged and the following day, the 28th, found it heading towards the coast, marching amidst 'gusty showers' and exposed to air attack. As it neared Dunkirk, the roads became ever more congested, while news of the surrender of the Belgian Army, broadcast by the BBC at midday, added to an incipient sense of panic. With its route taking it back across the border into Belgian Flanders, the pandemonium in the town of Poperinge was especially unsettling. According to Bootle-Wilbraham, here the scene was 'indescribable', the streets clogged with debris, British motor vehicles and French horse-drawn wagons – much of the latter 'quite uncontrolled'. The chief cause of this bottleneck was a damaged bridge over a canal and, once cleared (partly due to the efforts of Bootle-Wilbraham himself), his Guardsmen passed through in good order.[90] On the other side, and with the distance to Dunkirk closing, he was intercepted by Merton, who had somehow procured some transport for his battalion:

> Just to the north of Poperinghe Brigadier Becky stopped me and told me that a number of lorries would meet the battalion south of Proven and would lift us to Hondschoote. I was indeed grateful for this. We embussed outside the Château de Couthove. There were then three miles of traffic abreast on the Dunkirk road.[91]

It was at this point that the single most famous episode in Merton's career took place. The scale of the disaster unfolding in northern France dismayed and demoralized many Allied commanders and there were notable casualties among Merton's peers. According to David French, even 'Budget' Loyd 'broke down under the strain',[92] and their immediate superior, the commander of I Corps, Lieutenant-General Michael Barker, was also overwhelmed. On 18 May, Sir Alan Brooke, GOC of II Corps, complained:

Barker [is] in a very difficult state to deal with, he is so overwrought with work and the present situation that he sees dangers where they don't exist and cannot make up his mind on any points. He is quite impossible to cooperate with. He has been worse than ever today and whenever anything is fixed he changes his mind shortly afterwards.[93]

None of this was true of Merton, though, who evidently rose to the novel challenge of commanding a brigade in action, even under these circumstances. An early sign of Merton's combativeness was evinced in Brussels in the first stages of the retreat. Watched by despondent and even hostile crowds of civilians, who now faced the prospect of a second German occupation in 25 years, according to one British officer the retreating BEF seemed 'like rats escaping through a hole'.[94] However, when one spectator spat at his staff car, this triggered an uncharacteristic outburst of rage. It was a reaction born of anger and frustration, as an accompanying despatch rider, Don Ellingworth, remembered: 'The Brigadier did his nut, in fact he was going to pull his revolver.'[95]

Yet there were different words for Merton's brigade as it retreated from Poperinge towards Dunkirk, pounded and harried (like the human tsunami of which it was a part) by a triumphant Luftwaffe. According to Walter Lord, whose classic account of the Dunkirk evacuation, *The Miracle of Dunkirk*, was first published in 1982:

[A]ll the while the Stukas continued their assault. 'Stand up to them. Shoot at them with a Bren gun from the shoulder. Take them like a high pheasant . . .' The advice came from Brigadier Beckwith-Smith, a throwback to the glory days of the Empire. But even those who understood what he was talking about found it hard to grasp the analogy. The Stukas had an implacable ferocity all their own.[96]

But, the condescension of Lord's judgement is clear, for it plainly had a very different effect on those whom Merton addressed. Nor were these the words, as Simon Sebag-Montefiore has put it, of just 'a jolly character with a partiality for shooting pheasants'.[97] Stressing the vital need to strike back at their assailants, if only to boost morale,[98] the idea of shooting at Stukas with Bren light machine guns (when they were pulling

up from their dive, and nearest to the ground) was far from absurd –
and, indeed, was urged by Merton on several occasions. Furthermore,
Merton's cheery exhortations modelled a confident style of command
intended to brace spirits despite dire conditions. As J. M. Langley, a
subaltern in the 2nd Coldstream, remembered, his platoon received
a memorable visit from Merton as they were resting outside Poperinge.
Although the news of their allotted role was fundamentally ominous, it
was delivered with typical gusto and an infectious enthusiasm:

Suddenly Brigadier Beckwith Smith ('Becky' to all) . . . drove up in
his car.
  'Marvellous news, Jimmy' he shouted. 'The best ever!' Short of the
German army deciding to call it a day, which seemed improbable, I
could think of no news deserving the qualifications of 'marvellous'
and the 'best ever'.
  'It is splendid, absolutely splendid. We have been given the supreme
honour of being the rearguard at Dunkirk. Tell your platoon, Jimmy –
come on, tell them the good news.'
  After all the months together I knew 15 Platoon very well, and
had not the slightest doubt that they would accept this information
with the usual tolerance and good humour they displayed in all
the vicissitudes of life 'on active service' or 'in action'. However, I
did not think that they would class it as 'marvellous' and the 'best
ever'.
  'I think it would come better from you, sir.'[99]

Undaunted by what might have seemed a weary if implicit challenge,
Merton was perfectly happy to communicate these tidings in person:

'Right, right', he replied as he strode across, and after telling them to
remain seated, made known to them the change in plan.
  Then, to my delight, since I had never heard this from him direct,
he recalled his earlier instruction, which had become a by-word
during the retreat, as to how to deal with Stuka dive-bombers.
  'Stand up to them. Shoot at them with a Bren gun from the
shoulder. Take them like a high pheasant. Give them plenty of lead.

Remember, five pounds to any man who brings one down. I have already paid out ten pounds.'

High spirits and optimism are very infectious, especially when they are not forced. Becky genuinely regarded the task as a supreme honour and I could see that much of his enthusiasm was shared by 15 Platoon.[100]

In Langley's view, together with the example of the Belgian Boy Scouts who had guided them through and beyond Poperinge, Merton's words acted as a genuine tonic:

A meal in the morning, the superb example of 'keeping your head when all about are losing theirs', so courageously displayed by the Belgian Boy Scouts in Poperinge, and Becky's words did much to help 15 Platoon through the next 24 hours which it took to cover the remaining 20 miles to our last fighting line on the Bergues-Hondschoote Canal.[101]

As Jeremy Crang has noted in an essay entitled 'The Defence of the Dunkirk Perimeter', the crucial role which Merton's brigade was allotted is largely missing from public perceptions of Dunkirk:

The popular image of the British Expeditionary Force at Dunkirk in 1940 is of long lines of forlorn soldiers waiting patiently on the beaches to be rescued by the Royal Navy. Shocked by their rapid defeat, they snake helplessly down to the shoreline to meet the little ships. But a short distance inland a gallant rearguard battle was fought for several days to defend the Dunkirk perimeter and enable the evacuation to take place. Without this determined final stand many more British troops would have been captured by the Germans: the 'miracle' of Dunkirk might not have appeared quite so wondrous.[102]

As with the whole of the retreat to, and evacuation from, Dunkirk, this defence was an improvised affair. As it was extemporized, and German pressure mounted, units were shifted around according to need and the organization of many brigades and divisions simply dissolved. For example, on 26 May the 3rd Grenadier Guards was transferred from Merton's brigade to the 5th Infantry Division; likewise, many of the headquarters personnel of the 2nd Coldstream were siphoned off 'by some alien staff officer' to hold a bridge elsewhere. To offset these losses, and as retreating troops continued to pour into the perimeter, on 29 May Merton sent 120 men of the Lancashire Fusiliers to reinforce his depleted Coldstreamers.[103] However, the scale of the crisis also meant changes at the top. On 31 May, as Gort (unwillingly) left the perimeter for England under an express order from Churchill,[104] command of its I Corps, which covered the sector from the port to the Franco-Belgian border and which served as the rearguard of the BEF,[105] was given to Alexander. This was a harsh decision, but Barker, its previous GOC, had been 'showing signs of strain and it is possible that Gort believed that Alexander had a better prospect of getting the remaining troops away'.[106]

In any event, Alexander's promotion placed Merton in acting command of the 1st Division just as the German attacks on I Corps' front intensified. At this point, his command, which was covering Dunkirk itself, comprised 1st Guards Brigade, the 3rd Infantry Brigade and, due to the exigencies of the situation, the 126th Infantry Brigade, comprising the regulars of the 1st East Lancashire Regiment and two Territorial battalions from northern England, namely the 5th King's Own and the 5th Border Regiment.[107] Although the defenders were helped by the nature of the surrounding terrain (which was typically Flemish – waterlogged, low lying, dotted with solid farmhouses and criss-crossed by canals and drainage ditches), and by German exhaustion and the reining-in of German armoured units for rest and refitting,[108] by this stage the defences along the 'Canal Line' were paper thin, being little more than a loose barrier of strong points which were in places overlooked from the opposite bank.[109] Here, it was very much a soldier's battle – with leadership and small-scale tactics at a premium. As Daniel Todman has emphasized:

In the final battles around Dunkirk, all the combatants were running on empty . . . Much of the fighting around the Channel ports was small-scale, improvised stuff between infantry units operating at close quarters. Neither side had many chances to fight well-organized, carefully planned battles in which massed artillery pieces unleashed the full concussive potential of modern war.[110]

Still, the German attacks on the Dunkirk perimeter were fierce enough and were audible (in the lulls between air attacks) to those waiting for evacuation. As L. F. Ellis put it in the official history of *The War in France and Flanders 1939–1940*:

[T]he sound of distant firing was a reminder that behind the scenes there were divisions which still fought, without rest or respite, to hold the enemy at bay while their comrades sailed for home, divisions which still turned their backs on the sea in order to confront the enemy – the soldiers of the Allied armies who made evacuation possible.[111]

Hard pressed by German infantry and their supporting artillery, 'the British troops had bitter fighting during this, their final day on the canal. Shelling and mortaring continued without pause and all units had heavy casualties.'[112] Emblematic of the ferocity and desperation of the fighting in Merton's sector were the exploits of Captain H. M. Ervine-Andrews of the 1st East Lancashires, who won the only VC awarded for the evacuation. In a feat of marksmanship which would have won Merton's warm approval, Ervine-Andrews climbed onto the roof of a blazing barn and picked off 17 advancing Germans with his rifle, before accounting for many others with a Bren gun.[113]

Such heroics, however, made no difference to the wider course of events and, on the afternoon of 1 June, Merton issued his final orders for the withdrawal to Dunkirk and its adjacent beaches. As Bootle-Wilbraham recalled, the French (who had been fighting bravely, mainly on the western end of the perimeter) would replace their British allies as they fell back to the shoreline. Non-essential personnel were to leave and embark for evacuation immediately, while 'troops awaiting embarkation were to be dispersed in small parties [and] dig in in the sand'. Some artillery support would remain in place until midnight and commanders were only to embark 'when approximately three-quarters of their force' had done so. Finally, and to emphasize that this was far from being a *sauve qui peut*, 'Brigadier Becky stressed that all sections were to embark armed with Brens and anti-tank rifles'. To underline his determination, Merton even forbade the beleaguered 2nd Coldstream from undertaking an early withdrawal to a less exposed position.[114] By dawn on 2 June an orderly retirement had taken place and the remnants of Merton's command were waiting to embark, either from the beaches or from the Mole in Dunkirk harbour. There then followed an anxious wait, for their losses the previous day (which included four destroyers) had forced the Royal Navy to suspend evacuations in daylight.[115] Nevertheless, and with the French still holding on:

> At 8.30 p.m. the British rearguard, about seven thousand strong, began to form up. With the remains of 1st Guards Brigade heading the column, they marched down to the Mole, there to embark. All Coldstreamers and Hampshires made a point of taking the Bren guns and anti-tank rifles, with which they had fought, on board with them. There were at least two Brens per section and two anti-tank rifles per platoon.[116]

It was at this point that Alexander and Merton embarked. It is not known which ship brought him back to England but, given the nature of the evacuation, Merton returned, like others, in the uniform he was standing in. Much to his regret, he even left behind the Prayer Book that Honor had given him on their engagement more than 20 years before.

The evacuation was, of course, a national, even global, melodrama. On Sunday 26 May, the day on which Gort was authorized to withdraw the BEF to the coast, a Day of Prayer took place across Great Britain and the Empire. Announced on 17 May and enjoying the full support of the churches, this day of supplication 'for the nation, empire and the allied cause' saw churches fill and the King, Queen and other public figures attend a high-profile service at Westminster Abbey. With the fate of the BEF hanging by a thread, the occasion reflected an acute sense of public and private anxiety.[117] This was clearly shared by Honor (prone to worry, as Merton had noted) who wrote a rambling, desperate letter to Georgina on 28 May:

> My darling mum . . . I think of you every moment of the day, often in the night when I am not thinking of my beloved one – we must keep strong [and] not fail in this tortuous time . . . Such glory as their epic tale of this week will outshine any in History, so for oneself one

mustn't think. I try not to think or listen and can hardly speak. I feel grateful and thankful to have been with you last weekend . . . Your spirit is so glorious and always has been, and I love you with all my breaking heart . . . it will be well if we can just hold to our Faith and trust in God.[118]

Her sense of relief was therefore tangible when she telegrammed Aberarder nearly a week later: 'Becky is home spoke to him 2 o'clock AM from Seaport. All too marvellous. Thank God for all his mercy going London to meet Becky.'[119] In contrast, Merton's telegram to Georgina, sent later that day, was much more laconic: 'Rough expedition but safely back at Dorchester with Honor. Bless you. Mert.'[120]

4

18th Division

On Sunday 30 June, and now stationed in the large and blessedly sunny Lincolnshire fishing port of Grimsby, Merton wrote a pensive letter to Georgina, reflecting on the mood of the country, the direction of his military career and the prospective course of the war. With the shambles of the recent retreat and evacuation behind him, and Britain and its empire now standing alone against the principal European dictatorships, Merton was struck by the incongruously carefree demeanour of the civilian population:

> It is just impossible to believe we are at war, and I don't wonder that the people don't realise. I walked along part of the beach south of Grimsby this afternoon and it was crowded with happy couples and children – no doubt not as crowded as in peace time and the wooden huts with which the beach is lined are nearly empty.[1]

Despite the country's straits, this pervasive sense of denial was apparent even in church, and this despite the recent sensation (and apparent success, if the Dunkirk evacuation was anything to go by) of the National Day of Prayer. On the very eve of a joint public statement by the archbishops of Canterbury and York (one which commenced 'The enemy is at the gate', and urged the nation to make 'every day, and especially every Lord's Day . . . a day of national prayer'),[2] Merton perceived only somnolence in this vulnerable coastal town:

> I went to church this evening in the very beautiful old building here – large enough almost to be a Cathedral – not full by any means and not many young people. Perhaps just as well they should be out in the open but one would like to think that they thanked God sometimes

out there for all that He has given them in this beautiful country of ours.[3]

Significantly, this reverie spoke of a concern that Merton had harboured well before Dunkirk. For among the items he kept until his death in Formosa nearly three years later was a reprint of a leading article first published in *The Times* on 17 February 1940. Entitled 'Religion and National Life', and pointing out the woeful ignorance of Christianity evinced by so many evacuees, it deplored the neglect of religious education in Britain's state-run schools. Touching on a major public and political issue that would be resolved – satisfactorily or unsatisfactorily in the longer term – by R. A. Butler's 1944 Education Act for England and Wales, its author (apparently the Revd Robert Catterall Worsley, an Anglican educationalist) spoke some hard and uncomfortable truths. It was, Worsley claimed, a:

grim fact that in a country professedly Christian, and in a country which at the moment is staking its all in defence of Christian principles, there is a system of national education which allows the citizens of the future to have a purely heathen upbringing.

As Worsley maintained:

The basis of good citizenship is character, and a man's character depends upon his beliefs. How, then, can the State afford to ignore these simple truths, and to view the teaching of religion as a task with which it has no direct concern?

What was plainly needed was bold, transformative action:

[I]f the war has emphasized the deficiencies of our present educational system, something more than war-time expedients will be needed to remedy them. More than before it has become clear that the healthy life of a nation must be based on spiritual principles. For many years we have been living on spiritual capital, on traditions inherited from the past, instead of providing for the future. Christianity cannot be imbibed from the air. It is not a philosophy but a historic religion, which must dwindle unless the facts upon which it is founded are taught, and such teaching made the centre of our educational system . . . The highest of all knowledge must be given frankly the highest of all places in the training of young citizens.

Worsley concluded with a salutary warning:

It will be of little use to fight, as we are fighting to-day, for the preservation of Christian principles if Christianity itself is to have no future, or at immense cost to safeguard religion against attack from without if we allow it to be starved by neglect from within.[4]

Even though it seemed to reflect the nation's parlous spiritual plight, Evensong at Grimsby Minster had a therapeutic value for Merton, for it poured balm on his nagging fear of being passed over, especially after being superseded in his command of the 1st Division by Major-General Kenneth Anderson who, in 1942, went on to command the British First Army in North Africa:

I was glad I went, for sometimes I feel a little hurt that people . . . have been promoted and I have not – yet anyhow – but when one hears that prayer about giving and not counting the cost or seeking any reward one feels fortified.[5]

(That this prayer of St Ignatius Loyola, the founder of the Society of Jesus, should have appealed to Merton is not surprising, but it is remarkable how this stray remark reflected the extent to which Loyola's prayer – 'Lord, teach me to be generous. Teach me to serve you as you deserve; to give and not to count the cost . . .' – had seeped into Anglican consciousness by this point, becoming a wartime staple of the RAChD.)[6]

Apart from incidental family news, Merton's reflection concluded with Britain's strategic predicament, especially the threat of invasion and the wider repercussions of the fall of France:

One keeps on going over in one's mind what their plan of invasion can possibly be. That it will contain some surprise there is no doubt, but however great it may be I feel they will have a tougher nut to crack than any they have met yet.[7]

As for France and its future, Merton wrote:

French politics may have been rotten but I don't think that had anything to do with the failure of the French Army to fight better than they did. I don't blame the French Colonies or Navy and Air Force for not going on fighting but I think the two latter might have taken bigger steps to see that less fell into German hands. I don't know how much we have got but it won't be long before the Germans put the screw on to get whatever of the Navy remains in French Colonial Ports.

Three days later, the dilemma of the future role of the French fleet under the terms of the recent armistice would be resolved by the abrupt seizure of French ships in British ports and by the Royal Navy's ruthless bombardment of the warships anchored in the Algerian naval base of Mers-el-Kébir.[8] Still, and as Merton fairly conceded, Britain itself was far from blameless for the recent catastrophe:

No doubt too as time goes on the French will feel more bitter against us for not being better armed after 9 months of war. How poor old Chamberlain can continue in the Government [as Lord President of the Council] I don't know. It just drives me wild when I think [of] the way his Government has gambled with our Empire.[9]

Arguably, due recognition of Merton's conduct in France never really came. Unbeknownst to him, Alexander attempted to have him appointed a Companion of the Order of the Bath (CB), his recommendation stating that:

This officer commanded the 1st Guards Brigade with conspicuous ability from May 10th to June 2nd, a period which it must be admitted was a tremendous strain on commanders. At all times, especially when the situation was most grave, he set a splendid example to his own troops by the cool and able manner he handled each different and dangerous situation. Particularly was this the case on the River [Scheldt] when the Germans succeeded in crossing the river and penetrated the defence. Without awaiting orders, Brigadier Beckwith-Smith acted with lightning rapidity in organizing counter attacks. These measures, well and quickly staged, were completely successful in saving a critical situation. Later, during the defence of Dunkirk, he showed the same commendable qualities as a soldier, finally withdrawing the whole of his Brigade in formed and disciplined bodies, properly armed and equipped, to the boats – and being the last himself to leave the shores of France. Personal bravery and calmness by a Commander in critical times has a great influence on soldiers – this splendid influence was exerted to the full by Brigadier Beckwith-Smith.[10]

Why this was never approved remains unclear, but Merton was eventually mentioned in despatches for a fourth time in December 1940 in recognition of his 'distinguished services in connection with operations in the Field'.[11]

Still, though no greater award was forthcoming, Merton's anxieties over promotion proved short-lived, for on 12 July 1940 – the day after his fiftieth birthday – he wrote an ebullient note to Georgina from Louth in Lincolnshire:

When I got back to my H.Q. at tea time today I found a message to say I had been appointed to command the 18th Division with acting rank of Major General and that I am to take it over tomorrow. So off I go to Sprowston Hall, Norwich . . . I have just spoken to Honor on the telephone. She is delighted of course. I'm naturally pleased I haven't been passed over altogether. One hopes one will prove worthy. As I told you, I have at moments been a little sad that I was not considered worthy before. However, all is well now and Pray God will continue so for all of us . . . You can say I've got a Division but better not say which or where.[12]

With a nod to his birthday the previous day, he added: 'Bless you for your birthday letter and telegram. No, it doesn't seem like half a century and

I don't think we show it as much as some.'[13] Merton's appointment, which officially commenced on 14 July, was published in the *London Gazette* on 16 July, and his acting rank of major-general was made substantive within a fortnight.[14]

Merton's appointment to the 18th Division was made under the aegis of Sir Edmund Ironside, a former CIGS, whose tenure as Commander-in-Chief Home Forces lasted just a few weeks, from 27 May to 19 July 1940. At this point, Ironside was wrestling with the problem of defending home soil with troops who were barely trained and desperately lacking in modern transport and equipment. The capitulation of France, which signed an armistice with Germany on 22 June, further complicated the challenge he was facing. With Holland and Belgium already overrun, Ironside's strategy identified the most vulnerable part of the English coast as lying 'between the Wash and Folkestone', his plans envisaging 'a largely static "crust" of beach defences, with blocks and stop-lines further inland and a small mobile reserve north and west of London to counter-attack landings in East Anglia or on the south coast'.[15] In view of the Army's lack of heavy equipment after Dunkirk, its limited mobility and its paucity of training, this was a reasonable approach in many ways, though it failed to take into account the vulnerability of the south coast after the fall of France, or the problems of ceding large parts of eastern England to the Germans in the event of an invasion. Ultimately, this failure of vision was instrumental in his supersession by Sir Alan Brooke in mid-July.[16] Nevertheless, Ironside's plans clearly favoured Merton, whose mettle on the defensive had already been showcased on the Scheldt and at Dunkirk, and the news of his promotion clearly thrilled his family. On 13 July, Honor sent a telegram to Georgina (who, from the fastness of Aberarder, was ever watchful of her son's career) which rejoiced, 'Thinking of your joy over Becky's promotion. All so happy today . . .'[17] For his part, Merton viewed this development as another promising step up the career ladder, confiding to Georgina at the end of August, and with no apparent irony: 'I hope . . . that you will be spared long enough to hear of Dunkirk from my own lips. I should like to think I will be spared long enough myself to be a field marshal.'[18]

However, after the drama and success of its last-ditch stand at Dunkirk, news of Merton's departure from 1st Guards Brigade met with a more muted reaction from his colleagues. On 17 July, his successor, Brigadier

F. V. Copland-Griffiths (or 'Cop', as he was known), wrote to express his disappointment that Merton was not staying with the 1st Infantry Division, which was now deployed along the north Lincolnshire coast: 'I am so delighted you have got promotion, but like everybody else here, extremely sorry that it is not to this Division.' Still, and despite its gruelling ordeal in Flanders, Copland-Griffiths' inheritance seemed in good shape. As he acknowledged, 'I know that I am taking over the best Brigade in the Army, so I have not much to worry about provided I can do my part!' Regarding Merton's parting advice, which appears to have been a characteristic blend of charm and efficiency, he wrote:

> Thank you for the tips which I find very helpful. I have paid hurried visits to everybody and done the Northern part of the sector in some detail and I suppose I shall get to know it all some day . . . The King came to see us last Saturday and he and the Major-General said some very nice things.

Nevertheless, Copland-Griffiths felt that additional mentoring from Merton might still be beneficial: 'If I get a chance I would like to come down and see you as we are not very far apart.'[19]

Indeed not. Under Ironside's defensive scheme, the 18th Infantry Division was deployed further to the south, along the Norfolk coast. However, though their functions had now converged, the 18th Division was very different in character from the 1st Infantry Division, and from the 1st Guards Brigade in particular. Formed on 30 September 1939, with its headquarters in Trowse House, Norwich, the 18th Division had not been part of the BEF evacuated from Dunkirk, nor was it part of the war's 'second B.E.F.' which was sent (briefly) to prop up the French after that storied withdrawal.[20] It had also missed the Norwegian campaign of April–June 1940, which had seen a small British force bundled out of Norway together with its French and Polish allies. And the fact that the 18th Division was largely untested was not the only major difference. Whereas the 1st Division had embarked for France in September 1939 as a division composed of regulars or reservists, the 18th Division was classed as 'a Second Line Territorial Army Division, [a] duplicate of 54th (East Anglian) Infantry Division'.[21] In other words, whereas the 1st Division had been composed of long-service professional soldiers, in accordance with plans laid down in 1920 the 18th had been raised on cadres supplied by the part-time, pre-war Territorial Army (TA).[22] While Merton had commanded Oxford University's OTC and was familiar with the TA in London in the 1930s, these units had at least been filled with willing volunteers. The same cannot be said of the human material that filled the ranks of the 18th Division – and much of the British Army – throughout the Second World War. As Alan Allport has calculated, of the 3.8 million men who served in the British Army between 1939 and 1945, 'all but 258,000 were civilians on the day war broke out'.[23] Of the remaining 3.5 million, fewer than half a million were in the TA on the outbreak of war and, of the remainder, three-quarters were conscripts.[24]

And the TA that generated the 18th Division had, like the Regular Army, gone through a lean period between the wars. Despite its modest size on 3 September 1939, it had experienced a surge in recruitment both before and after the Munich Crisis. Indeed, in March 1939, and by nothing more than 'a proverbial stroke of the pen', its size had been doubled by the Secretary of State for War, Leslie Hore-Belisha.[25] However, this expansion had the effect of creating 'enormous administrative problems due to shortage of drill halls, equipment, uniforms, and, most seriously, instructors',[26] for the foundations on which it occurred were narrow to say the least. During the 1920s and 1930s, and as Merton had discovered in London, the TA had suffered from chronic underfunding, a dearth of new equipment and a conspicuous lack of public interest. Significantly, in an era marked by the Depression, and with modest recruitment targets to meet, there had been an abiding scarcity of recruits. In part, this reflected the competition posed to part-time soldiering by less taxing leisure activities (notably Britain's booming cinema and dance hall industries), but it also reflected the emotional and psychological scars of the First World War, a natural incli-nation to pacificism (if not to outright pacifism) and, until the mid-1930s, the absence of any clear-cut military threat.[27] Of the rank-and-file recruits who did come forward, many were deemed to be of poor quality – often enlisting simply for the modest pay that the 'Terriers' afforded. Moreover, the financial costs of being a Territorial officer served as a social filter, with means rather than ability often proving the deciding factor. Consequently, amidst the extensive patchwork of local units that comprised the TA in

1939, only a few of the most prestigious – such as the Honourable Artillery Company and the London Scottish – were viewed as high calibre in military terms.[28]

The fact that the 18th Division was formed at the end of September 1939, barely a month after the declaration of war and the passage of the National Service (Armed Forces) Act, affords a further clue as to the quality of Merton's new division. Though supplied by the TA with its cadres of instructors and pre-war soldiers, the division was chiefly comprised of conscripts, men who, under the terms of the Act, were aged between 18 and 41 and were deemed eligible to serve. This reliance on conscripts, or 'National Servicemen', had major implications for the morale of the British Army throughout the Second World War. As David French has put it: 'The rapid expansion of the army during the Second World War presented the military authorities with three fundamental problems. Many recruits were suspicious of the army, did not want to join it, and did not want to fight.'[29] Certainly, the unwelcome burden of compulsory military service, the demands and pettiness of military discipline, lengthy spells spent languishing at home and a growing distrust of the capacities of its own commanders posed serious problems for the morale and discipline of the Army in the first years of the war. Indeed, and as Allport has elaborated, by 1942 the term 'browned off' had come to characterize the prevailing mood of the British soldier – a depressing cocktail of frustration, indifference and helplessness generated amidst a lengthening war by a colossal, dehumanizing military machine. According to Allport, 'The whole story of the British Army from Dunkirk till V-J Day was, in a sense, its grappling with its own Browned-Offness',[30] a feeling expressed in the candid admission of one Scottish veteran that:

> If Churchill instead of his blood, sweat and tears thing had said 'Any man or woman in the forces who would like to give it all up and go home, can' – he wouldnae have got the microphone out of his mouth before he'd been trampled to death in the rush.[31]

Under these circumstances, a special style of command was undoubtedly required of the Army's senior commanders. Hampered by their record of early defeats and dogged by the unflattering pre-war caricature of Colonel

Blimp ('the famously ruddy-faced reactionary created by the cartoonist David Low'),[32] effective generalship in Britain's field armies demanded a strong degree of personal presence and appeal. As David Fraser has put it:

> Such a generation and such an army had to be led rather than driven. To become truly disciplined, as an army must, discipline had to be combined with a certain charisma in those who demanded it, or in enough of them. Mechanical processes could achieve something – and something necessary – but only if combined with those touches of human communication, inspiration and example men call leadership.[33]

Ultimately, and as Correlli Barnett noted, Britain's best generals knew the value of good public relations and aimed to be 'immediate and personal figures to the troops, not merely remote embodiments of command to whom was owed unquestioning respect and obedience'.[34] And, among the assets of an effective leader was the key but elusive quality of likeability. For, as Fraser has observed:

> And in this army not only respect for competence, fairness and even strictness, but liking – however roughly disguised or disclaimed – was an important factor. Montgomery, sometimes regarded as inhuman in his judgments of ability, always recognised this. 'I don't agree,' he used to say after visiting a command whose chief was reported to him as no good, 'I don't agree. And they *like* him. That's important. They're good judges.' Suspicious of mere charm, Montgomery knew the strength affection could bring to the military bond, how it could warm necessary respect, how it could stimulate confidence of the led in the leader.[35]

A key token of familiarity and approval among the ranks of 'the led' was the coining (or adoption) of an affectionate nickname. Among the roll call of distinguished British generals to be honoured by such monikers was 'Monty' himself, together with 'Bill' Slim (General Sir William Slim, victor of the Burma campaign), 'The Auk' (namely Sir Claude Auchinleck, victor of the First Battle of El Alamein in July 1942) and 'Alex'

(Sir Harold Alexander, Supreme Allied Commander in the Mediterranean). In contrast, Kenneth Anderson, who became GOC of the 1st Division on its return from Dunkirk, was tactfully described by Merton as 'not such an attractive personality as the last one', namely the famously charming Harold Alexander. Later, Anderson also failed to endear himself to the First Army in North Africa. As General (later President) Dwight D. Eisenhower tellingly remembered:

General Anderson was a gallant Scot, devoted to his duty and absolutely selfless. Honest and straightforward, he was blunt, at times to the point of rudeness, and this trait, curiously enough, seemed to bring him into conflict with his British confreres more than it did with Americans. His real difficulty was shyness. He was not a popular type, but I had real respect for his fighting heart.[36]

Much worse, and as one British veteran of the Malaya campaign and the fall of Singapore reflected, Lieutenant-General Arthur Percival, who as GOC Malaya presided over the whole debacle, was either unknown or disdained by those under his command. As Sergeant Harry Blackham put it:

He just didn't look the part . . . And how he could make his appearance even worse by wearing that long obsolete Wolseley helmet, God alone knows . . . I have always felt sorry for him. He was not a known general like the Auk or Alex. Can you possibly think of Percival as 'Perce'?[37]

However, this was never a problem that applied to 'Becky', though his résumé was otherwise typical of those who rose to command divisions in the field. As Jonathan Fennell has noted:

The men who went on to command field-force divisions of the British Army against Germany and Italy in the Second World War were typically young and up-and-coming thrusters . . . The vast majority, 92 per cent, had served in the Great War . . . Most divisional commanders in the Second World War, therefore, had relatively recent 'personal knowledge of front-line service' and possessed what Napoleon referred to as one of the greatest attributes that any general required, luck.[38]

If that luck was signalled by the fact that they had served in, and survived, the First World War as junior officers, 'they were also broadly competent; 92 per cent of divisional commanders who had served in the First World War had been awarded medals for gallantry or leadership of a high order'.[39]

Despite its tricky composition, and the shifts that were occurring in the requirements and nature of command, in July 1940 Merton brought his talents, experience and personality to bear on a division with a gilded reputation to uphold. Its precursor, the original 18th Division, had been raised in September 1914 as one of the divisions of Lord Kitchener's all-volunteer 'New Army'. The 18th (Eastern) Division, as it was then styled, had been trained and led until January 1917 by Frederick Ivor Maxse, one of the British Army's best divisional and corps commanders on the Western Front.[40] On 1 July 1916, the tragic opening day of the Battle of the Somme and the bloodiest day in the history of the British Army, the 18th Division achieved the rare distinction of taking all its assigned objectives. In the subsequent months of the Battle of the Somme, it went on to cement its 'growing reputation as an elite division', taking (for example) the formidable Schwaben Redoubt that September, a task that had eluded the famous 36th (Ulster) Division on 1 July.[41] Key to its performance was the exceptional emphasis that Maxse placed on thorough and appropriate training, an emphasis he maintained as a corps commander in 1917 and which transformed his division of citizen soldiers into one of the most proficient formations in the British Army. In April 1918, Maxse was appointed to the new role of Inspector of Training for the BEF, a role intended to eliminate the persistent problems posed by 'the varied nature of training within different formations and the diversity of command approaches'.[42]

Furthermore, the elite 18th Division proved to be a nursery of some of the most prominent leaders of the British Army in the Second World War. Sir Alan Brooke, who was a corps commander in the BEF in 1939–40; Commander-in-Chief, Home Forces from July 1940 to December 1941; and CIGS from December 1941 to January 1946, served as a Brigade Major

Royal Artillery with the 18th Division during the Battle of the Somme,[43] reputedly introducing the creeping barrage – a tactic borrowed from the French – into the BEF.[44] Ironically, another officer to enjoy a distinguished career with the 18th Division was Arthur Percival, who was commissioned into the 7th Bedfordshire Regiment as a second lieutenant in 1914 and rose to command the 2nd Bedfordshires in 1918, a year in which he also took temporary command of the division's 54th Brigade. Earning the MC and the DSO in his ascent through the ranks, at the end of the war Percival was described by his brigadier as 'an excellent and most efficient officer, beloved by his officers, NCOs and men',[45] attributes that failed to re-materialize in the Malayan campaign of 1941–2.

It is worth dwelling on the history and renown of the old 18th Division, as Merton's appointment as its GOC was a remarkable case of history repeating itself. For Maxse (on whose staff Merton had served in 1918) was not only a Coldstreamer who had commanded the regiment's 2nd Battalion from 1903 to 1907, but had also served as the commander of the 1st Guards Brigade in the original BEF, returning from France (and the Mons and Aisne campaigns) to take command of the 18th Division at the end of September 1914.[46] Despite his background as a Guards officer, Maxse had recognized the worth of its civilians-in-arms from the moment he took command in Colchester. As Clifford Kinvig has remarked:

> From the outset he showed none of the antipathy to the unmilitary and at times querulous citizen soldiers which many regular officers initially displayed, and which some were to exhibit for the duration. He saw the New Armies as first-class raw material and quickly appreciated the excellent physical and moral qualities of the subaltern officers as well as the standard of the rank and file which he averred was 'undoubtedly higher than that of the men we recruited to the old Army'.[47]

Given the circumstances of the late summer of 1940, and his credentials as one of Maxse's staff at the end of the First World War, it appears that Merton's appointment was an attempt to repeat the manifestly successful experiment of sending a thrusting and ambitious Guardsman, a fighting officer and a proven trainer, to prepare a new generation of citizen soldiers (and a second iteration of the renowned 18th Division) to wage a modern war against the most formidable army in Europe.

However, when Merton took command in July 1940, the 18th Division was poorly equipped and widely dispersed in coastal defence duties. With its headquarters in Norwich, its units were spread along the coast, with the 54th Brigade (for example) covering the 25-mile stretch of coast between Cromer and Lowestoft, the 5th Suffolks being billeted in 'holiday bungalows' among 'the sand dunes of Hemsby'.[48] It was also a much larger and more complex entity than he had previously commanded, a fact for which his background as a staff officer in the First World War stood him in good stead. Whereas the 1st Guards Brigade had consisted of three infantry battalions plus an anti-tank company, the 18th Division comprised nine infantry battalions in three brigades (53rd, 54th and 55th). These were supported by a host of 'Divisional Troops' which, on leaving Britain in the autumn of 1941, comprised three regiments of field artillery (118th, 135th and 148th Royal Artillery), a regiment of anti-tank guns (125th Royal Artillery), four companies of Royal Engineers (287th, 288th, 560th Field Companies and 251st Field Park Company), a signals unit, a machine-gun battalion (the 9th Royal Northumberland Fusiliers) and the 18th Battalion, Reconnaissance Corps. It also mustered four companies of the Royal Army Service Corps (RASC), a unit of the Royal Army Ordnance Corps (RAOC), three field ambulances (196th–198th) of the Royal Army Medical Corps (RAMC), the 44th Field Hygiene Section and a provost company of the Royal Military Police (RMP).[49]

Despite its complexity, the core of the division was its nine infantry battalions, whose mainly East Anglian origin was advertised by the divisional insignia of a stylized windmill. The 53rd Brigade was composed of the 5th and 6th Battalions of the Royal Norfolk Regiment and the 2nd Battalion of the (all-Territorial) Cambridgeshire Regiment; the 54th Brigade comprised the 4th Battalion of the Norfolks, as well as the 4th and 5th Battalions of the Suffolk Regiment; and the 55th Brigade mustered the 1st Battalion of the Cambridgeshires, the 5th Battalion of the Bedfordshire and Hertfordshire Regiment and the 1/5th Battalion of the Sherwood Foresters.[50] As the composition of the 55th Brigade intimated, the East Anglian identity of the division was always more notional than real, and its divisional troops gave it a truly national character. Indeed, it could scarcely have been otherwise as the multifarious needs of an infantry division usually meant (much to Churchill's chagrin) that fewer than half of its soldiers were 'frontline infantrymen'.[51] Besides an East Midlands (Derbyshire) presence in the form of the Sherwood Foresters, when the 18th Battalion, Reconnaissance Corps arrived in January 1941 (an addition dictated by the failure of tactical reconnaissance during the Dunkirk campaign)[52] it was actually the repurposed and rebranded 5th Battalion of the Loyal North Lancashire Regiment. Likewise, the divisional machine-gun battalion (intended to supply, as needed, additional firepower to its infantry brigades) had seen action in France with the 23rd (Northumbrian) Division, a TA division disbanded after Dunkirk.[53]

As a microcosm of British – and especially English – society, the personnel of the 18th Division came from a wide range of occupational, social and religious backgrounds and reflected all the diversity, hierarchies and cross-currents of civilian and military life. Among the individual soldiers of 18th Division who earned distinction after the war was the Cambridge-based artist and cartoonist Ronald Searle, who joined the TA in April 1939, 'registering as an architectural draughtsman with the Royal Engineers'.[54] As for the former colliers of the 9th Northumberland Fusiliers, 'easily one of Beckwith-Smith's most tightly knit Territorial units', one prisoner of war (POW) noted after the fall of Singapore that:[55]

> The Fusiliers happened to be of good stock, tough and hard working. When faced with a job of work [at Keppel Harbour], they got down to it, and finished it off honestly. Not because they were Jap-happy, as some of the less fortunate flung at them, but because they had always looked at work as something to be done, not as something to be avoided.[56]

If a 'pecking order of prestige . . . enforced in a spirit of withering snobbery' had always been characteristic of the Regular Army,[57] this was also a trait of the TA. Though all combat soldiers 'looked down on the non-combat branches',[58] the gunners of the 135th Field Regiment belonged to a unit that was 'more distinguished socially than militarily', having once been the North Hertfordshire Yeomanry.[59] Chiefly recruited from Hitchin and Peterborough, its gunners looked askance at the East Anglian 'swede-bashers' who filled the infantry battalions of the 53rd Brigade.[60] In keeping with their pre-war status, its regimental chaplain was a Church of England rector from Somerset – 'as gentlemanly a padre as anyone could wish'.[61] Diversity was also the keynote in religious terms. The medical officer of the Northumberland Fusiliers, Captain H. Silman, was Jewish and, writing to his mother from Norwich in July 1940, Merton remarked that his division's 'senior chaplain' was a Methodist, 'simple and earnest'. (Perhaps reflecting Georgina's Low Church, Church of Ireland heritage, he took care to add: 'I thought the same about [Norwich Cathedral] as you do about the one in Inverness – but I suppose it can't be helped in a Cathedral where pomp and circumstance are necessary.')[62]

With the country braced for invasion, and the Battle of Britain raging in the skies, the early weeks of Merton's command were marked by a flurry of visits from Brooke, Churchill, Anthony Eden (the Secretary of State for War), Gort (now Inspector of Military Training) and the King himself. On 30 July, Brooke recorded his tour of inspection in the following terms:

> Flew to the Wash . . . Then inspected beach defences from Wash to Yarmouth, visiting 18th Div and seeing Beckie [sic] Smith. Unfortunately weather was bad and had to motor back from Norwich instead of flying which took 3 hours instead of 40 mins![63]

Better fortune attended Churchill's visit a few days later, in which he 'inspected troops and gun positions in 53rd Infantry Brigade area'.[64] Subsequently, Merton wrote to Georgina to report on 'the usual hectic week, the outstanding features of which were visits from Winston [on 7 August] and Anthony Eden [on 9 August]':

> The former when he got out of his plane advanced and shook me warmly by the hand and said 'I am pleased to see you again, Becky – Clemmie [Clementine] has been asking when I was going to see you.' He brought his brother [John] and son [Randolph] with him. The former said, 'I haven't seen you since the naval manoeuvres of 1913' (when you remember I spent a few days in the *Enchantress* with them).[65]

Though clearly gratified by John Churchill's recollection of their time spent on the Admiralty yacht nearly 30 years earlier (when Winston was

First Lord of the Admiralty), Merton was, characteristically, less impressed by the Prime Minister's son, something of a ne'er-do-well who was then, in theory, a serving officer in the 4th Queen's Own Hussars: 'Randolf [sic] has got very fat. He should be serving with his regiment.'[66] Despite this blunt assessment, 'Winston was charming. He had spent the morning with the 1st Guards Brigade and when he took off at 7.30 pm he said it was the best day he had had.' For Merton, who only weeks earlier had been struck by the prevailing complacency in Grimsby, Churchill's visitation proved to be a revelation:

> I travelled in the car with him some of the time and one could see he was almost as moved as I was by the reception he got from the people. News of his presence travelled fast. He kept on repeating 'brave people'. He saw one battalion on parade and enjoyed that as much as anything. He made a very good little speech to some Newfoundlanders, very different to Neville Chamberlain . . . Eden too was very charming. It seems funny to know such great men, even as well as I do, and to think that they came to listen to anything one has to say. Winston has a nap after lunch and then is prepared to work till all hours of the night, which I don't think his colleagues appreciate.[67]

Although it proved tricky to forge relations with the scholarly Bishop of Norwich, Bertram Pollock, who had somehow got Merton's 'whereabouts wrong',[68] the King's whirlwind visit to the division on 23 August was no less memorable than Churchill's. Arriving at Norwich Thorpe station that morning, where he was met by Merton, the King visited the Sherwood Foresters, the 4th Norfolks, the 5th Bedfordshire and Hertfordshires, the 196th Field Ambulance, the 5th Suffolks, the 1st Cambridgeshires and 'trawler personnel at Yarmouth'.[69] As Merton recounted to Georgina:

> The King's visit was a great success I think – and he was splendid the way he (pretended anyhow) to take an interest in all he saw. I spent most of the morning alone with him in his car and he chatted away about . . . all sorts of things and people, Sandringham [and] his shooting until towards the end of the morning he fell asleep on my shoulder. I had lunch in his train.[70]

A frisson of professional tension was, however, provided by Lieutenant-General Edmund Osborne, GOC of II Corps, of whom Merton wrote:

My superior is a man called Osborne who is very nice to me but is fond of sacking people. However, he's sacked so many already that they may get sick of him before he gets sick of me! ... The great joke of the day was that Osborne was bragging how he had commandeered Egerton House at Newmarket for something – not knowing it belonged to the King, who simply remarked that it was the first he had heard of it.[71]

Besides these visits, Merton's initial weeks in command were punctuated by air raids and by command exercises such as BUSTER. Directed by Home Forces, this was intended to test the reaction of its various headquarters in the event of 'the landing of German troops in large numbers by sea and air'.[72] However, a priority for Merton was to get to know his new and diverse command, which at first included the gunners of the 57th (Newfoundland) Heavy Artillery Regiment.[73] Despite its having only formed the previous autumn, such was the churn of personnel in the early months of the war that he was, in fact, the *eighth* successive commander of the division, his longest-serving predecessor, Major-General Bernard Paget, having been with the 18th Division for only five months.[74] Perhaps with this in mind, Merton was keen to make his presence felt. He held his first divisional conference on 20 July, having inspected artillery positions and logistical arrangements two days earlier.[75] Focusing on his divisional troops, he promptly turned his attention to the matter of supplies and, on 30 August, swooped to inspect the 291st Company RASC, which was then serving as the divisional supply column at Kimberley Park, just west of Norwich.[76] As the autumn set in, and the threat of invasion receded (notwithstanding the state of high alert on 7–8 September, when Brooke issued the warning order for CROMWELL, i.e. a 'state of readiness in Eastern and Southern Commands'),[77] Merton was concerned to improve the amenities available to his men. Never a puritan, the enduring Sabbatarianism of British society proved to be something of an obstacle to him in this respect, for on 3 December 1940 it was noted at divisional headquarters that:

Information was received indirectly . . . that legislation enabling the opening of Sunday Cinemas was likely to be delayed in consequence of the pressure of business in Parliament. The introduction of Sunday Cinemas has been advocated by the Divisional Commander as a welfare calculated to assist the relief of monotony and to cater for the entertainment of soldiers on leave.[78]

To help alleviate the drabness of the East Anglian winter, a Norwich Services Club was opened on 28 December in St Andrews Hall, a large fourteenth-century building in the middle of the city. A major civic occasion, the Lord Mayor was present and speakers included Merton, Honor and Major-General William Rozanne, formerly commander of 55th Brigade and now GOC of the new-fangled Norfolk County Division.[79] This was one of ten new 'County Divisions' created specifically for coastal defence,[80] its creation signalling that 18th Division was now slated for a more active role in the war.

Although Alan Brooke noted on 8 November that he had visited '3 of the new Brigades which have replaced the 18th Division',[81] the 18th's next destination remained unclear for some time. However, on 13 December it was instructed that it 'would move to Scotland for mobilization in mid-January, for service in [a] tropical climate'.[82] A week later, a divisional conference was convened in which Merton relayed the 'details of ensuing moves and mobilization'.[83] The complexity of this manoeuvre in the depths of winter can be readily appreciated, especially given the distances involved and the problems posed by the blackout, the weather and even the possibility of German air attack. Consequently, after divisional headquarters had moved to Didlington, a small village 40 miles to the west of Norwich and closer to the division's intended route, orders were finalized on Boxing Day.[84] As the war diary of the division's Deputy Assistant Adjutant General and Deputy Assistant Quartermaster General elaborated, the redeployment was involved and protracted:

During the first days of January the Division left Norfolk and moved to the Scottish Borders. The move was partly by road and partly by rail . . . The rail arrangements were good throughout. The road move was done under the worst of weather conditions, snow, rain and ice. Over 40 degrees of frost were recorded in Melrose on the day the first parties moved in . . . The stages fixed made driving before dawn and after dark necessary . . . The move was the first major move of the Division and entailed the movement of 1100 vehicles and 600 motor cycles over more than 300 miles of road.[85]

However, it was a testimonial to the quality of the staff work, the diligent maintenance of divisional vehicles and the care of its soldiers that little damage – and apparently no serious injuries – were sustained. In fact, 'the only non-arrivals were two mechanical breakdowns, and only two accidents occurred'.[86]

With divisional headquarters now based in Melrose, in the eastern reaches of the Scottish Borders, and its units settled in locations as far removed as Dumfries in the west, the second phase of the 18th's transformation could begin: 'As soon as the Division was concentrated [a relative term], Mobilization took place.'[87] This second phase meant ensuring that the division, which had long led a static existence on the East Anglian coast, had its full complement of troops and equipment. Although British industry was now making up for the huge losses of equipment sustained at Dunkirk, the situation remained precarious:

The bad weather held up deliveries of stores etc. within the Division. Outside the Division further hold ups occurred for various reasons, and as a result the Division was not in any way complete . . . Equipment continued to arrive in considerable quantities up to the end of the month.[88]

In terms of manpower, and again reflecting the wider war effort and the voracious requirements of British industry, it was also lacking in the skilled, older tradesmen needed for its supporting services: 'Both in officers and other ranks all units were practically up to strength . . . except for R.A.O.C. personnel. All R.A.O.C. specialists are difficult to obtain and when they come are often of low medical category.'[89] The situation remained unresolved throughout February:

By 0100 hours 1st February the last units of 18th Division were intended to report mobilisation complete. Reports received showed quite clearly that there were many deficiencies both in major and minor items, consequently every unit sent in large deficiency lists, which eventually resulted in the visit of Brigadier Macpherson, Deputy Director of Recruiting and Mobilisation, to the Division on 12th, 13th and 14th February. Brigadier Macpherson toured all areas with the A.A. and Q.M.G. and visited the majority of units and their Commanding Officers.[90]

Consequently, 'a certain number of stores came forward more quickly than had previously been the case', but delays in the delivery of equipment persisted, especially from outside the division, and 'many units were still far from complete at the end of the month'.[91]

It was an unpropitious start for the daunting task of training the division for active service overseas. And, as indicated on 13 December, it seemed obvious where that service would be. As the 18th Division was concentrating and re-equipping in the Scottish Borders, fighting was raging against the Italians in East Africa and Libya, where much-needed British victories triggered the arrival of Rommel's *Deutsches Afrika Korps* (DAK) early in 1941. With many hard lessons from the Dunkirk campaign to apply, and North Africa the only theatre of war in which the Army was engaged in a ground war against Germany, it was inevitable that the training of the 18th Division would be shaped with the desert war (and Hitler's *Wehrmacht*) in mind. The unfolding war in this supremely mobile arena accentuated the British Army's post-Dunkirk emphasis on 'mechanized fire-power',[92] one that drove the conversion of infantry battalions into armoured and artillery regiments on an extravagant scale.[93] The stinging lessons of the Dunkirk campaign (identified and digested over the summer of 1940) also led to a heightened emphasis on mobile reconnaissance, tactical co-operation with the RAF and speedier means of communicating orders.[94] However, as the latter intimated, the old, pre-war emphasis on commanders fighting controlled, methodical battles on their own terms remained – contests in which 'combined arms action and the generation of overwhelming fire-power' were the keys to victory.[95] Under the terms of *Army Training Instruction Number 1*, which appeared in January 1941, just as the 18th Division began its new training regime, the responsibility for orchestrating these elements was devolved from the division to its component brigade groups, now increasingly viewed as 'the army's basic tactical formation'.[96] Added to these tactical refinements was a heightened emphasis on promoting high morale, a task that hinged on a variety of factors ranging from decent service conditions to the personal confidence that commanders could inspire.[97]

Still, the intrinsic limitations of this training regime need to be appreciated. First of all, and as David French has stressed, 'The military authorities were in no doubt that, compared to the Germans, Home Forces had a serious training deficit to make up.'[98] This was not helped by some basic facts of geography: ground suitable for large-scale training was in short supply, especially given the nation's agricultural needs, and the constraints imposed by billeting meant that units were often widely dispersed, making such training harder to accomplish. Equipment, ammunition and experienced instructors were scarce, while commanders retained their pre-war habit of following their own interpretations of general training principles. In addition, such was the volume of instructions flowing from an anxious War Office that they often went unread or even unnoticed.[99] Also, a laissez-faire approach applied to training in small unit tactics. Combat drills designed to inculcate an instinctive response to enemy action (and especially to such threats as enemy infiltration) were often discouraged on the grounds that they suppressed individual initiative – a quality hard to summon by frightened and inexperienced troops in the searing heat of battle.[100] Furthermore, divisional battle schools, intended to hone small unit tactics and provide 'battle inoculation' by exposing soldiers to live-firing training, were a belated product of the latter half of 1941, the first being opened by 47th Division that July.[101]

Despite these inherent problems and shortcomings, prevailing conditions in 1941 did allow some large-scale training exercises to take place. For example, that autumn Exercise BUMPER involved a dozen armoured and infantry divisions, a quarter of a million troops, and was intended to test Britain's mobile defences and gauge the best configuration of another European expeditionary force. Its results were mixed: communications were poor, liaison with the RAF faulty, and the new emphasis on the brigade group proved to be flawed.[102] Nevertheless, such exercises were fiercely competitive and, under Brooke's stern gaze, and his policy of removing inadequate commanders, the penalty of failure could be fatal in professional terms. In the aftermath of BUMPER, for example, the GOC of Eastern Command was sacked and he was followed by two corps commanders, including the rebarbative Osborne.[103] In this context, it was no small achievement that Merton succeeded in holding on to the 18th Division until it went overseas for, as French has remarked, under Brooke:

> Senior officers enjoyed a leasehold, not a freehold, on their commands . . . the average divisional commander had too little time to impose their own ideas on his command before he was either dismissed or promoted and a new commander, with new ideas, was imposed on the formation.[104]

Until his division embarked that October, Merton was wholly absorbed in training matters. Unlike during his time in India, the period of the 'Phoney War' or his months in captivity, there was no stream of letters to Georgina or Honor. Stationed at home, it may have been that easy communication favoured the telephone.[105] Arriving in Scotland on 11 January, where he was billeted in Prior Wood House, Melrose, Merton convened a divisional conference the very next day. Here, he divulged that the division would not be embarking 'for some time' but that this 'was to be kept secret', presumably to forestall a mood of complacency setting in. Three phases of training were then outlined for the period until mid-March, progressing from an emphasis on individual training to battalion- and brigade-level exercises. A caution was issued about 'Assistance to Civil Powers in the event of Air Raids' and, for the sake of discipline, Merton warned against 'the undesirability of officers fraternising in public with [female] ATS [Auxiliary Territorial Service] personnel'. On more tactical matters, Merton stressed that, if dedicated 'Tank Hunting Platoons' were to be abandoned, 'the art of seeking out the tank should not be forgotten'.

On 21 January, formal operational and training instructions were issued. Commencing on 22 January, the division took part in GHQ's four-day Exercise VICTOR (which Merton judged to be 'very valuable training'), and on 26 January he attended the 55th Brigade's TEWT (i.e. Tactical Exercise Without Troops). More divisional training notes appeared the following day. On 29 January, yet another divisional conference was convened; the 18th Battalion, Reconnaissance Corps was visited on the 30th;

and on 31 January the 18th Division was inspected by the GOC of Scottish Command.[106] And Merton's approach was typically thorough. On 29 January it was decreed at the divisional conference that each field regiment would attend the Royal Artillery's practice camp at Beattock for three days in February, with the relevant brigade commanders at hand on the third to 'give orders for artillery support'. A schedule of other exercises was also laid out: a signals exercise would take place on 17–18 February and brigadiers would attend a Command exercise at Edinburgh on 19–22 February. A divisional exercise would be held in the first week of March, followed by an inter-brigade exercise in the second week, an inter-divisional exercise in the third and another brigade exercise in the fourth.

After Merton's visit to the 18th Battalion, Reconnaissance Corps, formerly the 5th Loyals, a detailed memorandum summarized the many shortcomings he had promptly identified. Although its regimental training programme seemed 'well drawn up', more 'supervision in its execution' was necessary: in one company, no officers or senior non-commissioned officers (NCOs) had shown up for parade and the instruction on light machine guns delivered by one hapless corporal was simply 'bad'. In another, 'the drill was of poor quality and the elementary faults were allowed to pass without comment'. Hence, it was evident that 'the instruction of officers must receive special attention in view of the unit's new role'. If billets and dining rooms were in a good state, sloppiness was apparent among the quarter guard (whose turnout and arms drill were 'poor') and in the guard room itself, which was 'dirty and untidy as were the surroundings'. The wash houses were, it was also noted, 'not in working order'. All in all, it was evident that 'a much higher standard of training and turnout' was 'necessary', a verdict borne out by the facts that 'the men's hair is too long', that too many soldiers were excused duty or absent from parade, and that 'the contract for the repairs of boots' was unsatisfactory.[107]

Merton's handling of the division during this critical phase can be followed in the correspondence of one of his brigadiers, namely Tristram Hugh (or 'Tim') Massy-Beresford, who took command of the 55th Brigade in December 1940. A younger Old Etonian who had been commissioned into the Rifle Brigade, Massy-Beresford had (like Merton) been wounded and awarded the MC in the First World War. In a letter to his wife from Tidworth on 16 December, Massy-Beresford's reaction to his promotion highlighted the challenges which senior officers of the Regular Army, more familiar with the insular and tight-knit world of regimental life, now had to confront:

> I have no illusions that it is going to be a very lonely existence from now on until I get back to you. A Brigadier lives in a very small headquarters with only half a dozen very respectful young officers around him and after these months of chaps of my own age and kind, it will be a serious contrast.[108]

Nor, at this stage, was he any more than lukewarm at the prospect of joining Merton's division:

> The Divisional Commander will be one Beckwith-Smith who was my immediate superior at Eton and one of my Fag masters. I don't really know what he will be like in this exalted position. He was a bit of a fuss-pot in younger days. The last time I saw him was when I was in the War Office and I had to get him and his family to India.[109]

Still, the early signs were encouraging. Though ordered to 'report immediately', in a telephone call to his 'new master' he was told by Merton to report in just over a week, when Christmas would be over and the move to Scotland under way.[110] In February, and with the division assailed by heavy snowfalls, Massy-Beresford noted that 'certain exercises had to be cancelled instead of being carried out in very unpleasant conditions'. Nevertheless, and to Massy-Beresford's surprise, Merton duly appeared in Galashiels to observe an improvised river crossing.[111]

While training continued throughout February, with plans hindered and enthusiasm dampened by the prevailing 'Canadian' conditions,[112] the division's transfer to Western Command lifted the general mood. Intimated from late March and implemented by road and by rail from 1 April, this move 'was undertaken at short notice', with units moving 'unit by unit' over a period of two weeks.[113] However, once back in England, the constraints of space and billeting still meant that the 18th was widely dispersed, now across Lancashire, Cheshire and Staffordshire. Based at

Swinfen Hall near Lichfield, Massy-Beresford had a four-hour journey by car in order to confer with Merton at Hazelfield House near Knutsford.[114] However, as his dealings with his former 'Fag master' developed, so too did a liking and respect for Merton, whom Massy-Beresford now began to refer to as 'Becky'. A sharp judge of character, and not averse to gossipy digs at mutual acquaintances in his letters to his wife, on 24 May 1941 Massy-Beresford wrote of a conference at 'Becky's H.Q.': 'He was MOST agreeable as usual and asked me to lunch. Had an excellent meal and much jesting one way and another. I like his sense of humour. It is infectious and makes me say funny things.'[115] Still, beneath this geniality lurked the same, rather steely professional outlook. A few weeks later, Massy-Beresford noted a difference of opinion over one of his battalion commanders (apparently, Lieutenant-Colonel Gerald Carpenter of the 1st Cambridgeshires). As he wrote to his wife in mid-June:

Today I spent with another of my Units but it was not nearly as agreeable as other such visits. 'Tis not such a happy crowd and I had an unpleasant job to do . . . I had to make it plain to the C.O. that I was not pleased with him. I've discovered that he is not being very loyal or helpful and was heard complaining of certain criticisms of mine . . . I had to make it clear that he would be out of it if there was anything of that sort again.[116]

Later, he added that:

The only occasion when Becky and I were not in agreement was over this C.O. Becky wanted me to sack him and, in a way, I wanted to do so too, but, although I disliked him I felt he would be stout in battle. (He had a D.S.O. in the last War). In the event, his was the one and only unit within my sphere of knowledge, which held on where I had put it right up to the moment when we surrendered and I got him a Bar to his D.S.O. Nasty man all the same.[117]

Merton's repeated appearances in Massy-Beresford's correspondence rather belie his impression of Merton's duties and activities. As Massy-Beresford opined in another missive from Swinfen Hall:

Little Becky suddenly appeared here for lunch today. He IS a charming little man (about 4ft nothing). We came up here after lunch and had a long talk, all most natural and friendly. I'm surely in luck in having such a master. We see eye to eye on all matters, have the same ways and there is no question of superior officer with 'telling offs' and the like. He trusts me and just says what he would like done and is interested in all that I do. It happens that I am in a far more interesting position than he is since he, literally, has no troops to Command these days except me and the other two Brigade Commanders. All the Division is divided between the three of us in our various areas, so Becky has nothing left except heavy Divisional Artillery etc. . . . It is completely spoiling to have such an understanding master for such a long time.[118]

Merton's ubiquity was noticed by other units too. After a 'two-day endurance test' near Blackburn in mid-April, the 4th Norfolks were warmly congratulated by Merton.[119] Similarly, having trekked from Duns in the Scottish Borders to Altrincham in Cheshire, 291st Company RASC was once again surprised by a visit from the GOC on 17 April, its diary noting another 'unexpected inspection by Maj. Gen. Beckwith-Smith'.[120] Likewise, while encamped at Madeley in Staffordshire, the Reconnaissance Battalion, previously marked as a problem case, was visited by Merton on at least four occasions from mid-April to mid-October. On 2 May, the inspection was especially thorough:

Major General D.G. Johnson, V.C. C.B. D.S.O. M.C. Inspector General of Infantry accompanied by G.O.C. 18 Div, Maj Gen Beckwith Smith D.S.O. M.C. visited this Unit and spent the greater part of the day enquiring into the state of training and interviewing the various Officers who were present.[121]

And this regimen clearly worked, as there were major signs of improvement. In contrast to his damning visit that January, when Merton arrived on 14 August he 'complimented the Battalion Main Gate Guard'.[122] And again, in his divisional conferences and instructions, Merton showed an unerring eye for detail. In Administrative Order Number 14, for example, issued in preparation for the division's movement from Scottish to Western Command, it was stated that:

> At all times on the move, at the halt and at rest, full Anti-Aircraft precautions will be taken. It is emphasized that the Division is moving into highly developed industrial areas where attack from the air is always an immediate contingency. Blackout and other . . . measures will be strictly enforced and Anti-Aircraft weapons will be constantly at instant readiness to attack low flying aircraft.[123]

A handwritten note on the copy kept by 291st Company RASC added: 'G.O.C. very insistent on this. Black Out. Magazines on always.'[124]

Nevertheless, Merton's most important contribution lay in overhauling the division's artillery, and especially in reforming the languidly 'seigneurial' 135th Field Regiment. As Stephen Alexander remembered, even after it had abandoned its motley and ageing ordnance on the Norfolk coast and been re-equipped with modern, 25-pound field guns and Morris tractors, all was not well with his unit. In fact, as he admitted:

> All this new machinery made us feel much more glamorous . . . We headed north [to Lockerbie], conscious of our new fighting power but subconsciously expecting too much of our new acquisitions. Perhaps we thought technological advance called for less rather than more physical toughness and enterprise.[125]

Its technical failings were apparent during the regimental firing exercise held at Sennybridge camp in Brecknockshire that August where, even after months of training, its performance was 'very disappointing'.[126] As Alexander remembered: 'On a night shoot one troop fired 180 degrees off target, rattling a few dustbins in the village.'[127] To compound this, a few days earlier, and under Merton's gaze, the 118th Field Regiment had executed an 'outstandingly successful' fire-plan which had featured the laying of a smokescreen.[128]

With one of the division's three field artillery regiments failing badly, its new Commander Royal Artillery, Brigadier Hubert Servaes ('a thrusting Liverpool businessman before the war'),[129] found a new commanding officer in the form of Philip Toosey, previously his second-in-command in the 59th (4th West Lancashire) Field Regiment.[130] Like Servaes, Toosey was a Territorial and a veteran of the Dunkirk campaign; he had also earned some distinction in the pre-war years, where his battery had won a string of gunnery competitions.[131] As Servaes remembered:

I went to the 18th Division . . . and found that one of the Regiments had got into a very bad state and needed a new commander. I applied quickly for Phil, and only just in time, as General Osborne had also applied for him . . . By pulling every string I knew of, I managed to secure him (to the chagrin of Osborne!) and he came to us about two months before we started our ill-fated trip abroad.[132]

And the transformation of the 135th was remarkable once Toosey had joined it at Macclesfield. First, however, there was its dreadful perform-ance at Trawsfynydd in North Wales, where (as Toosey recalled):

All that happened was that during the whole day's firing we succeeded in hitting two villages outside the ranges and very rarely any of the chosen targets. The results were disastrous, and it was clear that a great deal of training was needed, and needed as quickly as possible.[133]

Consequently, Toosey imposed a strict new regime which ensured the speedy revival of the regiment. As Stephen Alexander put it:

[Toosey's] bearing went down well with the troops, and the officers soon found they could take it or leave it. The older ones departed, and everyone else now felt Toosey's keen dark eye upon their successes and failures . . . With Toosey's arrival the feeling of fiddling while Rome burned left us.[134]

And, as Servaes stressed, all this occurred under Merton's aegis for, as he said with reference to Toosey after the war: 'My General, Beckwith-Smith, whose standards were extremely high, was most delighted with him.'[135]

As the tempo and quality of training picked up, those in the ranks of the 18th Division also felt the change. Kenneth Bailey of the 5th Suffolks remembered that:

[W]e were introduced to the dangerous and frightening weapons of war, at one stage taking part in a Brigade exercise where we, the infantry, had to advance under live artillery covering fire, shells from which were fired at targets in front of us as we moved forward. It was on this exercise that we experienced what could happen in real combat when a shell dropped short amongst us, resulting in a number of serious injuries and the death of a Lance Corporal . . .[136]

Despite such 'stiff training' and the onerous demands of military discipline, Bailey recalled that morale was high, even among the great majority who were not serving by choice: 'Surprisingly, everyone [*sic*] of we conscripts appeared to take these measures . . . in very good spirits, and after parades and other duties there were always evening visits to the local public houses where we could relax and curse about the sergeant major!'[137] A further feature of divisional life was the unrelenting stress on organized sport – football in the winter and 'mainly athletics' in the summer, 'whether one liked it or not'.[138]

By August 1941, the division's heightened emphasis on training, physical exercise and the competitive spirit was plainly paying dividends, with the war diary of the once-slothful 18th Battalion, Reconnaissance Corps recording that:

Enquiry into courses on Modern Languages proved that there is a lively interest in the Battalion particularly in French and German. Guard Mounting Competition for best turn out and drill commenced today, judging by the R.S.M. and the Adjutant. Divisional Sports Meeting held. Representatives of the Battalion take part and attend. 2 events won – 300 yds and obstacle race. Took 3rd place in Sports. Map showing the War situation in Russia put up in NAAFI [Navy, Army and Air Force Institutes] Canteen. Great interest shown by the men. This is marked daily from 'The Times'.[139]

Such interest in French and German, and in the unfolding war on the Eastern Front (the Soviet Union had been invaded by Germany and its allies on 22 June), reflected the intellectual curiosity of the citizen soldiers of this era, an interest reflected in the creation of the Army Bureau of Current Affairs (ABCA) in June 1941, with its pattern of weekly, army-wide bulletins and discussion groups intended to 'educate and motivate Britain's conscript army . . . in a prolonged ideological conflict'.[140] As Alex Danchev noted, in ABCA 'we catch the echo of Cromwell's plain russet-coated soldier, who knows what he fights for and loves what he knows: an ideal invoked mistily and often at the time'.[141] Yet, even before ABCA, Merton had already grasped the value of this kind of education for his khaki-clad soldiers, addressing the issue as early as his divisional conference on 12 January. Grounded in an appreciation of the value of education which had crystallized in the British Army during the First World War (as a means of raising morale as well as enhancing military efficiency) and conscious of the time available once the division embarked for war,[142] here Merton had ruled that:

An education officer [is] to be appointed in units forthwith. He will select a team of instructors. No text books will be available on board ship and therefore a good deal of preliminary work is necessary. There will be ample time on voyage for education. In addition preparation will be made to keep men interested on board ship, and information acquired of places that may be visited.[143]

In the spirit of these instructions, orientation lectures also marked these months of training. In May, for example, the 291st Company RASC heard a lecture on 'Our English Heritage', which was given 'to all available personnel'.[144] Likewise, in August alone the 18th Battalion, Reconnaissance Corps heard a lecture on 'Nazi War Aims' on the 14th and, two weeks later, a lecture (by a 'lady lecturer') on the 'Political and Geographical importance of the Mediterranean in the present war'.[145] However, other, more fundamental educational needs and deficiencies were also addressed, it being noted in July 1941 that:

It was found on enquiry that there were approximately 150 men in the Division who were illiterate. Arrangements were made for some 40 of these who were said to be intelligent to be taught to read and write under unit arrangements. The remainder to be transferred to the Pioneer Corps, if possible.[146]

In addressing the needs of body, mind and spirit, Merton also placed a premium on entertainment, for on arrival in Scotland:

The Divisional Commander decided to keep the Divisional Concert Party in being and their Show continued to entertain all ranks on every possible occasion. In addition many local people assisted at giving Shows to the troops, and with the help of two mobile Cinemas it was possible to start the basis of giving entertainment for all ranks in their new locations.[147]

If the Sunday opening of cinemas had proved awkward in East Anglia, this push on entertainments had even greater implications for austerely Presbyterian and Sabbatarian Scotland. As Massy-Beresford wrote to his wife from Galashiels on 5 February:

On Sunday night I attended the Divisional Concert Party's performance in the local cinema. 'Twas not as good as Divisional Concert Parties which appeared in the last war but it was quite entertaining in spots. At the end I had to get up on the stage and make a speech thanking the cinema management for allowing us to use their premises each Sunday night. 'Tis not usual in this country to allow such things and the City Fathers had to be handled very carefully.[148]

Though convention may have inhibited leisure pursuits on the Sabbath, religion also played a significant part in Merton's agenda for the division, a concern that Worsley's strident article in *The Times* may well have fuelled. As early as 8 November 1939, a divisional chaplains' conference had taken place at the Bishop's Palace in Norwich, a conference attended by the 18th's original GOC, Major-General T. G. Dalby.[149] The fundamental importance of religion in general, and Christianity in particular, stemmed from three key factors.

Firstly, throughout the 1940s Britain remained a self-consciously Christian society. Despite the fears stirred by declining church attendance and perceived threats to the traditional British Sunday, professed atheists and agnostics were few and far between and Christian belief and morality remained normative. The monarchy stood as a thoroughly Christian and conservative institution (as Edward VIII had found out to his cost) and Christian moral standards were entrenched in English and Scottish law. In childhood, Christian socialization was once again the norm: Sunday schools still attracted the great majority of working-class children; church schools (chiefly Anglican and Roman Catholic) comprised a large proportion of the nation's elementary and secondary schools; and hymns and biblical tropes were deeply woven into popular culture and the English language itself. Indeed, under the existential threat posed by the pagan might of Nazi Germany, this cultural Christianity was hugely reinforced by the sustained religious output of the BBC; by government propaganda (notably the image of St Paul's Cathedral standing undamaged amidst the London Blitz); by the combined literary endeavours of C. S. Lewis, T. S. Eliot and Dorothy L. Sayers; and by the religious provisions of the 1944 Education Act. In short, Christianity remained a core aspect of British national identity, its purchase reflected in successive National Days of Prayer called by King George VI, in the rhetoric of Winston Churchill and in the perceptions of foreigners ranging from Joseph Stalin to the anti-Nazi Swiss theologian, Karl Barth. Secondly, reflecting the society from which it came, and the attitudes and mores of its ruling class, the British Army remained an institutionally Christian organization. In addition to the RAChD, which had been in existence since 1796, its officers and other ranks had to attest a religious allegiance, which was borne on their identity discs. Christian Scripture was issued to the Army at public expense and, until 1946, weekly church attendance (often accompanied by the controversial church parade) was mandatory, in theory at least. The lessons of the First World War had, if anything, confirmed the value of religion in the eyes of professional soldiers, as they seemed to vindicate the centuries-old belief that strong religious convictions made for higher morale and more courageous and better disciplined soldiers. Thirdly and finally, its importance in the 18th Division also stemmed from more local factors, for traditional rural areas such as East Anglia were widely perceived (and idealized) as much more susceptible to the lingering influence of church or chapel than teeming industrial centres such as London, Manchester or Birmingham.

Besides the routine church services (mandatory or otherwise) recorded in the unit war diaries of the 18th Division, the importance of religion was manifested in other respects. For example, following a typically leisurely field exercise in the Lake District with the 135th Field Regiment, Stephen Alexander wrote to his mother of their recent 'Service in the field', an event which had accompanied an idyllic day.[150] With the prospect of overseas service looming, special church parades were held throughout the division on the National Day of Prayer appointed for Sunday 7 September 1941, an occasion which marked the second anniversary of the outbreak of war.[151] The following month, as preparations for embarkation quickened, the division had two episcopal visitors. The first was the Bishop of St Albans, Michael Furse, whose primary interest was in the 5th Bedfordshire and Hertfordshires of 55th Brigade. As a former infantry chaplain and an Old Etonian, he naturally hit it off with Massy-Beresford, who wrote from Whittington Barracks:

Yesterday, the Bishop of St Albans came to see one of my lot and gave a most heartening address in the church. He is a truly charming man and I was asked to lunch to meet him. He sat next [to] me and we talked ten to the dozen all through the meal, chiefly on the problem of Army Chaplains in relation to Bishops. He was Bishop of Pretoria many years ago before 'Tiny' Talbot [i.e. Neville Talbot] (our Battalion Chaplain in the first war). Also, he left Eton in 1889 which made me feel the devil of a chicken.[152]

The following week, it was Massy-Beresford's turn to host the Bishop of Ely, the newly consecrated Edward Wynn. Another veteran of the First World War (in which Wynn had served as an army chaplain in France and Italy), on meeting Massy-Beresford he reverted to his old army habits. As Massy-Beresford described it:

I told you of our Bishop last Sunday. Last night I had another one, this time the Bishop of Ely and such a nice man too. He had been to see his own people (The [1st] Cambridgeshires) and looked in here after dinner and stayed quite late talking to us. We discussed all manner of things . . . My dear wife, he called me 'SIR'!!!! Did you ever think that you would ever live to hear me being called 'Sir' by a Bishop[?] That tickled me more than anything that has happened for a long time. I MUST be getting venerable . . .[153]

However, such was the enduring influence of religion that its representatives and expressions required some management. Despite Toosey's wider shake-up of the 135th Field Regiment, its chaplaincy arrangements (in his eyes at least) remained unsatisfactory. As he recalled:

At that time I had a row with my Padre and I discovered he was leading the Subalterns in riot and song and failed after a night exercise to turn up and see the men get their breakfast. He was hogging it in the Mess having a very good meal himself. So I sacked him. I got a terrific rocket from the Bishop of Chester who said that I had no right to do such a thing and I said 'I am not taking that man to War with me.' I got another Padre but he, unfortunately, turned out to be no better.[154]

Before embarkation, other units also encountered problems in the religious realm. In the Reconnaissance Battalion, the RMP were summoned in mid-October to 'investigate certain religious tracts found in [a] mail bag'.[155] Although the nature of these tracts was not specified (presumably pacifist, sectarian or both), the Janus-like character of wartime society was reflected in the donations, both sacred and profane, made to the 55th Brigade as it entrained for Liverpool:

Just before OUR train started [wrote Massy-Beresford], a couple of 'Do Gooders' appeared at our carriage door, each with a carton of 'Comforts' for the troops. When the train started we had a look inside these cartons. One contained prayer books, the other 'Contraceptives'!!!!!![156]

By the summer of 1941, through sustained effort on many fronts, the division (with the belated exception of the 135th Field Regiment) had reached a high state of training and readiness, a state that was matched by its overall morale. Since January, alongside intense unit training, a series of exercises had marked its evolution from a motley collection of static coastal defence units into a cohesive and highly mobile division capable of taking the field against Rommel. Among these exercises were MARK (in mid-March, the 18th squaring up to the 52nd (Lowland) Division in 'the role of an invading German force having EDINBURGH, and the cutting of [the] EDINBURGH-CARLISLE railway communications as its objective');[157] HOPS (29 May – 1 June, in which the division's 54th Brigade went to the defence of Shropshire, alongside a Czech brigade);[158] MOOR (in early July, in which the 18th joined the 2nd Division in repulsing a German invasion of Yorkshire);[159] WESSEX (a staff 'telephone battle held at DODDINGTON HALL' in Lincolnshire later that month); CANNON (in early August, designed to put the divisional artillery through its paces); and LEEK (in mid-August, in which 54th Brigade had moved from 'the Hereford Area to resist an enemy landing at SWANSEA', a feat that 'involved a move of 60 miles over bad and hilly roads').[160]

In early June, the division's sense of cohesion and self-confidence was crowned by the decision to introduce the divisional insignia 'for wearing on Battle Dress throughout the Division'.[161] That summer, its thriving state was also reflected in its disciplinary record: 'The high standard of smartness and discipline within the Division is evident by the fact that during [July] the number of men charged by [RMP] personnel in Western Command amounted to approximately 1% of the Division.'[162] More positively, and as Kenneth Bailey of the 5th Suffolks remembered, by the autumn of 1941 his battalion was 'a fully trained, most efficient and well-equipped fighting unit'.[163] More ruefully, Reginald Burton, a Regular officer who had transferred into the 4th Norfolks, came to the conclusion that the 18th Division ultimately proved to be the victim of its own (and Merton's) success. In particular, by besting the veteran (and originally Regular Army) 2nd Division in Exercise MOOR (in which Merton's plans were 'successfully carried out in action', the 'Germans' being caught in a pincer movement),[164] it had put itself in pole position for deployment overseas – just as the war was about to widen in the Far East. As Burton wryly remembered: 'It is interesting to note that had the 2nd Division won the exercise they would have finished up in Malaya and the 18th Division would have gone to Burma: so much for the hinge of fate.'[165]

5

The great misadventure

For the 18th Division, 'the hinge of fate' began to turn in mid-October 1941, the previous month having seen some of its troops detailed to render 'assistance to farmers' in gathering their third wartime harvest.[1] Merton convened his final divisional conference before embarkation on 9 October, the venue being Ribbesford House in Bewdley, Worcestershire, 'a niceish house by the Severn'.[2] The previous day, many of his soldiers had heard a lecture on the 'Conduct of Prisoners of War', the speaker being a civilian from MI9, a branch of the British Directorate of Military Intelligence responsible for helping POWs to escape and fugitives to evade capture. None could have appreciated the irony of the occasion, or of its subject matter. Three days later, all divisional transport was ready for movement and, by 20 October, mobilization was complete.[3] With embarkation imminent, and rumours abounding, absenteeism began to increase, as individuals deserted or went temporarily absent without leave.[4] At this point, the destination of the 18th Division was still unknown, though a series of lectures on the recent Syrian campaign against the Vichy French seemed to suggest (as widely anticipated) the Middle East, as did a divisional instruction that 'jerkins, gum boots, oil skins etc. will be handed in at once' and that all units would be inspected in tropical kit before departure.[5] On 22 October, the King paid his second visit to the division, showing (as he inspected the 18th's Reconnaissance Battalion at Madeley) a special interest in its new armoured cars.[6] In fact:

Although it had been arranged in the programme that the King should drive past certain units drawn up on the road, His Majesty decided he would get out of his car and walk down inspecting the troops. This gesture was greatly appreciated by the officers and men of the units concerned.[7]

Besides the Reconnaissance Battalion, the King was also keen to meet the 4th Norfolks, who had 'provided the guard for SANDRINGHAM in the autumn of 1940'.[8] On 25 October, a 'special order of the day', written by Merton, went out 'to all units'. Though its text has not survived, its timing was unmistakable, signalling as it did the first step in the division's long and immensely costly *via dolorosa*.[9]

The 18th Division's 'great misadventure', as one survivor called it,[10] was launched from several ports of embarkation, with units sailing from Avonmouth (18th Reconnaissance Battalion), Gourock (53rd Brigade) and Liverpool (54th and 55th Brigades, plus the 9th Northumberland Fusiliers). Some of its vehicles and guns were also shipped from Swansea and Birkenhead. While the embarkation of troops took two days (28–29 October), the loading of its heavier equipment was more protracted, requiring a whole week. Nevertheless, it was a testimonial to its staff work that 'all arrangements worked smoothly and without delay'[11] and that secrecy was maintained to the last. Up until the moment of embarkation, its destination remained unknown even to some of the division's most senior officers. As Massy-Beresford remembered, he had to entreat the Embarkation Commandant to divulge this all-consuming secret as he boarded his troopship, the *Orcades*, in Liverpool – being told, in a whisper, 'Halifax'.[12] Although some of its transports – such as the Polish liner *Sobieski* – were small and uncomfortable on the Atlantic swell,[13] Massy-Beresford found his suite on the *Orcades* 'delightful', while Merton, with Divisional Headquarters, sailed from Liverpool on board the *Reina del Pacifico*, a 17,000-ton modern liner that had plied the route from Liverpool to Valparaiso.[14] From 30 October, the convoy – codenamed 'William Sail 12X' and comprising seven transports under a Royal Navy escort – sailed westwards, en route to Nova Scotia.[15] On 2 November, it rendezvoused with a huge convoy of merchant ships sailing eastwards under a strong US Navy escort, one that comprised 'the Aircraft Carrier YORKTOWN, 2 battle ships and a strong destroyer force' – 'a real Metro-Goldwyn-Meyer' show, as Merton's senior liaison officer, Ken Tomkinson, described it.[16] At this point, their Royal Navy escorts turned east and the division was taken under the wing of the US Navy for the latter stage of its voyage to Halifax.[17]

Unbeknownst to the soldiers of the 18th Division, who marvelled at these impressive manoeuvres in the mid-Atlantic, they were witnessing a major escalation in Anglo-American naval co-operation in the wake of the Placentia Bay Conference of August 1941, one intended to safeguard British convoys and supply lines while preserving the technical neutrality of the United States. Obliged by the hazards of the Mediterranean to take a highly circuitous passage to their (presumed) destination in the Middle East, by 11.00 a.m. on 8 November the 18th Division had arrived in Halifax, 'the first city without a blackout' its troops had seen since the summer of 1939.[18] There, another facet of Anglo-American co-operation manifested itself, as (under sealed orders opened on 1 November) the division began its rapid transhipment to 'six American troopships' waiting in the harbour, three of which were recently converted – and renamed – luxury liners.[19] These were to convey most of the division to its presumed destination via the South Atlantic and the Indian Ocean, thereby affording their passengers a 'well-cushioned odyssey in the borrowed floating palaces of the idle rich'.[20] (In fact, such was the dissatisfaction of the 9th Northumberland Fusiliers on being allotted the *Orizaba*, a much less desirable transport, that a minor mutiny ensued, one that resulted in the collective punishment of the battalion – i.e. extra route marches – once it had reached India.)[21]

For Merton, however, there were broader problems of Anglo-American co-operation to take into account, especially given the unprecedented nature of the situation. In orders issued prior to re-embarkation, Merton explained that:

> [T]his is the first time British troops have been transported in American ships [and] on the maintenance of good relations between all ranks on board and the American merchant officers and seamen may depend the continuance of the offer of the American Government to make further shipping available to the Empire . . . The routine on American ships may be different to that on British ships and all ranks must adapt themselves to the new conditions as quickly as possible. It must be impressed that the standard of the British Army will be judged by the behaviour and discipline of the troops on board.[22]

Most significantly, though Prohibition had ended in 1933, the US Navy remained firmly teetotal, an institutional foible that now had to be respected by 20,000 British soldiers:

The American ships are 'dry' and it is understood that no beer or spirits for consumption on board can be taken. This may be a hardship but it must be explained to all ranks that the American troop ship regulations must naturally be observed to the letter.[23]

Re-embarked and duly admonished, the convoy set sail at 8.00 a.m. on 10 November, transhipment having taken just 36 hours. Steering a southerly course, the transports were furnished with a formidable escort by the US Navy – including the aircraft carrier USS *Ranger*, two cruisers (USS *Quincy* and *Vincennes*) and eight destroyers.[24] With the notable exception of the Northumberland Fusiliers, for most of the division their new accommodation seemed to be excellent. Sharing the USS *Wakefield* (previously the SS *Manhattan*) with Merton and Divisional Headquarters, as he had earlier shared the *Reina del Pacifico*, Kenneth Bailey of the 5th Suffolks remembered that 'compared to the previous ship this was a magnificent looking transport, everything about it being first class, accommodation and food excellent and [the] friendliness of the American crew could not have been better'.[25] Like the passage to Halifax, the month-long voyage to Cape Town saw no interventions by the *Kriegsmarine*, but this was not just a matter of luck for, by virtue of ULTRA decryptions of German naval signals, the whereabouts of every U-boat was known to those plotting the course of the convoy from the Admiralty.[26] While the ships refuelled at Port of Spain on 17 November, during a 48-hour pause in which shore leave was not widely allowed, Merton dined at Government House with the Governor of Trinidad, Sir Hubert Young, the American consul, and Rear Admiral Arthur Byron Cook, the commander of the US naval escort.[27]

In fact, the greatest dramas to occur in this part of the voyage were the 'Crossing the Line' ceremonies on the Equator.[28] On the *Wakefield*, Commander W. K. Scammell of the US Coast Guard honoured the occasion in the customary fashion, a proclamation being issued under the name of 'NEPTUNUS REX, Ruler of the Raging Main', and soldiers of the 18th were initiated into the 'Solemn Mysteries of the ANCIENT ORDER OF THE DEEP' with much raucousness and hilarity.[29] On the *West Point*, however, formerly the SS *America*, things got out of hand, with Anglo-American relations becoming decidedly strained. As Massy-Beresford remembered:

I knew that this was, traditionally, the occasion for certain ceremonials but these American Sailors had strange ideas on the subject. They went quite crazy, dressed themselves up and roamed round the decks shouting and singing. Not only that, they were vicious . . . They seized on the occasional soldier and chained him to the deck rails and left him there in the sun. They thought they were being amusing but there was not one atom of humour at any moment. They set up a huge tank with tarpaulins and filled it with water, presumably for bathing and water games . . . Instead, they poured garbage into it – all sorts of muck – and then pushed the troops in. I was so disgusted with this process – it was obviously upsetting the troops – that I took off all my clothes and jumped in myself. This caused such astonishment that that particular 'Amusement' was abandoned.[30]

However, the nascent Anglo-American 'special relationship' bore the strain of these excesses, and on 27 November Merton exchanged compliments with Rear Admiral Cook, with whom he had dined on USS *Ranger* and at Trinidad's Government House. From the *Wakefield* came the signal:

ALL RANKS UNDER MY COMMAND SENSIBLE OF HONOUR OF YOUR SPLENDID ESCORT AND ADMIRE BOTH THE SPIRIT AND MANNER IN WHICH YOUR UNIQUE AND DIFFICULT TASK IS BEING EXECUTED. WE HOPE TO PROVE OURSELVES WORTHY OF YOUR LABOURS AND THAT SUCCESS WILL BE YOURS IN WHATEVER TASKS MAY LIE BEFORE YOU. PERSONALLY REGRET YOUR IMPENDING DEPARTURE AND HOPE WE MAY SOON MEET AGAIN UNDER MORE FAVOURABLE CONDITIONS.[31]

From the *Ranger* came the response:

MANY THANKS FOR YOUR GRACIOUS MESSAGE. THE OFFICERS AND MEN OF THE RANGER, RHIND, AND TRIPP, MYSELF AND STAFF, WISH YOU AND THE TROOPS UNDER YOUR COMMAND A PLEASANT VOYAGE AND ALL THE

GOOD FORTUNE YOUR NOBLE CAUSE DESERVES. GOODBYE,
GOOD LUCK AND SUCCESSFUL CAMPAIGNING.[32]

Even on the *West Point*, the unseemly scenes on 'Crossing the Line' were
soon forgotten, with the British officers on board subscribing £100 for
silverware – bought in Cape Town – which was duly presented to its
captain and mates by Massy-Beresford himself.[33]

After nearly three weeks at sea, the convoy anchored at Cape Town on 9
December. There, the division was royally received by the city's inhabitants.
Perhaps because of Afrikaner hostility towards the war, the hospitality
extended by its Anglophone residents was pointedly demonstrative. For
Merton, there was the inevitable round of official engagements. On the
evening of 9 December, after lunch at Cape Castle with the local commanding officer, he was presented to Field Marshal Jan Christiaan Smuts, Prime
Minister of the Union of South Africa. The following day, Merton was
lunched and entertained by Henry Stephan, a senior South African liaison
officer and former Lord Mayor of Cape Town, and dined that evening
with the captains of the *Wakefield* and *Mount Vernon* (formerly the SS
Washington). After a welcome break on the 11th, he paid a courtesy call on
the sitting Lord Mayor on 12 December.[34] Amidst all of this, as his chief
liaison officer, Ken Tomkinson, remembered (albeit in the third person):

> Ken had one day as duty ADC with Becky, who was as usual charming.
> They did a few duty calls handing out appreciation and thanks to the
> huge WVS [Women's Voluntary Service] canteens and clubs that gave
> the troops parties, to the chief of Police and other Civic dignitaries,
> in the fine beflagged car lent to Becky by the Town.[35]

As for his division, its stay at Cape Town reflected its implicit role as a
goodwill ambassador to Britain's allies and Dominions:

> Four days' stay in CAPE TOWN provided all ranks with a most
> welcome break from the monotony of a long sea voyage. No
> trouble seemed too great for the inhabitants of CAPE TOWN,
> whose hospitality and generosity combined to make these four
> days most enjoyable for all concerned. Before leaving . . . the sum

of approximately £300, subscribed by all ranks of the Division, was presented to the Mayor for distribution to such charities as he thought fit. This money was most gratefully accepted, particularly in view of the fact that from among the many convoys that have passed through CAPE TOWN since war was declared no donations had previously been made.[36]

According to Massy-Beresford, not one of the division's soldiers went without 'lodging or entertainment'.[37] Kenneth Bailey, who was struck by the natural beauty (and by the racial segregation) of the city, also recalled how friendly its white inhabitants seemed to be towards their British visitors:

Here at Cape Town in glorious warm weather, we enjoyed three days shore leave, most of the troops being met at the docks by local people and being invited to their homes for meals . . . During our walks in the centre of Cape Town we marvelled at the huge skyscraper office blocks, the like of which most of us had not seen before. From the sky-high windows of these imposing buildings as we walked the streets, we were greeted with waving hands and handkerchiefs from the occupants of the offices.[38]

However, even as Merton and his division were being feted in Cape Town, the whole course of the war – together with the purpose of their voyage – was being transformed. On 7 December 1941, with devastating effect, carrier-borne aircraft of the Imperial Japanese Navy struck the US Navy's Pacific Fleet at Pearl Harbor. An hour before, and after shooting down a British reconnaissance plane, the Japanese commenced a seaborne invasion of the Malayan peninsula and southern Thailand. On 10 December, the battlecruiser *Repulse* and the battleship *Prince of Wales* were sunk by Japanese aircraft off the east coast of Malaya. The day after this stunning Japanese success against the Royal Navy's 'Force Z' ('In all the war, I never received a more direct shock,' so Churchill admitted),[39] Merton convened a conference 'to discuss administrative questions', announcing that 'according to his original instructions the Division was destined for EGYPT'.[40] However, all of this was now thrown into doubt. Although the British Eighth Army was involved in heavy fighting with the Germans and Italians in Libya as part of Operation CRUSADER, the need to bolster the Empire's flimsy Far Eastern flank (which had long been neglected in favour of home defence, the war in the desert and supporting the Soviet Union)[41] was growing ever more urgent.

After its welcome sojourn in Cape Town, the convoy sailed on 13 December, a reduced American escort handing over to the British cruiser HMS *Dorsetshire* the following day. Once again, there was a fulsome exchange of courtesies, with Merton's valedictory running:

ALL RANKS UNDER MY COMMAND APPRECIATE THE HONOUR OF HAVING BEEN ESCORTED SO SUCCESSFULLY OVER SO MANY THOUSANDS OF MILES BY THEIR COMRADES IN ARMS IN THE UNITED STATES NAVY. WE WISH THE OFFICERS AND CREWS OF THE QUINCEY [*sic*] VINCENNES AND THE DESTROYERS SUCCESS IN WHATEVER TASKS LIE BEFORE THEM. FOR OUR PART WE SHALL ALWAYS REMEMBER THIS UNIQUE VOYAGE AND ADMIRE THE MANNER IN WHICH YOUR TASK HAS BEEN CARRIED OUT.[42]

This elicited the signal: 'WE DEEPLY APPRECIATE YOUR MES-SAGE AND HOPE SOME DAY WE CAN RENEW CONTACT WITH YOU AGAIN WHEN THE JOB AT HAND IS SUCCESSFULLY COMPLETED.'[43]

But for the 18th Division, the 'job at hand' was about to change pro-foundly. Ever since it sailed from Trinidad, the War Cabinet's Chiefs of Staff Committee had been pondering what to do with what seemed to be a spare division. On the morning of 21 November, Sir John Dill, who was about to retire as CIGS, informed his peers on the Chiefs of Staff Committee (namely Admiral Sir Dudley Pound and Air Chief Marshal Sir Charles Portal) 'that it was necessary that a decision should be taken now whether the 18th Division should go to the Middle East or to Iraq'. Accordingly, the Chiefs of Staff instructed their secretary to refer the matter to Churchill.[44] That evening, Churchill chaired a further meeting of the Chiefs of Staff Committee in which it havered over the question of whether to send the 18th to Bombay or to Suez for transhipment to Basra. Eventually, this logistical question was referred to the War Office, it being thought that there was plenty of time to make the final decision before the convoy reached Durban.[45] However, Japan's entry into the war threw this projection into disarray. On 8 December, the Chiefs of Staff concluded that 'it would be unwise to divert the 18th Division to the Far East'. Nonetheless, three days later Churchill raised the question of sending the division to Burma, but the salutary fate of 'Force Z' counselled caution: nothing was resolved by the Chiefs of Staff, 'primarily because the naval situation in Far Eastern waters required study'. The following day, 12 December, they informed Sir Archibald Wavell, the Commander-in-Chief in India, that 'the policy was now to send all reinforcements we can to India and the Far East, subject to our not withdrawing units or equipment now in [the] Middle East and Iraq'. Wavell was also informed that Burma was now under his command and that the 18th Division was being diverted to India. On 13 December, Wavell was informed it was heading for Bombay, a destination confirmed the next day.[46]

Naturally, while in Cape Town, and for several days afterwards, uncertainty reigned in the 18th Division. As the war diary of Divisional Headquarters noted:

> Whilst in CAPE TOWN the embarkation authorities had been unable to give the GOC any information as to the Division's eventual destination. The American Naval Officer in command of the convoy had, however, received instructions from the US Navy Department to the effect that the convoy would proceed via ADEN to BOMBAY. It was not until 17 December that any instructions were received from the British authorities. On this day the Captain of HMS DORSETSHIRE received orders from the British Admiralty for the convoy to proceed direct to BOMBAY. This information was made common knowledge.[47]

However, this unforeseen development served to split the convoy. Firstly, the *Orizaba*, a transport with a 'small fuel storage capacity', was obliged to head to Mombasa to refuel, taking the 9th Northumberland Fusiliers with it.[48] Consequently, it did not reach Bombay until 6 January.[49] Secondly, after haggling between Wavell, the War Office and the Commander-in-Chief of Far East Command (namely the RAF's Sir Henry Brooke-Popham) over the accelerated deployment of 53rd Brigade, on 22 December Brooke-Popham told London that Malaya Command now deemed the 'earliest possible arrival of 53rd Brigade Group essential, even if without transport or guns'. Consequently, on 23 December, the *Mount Vernon*, with 53rd Brigade on board, was abruptly ordered to 'an unknown destination' (in fact, Singapore) and headed north. Significantly, although permission was obtained from the Americans to put *Mount Vernon* in harm's way, the only explanation received by Divisional Headquarters was an opaque and rather 'terse message from HMS [DORSETSHIRE] saying "MOUNT VERNON has orders to go to MOMBASA"'.[50] On Christmas Eve, the Chiefs of Staff assured Wavell and Brooke-Popham that, while the deployment of the rest of the 18th Division had not yet been decided, 'We feel that we must get reinforcements into Malaya while the situation permits.'[51]

Over the festive season, in which 'Christmas day was celebrated in traditional fashion' on the *Wakefield* (and a pantomime performed, produced by its 'hard working Entertainments Committee'),[52] it and the *West Point* steamed at full speed for Bombay, the *Dorsetshire* bringing up the rear with the two remaining transports, the *Leonard Wood* and *Joseph T. Dickman*. On the evening of 27 December Merton disembarked at Bombay, duly piped ashore by the crew of the *Wakefield*.[53] On arrival, he was told by the embarkation officer that 'all units . . . would be quartered in the area of AHMEDNAGAR, with the exception of 148 Field Regiment who would be in the area of POONA'. As and when they arrived, the 9th Northumberland Fusiliers would also go to Poona, as would the 53rd Brigade, whose whereabouts remained unclear. In contrast to the speedy conduct of business at Halifax and Cape Town, disembarkation would take five full days. At this point, as the war diary of Divisional Headquarters noted with dismay, still 'the GOC has had no information regarding the USS MOUNT VERNON, and therefore does not know where 53 Infantry Brigade Group has gone'.[54]

Apart from the loss of one of its three infantry brigades, during its two-month voyage to India the 18th Division was also weakened in other respects, and not least by the length and conditions of its passage. Decades later, John Nixon of 196th Field Ambulance recalled his voyage on board the SS *Oronsay* (to Halifax) and the *Joseph T. Dickman* (to Bombay, via Cape Town), a sojourn by which the division transitioned from winter into summer. En route to Halifax, despite storms and seasickness, he came to revel in 'the fresh sea air'; he was thrilled by 'hundreds of troops in Halifax docks singing patriotic songs while waiting to embark'; he was fearful of his ship capsizing as it was hit by the Roaring Forties in the Southern Ocean; and, at Cape Town, he welcomed the hospitality of a retired British seadog and his attractive daughter.[55] Similarly, Ronald Searle remembered that 'even fishy Halifax smelt like an exotic Spice Island' after 'eleven sweaty, seasick days below the water-line' of the Polish transport *Sobieski* and that, on board the *Mount Vernon*, 'our lives took on the sort of fantasy that comes with interminable suspense between sea and sky', a torpor fed by plenty of free Camel cigarettes and 'gargantuan helpings of American peacetime navy food'.[56] So far south had the *Mount Vernon* sailed by mid-November that 'rumour had it that we were to be dressed as penguins and quietly distributed about the Antarctic on secret missions that would be revealed only when Roosevelt and Churchill signalled that the seals on the envelopes could be broken'.[57]

Amidst this air of unreality, 'the terrible news of the sinking of HMS *Prince of Wales* and HMS *Repulse*, two of the Royal Navy's most famous battleships', had a profoundly sobering effect.[58] As Massy-Beresford noted:

> I've forgotten the actual day . . . that we read the news of the sinking of the *Prince of Wales* and the *Repulse*. It came as a terrific shock. I had no idea at the time what this loss would mean in terms of the defence of Singapore but I had a fearful feeling that if this could happen in a few minutes, what chance of survival had the rest of our Battleships in other parts of the world.[59]

Despite this body blow to British naval power and prestige, for the 53rd Brigade on board the re-routed (and comparatively 'luxurious') *Mount Vernon*,[60] the looming prospect of facing the Imperial Japanese Army caused no alarm. On the contrary, and as Searle remembered, there was a dreadful mood of complacency:

> We reached Mombasa on Christmas Day . . . It appeared there had been a change of priorities. We were no longer required to restore order to North Africa. Instead, we were to be diverted to the Far East, where we were to shove some (by now rapidly advancing) Jap dwarfs

out of Malaya and back onto their own rotten rice patch where they belonged.[61]

He continued:

> After all the excitement of our two African halts, and with two more weeks at sea before being tossed lightly into a battle that was already lost, we, the awaited reinforcements, settled down peacefully for the long journey across the Indian Ocean. We were disturbed only by the occasional lecturer who cheerfully told us that the Japs, being physically unable to close one eye (honest), could neither take aim nor shoot straight and (seriously) we'd got it made.[62]

According to Searle, far more 'demoralizing' than the prospect of closing with a largely unknown enemy in a wholly alien environment 'was the fact that, to settle comfortably on the shady side of the deck, we now had to undo the two top buttons of our tropical shorts'.[63] If tinged with a bitterness born of defeat, capture and captivity, these recollections were confirmed by William Naylor, a gunner in Philip Toosey's 135th Field Regiment, who concurred that:

> I don't think at the time it made any difference ... We were going to fight somebody; we were going into battle somewhere. Whether we were going either to face the Germans or the Japanese I don't think we were particularly worried.[64]

Moreover, despite the fate of 'Force Z' (described by Ken Tomkinson as 'a shatterer'),[65] Naylor also noted, like Searle, that a pronounced strain of racial arrogance bedevilled the brigade's approach to the Japanese in general:

> [W]hen we first arrived [in Singapore] the sense was that these little yellow so-and-so's were badly organised, they had got no equipment and weren't able to do very much. They were coming down [the Malayan peninsula] on bicycles and it sounded quite laughable ... nobody took them very seriously ... There wasn't the feeling that we were in a hopeless situation from the beginning.[66]

Nevertheless, on other ships, among the rump of the division, the mood was not so sanguine. This was true of Massy-Beresford who, though commanding an entire brigade on the *West Point*, noted that it was some days after leaving Cape Town that its American captain told him that 'he had received instructions to sail for Bombay. The whole convoy was changing course except one liner carrying the 53rd Brigade which was sailing straight for Singapore.' Instead of elation, this induced

> a sick feeling in my tummy. I didn't realise until much later that we were DOOMED but I had no liking for the prospects, seeing that we were totally ignorant of any form of jungle warfare, were not suitably clad or equipped and were all soft from the long cramped voyage.[67]

Indeed, although the voyage to India had in some ways been a huge success, with fewer than 40 casualties ('deserters, sick and V.D.') and 'excellent behaviour' displayed throughout,[68] the months at sea had dulled the fighting edge which Merton had honed for so many months in Great Britain. To an extent, this was only to be anticipated and it had been foreseen by Merton. Three weeks before embarkation, he had issued '18 Div Training Instruction No. 7', a document which laid down 'principles' intended 'to keep troops mentally and physically fit, and to improve and maintain the present standard of military training'. Besides the half-hour set aside each day for Physical Training (or 'PT'), Unit Education Officers were to identify speakers who could keep men alert through lectures, debates and language classes (with, significantly, 'elementary instruction in Arabic' strongly recommended). 'All ranks of all arms', whether issued with a rifle or not, were to be trained in its use, and the importance of 'Map Reading' and 'Bayonet Fighting' was underlined. Under the heading of 'Know your Enemy', instruction was also to be given in 'German Army Organisation', 'German Army Equipment', 'German Army Tactics' and in the 'Identification and handling' of German prisoners of war.[69] Still, it soon transpired that conditions aboard its crowded troopships were not conducive to such an ambitious training regime, even when the weather allowed, and it was curtailed long before the division docked at Cape Town. As the war diary of Divisional Headquarters conceded at the end of November 1941:

By this time training was in full swing on all ships. Every inch of desk space being occupied with training of one kind or another. Deck space was however extremely limited and the scope for training therefore much reduced. In USS Wakefield every man on board had approx. ½ hours organised exercise every day and ¾ hour for lectures. Conditions were approx. the same in every ship . . . Entertainments in the form of boxing contests, concerts, sing songs etc were organised daily.[70]

For Kenneth Bailey, a PT instructor on board the *Wakefield*, daily physical exercise took the form of 'a few laps around the long and spacious deck'. Beyond this, apart from some boxing, 'much of the leisure time each day was spent on deck soaking up the sun and being thoroughly engrossed in watching the manoeuvres of the escort ships'.[71]

Furthermore, the division's stopover in India, which lasted barely a fortnight, inclusive of the long train journeys to and from Ahmednagar, could not compensate for its idle weeks at sea, nor for the division's grave deficiency in jungle warfare training (a deficiency which, it must be said, was common to many units stationed in pre-war Malaya). Widely dispersed in the areas of Ahmednagar and Poona, combined arms training proved impossible, and 'in the light of unit dispositions the GOC decided that training could be most satisfactorily carried out by arms instead of by Brigade Groups'. Given the shortage of time and the prevailing ignorance of 'what jungle warfare might consist of',[72] training chiefly took the form of long route marches designed to toughen and acclimatize their participants. As the divisional history put it: 'During this period units were directed to pay attention to "hardening up" troops after the long voyage.'[73] For Kenneth Bailey, the training regime in Ahmednagar was characterized by 'route marches', 'football matches on grassless, dusty pitches', 'guard mounting, field training and company drill, and on the two Sundays spent here, attending church parades'.[74] Gunner Jack Chalker, of the 118th Field Regiment, had similar recollections:

In India we spent our time polishing boots and blancoing belts to beyond perfection, had *dhobi wallas* wash and press immaculate creases in our idiotic 'let-down' shorts, and attended endless futile parades without any preparation for the fighting that was to come.[75]

However, it should be stressed that Merton did not neglect the looming prospect of jungle warfare. With a thoroughness that had always characterized his approach to training, the divisional history records that:

Although the destination of the Division was still unknown, efforts were made to obtain all possible information on the Japanese Army, forest warfare and fighting conditions in MALAYA. [India's] Southern Command arranged for a training cadre to be attached to Divisional HQ. The cadre was designed to help in the preparation and running of schemes. Orders to move, however, were received before the cadre got going.[76]

According to Ken Tomkinson, in an effort to implement this training, Merton's staff 'worked 18 hours a day'. However, 'it was all rather a nightmare disorganised rush. On the one hand lists of G 1098 equipment the division should have, which weren't obtainable [and on the other] programmes of training under tropical conditions which it was impossible ever to carry out.'[77] Subsequent training, delivered en route from Bombay to Singapore, was of limited usefulness, with Massy-Beresford (for example) providing 'a series of lectures and discussions' on jungle warfare.[78] However inadequate, it was at least more than that provided for 53rd Brigade on board *Mount Vernon*. Without even the benefits of a fortnight in India, news of the fate of 'Force Z' encouraged its commander, Brigadier C. L. B. Duke, to initiate instruction in tactical withdrawals, which Toosey, understandably, deemed bad for morale.[79] Other than that, shipboard training (with its shortcomings) simply continued, leading Stephen Alexander to recall that 'A less suitable preparation for jungle fighting could scarcely be imagined.'[80]

And the campaign which engulfed the 53rd Brigade, and eventually the whole of the 18th Division, went disastrously wrong from the outset. Apart from the rapid destruction of 'Force Z', and its confirmation of Japan's aerial and maritime dominance, Malaya and Singapore were always highly exposed to a Japanese offensive which, until the middle of 1942, carried all before it, whether in the Far East or in the Pacific. Indeed, although they struck hard at Pearl Harbor, the Japanese prioritized knocking the British Empire out of the war. This pursuit of a 'Britain-first strategy' placed Hong Kong, the Malayan peninsula and Singapore in a particularly vulnerable situation,[81] especially given the overriding priorities of the war against Germany. The Japanese onslaught against Hong Kong commenced on 8 December, with the colony surrendering on Christmas Day. Under heavy bombardment, with no prospect of relief, its morale sapped by defectors, saboteurs and Fifth Columnists, its water supply cut, and the prospect of an orgy of violence being unleashed should resistance continue, the situation in Hong Kong prefigured that in Singapore barely two months later. Even Churchill's exhortations to continue the fight, and the deployment, to no avail, of last-minute reinforcements (in this case, two battalions of Canadians), were precursors of what was to follow.[82] On 8 December, the Japanese also launched their first air raid on Singapore. While Brooke-Popham failed to initiate Operation MATADOR (a planned invasion of southern Thailand, which would have denied the Japanese forward airfields), and the troops of Malaya Command struggled in vain to defend British airfields in northern Malaya, the power and momentum of the Japanese invasion only increased, helped by a sophisticated intelligence network which had been active in Malaya for some time. The retreat down the 700-mile-long Malayan peninsula quickly assumed the character of a rout. Deprived of adequate air cover, lacking in tanks, poorly trained, badly commanded and with morale eroded by repeated withdrawals, Malaya Command's raw assemblage of British, Indian, Australian and Malay troops was unable to halt the advance of a more experienced, determined, better led, yet numerically inferior enemy.[83]

While the Malayan campaign has been hailed as 'the Japanese Army's most brilliant campaign of the war',[84] in John Keegan's words, 'The collapse of the British defence of Malaya has rightly come to be regarded as one of the most shameful Allied defeats.'[85] And it was as if to compound this unfolding catastrophe that the untried 53rd Brigade arrived in Singapore on 13 January 1942, part of Convoy DM1 which also brought three artillery regiments (one anti-tank, two anti-aircraft), an RAF squadron and 50 (perhaps 51) crated 'Hurricane' fighters.[86] It was less than a week after the Japanese breakthrough on the Slim River in central Malaya, and two days after the fall of Kuala Lumpur marked a further stage in the relentless advance of General Yamashita's Twenty-Fifth Army. Docking in the Naval Base, on the northern coast of the island, in pouring monsoon rain which at least hampered the Japanese air attack, three days were spent 'in a hectic turmoil of unloading ship, attempting to sort out equipment, drawing rations etc.'.[87] (For Philip Toosey, whose regiment had arrived with neither its guns nor tractors, it was even a case of lobbying Malaya Command for local replacements, which entailed the commandeering of civilian refuse trucks for its brief campaign in Johore.)[88] With no time for acclimatization, let alone further training, given what Percival termed 'the swift march of events',[89] the brigade was promptly pitched into the fighting on the peninsula, fighting which had now reached the state of Johore on its southern tip. While there was no chance to adjust to the humidity of the local climate, which even Indian troops found debilitating,[90] or to overhaul (or even maintain) its vehicles, the lack of recent or relevant training proved a much greater problem for the 53rd Brigade, especially after weeks at sea. Committed to an alien environment, facing an unfamiliar enemy and wholly untrained in even the basics of jungle warfare, its deployment defied a maxim forcefully propounded by Field Marshal Montgomery after the war:

New and untried troops must be introduced to battle carefully and gradually with no failures in the initial ventures . . . Great and lasting harm can be done to morale by launching new units into operations for which they are not ready trained.[91]

Amidst a worsening situation, the results were predictable. By 18 January, and now part of 'Westforce' (which had been improvised to halt the Japanese advance down Malaya's western coast), the bulk of the 53rd Brigade was 'attempting to cover an immense front' in northern Johore, its two remaining battalions 'separated by an unbridged river' and the road connecting them stretching for 40 miles.[92] Thinly spread, assailed by Japanese tanks as well as aircraft, and always in danger of being cut off by the outflanking and infiltration tactics of their adversaries, the brigade was badly mauled in the Battle of Muar. Though it avoided the fate of the equally raw 45th Indian Brigade, part of the 17th Indian Division, which had arrived in Singapore from Bombay ten days before and was 'smashed to pieces' in the fighting in Johore,[93] on 20 January a planned counterattack by the 53rd Brigade foundered in the face of Japanese resistance and poor co-ordination on its own part.[94] It was all a very far cry from the successful – even triumphant – field exercises conducted under Merton the previous summer. Nevertheless, historians of the Malaya campaign have recognized the problems that beset the brigade, problems that were to be shared and amplified when the rest of the 18th Division entered the fray. According to Stanley Falk, the 53rd was 'reasonably well-trained, though for desert rather than jungle warfare' and 'none of its troops had any combat experi-ence'. Furthermore, its 'unpracticed troops, ill at ease in the strange jungle and distressed by the tropical heat, were not ready for an early fight'.[95] In sum, 'the ill-prepared and tired 53rd Brigade could probably not have pre-vailed. The Japanese forces building up before it were strong; the terrain fa-voured them, and they had air support.'[96] (Louis Allen has concurred with this verdict: '53 Brigade should have been allowed to train and acclimatize itself, but there was not time for normal delay, and it was flung into the bat-tle almost at once, after being at sea for nearly three months.')[97]

In the wake of the Battle of Muar, the long and difficult retreat towards the Straits of Johore and Singapore Island continued, the cohesion of the brigade sapped still further by the strain of defeat and – a function of desperation – the transfer and re-transfer of its units. Toosey's 135th Field Regiment, for example, was put under the command of the 11th Indian Division, where it remained until after the fall of Singapore.[98] Moreover, by 28 January, as the brigade was poised to retreat across the causeway linking Johore to Singapore Island, the 6th Norfolks, 'as far as a fighting force was concerned, did not exist'.[99] The following day, the brigade received orders to cross the causeway. As the divisional history of the 18th stated:

> The relief and withdrawal were carried out without incident. On arrival on the island the Brigade gave up control of all 11th Indian Division units and HQ went to TANGLIN BARRACKS with orders to take over the Brigade *as originally constituted* [my italics] for re-organisation and refitting.[100]

In short, the 53rd Brigade had achieved nothing amidst the larger and in-creasingly desperate attempt to shore up the defence of Malaya – basically by throwing whatever units were available (however unprepared and untrained) into the path of the Japanese advance. And the cost to Merton's division, even before it arrived, was severe. One-third of its fighting strength had been subjected to a blistering defeat and demoralizing retreat, its units had been cannibalized (a portent of what was to come) and one of its nine infantry battalions had been shredded, with no prospect of replacements ever arriving.

It was, in short, a dire situation for Merton to inherit once the bulk of his division arrived in Convoy BM11 on 29 January, the same day on which the 'much reduced' 53rd Brigade recrossed the causeway onto Singapore Island.[101] The remainder of the division, consisting of its divisional troops, arrived a week later on Convoy BM12, though not without losing the elderly, coal-burning transport *Empress of Asia* (carrying its Reconnaissance Battalion, anti-tank gunners and many RAOC and RAMC personnel) to Japanese air attack.[102] With the sinking of the *Empress of Asia* just off Singapore, 18th Division lost many of its vehicles and most of the guns of the 125th Anti-Tank Regiment.[103] However, there was one bright spot in the arrival of Convoy BM12. Now aboard the Free French ship the *Felix Roussel*, which had run between Marseille and Saigon before the war, the 9th Northumberland Fusiliers had deployed their many machine guns to good effect in an improvised anti-aircraft role.[104] Their earlier truculence now forgiven, Merton wrote to Honor three days after their arrival:

The last of my family (Division) to arrive here two or three days ago, had a pretty bad experience, but behaved magnificently. Their ships were dive bombed for an hour on two successive days. After the first, I think the Navy got a bit short of ammunition, anyhow on the second day, the defence of their transports fell almost entirely on my chaps with their light machine guns, and they fairly stuck to it, but one ship [the *Empress of Asia*] got hit and set on fire, and the Navy has sent the troops a message of congratulation on their behaviour, while the Captain of another ship told the troops that it was entirely owing to them that his ship was still afloat.[105]

Still, the arrival of the 18th Division stood no chance of turning the tide of defeat. As recognized in the British official history of *The War against Japan*:

The 18th Division had been destined for the Middle East where it had been intended that it should complete its training. It was not therefore tactically loaded and would arrive at the end of a long and tedious voyage without transport, supporting arms, or adequate maintenance facilities. It would not be an efficient fighting formation ready for action for some time. The troops would be soft after several weeks at sea in crowded transports; and they had had no training in jungle warfare.[106]

Significantly, as it was disembarking at Bombay, Wavell had lodged a request with Sir Alan Brooke, now CIGS, that the 'remainder of 18th Division would be allowed to remain with him for [the] defence of India and Burma'. After a tussle between India and Far East Commands, on New Year's Day the War Office confirmed that 'the whole of the 18th Division was definitely allotted to Malaya'.[107] However, such was the sheer speed of the Japanese advance that the intended role of the 18th Division in Malaya was rendered redundant over the ensuing month. On 5 January, at a Malaya Command conference convened by General Percival, it had been envisaged that the 18th Division would be used to stiffen a defensive line north of Johore. By the time of its re-embarkation at Bombay (15–18 January) and its departure in two convoys the following day, the decisive Battle of Muar had already been fought (and lost) and, by the time of its arrival in Singapore on 29 January, Malaya's southernmost state of Johore had already been overrun.[108] In other words, the division arrived far too late to have been of any strategic use.[109]

However, in terms of its quality, it was certainly no worse (in fact, probably much better) than the other ill-starred reinforcements that flowed into Singapore at this time. In addition to the 45th Indian Brigade (which Percival argued 'had never been fit for employment in a theatre of war'),[110] on 25 January the 44th Indian Brigade, another brigade of the 17th Indian Division, arrived on Convoy BM10 together with a draft of 7,000 Indian replacements. The day before, an Australian machine-gun battalion and 1,900 replacements for the 8th Australian Division had arrived on Convoy S2. However, as the official history acknowledged:

The 44th Brigade was no better trained than the ill-fated 45th, and on arrival was retained on the island for further training. The 7,000

Indian reinforcements were made up largely of young and only partly trained recruits ... That the reinforcements sent from India were only partly trained was unavoidable, for at the time nothing better was available. India had strained every nerve to expand her army quickly to meet the demand for field formations to provide garrisons for the Middle East, Iraq, Persia and Malaya. The country was drained of trained officers and men other than those required to staff the greatly enlarged instructional establishments and to provide cadres for the new formations to replace those sent overseas.[111]

If, therefore, 'the Indian contingent was strong only in numbers',[112] 'the fighting efficiency of the 1,900 Australian reinforcements was [also] a grievous disappointment'. Although the machine-gun battalion was 'well-trained', such were the mechanics of the Australian Army's training and deployment system that, while better trained troops were left in the Dominion, or were available in training camps in the Middle East, 'some of them sailed within a fortnight of enlistment and had not even learnt how to handle their weapons, few of them had had any time to assimilate even the rudiments of discipline or were in any sense trained'.[113]

In other words, despite their numerical significance (the five infantry brigades which arrived in Singapore that January represented half the number available to Malaya Command on 7 December),[114] it is highly doubtful whether the tens of thousands of reinforcements poured into Singapore in the six weeks prior to its capitulation were any kind of force multiplier. As the official history put it, these were 'the equivalent of a physically unfit British division, two almost untrained Indian brigades, a number of partially trained Indian and Australian reinforcements and aircraft which could be but a wasting asset'.[115] According to Brian Farrell, after successive defeats on the Malayan peninsula, on the eve of the battle for the island:

Malaya Command was more makeshift than ever. Full strength units were raw and just arrived, neither acclimatized nor fit to fight. Veteran units were worn down or lacked equipment. The raw replacement drafts could not replace the combat power lost on the mainland ... the field army was dead. Malaya Command was now a collection of units with little confidence left in their high command or each other. Some were still full of fight. Others were broken.[116]

Moreover, at a tactical level, Daniel Todman has emphasized that it was more than a lack of jungle training that hampered the defence of Malaya. While the Japanese, too, were often unfamiliar with the jungle milieu, their troops and commanders (most of whom were veterans of the war in China) made up for this deficiency by initiative, flexibility and aggression.[117] In contrast, and regardless of their level of training, British, Australian and Indian tactics were derived from 'the highly structured infantry and artillery battles that had characterized the Western Front in 1917', an orientation 'poorly suited' to the tactical situation on the Malayan mainland, 'where troops were less densely concentrated and the jungle terrain encouraged outflanking and infiltration'. Consequently, though British and imperial troops 'often fought hard from behind prepared defences', once their lines were breached, as they were recurrently, 'they were thrown into disarray'.[118]

But how had Merton and his division, so well-prepared for the war against Germany, found themselves reinforcing this failure in Malaya? Apart from the economic value of the region, the answer lies in imperial defence policy and the state of Anglo-Australian relations when Japan invaded Malaya. In 1941, Malaya generated nearly 40 per cent of the world's rubber, and 60 per cent of the world's tin. Given the importance of these raw materials for the British Empire's entire war effort, and their significance as the foremost 'dollar-earner' in its trade with the United States, the peninsula itself (a long patchwork of protectorates and colonies, four-fifths of which was covered in rainforest) was well worth defending.[119]

However, apart from Malaya's importance as 'Britain's richest colony',[120] in strategic terms Singapore Island (since 1867, part of the Crown Colony of the Straits Settlements) was home to the Empire's most important naval base east of Suez, located astride the sea lanes to the Dutch East Indies, the eastern approaches to the Indian Ocean and the northern approaches to Australia. Japan's emergence as a leading naval power in the early twentieth century had, in the interwar years, prompted the development of a major new naval base on Singapore Island. Commenced in the 1920s and built (albeit sporadically) at vast expense (some £63 million) in a straitened economic climate,[121] it was intended to shelter and support a major British surface fleet in the event of war with Japan (or, as the Imperial Conference of 1923 put it, 'to provide for the security of the territories and trade of the Empire in Eastern waters').[122] A forward bastion in the maritime defence of Australia and even New Zealand, the naval base at Singapore symbolized Britain's determination to protect its far-flung colonies and dominions. However, in the mid-1930s, as Mussolini's Italy and Hitler's Germany emerged as prospective adversaries, the strategic approach to Singapore became more flexible, an acceptance dawning that, should war also break out in Europe, Singapore would get only what the Royal Navy could spare. In the event, the situation proved worse than this, for in June 1940 the Australian and New Zealand governments were informed that no fleet could be sent to Singapore for the 'foreseeable future', a revelation that reversed previous assurances and caused huge concern in Canberra and Wellington.[123]

Given the governing assumption that Singapore Island would be attacked from the sea (one rehearsed by Colonel Arthur Percival, then a senior staff officer in Malaya Command, in a 1937 lecture on 'The Strategical Problems of Singapore'),[124] the batteries and installations of Singapore's interwar defences faced seaward. However, from the summer of 1940, and as the prospect of war with Japan increased with its signing of the Tripartite Pact with Germany and Italy, the task of defending its vast Malayan hinterland was entrusted to the RAF, to the Army and to the natural climate and terrain of Malaya itself.[125] Despite its weaknesses, and echoing the kind of language used with reference to Britain's naval fastnesses of Malta and Gibraltar, in military and administrative circles it became habitual (if careless and misleading) to refer to Singapore as a 'fortress', the 'Gibraltar of the Far East' and even as an 'impregnable citadel'. (This language, for example, was used recurrently in Percival's lecture of 1937.) Singapore was emphatically not a 'fortress' in the sense of being capable of all-round defence: its landward defences were non-existent and, should the Japanese establish airfields on the Malayan mainland, its naval base would be rendered all but useless.[126] Indeed, in recognition of Singapore's fundamental vulnerability, the Royal Navy's Eastern Fleet headquarters were moved from Singapore to Java in the first week of 1942, signalling that the Navy now saw the Indian Ocean as its main line of defence against Japan.[127] Writing a few days later to General Sir Hastings Ismay, his key liaison officer with the Chiefs of Staff

Committee, Churchill described the state and configuration of Singapore's defences as 'one of the greatest scandals that could possibly be exposed'.[128] As he famously lamented in his history of the Second World War, in early 1942 Singapore was an 'almost naked island' and, though he accepted responsibility for not being curious enough about its defences, Churchill insisted that 'the possibility of Singapore having no landward defences no more entered into my mind than that of a battleship being launched without a bottom'.[129]

However, though the naval base at Singapore had 'lost its *very raison d'être*' by the summer of 1940,[130] its symbolic importance remained very real, and what helped to seal the fate of the 18th Division was the increasingly strained relationship between London and Canberra over matters of imperial defence in the winter of 1941–2. Appalled and alarmed by Japan's blitzkrieg across South-East Asia and the Pacific, Australia's new Labor government grew increasingly fearful of a Japanese invasion, fears stoked by frantic reports from Australia's Commonwealth Commissioner in Singapore.[131] On 27 December, its Prime Minister, John Curtin, voiced his concerns in a speech in which he announced that Australia would, if necessary, turn to the United States for its defence. Though London agreed on 6 January to reinforce Malaya with the 6th and 7th Australian divisions and the British 7th Armoured Brigade from the Middle East, the inevitable delay meant that those reinforcements already slated for Singapore and Malaya would arrive as planned, a commitment confirmed by shrill Australian insistence that any evacuation of Singapore – 'this central fortress in the system of the Empire' – would be regarded as 'an inexcusable betrayal'. Consequently, in Daniel Todman's words, 'London could not . . . be seen publicly to have forsaken Singapore. The servicemen sailing there would pay the price.'[132]

But there was, nonetheless, a real understanding of the situation in London, and even a fleeting opportunity to pluck Merton's division from the maw of catastrophe. However, in combination with pressure from Australia, this was passed over due to the creation of a new Allied command structure in the Far East. Building on the Anglo-American Arcadia Conference of December 1941, in January 1942 a joint Allied command was activated which broadened and superseded the functions of Far East Command, of which Malaya Command was part. Christened ABDA

Command (American-British-Dutch-Australian), it was placed under Wavell who, after his successes against the Italians in the Western Desert, was Britain's most accomplished battlefield general. For Wavell, no less than for the Australians, a vigorous and protracted defence of Singapore was imperative, buying time for him to build up Allied forces in the Dutch East Indies.[133] Accordingly, and fresh from visiting the island, Wavell cabled Churchill on 21 January, admitting the grave weaknesses of its defences but stating that the arrival of the rest of 18th Division would help Singapore's 'prolonged defence'. As Wavell put it:

I hope to get [44th] Indian Brigade and remainder of 18th Division into Singapore. After allowing for losses, this should give equivalent of approximately three divisions for defence of island, if we are driven into it. Subsequent reinforcements will probably have to be used for defence of Java and Sumatra, which are both weakly held.[134]

Churchill, with Alan Brooke,[135] was unconvinced. The 18th Division could, the Prime Minister thought, be better used for the defence of Burma: 'I began to think more of Burma and of the reinforcements on the way to Singapore. These could be doomed or diverted. There was still ample time to turn their prows northwards to Rangoon.' Churchill, in fact, wrote to Ismay in response to Wavell's plans: 'His message gives little hope for prolonged defence. It is evident that such defence would be only at the cost of all the reinforcements now on the way.' Still, the pressure of Anglo-Australian relations and the imperatives of imperial (and Allied) solidarity proved irresistible – nothing was done (especially under Curtin's stinging admonitions) and the 18th Division maintained its fateful course towards the beleaguered island.[136] However, and as Churchill later accepted, 'there is no doubt what a purely military decision should have been'.[137] Seen from the perspective of the 18th Division, which was still at sea:

The Japanese crawled . . . with such alarming speed down their intelligence maps of Malaya, that 18 Div. staff started getting out the Netherlands East Indies sheets! All the voyage Becky saw to it that training went on as flat out as possible. Then suddenly one day came the shout, 'Orders!' 'It's Singapore.'[138]

6

The battle for Singapore

When Merton arrived, his task was clearly an impossible one: to take a battered and depleted division, consisting mainly of inadequately trained and unacclimatized troops, into a battle there was no chance of winning. However, and in a letter written to Honor on 29 January, he remained undaunted:

> After crossing the equator for the fourth time yesterday, we said goodbye to the Captain and many of the officers [of the *Wakefield*]. The Sirens were soon going and the A.A. guns, but luckily we were not the target, though we should have made a good enough one. Apparently, the report got about that we were being heavily bombed; all due to the very doubtful dropping of a couple of bombs near our tail . . .[1]

On docking at Singapore:

> A Staff Officer came on board and took me straight to General Percival's Headquarters . . . Percival asked me to lunch and to stay, and as he seemed to mean both, I am writing to you from Flagstaff House . . . Percival was with Sir John Dill as his Chief of Staff at the beginning of the War. He is charming but has no easy task. However, I am not going to talk about that.[2]

Merton and his troops disembarked in an atmosphere of encroaching chaos and incipient panic. On disembarking from the *West Point*, the commanding officer of the 18th Cambridgeshires, a holder of the DSO from the First World War, was told by 'a number of high-ranking officers' that they had arrived too late to make any difference.[3] And even to the inexperienced soldiers of the 18th Division, the demoralization of Singapore's defenders was apparent. Painfully conscious of the loss of the *Prince of Wales* and *Repulse*, the debacle in Malaya and Japanese dominance of the skies, their spirits sank still further at the sight of RAF personnel heading in the opposite direction. As Kenneth Bailey remembered:

On disembarking at Singapore on 29 January, we saw that another ship was about to leave the docks when we were surprisingly informed that on board were the remnants of the R.A.F. which were leaving the island to take up station on Java. At the very time of disembarking we were under attack from Japanese aircraft, and with the knowledge that the R.A.F. were leaving the island, it was unmistakably and painfully obvious, although not readily admitted, that we were doomed.[4]

Significantly, some of those who saw the 18th disembark (its transports, when 'unloaded and ready for sea', promptly filled by civilian evacuees)[5] felt a pang of sympathy. Interviewed in 1975, Charles Elston, who served as an officer in the 1st Indian Anti-Aircraft Regiment, was asked whether the arrival of the division gave him any feeling of confidence. He answered:

No, it didn't because by then it didn't really seem to be a matter of troops being required, as far as I could see. You really needed a massive Air-force to arrive and a massive Naval support. I well remember the 18th Division arriving . . . I think they must have thought it quite extraordinary to be arriving in conditions such as they were.[6]

And they got more extraordinary still. Arriving a few days later with the 9th Northumberland Fusiliers, and alluding to the British failure to hold Greece and Crete against the Germans the previous year, Richard Sharp recalled that:

As we came down the gang-plank we were told, 'We're evacuating the mainland to-day', and we said 'Christ, have they never heard of

Crete out here?' and stepped ashore. But you shoved that out of your mind – you had to. You were no good to anyone except the enemy if you went into a fight, knowing it was useless.[7]

Even in these dire circumstances, Merton sought to lift the spirits of his division, efforts that recall his approach to the 1st Guards Brigade during the retreat to Dunkirk. As Sir John Smyth put the challenge in *Leadership in War*: 'Montgomery has so rightly said that there is no greater morale-raiser than unbroken victory. And he himself proved that this was true. But what about unbroken defeat? Where does that get you?'[8] Still, Merton sought to stoke a more confident mood by singling out for commendation those who had distinguished themselves in the fight for the mainland, praising in particular the conduct of Philip Toosey, whose 135th Field Regiment had performed well (despite the odds) in Johore. Just after Merton arrived, he took action, as Servaes testified: 'My General sent for [Toosey], and personally congratulated him not only on the part his regiment had played, but on his own personal showing, and told him how proud he was of him.' This was a characteristically buoyant and generous gesture amidst an otherwise deplorable situation, for as Servaes went on: 'I cannot describe to you the state of things at Singapore at that time', the atmosphere among its defenders being one of 'defeatism, panic and complete loss of morale'.[9]

Ten days before Merton's arrival, in a message to the Chiefs of Staff Committee, Churchill had dictated some urgent measures for the defence of Singapore Island. In order to remedy decades of neglect – even negligence – he urged the wiring and mining of potential landing sites, the construction of field works with interlocking fields of fire, the seizing of 'every conceivable small boat' in the Straits of Johore, the creation of new 'field batteries' covering the length of the Straits, the formation of 'mobile counter-attack reserve columns' and the conscription of the entire male population in 'constructing defence works'. Urging that 'the whole island must be fought for until every single unit and every single strong point has been separately destroyed', he concluded by pronouncing that 'the city of Singapore must be converted into a citadel and defended to the death. No surrender can be contemplated.'[10] In other words, Singapore was to become a Far Eastern Verdun – and Merton wasted no time in preparing the division for its ordeal. As the divisional history recounted:

On the morning of 29 January 1942, immediately after disembarkation, the G.O.C. visited H.Q. Malaya Command. He was informed that the decision had already been taken to make SINGAPORE a beleaguered fortress. By midnight on 31 January all troops would have been evacuated from the mainland, and the Causeway would then be breached. 18 Division was to be prepared to move up 'as early as possible' to relieve the Indian Divisions in the Northern Sector of the island [which] was taken to mean as soon as units were equipped and issued with transport.[11]

By this stage, the island was already divided into three sectors: Northern (running from the Causeway to Changi, held by III Indian Corps' 9th and 11th Indian Divisions); Western (running from the Causeway to Sungei Jurong on the south-west coast, held largely by the Australians); and Southern (from Sungei Jurong eastward to Changi, held by Singapore's original 'Fortress' troops). There was also a Command Reserve of British and Indian battalions, including some mauled by the fighting in Johore and drafts of newly arrived, 'semi-trained' recruits. Significantly, instead of being returned to Merton, his estranged 53rd Brigade was added to this reserve on 30 January.[12] Nevertheless, the importance of Merton's division can be gauged by the fact that its infantry battalions comprised nine of the 13 British battalions on the island and almost a quarter of the total available for Singapore's defence (in addition to the British battalions, there were 17 Indian, six Australian and two Malay battalions).[13]

The challenges of defending the island were, however, formidable (see Figure 1). Besides faltering morale and unrelenting Japanese air attack, Percival felt obliged to cover all eventualities, which included (whether severally, or in combination) seaborne landings, an attack across the Johore Straits, and even the prospect of an airborne assault (Japanese paratroopers had captured the key airfield at Menado, in the Dutch East Indies, in January 1942).[14] On the northern and western shores, a front of around 30 miles, a maze of mangrove swamps and inlets complicated the defenders' task, while enemy movements on the opposite shore (a distance of between 600 and 2,000 yards) were masked by rainforest. Inland, much of the island was covered by forest and plantations, but 'of prime importance' to the defenders were, firstly, the central village of Bukit Timah, where 'crucial high ground and supply dumps' lay only five miles from Singapore City, and, secondly, three large reservoirs (Seletar, Peirce and MacRitchie) which maintained the water supply to its population, now swollen to about one million inhabitants and refugees.[15]

Shocked by the size of the Northern Sector, Merton visited Malaya Command HQ once again on 30 January, where 'he represented that the Northern Sector was too big for the Division to hold, even if 53 Infantry Brigade rejoined', a point that was acknowledged 'in principle'. Having made his point, the following day, 31 January, Merton attended a conference of Lieutenant-General Sir Lewis Heath's III Indian Corps, under which the 18th Division had now been placed. Here, he learned that his division 'would relieve 9 Indian Division on the [north-east] coast that night'. While the 9th's artillery would remain in place, now under the command of 18th Division's Commander Royal Artillery (CRA):

> The decision to put 18 Division into the line so suddenly was taken because the 22nd Indian Infantry Brigade of 9th Indian Division, which incidentally had only two brigades, had been cut off in JOHORE and had not crossed to the island before the Causeway was blown.[16]

After the conference, Merton visited the headquarters of the 54th and 55th Brigades 'and gave verbal orders . . . to move to the coast that night'. On arrival, 54th Brigade took position on the right and 55th Brigade on the left, deploying to the right (or south-east) of 11th Indian Division. Divisional headquarters was established that afternoon 'near the southern crossroads at PAYA LEBAR', halfway between the north-east coast and Singapore City.[17]

Facing the Johore Straits, the 18th Division's sector comprised Seletar airfield on the left, 'which ran to the water's edge', the Punggol Peninsula in the centre and Loyang Beaches on the right. Its frontage was a mixture of mangrove swamp and open beach, including a stretch of 500 yards at the tip of the Punggol Peninsula.[18] However, though very far from the East Anglian coast in 1940, the 18th Division was well-practised in the art of coastal defence, and Merton swiftly identified the strengths and weaknesses of its position:

> The G.O.C. considered the relative importance of these three sectors was from west to east. He judged SELETAR AERODROME the most

attractive objective for the Japanese, since here an airborne and seaborne attack could be combined. PUNGGOL PENINSULA was the next in importance, since it could be cut off by landings . . . thus forming a bridgehead for future operations. The LOYANG BEACH sector, although suitable for a landing, presented no particularly attractive objective inland.[19]

There were, however, some grave practical problems to overcome. Captain Tufton Beamish, Merton's GSO 3, noticed the parlous state of the makeshift coastal defences the division had taken over. Blockhouses, constructed from tree trunks and lacking camouflage, lay thinly spaced every 400–500 yards, were sited away from the water's edge and lacked clear fields of fire. These were complemented by inadequate gun emplacements, constructed of earth and sandbags and, once again, devoid of camouflage. There was no barbed wire – and very little was available – and 'the supply of anti-tank mines was totally inadequate'. In the event, fields of fire had to be cleared using whatever machetes were available, and even bayonets were put to use.[20] According to Lieutenant-Colonel Alfred E. Knights, the commanding officer of the 4th Norfolks, 'It was a practical impossibility to put this sector in anything like a reasonable state of defence in the time available for doing so.'[21] In terms of its communications, the division's signalling equipment 'had not yet arrived' and contact between its two brigades proved 'very difficult' until 'some buried lines of the existing system were allotted to the Division'.[22]

The enormous challenge facing the 18th was clear at divisional headquarters. As Ken Tomkinson reflected:

18th Division had formed in 1940 [as] part of the East Anglian coastal defences. Her men were accustomed to a high standard of coastal impregnability. Imagine, therefore, their amazement to find on the [north-east] coast of this renowned fortress of Singapore almost no wire, almost no searchlights, mines or communications, on a perfectly accessible coast within 2 miles of an active, strong and so far highly successful enemy.[23]

Still, with his usual briskness, Merton set about organizing the defence-in-depth of his allotted sector, resolving 'to hold a daily conference at

0930 hrs, to be attended by [CRA], [Commander Royal Engineers (CRE)] and [both] Brigadiers to deal with defensive arrangements'. At the first of these, on 1 February, he enunciated the governing principles which would ensure a deep, all-round and vigorous defence. Any Japanese landing would be repelled on the beaches while any breakthrough (or airborne assault) would be 'dealt with by reserves'. The core of the division's shore defences were its observation posts and artillery and machine-gun emplacements, but 'behind these forward localities would be support and reserve localities'. All 'defended localities', including artillery positions, had to be capable of 'all-round defence' and 'be stocked with water, food and ammunition for seven days'. However, rather than simply wait for their attackers, in each locality 'a proportion of the garrison must always be available to move out, hunt and destroy any enemy who had penetrated the area'. Similarly, aggressive patrolling would be carried out 'at dawn between forward localities' and, at the same time of day, to ensure that 'main roads' were clear. Artillery pieces and machine guns would be supported by searchlights once they 'became available', while 'priority of issue of wire would be given to forward localities'. A single battalion, the 1/5th Sherwood Foresters, 'would be regarded as Divisional reserve and could not be used by 55 Infantry Brigade without reference to Divisional HQ'.[24] Other, non-divisional units were present in support, including four Field Regiments of the Royal Artillery, three companies of Indian Engineers, and other Indian troops and armoured cars at Seletar airfield.[25]

Though deemed by Percival to be as 'soft as jelly after three months at sea',[26] what the 18th Division (or at least its 54th and 55th Brigades) accomplished in the space of just five feverish days was remarkable (see Figure 2). These 'were spent in organising defences and making adjustments' (including building breastworks where a high water table precluded digging trenches) and, notwithstanding the scarcity of barbed wire, 'all localities were wired in with a double apron fence'. Anti-tank mines were sown at Seletar airfield and on the beaches of the Punggol Peninsula; creeks were rigged with 'anti-boat' devices (including booms, explosives and even a 'flame trap'), while 'piers, slipways and cranes' were duly demolished. Furthermore, a detachment of Chinese volunteers (from what was known as 'Dalforce', named after its founder, Lieutenant-Colonel J. D. Dalley of the Federated Malay States Police)[27] was attached to the 54th Brigade with the aim of preventing infiltration by maintaining 'listening posts in the mangrove swamps'. Furthermore, the division liaised with a nightly Royal Navy 'Straits Patrol' (whose engines would, it was feared, alert any attackers to its presence) and a flotilla of small boats was collected with which the division, with the help of attached naval personnel, could mount its own patrols of its sector's numerous creeks and inlets.

However, three problems soon presented themselves. Firstly, given the degree of congestion on Singapore Island, there was little room for manoeuvre: 'The rear area of the Division was overcrowded with extra-divisional units and establishments.' This included two RAF transit camps, two reinforcement camps and an RAOC vehicle park. (On one occasion during the subsequent fighting, divisional headquarters and the divisional reserve were overrun by RAF personnel fleeing Japanese shelling.)[28] Secondly, 'to avoid damage to civilian property on the mainland', Malaya Command decreed that its artillery was permitted 'to open fire only on known enemy localities' – a restriction aimed at not alienating the Sultan of Johore, and which was not rescinded until 5 February. Thirdly, it proved difficult to control or even channel the movement of civilians, a worry-ing factor given the number of refugees on the island and longstanding – and all too justified – fears of pro-Japanese spies and saboteurs.[29] Besides fears of Fifth Columnists, Reginald Burton noted how the soldiers of the 4th Norfolks, as new arrivals and as men 'whose normal horizons were bounded by King's Lynn in the north and Southend in the south', were be-wildered by the sheer diversity of the tide of refugees – 'Chinese, Malays, Tamils and others' – and how Chinese demands for weapons seemed dis-tinctly 'unfriendly'.[30] As the divisional history noted:

> Civilians were always a difficulty and although they were prohibited from going within a mile of the coast from 1 February it was some days before this order became effective. A curfew was in force from 2130 hours to 0630 hours, nevertheless civilians were constantly passing through reserve areas and gun positions. Thus there was every facility for fifth column activity.[31]

Away from these preparations and Merton's direct oversight, the 53rd Brigade ('re-equipped, in the main, at the expense of the rest of the

Division') moved up to the coast on 2 February, now under the command of 11th Indian Infantry Division and relieving the 15th Indian Infantry Brigade. Three days later, the guns and vehicles of the 118th and 148th Field Regiments were, after a week's delay, disembarked – and were promptly employed in counter-battery fire by Malaya Command. The same day saw the arrival of Convoy BM12 and the 9th Northumberland Fusiliers, who were fed, company by company, into the 18th Division's defences on 6 February.[32] However, what Merton seems to have feared most at this stage was an airborne assault on Seletar airfield. On 4 February, he 'discussed the general artillery policy with the C.R.A.', ensuring that as many batteries as possible could be brought to bear on the airfield in the event of a Japanese landing. He also ensured that almost a million gallons of aviation fuel was drained from the airfield's storage tanks. Still, he remained anxious over the vulnerability of the airfield. On 5 February, the artillery's fireplan was revised, with Merton ordering 'the C.R.A. to arrange for as many guns as possible to bring fire to bear on the landing ground'. Consequently, 'a concentration of fifty guns' was arranged 'to be available at call' by the officer in command of the airfield's defences. To supplement this, 'a plan for a counter-attack on SELETAR AERODROME' by the 1/5th Sherwood Foresters 'supported by artillery was prepared and the necessary reconnaissance carried out'.[33]

Despite his preoccupation with Singapore's defences, in the days after his arrival Merton still found time to write to Honor. On 3 February, he gave his impressions of the mood on the island, and at his headquarters. Struck by the inundation of refugees, he wrote how the local population had risen suddenly 'from 400,000 to about a million' – 'how everyone manages to crowd in and find food, I don't know.' He had also explored the ground in the vicinity of his headquarters, reporting that 'I have had a walk in what seems to me to be real jungle, though I suppose the up-country "wallahs" would laugh at us for saying this.' He had met Wavell, 'who seems quite pleased to see one, chiefly no doubt on account of what I brought with me. He accused me of having put on flesh which shows I must be well.' Singapore's climate was such that 'I have parked all my kit at Flagstaff House and am travelling light. One wants nothing but a pair of shorts, shoes, stockings, and a shirt.' In terms of his division, 'everyone is well, and in good heart' and he had (temporarily) 'got Bulger Duke (Brigadier

Commanding 53rd Brigade) and his lot back somewhat thinned'. Honor's messages, to his mess cook and to his mess sergeant's wife, had been received and appreciated. All in all, he averred, 'The whole situation here is quite extraordinary, and would be comic if it was not so tragic.'[34] A briefer note followed the next day. His headquarters had been relocated and he now had 'a tent for my office, and a ballroom for my bedroom!' He also reported that: 'I ate my lunch to-day on the edge of a lagoon, and mangrove swamp, looking across to another island [Pulau Ubin]. I had a good walk too, and I know what a Rubber tree looks like now. All well.'[35] On 5 February, he noted that the site of his present headquarters, 'under different circumstances . . . might be very pleasant'. The bombardment of Singapore was also intensifying:

> It's not too bad as it is, only gets a bit noisy, on the ground as well as in the air now. We are lucky to have had the days of quiet which we have had since coming in the area. It seems a month since we got off the ship, in fact it is barely a week . . . I now have a sailor, Lieutenant Commander Reed, attached to my Staff, also a policeman, Harrison, from up-country. The latter knows a good many of the languages, and a lot about the people.[36]

On 5 February, Japanese shells began to fall in the divisional area from across the Straits of Johore, with 'any movement on the beaches, especially around the tip of PUNGGOL PENINSULA' being 'certain to draw fire'. Seletar airfield was also targeted by Japanese bombers, the latter unmolested by the RAF ('The lack of air support on our side was most notable,' as the divisional history noted sourly).[37] For a few days it seemed as if a classic siege of the kind envisaged by Churchill might still transpire, and that 'a situation comparable to trench warfare was developing'.[38] Japanese artillery fire began to intensify, and by 7 February it was raking the roads 'in the vicinity of Divisional H.Q.', which had relocated to 'the rubber plantation N.W. of PAYA LEBAR, some 250 yds west of the PAYA LEBAR – SELETAR AERODROME ROAD'.[39] Moreover, in an echo of countless skirmishes in the no-man's land of the Western Front a generation earlier, on the night of 7/8 February the Japanese ousted 'the standing patrol' of the 4th Norfolks on Pulau Ubin, a small outcrop in the eastern reaches of the Johore Straits.[40] Though this was just a feint, intended to fix the defenders on the north-east coast while the main assault went in elsewhere,[41] Merton continued to bolster his defences, deploying the survivors of the *Empress of Asia* (namely the Reconnaissance Battalion and the 125th Anti-Tank Regiment – minus their original equipment, with the latter serving mostly as infantry)[42] to the rear of his divisional area.[43]

By 8 February, despite continuing Japanese shelling from the mainland (Merton wrote to Honor, 'Not quite one's idea of what Sunday ought to be, for it has been anything but peaceful . . . they are making a beastly noise'),[44] the situation on the divisional front seems to have stabilized to the point at which an ambitious *offensive* action was being contemplated. As Merton continued to organize ad hoc 'reinforcement companies' for his two brigades, Malaya Command bestowed a mark of confidence on his division and its capabilities:

> Orders were received that there was to be a raid on the mainland by a force of approximately two companies. The raiding party was to land in the area of PASIR GUDANG and attempt to destroy the hostile guns reported to be about 2000 yds inland. The raid was to last 24 hours. The landing area was opposite 55 Infantry Brigade, who were ordered to carry out the operation, and [1/5th] Sherwood Foresters were detailed by the Brigade.[45]

This plan, however, faced immediate problems:

> The raid was ordered to be carried out as soon as possible, but owing to the short notice given and the difficulty in obtaining suitable craft, it was decided that it could not be carried out before the night [of] 10/11 February. Consequently, it never materialised.[46]

What stymied this bold (and possibly unwise) foray across the Johore Straits was not a lack of boats but the all-out Japanese assault on the north-west coast of the island which erupted on the night of 8/9 February. This was preceded by a 'really massive' aerial and artillery bombardment which battered the defences and communications of the 22nd Australian Brigade.[47] As the 18th's divisional history noted, on the afternoon of

135

8 February 'artillery fire ceased and there was an ominous quiet on the Division front, although a great deal of activity could be heard on the west of the island'. That evening, sporadic Japanese shelling broke out once again, to which '18 Division artillery replied [with] intermittent bombardment and harassing fire' but, in the event, 'no attack developed'. A patrol of the 4th Norfolks ventured over to Palau Ubin but 'reported it clear of the enemy, who had apparently left in a hurry'.[48]

The disaster which unfolded over the next few hours, and which ultimately engulfed the island, was, arguably, directly attributable to Percival's failure to deploy the 18th Division where it would have been of most use: as it was, it was holding the wrong sector at the wrong time. With two of its brigades intact, and under the leadership of a general with a clear grasp of coastal defence and a record of fighting dogged rearguard actions against the Germans, the 18th Division was undoubtedly the strongest formation in Malaya Command, and yet when the storm broke it was holding the least vulnerable, eastern half of the Northern Sector of the island's defences. Despite the seven-mile length of its line, to its front the Straits of Johore were much wider than they were to the west, beyond the Causeway, where they narrowed in places to less than half a mile.[49] Here, as part of the Western Sector, the line was held by the inexperienced 44th Indian Brigade and by the comparatively weak 22nd and 27th Australian brigades of the 8th Australian Division, stiffened (if that is the term) by the recent replacements from Australia. Although later accounts are conflicting, it seems that the greater potential of the 18th Division to hold the more vulnerable Western Sector had been discussed by Percival and Wavell when Wavell visited Singapore on 20 January. On balance, the evidence indicates that Wavell advised, though he did not insist, that the 18th Division be sent to the more vulnerable Western Sector.[50] That this did not happen was due to an absence of reliable intelligence about Japanese intentions, a predicament that was not helped by the fact that Japanese dominance of the skies rendered aerial reconnaissance all but impossible. Convinced that the Japanese forces facing him were much larger than they were, that they could strike anywhere along the northern coast and that a seaborne invasion could still be mounted on the southern coast, Percival's dispositions remained unbalanced and, as events were to prove, fatally misjudged.[51]

With his forces deployed along 70 miles of coastline,[52] or held inland awaiting developments, Percival fell foul of one of the cardinal rules of generalship, an error for which Merton's 18th Division would pay a heavy price. As Frederick the Great put this principle: 'Who defends everything, defends nothing',[53] a point demonstrated by the Japanese Twenty-Fifth Army when its 5th and (confusingly) 18th Divisions crossed the Johore Straits on the night of 8/9 February, outflanking, infiltrating and scattering the Australian 22nd Brigade in its path. Despite some fierce resistance, such was the success of their assault crossing that by dawn on 9 February 13,000 Japanese troops were ashore, reinforced by a further 10,000 within a few hours.[54] By that evening the Japanese had reached Tengah airfield, while the Imperial Guards Division made another successful crossing of the Johore Straits further east, this time routing the 27th Australian Brigade.[55] A major reverse in itself, the appearance of the Imperial Guards also un-hinged the so-called 'Jurong line', a three-mile front between the Kranji and Jurong rivers along which Australian Major-General H. Gordon Bennett had hoped to stem a Japanese attack from the west.[56] (See Figure 3.)

Although a sympathetic biographer, even Clifford Kinvig has criticized Percival for his failure to mount a major counterattack once the Japanese had established their bridgehead. Instead, he squandered his few combat-worthy formations in local, piecemeal counterattacks which frittered away the strength and cohesion of the 18th Division while having no effect on the overall situation. As Kinvig has summarized Percival's mistakes:

First, his Command Reserve and then Heath's were put under Bennett's command; later, he allocated the three-battalion 'Tomforce' – all drawn from different brigades – to the fight in the west and followed this with two single battalions, and finally the three-battalion 'Masseyforce' [*sic*]. His failure to organize a larger, concerted counter-attack more quickly and his piecemeal employment of the largely fresh, if ill-prepared, units of 18th Division to support different localities drew subsequent criticism even from his own staff. A counter-attack was certainly required, but it is doubtful whether this unfortunate division would have been able to move and act with the necessary speed and resolution. *In extremis* as Percival now was, perhaps it should have been given the chance.[57]

But Merton wasn't given the chance to exercise effective command of his division. Hence, on 9 February, taking advantage of the relative quiet to the division's front, he remained busy organizing reinforcement companies (this time from soldiers of the RASC) and refining his plans for holding Seletar airfield (which were never put to the test). Counter-battery fire continued against the Johore shore while the 1/5th Sherwood Foresters prepared for another foray to Palau Ubin. That night, however, a group of Merton's senior staff officers were called to headquarters of the III Indian Corps, 'where a scheme for the inner defence of SINGAPORE was propounded', one that stressed the 'importance of the water supply [which] had to be protected at all costs'. At this stage, 'the meeting was of an informative nature and no immediate action was required'.[58]

With the breaching of the 'Jurong line', however, the situation quickly deteriorated from 10 February, when it was decided to milk 'the reserves of 18 Division and form them into a composite force to operate under orders of H.Q. Malaya Command'. In consequence, at his usual daily conference, and in obedience to this flawed defensive strategy, Merton ordered the commander of the 9th Northumberland Fusiliers, Lieutenant-Colonel L. C. Thomas, to take command of a substantial force that comprised the Reconnaissance Battalion, the 4th Norfolks, the 1/5th Sherwood Foresters and a battery of the 85th Anti-Tank Regiment. Dubbed 'TOM FORCE', it was duly placed under Malaya Command and the divisional reserve (so carefully mustered over recent days) simply 'disappeared'. While this obliged Merton to comb out his divisional troops to form another, ad hoc reserve (eventually formed from RAOC personnel, who were marshalled into two companies and dubbed 'ALAN FORCE'), that evening Malaya Command took the further step of commandeering the 5th Bedfordshire and Hertfordshires too. These were withdrawn from the 55th Brigade, transferred to Malayan Command Reserve and then sent to reinforce Southern Area, spending the rest of the battle with 1st Malay Brigade.[59]

That afternoon, as much of Merton's division melted away, his headquarters was visited by Wavell, who had flown in from Java for 'twenty-four hours in Singapore'. Before he left for the stricken island, he had received an impassioned cable from Churchill, part of which ran:

[T]he defenders must greatly outnumber Japanese forces who have crossed the straits, and in a well-contested battle they should destroy them. There must be at this stage no thought of saving the troops or sparing the population. The battle must be fought to the bitter end at all costs. The 18th Division has a chance to make its name in history. Commanders and senior officers should die with their troops. The honour of the British Empire and of the British Army is at stake. I rely on you to show no mercy to weakness in any form. With the Russians fighting as they are and the Americans so stubborn at Luzon, the whole reputation of our country and our race is involved. It is expected that every unit will be brought into close contact with the enemy and fight it out. I feel sure these words express your own feeling, and only send them to you in order to share your burdens.[60]

These sentiments, Wavell assured Churchill, had been duly relayed to 'all divisional commanders and [to] the Governor', with a 'written message' to the same effect left for Percival.[61] In fact, in his 'Special Order of the Day' issued in Singapore on 10 February, Wavell paraphrased Churchill's telegram for the benefit of Singapore's defenders, urging them to emulate the Americans in the Bataan Peninsula and the Chinese in their four-and-a-half-year struggle against the Japanese. Declaring that 'It will be disgraceful if we yield our boasted fortress of Singapore to inferior enemy forces', it concluded by pronouncing, 'I look to you and your men to fight to the end to prove that the fighting spirit that won our Empire still exists to enable us to defend it.'[62] However, the force of such rhetoric had no appreciable impact on the fighting around Bukit Timah, which fell to the Japanese on the night of 10–11 February, when the intervention of TOM FORCE failed to push the Japanese back.[63] Still, it did mount 'the only serious counterattack Malaya Command made on Singapore island', and its soldiers put up a sterling fight. Advancing – significantly – 'in extended line', with bayonets fixed, and with close artillery support, their tactics were those they had learned under Merton's tutelage on manoeuvres in England, Scotland and Wales. They even roused the admiration of at least one Japanese spectator, however unsuited they were for 'the bush around Bukit Timah Hill'. In the event, TOM FORCE was halted by a concentration of Japanese tanks, guns, mortars and by 'their trump card: powerful close air support'.[64] Significantly, nearby Australians also failed to move up in support. As Wavell confided in 'unhopeful terms' to Churchill, the 'morale of some troops is not good'. While the nature of the terrain made it hard to defend, 'the chief troubles are lack of sufficient training in some of the reinforcing troops and [an] inferiority complex which bold and skilful Japanese tactics and their command of the air have caused'.[65]

Summoned the following morning to the headquarters of III Indian Corps, there Merton learned of the failure of TOM FORCE to halt the Japanese at Bukit Timah. The Australians were in disarray, the left flank of the 11th Indian Division lay exposed and there was now a growing 'danger of infiltration towards the reservoirs' from the north and from the west. 'Since the reservoirs were vital it was decided that further risks must be accepted on the Division front and more units withdrawn in order to try and secure the reservoirs' as, by now, 'an attack on the coastal sector held by the Division was regarded as most improbable'.[66] At his daily conference, held just after his return from this meeting, Merton 'ordered Brigadier T.H. Massy-Beresford MC to take command of yet another composite force, to be known as "MASSY FORCE"'. This was tasked with pushing westwards, halting Japanese infiltration towards MacRitchie Reservoir and linking up with the right flank of TOM FORCE in the area of Bukit Timah Hill. Besides the 1st Cambridgeshires of 55th Brigade and 4th Suffolks of 54th Brigade, units of the 11th Indian Division also formed part of the scratch ensemble that was MASSY FORCE, along with three light tanks, among the very few deployed by the British throughout the Malayan campaign.[67] Demonstrating that his drive had not deserted him, Merton visited the headquarters of TOM FORCE, MASSY FORCE and III Indian Corps in rapid succession, clarifying (after a confusing instruction from Percival) that the role of Massy Force was:

(a) to link up with the right flank of TOM FORCE.
(b) to push a fighting patrol through between the RESERVOIRS to ensure no enemy was in the area, this patrol joining up with the main body at the western end of MACRITCHIE RESERVOIR.
(c) to leave a detachment guarding the pumping stations in the area north of THOMSON VILLAGE.[68]

However, and in terms of tipping the balance, MASSY FORCE proved no more successful than TOM FORCE, which it absorbed on the afternoon of 11 February.[69] As their positions coalesced into a flimsy barrier of out-posts between Singapore City and the Japanese, by the end of the day it was clear to Massy-Beresford 'that this straggling line, none of it dug in or in any way approaching a position, could not hold for any length of time against the penetration tactics of the Japanese'.[70] Moreover, the expedients of TOM and MASSY forces had greatly eroded the strength and cohe-sion of 18th Division, afterwards causing the commanding officer of the 4th Norfolks to curse 'these hotch potch, thrown together at the last min-ute, Forces' – ad hoc creations whose component parts – crucially – barely knew each other.[71] Another effect of their creation was that 'some adjust-ment of troops in brigade sectors had to be made. Lack of any complete infantry units made improvisation necessary and again a very "make-shift" divisional reserve had to be organised'.[72] Indeed, so threadbare had the 18th Division now become, so attenuated was the line its units were required to hold, and so confused was its chain of command that:

> MASSY FORCE, although theoretically under 3 Indian Corps, was . . . comprised of practically the whole of the infantry of 18 Division. It could not in practice be divorced and therefore the G.O.C.'s responsibility, direct and indirect, was for a front of some fifteen miles, with his furthermost troops closely engaged with the enemy facing West, some seven miles away . . .[73]

Emblematic of the problem with the increasingly tangled chain of command was Massy-Beresford's impulsive plan (devised in response to Wavell's Special Order of the Day) to mount a counterattack 'using every available soldier' in the vicinity of Bukit Timah – with Massy-Beresford leading the charge, carrying a Union flag.[74] Merton, who 'did not agree with the project', felt that the go-ahead should be given by Lieutenant-General Heath of III Indian Corps. Naturally, Heath agreed with Merton and 'advised strongly against any such project, largely on the grounds of the failure of a similar effort by the [Australians] a day or so previously'.[75] And by this point such conflict and confusion were common to the defenders of Singapore, for 'much disorder was due to the repeated switching of formations from one command to another'.[76] To add to these woes, the enduring shortage of signalling equipment (a major problem, especially for an army whose units were being constantly shuffled and re-shuffled) greatly complicated Merton's communications with his widely dispersed units.[77] Still, amidst this confusion and near-chaos, it was the mark of a well-trained and functioning divisional staff that 'throughout the battle Becky's liaison went like clockwork', his three liaison officers ensuring 'that Becky was the best informed general in the field', to the point at which 'Malaya Command, Corps, A.I.F. and other formations frequently obtained their information from 18th Division H.Q.'.[78]

On 12 February it was made clear to Merton that he was now responsible for a major retreat, not a prospective counterattack. Visited by Heath, he was informed that he was responsible for the defence of MacRitchie Reservoir, and that his task was 'to shorten the front by withdrawing to a perimeter round SINGAPORE, which would provide protection for the water supply'.[79] The creation of this perimeter would involve a large-scale withdrawal of troops still on the northern coast, including those around Seletar airfield, but it did have the benefit of returning 53rd Brigade (still deployed between the Causeway and Seletar) to Merton's command, the brigade being earmarked to cover the withdrawal of the 11th Indian Division.[80] After issuing the orders for this manoeuvre (which was extremely hazardous under constant Japanese pressure – MASSY FORCE was under sustained tank attack throughout the day),[81] Merton 'went round the MACRITCHIE RESERVOIR front and endeavoured to co-ordinate the defence'.[82] Remarkably, despite the fighting around Bukit Timah, 'the moves were all carried out with no interruption or incident', and by midnight the division was concentrated for the first time in months, its brigades (53rd, 55th and 54th) running north to south respectively from Nee Soon village to Cluny Hill. While the guns of the 118th and 148th Field Regiments were now compressed into a much smaller area, which brought some benefits in terms of firepower, the divisional reserve had dwindled to a detachment of Northumberland Fusiliers and a unit of RASC drivers from the division's Field Ambulances.[83] As Brian Farrell has observed, Merton's dispositions show that he was aiming – too late, as events were to prove – to draw the Japanese into the kind of set-piece battle the 18th Division had *always* trained for, and into the kind of defensive fight that was familiar to him from the trenches of the Western Front and the campaign in France and Belgium two years earlier: 'Beckwith-Smith tried to pin the enemy down in a positional battle in mixed terrain: reservoir catchment scrub mingled with residential gardens and detached colonial houses.'[84]

It was not to be. The following day (Friday 13th, or 'Black Friday' as it became known to Singapore's defenders)[85] illustrated once again the persistence of Japanese air attack and artillery fire (this time directed by observation balloons), and what Massy-Beresford termed 'the expert infiltration tactics of the enemy'.[86] After 'some infiltration from the direction of the GOLF COURSE', it seems that 'false rumours were rife' in the divisional lines, British armoured cars being mistaken for Japanese tanks and a rumour spreading that the positions held by the 1st Cambridgeshires on the Adam Road had been breached.[87] While that was not the case, and as 'it was now quite impracticable to hold [his] daily conferences', Merton visited the headquarters of 54th and 55th Brigades in turn, directing that the remnants of the 3rd Indian Cavalry (part of the 11th Indian Division) now be absorbed into his scant divisional reserve. He also ordered his CRE to ensure that anti-tank obstacles were erected on key roads and side-roads and that the 288th Field Company of the Royal Engineers reinforced the 5th Norfolks of 53rd Infantry Brigade – yet another example of divisional troops being pressed into an unfamiliar infantry role.[88]

More ominously, Merton was summoned that morning to a conference at the headquarters of Malaya Command in Fort Canning, Singapore City. The Japanese had first issued Percival with a polite, air-dropped summons to surrender on the morning of 11 February, but this had been ignored.[89] Two days later, however, with the constant deterioration of the situation, the possibility of surrender loomed much larger. At this point, there were around one million civilians within three miles of Singapore's waterfront, the city was crowded with military transport and equipment (thus making it an even denser target for Japanese bombers), its water mains (most of them above ground) were heavily damaged, and the loss of the supply dumps at Bukit Timah had reduced the central stock of food supplies to only seven days' worth. Fuel was also running short.[90] Although capitulation was favoured by one Australian brigadier from as early as 9 February,[91] it was apparently Heath who persuaded Percival to summon his senior commanders to Fort Canning at 2.00 p.m. on 13 February for a conference 'attended by all area and divisional commanders and by the principal staff officers of Headquarters, Malaya Command'.[92] Here, they mooted a full-blooded counteroffensive, which was soon ruled out due to the sheer exhaustion of the defending troops, while Heath and Bennett urged surrender. Percival, however, was unconvinced and, having been directed that morning by Wavell to 'fight it out to the end as you are doing',[93] he ordered that resistance continue. Still, the window for naval evacuation was closing rapidly, the last opportunity being that night, and arrangements were made for the evacuation of essential staff officers, key technicians and nurses.[94]

What Merton contributed to this critical discussion is not entirely clear, as published accounts differ,[95] but according to the 18th's unpublished divisional history his position stood midway between Heath and Bennett's on the one hand, and Percival's on the other:

The G.O.C. confined his remarks to a statement, the gist of which was:

(a) That he was not concerned with higher policy, but only with the conditions appertaining to his Division.
(b) His Division was strung out on a wide front and units were hopelessly mixed up and not under their proper commanders.
(c) There was no reserve, although efforts were being made to try and organise a suitable Division reserve, and
(d) The men, not being acclimatised, were very tired, but if a twenty-four-hour respite could be obtained there was no reason why the present positions should not be held against a heavy attack, and later possibly a counter-offensive launched.[96]

If this was the position of the most powerful formation still under Percival's command, it did not quite warrant the tone of Percival's subsequent message to Wavell, in which he claimed:

In opinion of commanders troops already committed are too exhausted either to withstand strong attack or to launch counter-attack. We would all earnestly welcome the chance of initiating an offensive, even though this would only amount to a gesture, but even this is not possible, as there are no troops who could carry out this attack. In these conditions it is unlikely that resistance can last more than a day or two.[97]

He went on, rather misleadingly:

> My subordinate commanders are *unanimously* [my italics] of the opinion that the gain of time will not compensate for extensive damage and heavy casualties which will occur in Singapore town. As Empire overseas is interested I feel bound to represent their views. There must come a stage when in the interests of the troops and civil population further bloodshed will serve no useful purpose. Your instructions of February 10 are being carried out, but in above circumstances would you consider giving me wider discretionary powers?[98]

Wavell's response, sent on the following day, 14 February, was emphatic:

> You must continue to inflict maximum damage on enemy for as long as possible by house-to-house fighting if necessary. Your action in tying down enemy and inflicting casualties may have vital influence in other theatres. Fully appreciate your situation but continued action essential.[99]

However, sensing Percival's mood, Wavell also cabled Churchill to inform him:

> Have received telegram from Percival that enemy are close to town and that his troops are incapable of further counter-attack. Have ordered him to continue inflict maximum damage to enemy by house-to-house fighting if necessary. Fear however that resistance not likely to be very prolonged.[100]

In contrast to Percival, in the wake of the conference at Fort Canning Merton dutifully sought to implement its decisions in full. Firstly, preparations were made for the evacuation of key personnel: 'At a subsequent conference held at [III Indian Corps] H.Q. it was tentatively decided that a limited number of officers and men who were trained staff officers or good trainers of men should be evacuated that night.'[101] Secondly, in the spirit he had evinced during the Dunkirk campaign, he made determined preparations to fight on. Anticipating that an enemy tank attack might erupt on his front 'from the direction of the GOLF COURSE' and the adjacent racecourse in the area of Bukit Timah, which would give Japanese armour the benefit of open terrain, he arranged for anti-tank guns 'to be in position by first light next morning'. Also, concerned by the lack of a second line of defence, the machine guns of the 9th Northumberland Fusiliers were deployed to the rear 'to cover all the open ground to the West'.[102] That evening, Merton shortened the line of 54th Brigade, adding some depth to its positions while thinning the division's defences on the south side of MacRitchie Reservoir, where it was judged that the Japanese would lack the boats to cross it in force. Besides taking this risk, Merton received orders to form a divisional party 'of up to two hundred all ranks . . . to consist of trained staff officers and ranks whose qualifications would be an asset to the future conduct of the war'. With a careful eye to the morale and discipline of his troops, Merton decreed that only one in eight of the division's selectees would be officers, thus forestalling an impression of an *officers'* flight to freedom. In the event, the party departed at midnight, 'but, owing to some hitch, all did not get away that night and only a proportion succeeded in getting away the next night. The remainder returned to their units.' Among those who got away were the division's Assistant Adjutant and Quartermaster General (AA and QMG), Lieutenant-Colonel Francis Dillon MC, who was later taken prisoner in the Dutch East Indies, Lieutenant-Colonel L. C. Thomas of the Northumberland Fusiliers, and Tufton Beamish, who eventually reached India and safety.[103]

Valentine's Day 1942 brought no cheer to the defenders of Singapore, or to Merton's beleaguered division. According to the divisional history, 'Dawn broke with the usual alarmist reports that the enemy had broken through down THOMSON ROAD and along the BUKIT TIMAH ROAD.' This was not true, though heavy shelling forced the 4th Suffolks to fall back, while 'some misunderstanding' caused a delay in the deployment of the anti-tank guns and the 9th Northumberland Fusiliers: 'This was a serious matter and the G.O.C. ordered the [anti-tank] guns to be moved up at once and the [machine guns] to be in action by first light the next day without fail.'[104] Additionally, Merton was 'considerably perturbed about two points': firstly, that 'there was in fact no complete infantry unit in the divisional reserve' and, secondly, that the 54th Brigade was still stretched far too thinly. While a bigger reserve was scraped together in the residential area of Mount Pleasant (comprising Royal Artillery gunners, Royal Engineers (RE), RASC and RAOC personnel, plus some 4th Suffolks and Northumberland Fusiliers), as evening fell the anticipated Japanese thrust came 'from the direction of the GOLF COURSE'. Supported by tanks and an artillery barrage, this pushed the 4th Suffolks back to Mount Pleasant, leaving the 1st Cambridgeshires holding a salient astride Adam Road. However, though his division was clearly in desperate trouble, Merton would not concede defeat. In the wake of this latest advance, he appeared at the headquarters of 54th Brigade where 'it was agreed to stage a counter-attack' with a company of the 5th Suffolks, supported by 'a troop of Light Tanks, which was in the area'. According to Merton's plan, 'at first light this attack was to drive northwards up ADAM ROAD through the 1st Cambridgeshires, and so take the enemy in the flank'. Due to an administrative slip-up (the 2nd Cambridgeshires were somehow mentioned in the written orders, rather than their sister battalion), when they arrived in the 1st Cambridgeshires' salient the Suffolks were ordered to occupy a position 'from which [they were] shelled out soon afterwards'. As a result, this last defiant counter-punch 'never materialised'.[105]

However, the 18th Division, though battered, at least stood its ground.[106] For elsewhere the defence was collapsing, and the Japanese advance along the southern coast now threatened to turn the 18th's positions from that direction. If the tactical and strategic situation looked increasingly bleak:

[By] 14 February parts of Percival's forces were beginning to fall apart. Australian troops, whose battalions had borne the brunt of the fighting in Johore and in the west of Singapore, were prominent amongst those seen in the town and around the harbour. Some were merely lost, others determined not to go back, and a few were intent on an early escape from the island.[107]

In a letter passed on to Churchill through his father, who was Member of Parliament for Lewes, Tufton Beamish testified that Australian 'resistance as a whole can but have been feeble and half-hearted', and that 'several hundred Australians were in the docks days before the capitulation looking for a boat home'.[108] Elsewhere, urged on by Indian nationalists accompanying the Japanese, Indian troops were surrendering, or even defecting, in large numbers, a phenomenon witnessed by the 1st Cambridgeshires as early as 12 February.[109] Finally acknowledging the reality of the situation, Churchill cabled Wavell on 14 February: 'You are of course sole judge of the moment when no further result can be gained at Singapore, and should instruct Percival accordingly. C.I.G.S. [Alan Brooke] concurs.'[110]

And Percival was busy with his own assessments throughout 14 February, undertaking 'a long day of visits to the front, talks with Headquarters Staff and the Governor and the Civil Authorities'.[111] Under relentless Japanese bombing and artillery bombardment, the water supply was now extremely precarious: not only were Singapore's reservoirs in Japanese hands, but Malaya Command's Chief Engineer, Brigadier Ivan Simson, warned Percival that its infrastructure was on the point of collapse (even if the Japanese had inexplicably failed to turn off the flow). It was on those grounds alone, and the risk of disease that they raised, that the civilian Governor of the Straits Settlements, Sir Shenton Thomas, now urged surrender.[112] While the loss of vast dumps of supplies meant that stocks of food and many types of ammunition were now dangerously low, Percival was also advised to surrender by 'one of the few British commanders to enhance his reputation during the campaign', Major-General B. W. Key.[113] Now commanding 11th Indian Division, Key had been fighting the Japanese since their landing at Kota Baharu on the night of 7–8 December, and he dismissed Percival's proposal of one last-ditch offensive by reminding him of the likely fate of Singapore if determined (but futile) resistance was offered. Besides the fall of Hong Kong a few weeks earlier, the 1937 Rape of Nanjing and more recent events on Singapore itself (notably the massacre of patients and staff at Alexandra Hospital, which took place that day) already served as terrible warnings of what might be expected.[114]

At 9.30 a.m. on Sunday 15 February, after a Communion Service at his headquarters in Fort Canning (Percival, like Merton, was a solid churchman), Percival convened another conference of his most senior officers. Besides the Inspector General of Police and the Director of Civil Defence, 'the commanders of Northern, Western and Southern Areas and the anti-aircraft defences were present', in addition to other senior officers.[115] Merton was, significantly, the most notable absentee, being represented by a divisional liaison officer, Ken Tomkinson.[116] However, before its deliberations got under way, he did make a report, along with other 'formation commanders', on the parlous state of his division.[117] After sobering summaries of the state of the water supply and the levels of food and ammunition available, Percival stated that a Japanese breakthrough – with its 'disastrous consequences for the civil population' – was all but inevitable. There were only two alternatives: either mount an immediate counterattack to recover the reservoirs and the supply dumps at Bukit Timah, or surrender forthwith. As there was a consensus among those present that the former was impossible ('beyond the capacity of the exhausted troops', as Churchill later put it), the conference was unanimous in its decision to capitulate. Towards the end of the meeting, a further telegram arrived from Wavell, which began by reiterating the strategic need to fight on. Nevertheless, it continued, 'When you are fully satisfied that this is no longer possible I give you discretion to cease resistance.' Before hostilities ceased, all military equipment of potential value to the Japanese had to be destroyed, and every opportunity given to 'any determined bodies of men or individuals to try and effect escape by any means possible. They must be armed.'[118] Percival replied, 'Owing to losses from enemy action, water, petrol, food, and ammunition practically finished. Unable therefore to continue the fight any longer. All ranks have done their best and are grateful for your help.'[119]

As this fateful meeting proceeded, things were far from quiet on the 18th Division's front: 'Dawn reports indicated that the enemy had infiltrated on all Brigade sectors, but nevertheless the front was still holding.' In fact, such was the extent of this infiltration that elements of the 53rd Brigade had to be pulled back and, behind the 55th Brigade, 'snipers appeared to be everywhere'. As for the 54th Brigade, this was being menaced by Japanese troops who had filtered through to Mount Pleasant itself. Despite attempts to clear these footholds, the division's defences were plainly compromised:

The lack of any reserves in the nature of a formed unit made the staging of any organised counter-attack to restore positions impossible, and all that could be done was to try and fill up the gaps with some detachments from the various assortment of troops, which formed the so-called reserve.[120]

Furthermore, the divisional artillery continued to fire, in the early afternoon playing 'a large part in preventing the enemy from developing his attacks on a larger scale, and from penetrating our thin red line deeper than he did'.[121] It was only after visiting his brigades that Merton travelled to the headquarters of III Indian Corps to make his report on the situation, there being 'no telephone communication' at 18th Division's headquarters. From here, Merton was able to telephone Heath at Malaya Command, reporting

> the serious situation on the Divisional front, due to the [Japanese] penetration up to MOUNT PLEASANT ROAD, the tiredness of his infantry, all of whom had been fighting continuously for three, and some for five, days with no sleep, and also the lack of reserves suitable for counter-attacking.[122]

Ordered to await Heath's return, there followed the delicate and dangerous task of arranging and implementing a ceasefire, a task greatly complicated by the wholesale disruption of communications and by a two-hour difference between Japanese Army time and local time.[123] On his arrival, Heath instructed Merton to ensure that artillery fire would cease in the 18th Division's sector when an initial flag of truce passed down the Bukit Timah Road, an instruction that Merton relayed by messenger and (in person) by radio. After the arrival of Key at III Indian Corps headquarters, Heath

> explained that, in view of the fact that the enemy were virtually in control of the water supply, that gun ammunition was short, and that petrol and food stocks were very low, it had been decided to capitulate, but as from what hour it was not clear.

After more discussion, Heath decreed that this would take effect at 4.00 p.m. Returning to 18th Division headquarters, Merton issued written instructions at 2.00 p.m. 'to the effect that all resistance would cease at 1600 hrs, and that units would remain in present locations, and if attacked would show a white flag'. An order to destroy all field guns was also transmitted, but it was indicative of the chaos that threatened that 'in the case of one or two troops a counter order was received, its source never satisfactorily being traced'. The situation remained on a knife's edge as tense negotiations took place well into the afternoon between Yamashita and Percival. For Merton, it was his last task as a free man to oversee the ceasefire on the division's front, a task he accomplished amidst a dangerous whirl of conflicting information. As the divisional history recounted:

About 1600 hrs a vague telephone message from Corps suggested that an armistice had not been declared, but the action to be taken was never given before the telephone line went. Further counter orders emanating from various sources were received, culminating in one signed by the G.O.C., Southern Area, for the G.O.C.-in-C. [i.e. Merton], stating that resistance would continue. Ultimately, at about 1930 hrs, a written message from [Malaya] Command ordering hostilities to cease at 2030 hrs, and that there should be no further destruction of equipments, was received.[124]

Significantly, it appears that the sight of the white flag on the Bukit Timah Road had already had the effect of halting the fighting at 4.00 p.m., as originally instructed. While these instructions had 'a very real psychological effect on the fighting value of the troops', the Japanese seem to have responded in kind, with a peace of sorts descending on 18th Division's sector after the hour had elapsed.[125]

As the divisional history insisted, the fight which the 18th Division put up on Singapore Island, mainly under Merton's command, was determined, and its surrender far from abject: 'The total casualties in action [it claimed] – 29% of the officers and 16.3% of other ranks – is further indication that the 18th Division was not allowed simply to "walk into the bag".'[126] Although the editor of the Straits Times, Edwin ('Jimmie') Glover, spoke in 1942 of the 'disappointing' performance of the British troops 'who arrived after the campaign began', and Max Hastings has written of the 'swift humiliation' of the 18th Division in his history of the Second World War,[127] Colin Smith, in a much closer study of the fall of Singapore, recognized that its units learned 'fast' and that their 'morale was generally good'.[128] Far from being 'of little value', as Gordon Bennett claimed,[129] an officer of the 9th Northumberland Fusiliers even recalled that 'I think we felt that our division was all that was needed to put things right.'[130] The official history of the campaign agreed, noting the stubborn stand made by the 18th around

Bukit Timah as proof that 'there was little wrong with the fighting spirit of many of the troops when given the opportunity of meeting the enemy on reasonably equal terms'.[131] Inevitably, some of its units performed better than others. Whereas the 4th Norfolks and 1/5th Sherwood Foresters (both prime components of TOM FORCE) were close to breaking point towards the end,[132] the 1st Cambridgeshires turned out to be 'Beckwith-Smith's star turn' – and this despite the doubts entertained by Merton and Massy-Beresford about their commanding officer – distinguishing themselves in fierce house-to-house fighting 'amidst the tropical Tudor splendour of Adam Road'.[133] Inflicting four times the number of casualties they incurred, it was, by all accounts, 'a magnificent performance . . . from a division in which most of the high command had had little faith or had damned with faint praise'.[134]

Perhaps the best appraisal of the division's performance came from the escapee Francis Dillon. Writing with the benefit of hindsight coloured by '34 years' service [and] pretty good experience of war of all sorts', Dillon acknowledged that Singapore 'had been a most disheartening battle from the divisional point of view'.[135] Nevertheless, the preparations made by Merton for the defence of the island's north-east coast had been professional and thorough:

We knew the game of coast holding from our experience in England in 1940–41 and were properly organised with strong reserves for counter-attack purposes . . . I always felt that if the Japanese had made any lodgements on our front we would have had him [sic] off again without very much trouble and killed the lot.[136]

However, once the Japanese had gained a foothold elsewhere, and began to enlarge it:

Our Division was then dribbled away bit by bit to reinforce weaknesses or patch holes in the line . . . When we finally did get together again on the final perimeter, the Division was inextricably mixed up, but since it was in close fighting contact with the enemy, it was not possible to re-organise, and it was strung out [over] seven miles of perimeter.[137]

Still, on the perimeter itself, 'although the fighting swung back-wards and forwards in places, virtually no ground was given. The 2nd Cambridgeshires, for instance, had not given an inch by the time of sur-render.'[138] As Ken Tomkinson likewise noted:

A few 18th Division troops retreated in penny packets from the perimeter without orders [but the] 1st Cambridgeshires, the Northumberland Fusiliers, 6th Norfolks, and the divisional Artillery... put up a fine show. The break through on the perimeter was not on the 18th Division front.[139]

In its creditable but fruitless contribution to the defence of Malaya and Singapore, almost 2,000 officers and men of the 18th Division had been killed or wounded. In total, 16,192 of its officers and men passed into Japanese captivity on 15 February 1942, in units that varied in size from the 841 officers and men of the 5th Bedfordshire and Hertfordshires to the 26 members of the 44th Field Hygiene Section.[140] In the words of Peter Brune, their deployment had been 'nothing more than a dis-tant exercise in military expediency'. Fundamentally, the division was unprepared to fight 'an enemy as proficient as the Japanese', especially given its lack of acclimatization, of training in jungle warfare, of air support, and of competent leadership from Malaya Command.[141] As Clifford Kinvig has stated, with some exaggeration, the 'frustrated and bitterly disappointed' 18th Division endured 'two years' train-ing and a 20,000 mile journey across three oceans to end up as POWs with scarcely a fight'.[142] Although the total number of prisoners of war taken by the Japanese at Singapore is uncertain (a statistic complicated by the flow of reinforcements into the island, by the losses sustained during the campaign on the mainland, by defections and desertions and by the chaos of defeat), there was no concealing its magnitude, the overall figure being in the region of 100,000.[143] Of these captives, ap-proximately 27 per cent were British, 13 per cent Australian, 11 per cent Malay and 49 per cent Indian. It was, as Daniel Todman has emphasized, 'a very imperial calamity'.[144] Nevertheless, the 18th Division formed 'the largest British component',[145] estimated by Tufton Beamish at around half the total.[146]

Nor can there be any mistaking the shame, anger and despair of its van-quished officers and soldiers. Writing to his wife in June 1942, Massy-Beresford recalled how he had sat with Merton, recriminating with him-self, as the white flag made its doleful progress along the Bukit Timah Road. Feeling that he had risen to the challenges of command, despite his confessed laziness in 'reading or mugging military books enough in peace and during training', he noted that:

My dear friend and Commander, Becky, touched on the above during our final and very distressing conversation as we sat gloomily at his H.Q. while the 'White flag' was being carried out to the Jap Commander. There was nothing either of us could do because the 'Mix up' had reached a point where neither of us had any troops to command (I HAD A FEW BUT had no idea or means of telling where they had got to). It was a sorrowful meeting but the dear little man said the nicest things that any commander ever said to a subordinate.[147]

Further down the chain of command, Captain Richard Sharp of the 9th Northumberland Fusiliers despaired that 'This was the end of our two years of training, of 13 weeks on board ship, to spend a few days in miser-able fighting, and give in.'[148] Idris Barwick of the RASC, in Southern Area at the time, remembered how his company reacted after hearing the order to surrender: 'I felt a lump rise in my throat. Several of the men collapsed and many were sobbing. I had never seen such misery. The reaction was awful.'[149] For L. L. Baynes of the redoubtable 1st Cambridgeshires, the news came as 'the greatest shock of my life', especially as 'we had felt that we were holding our own, and anticipated pushing the Japs back off the island before many more days had passed'.[150] In 1946, fresh from captivity, John Coast, a subaltern in the 4th Norfolks, raged how the men of his battalion, like the rest of the 18th Division, had been 'sent to Singapore as a sacrifice on the altar of public opinion – horribly pitchforked into the mystery and menace of tropical jungle'.[151] The whole division, so H. E. I. Phillips, another veteran, claimed in a letter to *The Times* in October 1947, had been immolated as part of the 'unredeemed disaster' that was the fall of Singapore, and he called (in vain) for a 'Commission of Inquiry' into the whole fiasco.[152] In more restrained terms, Coast's commanding officer, Lieutenant-Colonel Alfred E. Knights, deplored a deployment that had 'served practically no military purpose' and decried the 'waste of a good Division which might have been usefully employed elsewhere'.[153] Decades after, Kenneth Bailey confessed his abiding bitterness that his battalion had 'travelled 20,000 miles simply to surrender', and that they had been 'badly and sadly let down, being left abandoned like thousands of "sitting ducks" without the necessary resources with which to put into practice that which we had been trained to do for our country'.[154]

It was to salve such feelings as these that, like other commanders, Merton issued a personal message to the 18th Division in the aftermath of the surrender. Whereas the messages issued by generals Percival, Simmons (commander of Singapore's Southern Area) and Key were comparatively formal (and, in the former case, notably stilted and self-justifying),[155] that issued by Merton was similar to the sentiments he had expressed, in very personal terms, to Massy-Beresford:

No commander has ever led a happier or more loyal team into battle. The division was sent into a theatre of war for which it was neither trained nor equipped, to fight a cunning and clever enemy who was on the crest of a wave. It was sent to fight a battle that was already lost and has passed troops whose morale had been badly shaken. It had to endure long periods of hardship, without food and rest. It fought with great courage and tenacity and inflicted heavy losses on the enemy. Every man can and I know will rightly uphold his head knowing that he has upheld the best traditions of the British Army. During the 18 months that I have been privileged to command the division at home and overseas, it has carried out every varied and exacting task it has been called to undertake and now I can only dedicate the rest of my life to helping in any way I can the officers, Warrant Officers, NCOs and men of the 18th Div. God bless you all and bring you safely home when victory is finally ours, with knowledge that you have played your part in the achievement.[156]

His message was accurate, and it resonated. In 1946, back from captivity, Lieutenant Geoffrey Burton of the 118th Field Regiment wrote:

About midday, we received the General's farewell message, in which he praised the spirit of the troops under his command, and apologised for the piecemeal way in which we had had to go into action, for the first time. We had never had a fair chance; of that we were all fully aware.[157]

And the scale of the defeat, as Merton no doubt recognized, was stupefying. Speaking in the House of Commons in April 1942, Commander Robert Bower, the Conservative MP for Cleveland, ascribed the biggest surrender in British military history 'to the worst strategy since Ethelred the Unready'. In the House of Lords, it was claimed that even the humiliating defeats at Gallipoli and at Kut 'during the last war' paled into 'insignificance' by comparison, and that 'There is a consensus of opinion in regard to this point.'[158] Acknowledged by Churchill, one of its architects, as 'the worst disaster and largest capitulation in British history', so damaging were its potential implications that the Prime Minister deemed it unwise 'to hold an inquiry by Royal Commission' while the war was being fought – a view which Parliament shared.[159] Nor, in fact, would Churchill even release 'the reports received from General Wavell regarding the loss of Malaya and Singapore', telling the House of Commons that they were unsuitable for publication in wartime, and that they 'would cause a great deal of ill-will throughout the British Empire'.[160] And, exacerbated by jaundiced national perspectives and by a lack of *contemporary* primary sources,[161] that bitterness, and the many myths it has spawned (such as the veteran Japanese jungle fighter, and the fortress guns that could not fire inland), have lingered for 80 years, leading Karl Hack and Kevin Blackburn to observe that there was not one, but 'Many Falls' of Singapore.[162] In any case, and though a Royal Commission never materialized, as 'both a paradigm of military incompetence and a synecdoche of imperial decline' the fall of Singapore had no equal.[163] In Max Hastings' words:

The photograph of a British officer named Major Wylde, in baggy shorts and helmet askew beside his general as they carried the Union flag to the Japanese lines, became one of the most memorable images of the war. It seemed to symbolize the bungling, blimpish ineffectuality of the men who had been entrusted with the defence of Britain's eastern Empire.[164]

Inevitably, those who were associated with it were badly – even irredeemably – tainted. As Duff Cooper, Churchill's Resident Minister in the Far East from September 1941 to January 1942, fully appreciated: 'It is damaging to be associated, however distantly, with a disaster.'[165] And, after his liberation in 1945, Percival was to feel this most keenly. According to John Keegan, owing to his apparently 'catastrophic mismanagement of the Malaya campaign', Percival 'became a "non-person", shunned by all in official life and excluded from every commemoration of Britain's belated Asian victory'.[166]

In one sense at least, that was unjust. Although given permission to leave by Wavell, Percival chose to stay in Singapore, negotiating the terms of an 'unconditional surrender' to Yamashita at the Ford factory near Bukit Timah, before joining his men in captivity on 'Black Sunday', 15 February 1942.[167] But not all generals who served in the campaign in Malaya and Singapore shared that fate. Major-General A. E. Barstow of the 9th Indian Division died in a Japanese ambush in Johore at the end of January,[168] whereas Gordon Bennett of the 8th Australian Division escaped by plane 'the moment the capitulation terms came into force'. Although he never faced formal charges of desertion after reaching Australia, a recent appraisal of his conduct throughout the campaign has noted that 'There is no avoiding the strong suspicion that Bennett's mind in the last weeks was more on escape than on commanding his troops.'[169] For Merton, on the other hand, for whom such conduct would have been anathema, the end of hostilities on Singapore served only to place him on the threshold of the greatest test of his career.

7

Changi

The position which Merton and 16,000 soldiers of the 18th Division found themselves in after the fall of Singapore should be understood within the legal framework of the Geneva Convention and the cultural context of their Japanese captors. Somewhat ironically, the terms of their treatment were laid out in 'the most extensive codification of POW law yet attempted',[1] namely the 97 articles of the Geneva Convention of 1929. Fundamentally, this echoed the Geneva Convention of 1906 in its 'basic assumption' that a detaining power would treat its prisoners in the same way it would its own troops (when not on active service) 'with respect to rations, clothing, living space, and other necessities'.[2] Crucially, though the Japanese delegates at the month-long conference which devised the Convention duly signed it, its provisions relating to POWs were not ratified by the Japanese government. A variety of reasons informed this refusal. Assuming that its soldiers would not be taken prisoner, the Japanese military (an increasingly powerful force in domestic politics) saw no benefit in reciprocity. Furthermore, the Convention's lenient terms were seen as potentially aiding the bombing of the Japanese homeland, especially as captured enemy aviators had no reason to fear reprisals. While the notion of an inspecting power freely touring its prison camps was also ill-received, still more absurd were the punishments permitted for POWs – punishments that were milder than those meted out to Japanese servicemen for the same offences.[3] In 1942, therefore, the Japanese government announced it would adhere to the Geneva Convention *mutatis mutandis*, but by then its treatment of Allied POWs had already exposed the hollowness of such a declaration.[4]

It did, however, take time for Japan to sort out the higher administration of its POWs. In December 1941, an Information Bureau was established by Imperial ordinance 'to act as a registry and clearing-house in line with the requirements of Article 77 of the Geneva Convention', which required that details of all prisoners be recorded and relayed by the detaining power. Three months later, a Control Bureau was set up to oversee general 'administrative matters' such as 'the housing, employment, feeding and transport of POWs'.[5] Oversight, however, was lax: the bureaux, technically separate, were run by the same (hitherto retired) military personnel and such were the priorities of the Japanese war effort that complete lists of prisoners of war were never sent to the Allied powers – even though, at a local level, Japanese records were 'kept meticulously'.[6] As for prisoners' post, an entitlement under Article 36,[7] its content was tightly controlled (the Japanese generally allowing only preprinted postcards) and its flow, in either direction, proved highly erratic. Consequently, 'some of the POWs were fortunate in receiving mail', however belatedly, whereas 'others were deprived of any news from home for the entire period of their captivity'.[8] Captain C. F. Blackater of the Indian Army wrote of the gnawing sense of isolation and anxiety this entailed, for there was

> always the homesickness, the yearning, the paining knowledge that our wives, our children, our mothers, would know of those last days before Singapore fell and wonder and fear, while month succeeded month and we knew they were still in ignorance whether we were alive or dead.[9]

Illustrating the obstacles and frustrations involved, L. L. Baynes of the 1st Cambridgeshires remembered that, when he was issued with a postcard with which to write home nearly five months after being captured:

> We were told to print our cards, and I printed mine in small letters. I was very upset when my card was returned to me with the message that I should have used capitals, and that I could not have another card so must miss my turn. I need not have worried as none of the cards got through.[10]

As far as the Japanese high command was concerned, its haul of around 140,000 British, Australian, Dutch, American and even Canadian prisoners of war in the first few months of 'the great East Asia War' (as Japan's powerful army minister, General Hideki Tojo, styled it) served three main purposes. Firstly, they were a potential reservoir of time-limited intelligence on the Allied war effort; secondly, they represented a large and expendable labour force; and, thirdly, their use as 'white' forced labour was of immense propaganda value in Japanese-occupied Asia.[11] If, as Tojo directed, POWs would not be 'permitted to eat the bread of idleness', and would help 'native peoples realize the superiority of the Japanese Race',[12] what also put them in jeopardy was the culture of their captors. Imbued with a strong sense of cultural and racial purity, and of their superiority over other Asians (as the Chinese, Formosans and Koreans had already found to their cost), the same instinct also applied vis-à-vis Europeans, who in Japanese propaganda were often portrayed as 'devils, demons and monsters'.[13] Although General Yamashita (dubbed 'The Tiger of Malaya' for his victories over the British) appealed out of a 'spirit of Japanese chivalry' when he summoned Percival to surrender,[14] he also claimed that 'while his own people were descended from gods, Europeans were descended from monkeys'.[15]

Despite the ingrained racism of European colonial societies in East Asia, through sheer desperation the Japanese soon proved to be, if anything, even worse than their predecessors: 'British racism in South-East Asia was now eclipsed by that of the Japanese. Tokyo's new regime was characterised by a brutality such as the evicted imperialists, whatever their shortcomings, had never displayed.'[16] Harumi Furuya has acknowledged how Japanese racial attitudes and their implications militated against Europeans and Asians alike:

> Japan's racial identity as reflected in its treatment of POWs in the Second World War reflected its inferiority complex vis-à-vis the real whites, which manifested itself in the forms of retaliation against the 'superior' whites and subjugation of the 'inferior' Asians.[17]

Compounding what Yoichi Kibata termed this 'twisted racial feeling'[18] was the Bushidō-infused ('way of the warrior'-infused) ethos of the Imperial Japanese Army (IJA). Enshrining the spirit of the samurai, and productive of the suicidal phenomena of the kamikaze, of hara-kiri (ceremonial suicide by disembowelment) and of the desperate 'banzai charge' (human wave attacks), this 'way of the warrior' was embodied in the Army's Field Service Code. This code absolutely forbade surrender, a 'moral precept'

160

1 Merton's father, Beckwith Beckwith-Smith (1849–1926).
Courtesy of Lucinda Fraser.

2 Merton's mother, Georgina Beckwith-Smith (c. 1861–1942).
Courtesy of Lucinda Fraser.

3 Merton, Georgina, and Muriel ('Cissy') Beckwith-Smith at Aberarder, c. 1900.
Courtesy of Harry Henderson.

4 Merton receives the Royal Humane Society's vellum parchment at Glynde Place, Sussex, February 1910. Courtesy of Lucinda Fraser.

5 Merton Beckwith-Smith as a pre-war second lieutenant in the Coldstream Guards. Courtesy of Lucinda Fraser.

6 Lieutenant Merton Beckwith-Smith wearing the ribbon of the Distinguished Service Order, 1915. Courtesy of the Imperial War Museum, HU 113585.

7 Merton and Honor Beckwith-Smith (second from right) with the Bicester Hunt, undated. Courtesy of Harry Henderson.

8 Merton (left) with King Edward VIII (centre) at Windsor Castle, 1936. Courtesy of Regimental Headquarters Welsh Guards.

9 Merton and Honor Beckwith-Smith in the Punjab, 1938. Courtesy of Harry Henderson.

10 Merton (seated fourth from left) with the staff of the Lahore Brigade, 1938. Courtesy of Harry Henderson.

11 Merton (right) with King George VI (centre), August 1940. Courtesy of Anne Beckwith-Smith.

12 Merton on exercise in Scotland, 1941. Courtesy of the Imperial War Museum, H 7700.

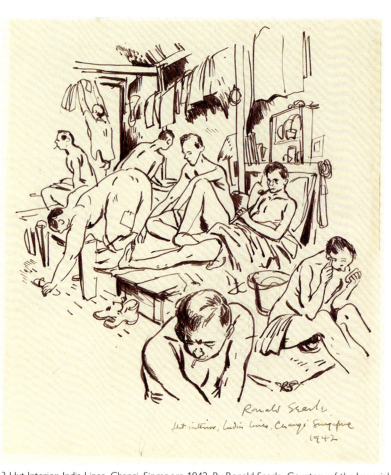

13 Hut Interior, India Lines, Changi, Singapore 1942. By Ronald Searle. Courtesy of the Imperial War Museum, Art. IWM ART 15747 36.

ST. GEORGE'S CHURCH, P.O.W. CAMP, INDIA LINES, CHANGI. SINGAPORE.
(1942- APRIL 1943.)
(PAINTED BY CPL. COOPER FOR ME. THE VIEW FROM MY ROOM FROM FEB. 42 - TO NOV. 42)

14 St George's Church, Changi, 1942, from the papers of Charles Wilkinson, 9th Royal Northumberland Fusiliers. Courtesy of the Imperial War Museum, Lieutenant Colonel C. Wilkinson, 81/7/1.

15 The last photograph of Merton, Karenko, November 1942. Though insignia of rank were apparently restored at Karenko, the ravages of malnutrition and of his tracheotomy are clear. Courtesy of Lucy Woodd.

16 Honor Beckwith-Smith in Sai Wan Military Cemetery, Hong Kong, 1949. Courtesy of Lucy Woodd.

that held soldier and civilian alike in a lethal grip as the war unfolded.[19] Stoked by a martial ethos that held both surrender and the surrendered in utter contempt; by the inherently brutal and brutalizing nature of Japanese Army discipline; and by an exalted sense of racial superiority, atrocities against Allied prisoners of war and civilians, European or Asian, were inevitable.[20] Such atrocities had been familiar to the Chinese since 1937 and would be visited on Singapore's Chinese population through a 'purification by elimination' after its surrender.[21] As Max Hastings has written:

> The Japanese army in its new conquests sustained the tradition of savagery it had established in China, a perversion of virility and warrior spirit which was the more shocking for being institutionalized. Soldiers of all nations, in all wars, are sometimes guilty of atrocities. An important distinction can be made, however, between armies in which acts of barbarism represent a break with regulations and the norm, and those in which they are indulged or even incited by commanders. The Japanese were prominent among the latter.[22]

Given the wretched state of Japanese logistics (the Japanese 'practised cannibalism on a wide scale' in the Pacific War, while more Japanese soldiers starved to death in 'the great East Asia War' than died at the hands of the Allies),[23] coupled with the growing lethality of Allied attacks on Japanese shipping, which killed as many as 12,000 POWs at sea, it is all too comprehensible how 27 per cent of all white POWs taken by the Japanese died in captivity. This figure stands in stark contrast to the 4 per cent of British, American and Commonwealth POWs who perished in German hands.[24] Still, the death rate among several million Asian forced labourers (or *rōmusha*) across the ironically named Greater East Asia Co-Prosperity Sphere could be even worse, with more than 100,000 Indonesians, Malays, Chinese and Burmese dying on the Burma Railway, half its entire Asian workforce.[25] If they were not, therefore, the most vulnerable victims of the Japanese military, the plight of these 140,000 POWs was still horrendous, being bleakly summarized in Jonathan F. Vance's *Encyclopedia of Prisoners of War and Internment*:

> No one can adequately impart the suffering most Allied prisoners endured during the three and a half years they were held captive.

They were beaten, kicked, robbed, clubbed with rifles and sticks, shot, had swordsmanship practiced on them, and were buried alive. Sadistic physicians experimented on them, and their corpses were mutilated. Some Japanese even practiced cannibalism on their bodies . . . When transported, they were herded along in 'death marches' at Bataan [Luzon], Sandakan [Borneo], and elsewhere, were crowded into insufferably hot boxcars, or were placed for days in the sweltering holds of 'death ships' with little room to move and nowhere to perform bodily functions . . . Worst of all they were starved and, as a consequence, suffered from almost every disease known to humanity.[26]

Although the full horrors of the Burma Railway and even of the 'Hell-ships' still lay in the future, few soldiers of the 18th Division harboured any illusions about their captors. As Kenneth Bailey remembered, in the first days of their captivity rumours spread about recent events at Alexandra Hospital, a place of notional safety 'where patients [including men of the 5th Norfolks] had been massacred, some whilst on operating tables, and also where nurses and other hospital staff had been bayonetted by the marauding invaders'.[27] And, as Ronald Searle grimly remembered:

The code of the Japanese soldier declares: 'Duty is weightier than a mountain, while death is lighter than a feather.' It was not only the Imperial Guard that still embodied the *bushido* spirit of the samurai. It was to be found in every ill-fed, ragged common soldier . . . One could understand, even admire at a distance, the spirit that drove these emotional, somewhat hysterical warriors to early victories and ridiculous feats of bravery. But it was infinitely preferable not to be – as we were – on the receiving end of it. It made things no easier for us that the Japanese and their prisoners were so far apart in basic thinking, let alone their military codes. This inability to communicate on the same wavelength was a disaster for us and, in our current circumstances, literally a matter of life and death.[28]

For more than 50,000 British and Australian POWs (mere 'gin-and-tonic warriors' in the estimation of the triumphant Japanese),[29] their captivity began with a lengthy trek from the area of Singapore City (soon to be renamed 'Syonan')[30] to the vicinity of Changi on the island's north-east coast, where a military cantonment had been in development since 1927.[31] On the way, many (including the 'desperately degraded' men of the 5th Suffolks) were free to contemplate the material and human detritus of a lost battle, a spectacle that did nothing to help their shattered morale.[32] As this was happening, Indian POWs were ordered to a separate camp at Nee Soon, where many thousands were suborned by recruiters from the newly created, pro-Japanese Indian National Army.[33]

Occupying an area of around 16 square kilometres, the POW complex at Changi embraced the pre-war military cantonment, a civilian prison, and Changi village itself, and more than 52,000 POWs had taken up residence by nightfall on 18 February.[34] While the Japanese sited their headquarters near to Changi Gaol, commandeering its warders' quarters and administrative building, the whole complex was wired in and subdivided into different areas, access to which was controlled by Japanese guards and, by the end of March, by 'renegade Sikh sentries' (or 'changelings', as Gunner Jack Chalker styled them).[35] By this point too, Changi's constituent areas had been separated by multiple belts of barbed wire.[36] With the Japanese aiming to maintain existing command structures, if only for administrative ease, a Camp Office was established to liaise with the Japanese authorities. This was staffed with personnel from Malaya Command and was still referred to by that rather tainted name.[37] Likewise, 'as far as possible the pre-war command and staff organisation was kept' for each of the camp's six constituent areas, all of which were 'run as independent units'.[38] In terms of population, the largest of these was the Selarang Area, 'containing 14,900 Australians' under Bennett's successor, Major-General C. A. Callaghan. Next came Merton's '18th Division Area', which held '14,000 men in and around the former India Barracks', followed by 'Southern Area', with 12,000 men of Singapore's former 'Fortress troops'. The smallest was '11th Division Area', comprising the 2,900 Britons of this Indian Army division, chiefly the officers and men of the 2nd East Surrey and 1st Leicestershire regiments.[39] (See Figure 4.)

Changi's pre-war cantonment area, which stood on 'a promontory thrusting out into the Straits of Johore', consisted of several barrack blocks complete with theatres, cinemas, playing fields, churches, officers' bungalows and warrant officers' married quarters. In fact, so lavishly endowed was the complex that one POW drily remarked that it was 'easy to see where much of the money voted for the Great Island Fortress went'.[40] Be that as it may, such comfort was deceptive, for 'the imprisoned army required ten times the living space Changi afforded',[41] with gross overcrowding a chronic and dangerous problem. In 18th Division Area, officers and other ranks 'lived in odd buildings, several units being under canvas'. Initially, the 5th Suffolks lived in bivouacs before transferring to more solid (but very cramped) barracks.[42] By the end of March, 7,000 POWs remained without 'proper shelter', while barrack blocks built for 150 now housed as many as 800. Inevitably, a great deal of hard physical work was required to make Changi even remotely habitable, a challenge complicated by a lack of tools and materials and 'by frequent alterations in the size and locality of the camp'.[43]

Sanitary arrangements and food and medical supplies posed severe problems from the outset.[44] Although the buildings at Changi were mainly intact, water, sewage and electricity systems 'had largely been put out of action' during the battle for the island.[45] For some time, therefore, water was 'very scarce', being 'limited to half a gallon a man each day for all purposes'.[46] As one 18th Division prisoner put it: 'Cleanliness was next to godliness, and also next to impossible, at least in the early days.' Though 'bathing parades' on Changi beach helped at first, these ended abruptly when it became 'an execution ground for Chinese and other anti-Jap elements'.[47]

In terms of food, though some could live on rations that had been hoarded or retrieved from the battlefield, shortages were inevitable. As Captain Richard Sharp of the 9th Northumberland Fusiliers said of his fellow prisoners: 'If they weren't ill they were hungry, and if they were ill, well, they were hungrier still when they became better.'[48] The Japanese issued rations from 24 February, on a daily scale of 500 grammes of rice per man, 50 grammes of meat or fish, 50 grammes of flour (which ended in September), 15 grammes of milk (ending in June) and tiny quantities of tea, sugar, salt and oil. Though wholly inadequate in nutritional terms (lacking in 'protein, fat and vitamin B'), the situation was worsened by the fact that rice was an unfamiliar food to British POWs and, to begin with, Army cooks struggled to make it palatable, even to prisoners who were always hungry.[49] In the interests of efficiency, and possibly reflecting the state of their own supply systems, at the end of February the Japanese announced that, within the space of the next two months, Changi had to

become self-sufficient in all foodstuffs except for rice. This led to the pro-
liferation of vegetable gardens throughout the camp which, in turn, put
further pressure on space.[50] Besides these gardens, by using 'private funds',
rations could be eked out by the purchase of food, either legitimately or
on the black market. In fact, 'purchasing parties' were soon allowed 'outside
the wire' to buy bread, tinned foods and fresh produce such as eggs, fish
and vegetables – which were usually channelled to the camp hospital.[51] In
mid-June, the Japanese enlarged this concession by paying amenity grants,
modest sums 'which enabled canteens to be established and local purchases
to be made for units and messes as well as for the hospital'.[52]

As for medical supplies, some were brought to Changi with Japanese
permission in mid-February, but 60 per cent of this stock was soon confis-
cated in order to supply the Indian camp at Nee Soon, and the turncoats of
the Indian National Army (INA). The camp's meagre medical stores were
further diminished by the need to supply a growing number of 'drafts and
working parties departing from Changi'.[53] While small quantities of drugs
could be bought in Singapore, and the Japanese 'made sporadic and small
issues of drugs and medicines, usually of those least required', by the end
of 1942 the situation was such that 'many important drugs were scarce and
others were unobtainable'.[54]

Given these conditions, disease was soon rampant: by the end of the year,
530 POWs had already died in Changi.[55] Dietary deficiencies resulted in an
outbreak of beriberi 'in an acute form' as early as April, an ordeal that fuelled
such novel 'dietetic experiments' as peanut meal biscuits, banana-skin pie
and an attempted 'extraction of vitamins from grass and leaves'.[56] If malaria
was kept in check in 1942 through a combination of local knowledge and
remaining stocks of quinine and other anti-malarial drugs,[57] it was a different story with dysentery. As one account of Changi put it:

Before the war there was almost no dysentery among troops in
Malaya, but cases began to occur during the fighting. When the
prisoners arrived at Changi there were present all the pre-disposing
factors for a major epidemic: low morale, inertia, gross overcrowding,
swarms of flies, lack of water and no sewage system. Within two days
the outbreak had begun; it spread rapidly and reached its peak in
March, when 1,196 cases were admitted to hospital in one week.[58]

Although the outbreak abated during the dry summer months, it flared up again later in the year due to the return of the rains, 'when flies bred', and the arrival of infected prisoners from the Dutch East Indies.[59] All told, February–December 1942 saw nearly 12,000 hospital admissions for dysentery. This exhausted supplies of emetine for the remainder of the war, while almost half the year's death toll in camp was due to either dysentery or 'dysentery and other causes'.[60] Besides dysentery, another epidemiological concern was a severe outbreak of diphtheria. This transmissible respiratory disease was 'endemic among the native population in Singapore' and, though normally quite mild and even asymptomatic, it became rife among a POW population weakened by malnutrition. By the end of September 1942, the outbreak had reached a peak of 309 cases, and it claimed 56 lives before subsiding from the middle of October. Significantly, the Japanese were sufficiently worried by this disease to be reasonably diligent in providing serum for twice-yearly inoculations, but they were initially lax in preventing its spread. According to one account, they were especially 'dilatory in allowing segregation of infected carriers in the Singapore working-camps',[61] a general neglect that could well have had fatal consequences for Merton.

A major driver of the spread of dysentery and diphtheria was the increasing mobility of Changi's population, a factor which stemmed from Japan's increasingly co-ordinated effort to put its vast pool of prisoners to work. In Changi, work parties were organized from March 1942, their initial function being to supply firewood for the camp's stoves. Given the sheer size of Changi's population this was a major undertaking, one that required tree-felling, with firewood hauled to the camp in trucks or on so-called 'Changi trailers', redundant vehicles pulled by teams of POWs.[62] This new, work-orientated regime was formalized from the beginning of June, when pay began to be issued to working prisoners at the rate of 10 cents a day for other ranks, 15 cents for NCOs and 25 cents for officers.[63] By this time, and despite the depredations of hunger and disease, the employment of POWs had grown exponentially. From March 1942 large numbers of prisoners were being put to work elsewhere on Singapore Island, their tasks including the clearing of debris; repairing and restoring infrastructure; mine-clearing; stevedoring; working in the Ford factory; and, perhaps most famously, building a Shinto shrine to '"Fallen Warriors" (apparently of both sides) on Test Hill at Bukit Timah'. This was consecrated on 7 May 1942, concluding a pharaonic task that required nearly 3,000 prisoners to complete. Although 29 April was observed as an official holiday in honour of Emperor Hirohito's birthday,[64] by the end of that month these labouring duties had become so widespread that the population of Changi had fallen to 32,000, with thousands of POWs in satellite camps such as Sime Road, River Valley Road, Adam Park and Serangoon. As at Changi, however, their accommodation was overcrowded and distinctly ad hoc: 'Transfers among the camps were frequent and the prisoners were housed in anything from barracks and bungalows to atap huts and tents, and at one point in the grandstand at the Racecourse.'[65]

By early April, POWs were also being sent much further afield. On 4 April, with just a day's notice, 1,125 British prisoners took ship for Saigon. Six weeks later, 3,000 Australians sailed for Burma, and five smaller contingents totalling 3,000 headed for Thailand towards the end of June. On 8 July, another contingent of 1,500 Australians was shipped to Borneo, and on 16 August a 'Special Party of all senior officers above the rank of lieutenant-colonel' (Merton included) sailed for Formosa. On the day of their departure, another thousand Britons and Australians sailed for Korea. Due to these movements, by the end of August the population of Changi had fallen to around 19,000, with fewer than 5,000, or one-third of its survivors, held in 18th Division Area.[66]

However, despite its dangers and hardships, it is a testimonial to what followed that these months at Changi came to be seen with something akin to nostalgia by survivors of the Burma Railway. As Christopher Bayly and Tim Harper have remarked: 'Changi was to be remembered as something of an idyll for the men who stayed there in its early days and experienced debased conditions in other camps.'[67] According to Massy-Beresford, these months were akin to a 'Phoney' captivity, and he even noted that:

When the first lot of orders came for a batch of troops to be moved elsewhere, it was greeted with cheers by the soldiery who were already getting bored with the type of life we were leading and assumed that better things were coming their way. Poor boobs. It was the railway in Thailand they were heading for.[68]

As for Massy-Beresford and other senior officers, life at Changi had a distinctly familiar feel:

I retained command of my entire Brigade and was able to keep discipline, organise sport and recreation. It was all too quiet and agreeable to be our final way of life as P.O.W.s. Surrounded by my devoted Staff and with plenty to do I was content enough. We even had a wireless of sorts to keep us in touch with the news – which wasn't all that encouraging at that time.[69]

Things appear to have been much the same at Divisional Headquarters, to which Lieutenant-Colonel Francis Dillon was returned after his abortive attempt to escape to Ceylon. According to Dillon:

The divisional staff were living in two messes in two semi-detached Warrant Officers' quarters on top of a little knoll overlooking the artillery parade ground beyond which there was an open padang [playing field] and then the blue sea. There was absolute minimum of furniture and both living and sleeping quarters were very cramped, but the whole place was spotlessly clean and there was a strong feeling of discipline and cohesion everywhere.[70]

In fact, what Dillon perceived as a newly returned, would-be escapee was hugely significant in the collective ordeal of the 18th Division, for it reflected the success of an attempt to revive a sense of order, discipline and morale among thousands of defeated, dejected and deprived officers and men. This policy was hindered by the Japanese and even resisted by prisoners themselves, but it proved its value on the Burma Railway and elsewhere. As Sibylla Jane Flower, the leading historian of the Far East POW experience, has emphasized, the retention of military discipline and of a functioning military hierarchy made a critical difference to survival rates on 'the railway of death'. Though some officers failed to rise to their responsibilities in captivity, some turning (in the words of one of their own) 'into selfish, mean and unscrupulous beings who will stop at nothing as long as their own ends are satisfied',[71] more commonly their extra pay subsidized the purchase of vital foodstuffs for the sick, while their role as intermediaries (whether in camps or in work parties, and often sandwiched uncomfortably – even dangerously – between POWs and their captors)[72] could shield their fellow prisoners from the worst excesses of the Japanese. As Flower has argued, and however invidious it may have seemed, the policy of 'limited co-operation' with the Japanese, one 'adopted by the most resourceful of the camp commanders', was 'the only conceivable way of ensuring the survival of as many POWs as possible'.[73] Indeed:

No one who saw the confusion and desolation of the camps of Asian labourers on the railway doubted that there was an advantage in being part of a predetermined military order. It was also an arrangement that the Japanese accepted and were prepared to work with.[74]

This bid to restore normal military discipline after the fall of Singapore stemmed from Percival, whose conduct as a POW partly redeemed his failings as a commander in the field. Though it went largely unrecognized by an unforgiving political and military establishment after the war, Percival's conduct in captivity showed that he was not lacking in moral or physical courage. If these seemed absent in the events preceding the fall of Singapore, his 'apparent feebleness in command in Malaya was in sharp contrast to his stoutness in captivity',[75] a stoutness that began with his refusal to leave the stricken 'fortress' despite having Wavell's permission to do so. Though the different areas of Changi were left to their own devices in subsidiary matters, military policy in captivity was still determined by Malaya Command (and always, of course, within the constraints of Japanese directives). Thus, 'on Percival's orders King's Regulations were strictly observed, the power of commanding officers being controlled and Courts-Martial regularly held'.[76] Still, the success of Percival's policy was in no sense a foregone conclusion, and much hinged on the personal authority and determination of his subordinates. In this respect, Merton came into his own, for as Ken Tomkinson recollected:

When one is young and well it's hard to shoot oneself, but that was about the mood at the time. However, Becky rose to the occasion magnificently. Officers, he pointed out, can still, as P.O.W.s, do an immense amount for their men. This idea of having a job to do was a most dominant and helpful factor throughout the whole P.O.W. period.[77]

The challenge that confronted Merton was, however, formidable. According to Richard Sharp, the mood throughout Changi in the early weeks of captivity was bleak to say the least:

We had lost a part of our self-respect with the capitulation. The feeling that British Arms had failed again, the disappointment, all the reaction to the surrender, possibly deep down, the feeling of disgrace, brought about a break down of discipline and a collapse of morale. Men, who had let down themselves, their officers and their regiment, felt themselves let down, and were contrarily self-assertive. Hunger added wings to a self-discipline already in flight, and thieving of money, and of food, became widespread. Disobedience was common, and mutiny not unknown.[78]

In fact, 'the collapse was genuine and very general'. Even in the hospital, 'there was chaos':

The doctors did what they could, but the direction from the top was non-existent. The wards were crowded, becoming daily ever more so; and wore a general air of dirt and neglect, and the smell was awful. The orderlies were infected by the same moral lassitude as the rest . . . Many patients went in, to come out ill-tended, having lost all they possessed.[79]

But there were some rays of light. As Sharp went on:

[N]ot everyone failed to play his part, nor was it everyone that gave in to indiscipline. It was these sound men, who formed the breakwater against the floods of disillusion and degeneration, and later became the foundation stone to the attempted organisation for captivity.[80]

In laying this foundation for the 18th Division, Merton had to overcome a profound psychological malaise. Perhaps its most challenging aspect was a sense of overwhelming despondency. Lieutenant Geoffrey Burton of the 118th Field Regiment admitted that: 'Psychologically, I found the greatest disinclination to do anything. The reaction from the strenuous days of battle was profound. I realise now that this was inevitable and attacked almost everybody, officers and men, junior and senior alike.'[81] However, Ian Watt, later a distinguished literary scholar but then a subaltern in the 5th Suffolks, recalled a dangerous psychosis that gripped many POWs in the early stages of captivity. As Watt recalled, a 'blind refusal to accept our lot' was commonplace, with some even refusing to eat their meagre rations of rice: 'a great many men swore that offering us rice was a calculated indignity: they hadn't liked rice before and they weren't going to start now (they did).'[82] For others, this 'rejection of present reality' proved more prolonged, inducing one prisoner to send precious postcards to a correspondent whom he knew to be dead.[83]

While an absence of communication with the wider world, and especially families at home, caused immense stress and anxiety, it also led to the spread of wild, even delusional stories. These were noted at the time by Captain Harry Silman, the medical officer of the 9th Northumberland Fusiliers, who wrote on 22 February – barely a week after the surrender – that:

Some most remarkable rumours spread round and are believed by many of the troops e.g. The Russians are fighting on German soil, there has been an invasion of England, we have landed in France, Rommel has been beaten etc. It is impossible to trace the source of these 'authentic' rumours.[84]

According to Geoffrey Burton, their sheer capriciousness was unsettling:

Contacts with the outside world were very few. Occasionally, working parties in Singapore would bring in fantastically optimistic stories of great Allied offensives which would set us free in a few weeks . . . Pseudo-news and rumours were passed around by many people either with the misguided idea of cheering us up with exaggerated reports of our own success or with the humorous intention of discovering just what people would believe and in what form their cock-and-bull stories would be returned to them. Of authentic news we had none.[85]

Most unsettling of all, such tales could acquire an apocalyptic edge, with L. L. Baynes recollecting that:

There was a fellow prisoner in the nearby Beds. and Herts. Regiment who was a 'gifted' Spiritualist Medium [and] we heard that the medium had gone into a trance the previous day, and that his spirit guide told him that we would all be off the island by the twenty-eighth of March, which was only a month away; he had also seen a vision of the ships carrying us leaving Singapore harbour, and was convinced there was no chance of error. It is comforting to hope, and thousands believed. Although I had left camp by the designated day, I was told when I returned that the hill in the camp from which the sea could be seen was crowded with believers all day awaiting a sight of those Blighty-bound boats, which alas, never materialised. Our boats were well and truly burned . . .[86]

Still, even this was not the end of this local soothsayer, for in April another prisoner wrote: 'Man claiming to be a Seer giving out prophecies in the Beds/Herts Regt. said his CO would be in hospital in a fortnight's time. Was punished for spreading malicious rumours, but . . . his CO went down with dysentery.'[87]

Besides such susceptibilities, POWs were naturally disposed to blame their senior commanders for their catastrophic defeat, and for their present plight. As Silman put it on 24 February: 'Idleness is a curse and is one of the worst features of the POW camp. It gives men too much time to sit and think and brood.'[88] While Gordon Bennett became an object of opprobrium for his premature departure,[89] Jack Chalker of the 118th Field Regiment, already stunned by the incompetence that had characterized the defence of Singapore Island, now had the leisure to contemplate how 'the civil and military authorities had consistently ignored warnings over the previous ten years that Japanese fifth-column agents were setting up subversive units throughout Malaya and surveying jungle tracks'.[90] According to Francis Dillon:

To many in [Changi], particularly the various Malayan Volunteer Corps, and to the vast majority of the non-regular officers and men in a territorial division like our own, the name 'Malaya Command' stank to high, high heaven . . . They blamed them for the unpreparedness in Malaya, failure to dig beach defences on the north coast of the island and the general lack of leadership . . . I watched with some surprise and not a little amusement, the development of a very first-class hatred such as can only be born under [POW] conditions.[91]

In this regard, it certainly helped Merton that, as a latecomer to Singapore, he was viewed more as a fellow victim, rather than as an author, of present misfortunes.[92] This sentiment was reflected by Harry Silman on 25 February, after the regimental adjutant of the 9th Northumberland Fusiliers had accompanied 'other senior and staff officers' for questioning. In the aftermath of these interrogations, Silman wrote sympathetically:

The GOC is feeling the position very keenly and is looking very worried. He is greatly to be pitied as he never had an opportunity of using his Division as such. Brigades, Battalions and Companies were taken away and the whole Division was scattered into odd bits which were thrown into the battle piecemeal. The Japs were surprised to get such a quick victory in an 'impregnable' fortress.[93]

But there was, nonetheless, still a moral victory to be won, and it was to that vital goal that Merton now applied his efforts.

8

Reconstruction and renewal

As Geoffrey Burton testified as early as 1946, the tide began to turn in Changi with the start of new initiatives that helped to shake prisoners out of their post-surrender torpor:

> When the first despair and disillusionment of capture had passed it soon became clear to everyone that something must be done to occupy our minds and bodies during the time, however long it might be, that we were likely to remain prisoners. Accordingly, lectures, debates, concerts, classes, games and many other pastimes were arranged. Everything was done on the presumption of a long stay in our present circumstances.[1]

However, these initiatives were not as spontaneous as Burton imagined, for they sprang from Merton's systematic reintroduction of divisional structures, institutions and discipline. As Silman noted, by 23 February a daily divisional conference had already been introduced by Merton, one mirrored in the 9th Northumberland Fusiliers – and, presumably, in other units – by local conferences of their own. From these sprang a reordering of divisional life: 'New orders come out each day about water, rations, equipment etc.'[2] (Remarkably, copies of some divisional orders, which were distributed to all units of the 18th Division, survive in the papers of Captain E. C. Dickson, who used them to keep records of the 88th Field Regiment, part of the 9th Indian Division.[3] How they came into Dickson's hands is not clear, though Dickson himself came to refer to Merton as 'our Divisional Commander'.)[4]

Despite his own frustrations and disappointments, to which we will soon turn, Merton was quick to recreate the familiar rhythms of divisional life. And, whatever his more private feelings may have been, in public this was smoothed by his personal charm and by a determination (as after the campaign in Johore) to praise whatever success his division had enjoyed against the Japanese. For example, Stephen Alexander remembered entering Changi in a truck on 17 February, to be met by Merton himself:

'Who are you?' said Becky.
'135 Field Regiment, sir.'
'Ah, Toosey's boys!'[5]

And Merton's praise was generous for Toosey himself, who, in the course of the siege, had been awarded a DSO in the field by Major-General Key of the 11th Indian Division. Consequently, within days of his capture, Toosey received a personal message from Merton at 18th Division Headquarters:

Dear Toosey, There seemed little chance of seeing you to congratulate you on a D.S.O., deserved many times over in a very short space of time. I would, however, like you to know what real pleasure this award brought to me.[6]

In addition to such marks of favour, John Coast of the 4th Norfolks noted how 'our little General . . . did all he could by going round talking to the men and trying to cheer them up, and this also helped to relieve our feelings of responsibility' for the fall of Singapore.[7]

Still, there was a harder and more controversial rationale to this policy. Apart from precedent and principle, a prime justification (especially with so little information from the outside world) was that the war was not over, and that the division might yet play a further part in it. According to a remarkably prescient 'full-dress appreciation' prepared for Merton by his intelligence staff, the Soviet Union would not strike against Japan until Germany was beaten; the United States would take two years to mount an offensive in the Philippines; and a push in the Pacific would coincide with an Allied invasion of France. Furthermore, should the Japanese be obliged to withdraw from Malaya, 'they would wipe us out before doing so'.[8] If keeping the division well-ordered, and as close as possible to fighting trim, offered better prospects for survival in that doomsday scenario, the concomitants of this new regime could prove irksome.

According to Francis Dillon, especially controversial were Merton's 'cadre classes for officers and NCOs', classes intended as a continuation of 'military education' but which were 'bitterly resented by many and were very unpopular'.[9] Among the refractories was John Coast, who complained of his quiet life being 'shattered' by 'the old boys at Divisional H.Q.', whose new course for subalterns involved pre-breakfast drill (on an empty stomach) and a series of 'tactical lectures, Sandhurst style'. If Coast resented their content ('a meander back to the plains of Salisbury' prior to the intrusion of tanks and aircraft) as well as their timing,[10] Ian Watt was more ambivalent. While he acknowledged that 'we absolutely needed a strict organization, and that the only possible form of it was a military one', he also regretted 'some rather foolish steps to restore our morale', steps that included a strict ban on beards and, 'despite my beri-beri feet', having 'to turn out before breakfast for saluting parades'. As Watt wryly noted: 'It seemed it wasn't enough to be prisoners; we had to be in the army too.'[11] Such feelings were shared by Stephen Alexander: 'No doubt in those early days the paraphernalia of military organisation was beneficial. Role-playing is safer than idleness, and make-believe morale better than demoralisation. But it looked peculiar to some outsiders.' An American sailor, for example, on arrival in Changi, was astonished to see British officers receive salutes and 'preen in full uniform as though they still owned Singapore'.[12]

However, in retrospect, and on the Burma Railway in particular, L. L. Baynes came to see the value of these efforts:

> As we recovered from the strain of battle, our Commanding Officer decided to tighten up discipline in the camp, and although it irked us to see the old 'bull' returning, looking back I can see that it was for the best: we would quickly have turned into a rabble without discipline, the strongest would have survived, and the weaker ones gone under.[13]

Apart from the tragic but salutary fate of tens of thousands of civilian labourers on the railway, Baynes also noted, rather cryptically, that 'later on we saw what happened to other troops who had not been subjected to discipline'.[14]

In April 1942, Sergeant Charles Steel of the 135th Field Regiment wrote an (unposted) letter to his wife which spoke of the 'high standard of internal organisation' in 18th Division Area. In particular, 'Regimental Gardens, Regimental Education Scheme, Changi "University", [a] Concert Party. Church Parades all in being.' He also acknowledged his disappointment that he hadn't won a prize for his 'bamboo serviette rings', which he had entered for 'a Battery Arts and Crafts Exhibition . . . judged by Major-General Beckwith-Smith'.[15] The revival of the divisional concert party and the creation of its celebrated venue, the 'New Windmill Theatre', lay in a divisional conference that took place on Sunday 1 March. As Captain Charles Wilkinson of the 9th Northumberland Fusiliers noted in his diary: 'Attended conference at Div. H.Q. about forming a Divisional Concert Party and a Garrison Theatre. I represented Divisional Troops.'[16] While also serving as the chairman of the 'Div. Troops Entertainments Committee', formed soon after with the aim of having 'a show every Wednesday on the Sports Ground',[17] Wilkinson kept diary notes tracking the evolution and success of the larger, divisional venture. On 8 March, he was back at Divisional Headquarters for a planning meeting, and on 18 March for an 'Entertainments Conference' at which it was learned that a show was now ready for production: 'It is "The Optimists" presenting "Rice and Shine". It starts tomorrow and it will take 19 performances for all the Div. to see it.'[18] Merton saw the show on 27 March, giving no opinion,[19] but the turn of the 9th Northumberland Fusiliers to see *Rice and Shine: A Topical Revue* came three days later, with Wilkinson deeming it 'a good show', including as it did sundry sketches ('The Soldier's Return' and 'A Food Fracas') and various musical solos. With spirits revived, each performance closed with a rousing rendition of the National Anthem.[20]

Succeeding weeks saw a growing programme of entertainment. Spurred by the success of George Bernard Shaw's *Arms and the Man*, staged in the open by officers of Malaya Command to 'a very high amateur standard',[21] variety concerts began to give way to more highbrow entertainment, with Wilkinson learning on 3 June that 'Div. H.Q. want a Dramatic Society formed in 18 Div., so arrangements are being made for one'.[22] With so many flowers blooming, and a growing concern that the comedy on display in this 'all male camp' was becoming gross and demoralizing,[23] Wilkinson learned the following day that Merton intended to get a grip on the situation:

Major Bowman came down to see me in the afternoon. He is in the Coldstream Guards and is Brigade Major to 54 Brigade. [The]

G.O.C. has detailed him to co-ordinate all the 18th Divisional Entertainments. Together with Archie Bevan (A.D.C. to the General) who is in the Welsh Guards and myself, the 3 of us will handle the whole situation and make all major decisions regarding concerts, plays and so on for the whole Division.[24]

On 5 June, in the interests of securing a suitable all-weather venue, Wilkinson and his new colleagues inspected a redundant NAAFI building, complete with its own stage, with Wilkinson noting that: 'It would be ideal for our purposes and make a first class permanent theatre. We are taking steps to get it.'[25] Within a week, this had been released and a stage manager appointed, with whom Wilkinson surveyed the stage to 'decide on the necessary structural improvements for next week's new Div. Concert Party show'.[26] In 24 hours, a joiner and bricklayer were at work, though 'electric light for the theatre [was] out of the question at the moment'.[27]

But what to perform? The resolution of this deceptively trivial matter revealed a good deal about Merton's judgement, and his sense of his soldiers' mood after four months of interaction in the close confines of Changi. Initially, the production scheduled to help launch the new theatre was a play entitled *The Island*, copies of which had already been laboriously typed up.[28] Apparently, this had been chosen on the simple grounds that its producer 'had himself been in the play on the London stage'.[29] However, it was controversial for an all-officer cast, for as Wilkinson wrote:

Went to what was to have been the first rehearsal of 'The Island'. Unfortunately, a certain amount of doubt as to whether the play was a suitable choice for the present circumstances was voiced by Lt. Col. Carpenter [of the 1st Cambridgeshires] and one or two other members of the cast. The result was it was decided not to do the play but to see if there were any more suitable ones available! A most unfortunate setback and a lot of useful time and labour expended for nothing.[30]

However, despite Wilkinson's exasperation, there was an important issue at stake in this selection, for as Francis Dillon, a cast member, explained about this 'tremendous local storm in the tea-cup', the plot of *The Island* 'turned on the love of a gunner CO for a junior officer's wife with the usual complications'. According to Carpenter (whom Dillon acknowledged to be 'a real stormy petrel', who 'thundered' his disapproval), the play 'would be bad for discipline, and would bring officers into disrepute'. With the matter referred to Divisional Headquarters, and aware of the delicate thread by which discipline hung, it was up to Merton to make the decision. As Dillon recalled, 'The GOC with his usual common sense, let everybody talk himself out, and then said quietly one morning, "I think you had better produce *The Dover Road*", and that was that.'[31]

The Dover Road, a darkly comic play by A. A. Milne, concerned a refuge for eloping couples en route from London to Paris, whose stay affords them the opportunity to discover the off-putting foibles of their prospective spouses. To resource this last-minute substitute, extra stocks of precious paper were released by Divisional Headquarters for the typing of scripts.[32] By 18 June the first rehearsal was being held and, according to Wilkinson, was going 'well'. On 4 July, the 'New Windmill Theatre' (a nod to the division's stylized windmill insignia) was officially opened with a 'Celebrity Concert' featuring, among others, the vocal talents of Padre John Foster Haigh of the 4th Suffolks, an acclaimed tenor in civilian life who had sung beside Paul Robeson.[33] The curtain went up on the first performance of *The Dover Road* at 7.30 p.m. on 11 July, its premiere timed to coincide with Merton's fifty-second birthday. According to Wilkinson, 'the G.O.C. made a speech at the end', following birthday greetings from his colleague, Major Bowman, and 'the whole thing had a real first night atmosphere'.[34]

Clearly, this whole theatrical venture proved a resounding success. Merton saw *The Dover Road* on at least three occasions, including its final night, 15 August, the eve of his departure for Formosa (or, ostensibly, Japan).[35] Harry Silman thought the play 'excellently done', with Wilkinson the star of the show (though 'Dillon appeared to be wondering what came next – this spoilt his acting').[36] Captain Ronald Horner of the RASC was, however, enthralled, and was even persuaded to play the role of 'a cockney salesman' in *I Killed the Count*, the next play to be performed, by 'Archie Bevan, Becky's ADC'.[37] As Horner wrote on 15 July:

Went to see 18 Division's presentation of *The Dover Road*, a really first class effort that helped to make one forget one's surroundings for a short time. Held in the new Windmill Theatre (the centre floor

179

of an old battle-scarred NAAFI block), it really recaptured the true theatre atmosphere.[38]

Though Merton never saw *I Killed the Count*, the 'New Windmill Theatre' remained a central part of life in Changi until its closure on 19 November 1942, by which point 'The Great Migration' of POW labour from Changi to other camps in the Co-Prosperity Sphere was well under way.[39]

Another venture that was emblematic of the revival of cultural and intellectual life, and of the care of mind, body and spirit which Merton had always evinced, was the creation of the '18th Division's University'. (Rather confusingly, another 'Changi University' was opened in Southern Area in 1942, so we will use this nomenclature to refer to Merton's creation.)[40] Announced in divisional orders on 22 March 1942, this was aimed at all ranks with the intention of benefitting those 'whose studies were interrupted by the war' and who wished to either enter 'a University proper', or prepare 'for a post-war career'. It would comprise seven faculties (Modern Languages, English Language and Literature, History, Geography, Mathematics, Economics, and Theology), syllabi had been prepared and each three-month course would consist of 'six to eight lectures a week, in addition to tutorial classes'. Further faculties would be established 'one by one, as the opportunity offers'.[41] By 11 April 1942, Charles Wilkinson could note that Military History had joined the roster of subjects on offer and that: 'The Div. University opens its first term tomorrow. I hope to go in for Military History when it commences.'[42] According to Geoffrey Burton, writing just after the war, of all the efforts made at this time

> [t]he most ambitious scheme was the foundation of [18th Division's] university. This by now well-known educational seminary was staffed by officers and men with teaching ability, and courses were started in English, History, Mathematics, Law, Military History, Theology, Languages, Art, Music and, I think, even Science. A library was formed with books from Raffles College in Singapore [later, the University of Singapore], and other sources.[43]

As noted by Wilkinson in his chronicle of life in Changi, Merton was keen to show his support for this new venture and, on its opening day,

Monday 13 April, 'Gen. Beckwith-Smith came down and listened to a number of lectures'.[44] Furthermore, he became a keen auditor of lectures on agriculture given by 'a pink, pop-eyed young landowner in a Gunner Regiment', always appearing 'followed by a perspiring [staff officer]'.[45] While the University's lecturers – all of whom were 'university men' – were 'excused all military duties' to devote themselves to their work, it was expected that students (all of whom were interviewed prior to admission) would 'be free to attend the lectures and tutorial classes at the time laid down'.[46]

John Coast, who played a key role in the early days of the University, saw Merton's interest at close hand. Wearying of regimental life in the 4th Norfolks, and of the chores devised by his CO as 'necessary for "morale"':

To escape from this boredom I obtained the job of Divisional Librarian. The chief function of the library would be to work [with] an embryo University – our General was very keen on the idea, for we had plenty of talent in the way of academic brains, and the plan was to open up with about a dozen normal faculties. Every day I worked there, helping build shelves, stealing furniture, and trying to amass books. The only times of contact with my Battalion were at meals and in the evening.[47]

For Coast, 'the one high spot in Changi was the gradual building up of the University', which was marked by the acquisition of teaching space in 'odd corners of huts' and by Coast's discovery of two professional musicians – a pianist and a violinist – who formed the core of a Music Faculty which, with the support of Divisional Headquarters, was duly brought into being.[48] Indeed, in his support for 18th Division's University, Merton was more than prepared to show a streak of ruthlessness, for as Coast recollected:

[T]he General asked me to combine my job of Librarian with that of University Adjutant; but for several reasons I turned the whole job in. The Library had so far not come up to my expectations, and I also suspected that 'Adjutant' meant office boy, and little spare time to learn anything myself. I found a deputy – but it seemed that the General didn't like my throwing the job over, and to my indignation and sorrow I found myself in the company of another dozen officers and 300 odd of our men, en route for the Nip working party at a place called Bukit Timah . . . the area over which our brigade had fought during the Battle of Singapore.[49]

As shown by his involvement in 18th Division's University, his appearances at the 'New Windmill Theatre' and even his adjudication of minor art and craft competitions, Merton became a very familiar figure to the inmates of Changi's 18th Division Area. In fact, given the diffusion of the division along the East Anglian coast, in Scotland, the North and Midlands of England, on various troopships and convoys, and across southern Malaya and Singapore Island, Merton was never more visible to its officers and men than during his six-month stay in Changi. All of this was accompanied by a highly personal touch, one that had already made him 'much beloved by his staff, and affectionately known among them as Becky'.[50] In May 1942, Horner noted how Merton had accepted an invitation to a dinner party at his mess, appearing late on the night in question and 'tearing over to the "A" Mess on a lady's bicycle!'[51] That Merton did not stand on his general's dignity (a wise choice, especially after such a disaster) was also shown by an anecdote related to Honor many years after the war by a soldier of the 287th Field Company, Royal Engineers:

I think every man of the Division thought the world of him, and would have gone anywhere for him. He was known of by us all, even though he held such a high ranking position as he commanded nearly 21,000 of us; he always had time for a word with the lower ranks of which I was one.[52]

He went on:

I remember so well about one month after we were taken prisoners in Singapore, he was walking amongst us with his riding breeches and leggings on, when someone shouted, 'Hye there "Becky", where's your horse?' His reply was, with a wave of his hand and stick, 'That's the spirit, boys, that's what I like to hear. We shall win through.' And even under these conditions every man would stand and salute him. Something the Japs could never understand.[53]

If relations between divisional headquarters and the 9th Northumberland Fusiliers had not always been cordial, especially over the question of maritime transport, even its rapport with Merton appears to have been close and genuinely affectionate. Harry Silman, who was Jewish, thought Merton was especially impressive on the Northumberland Fusiliers' regimental day, 23 April:

> St George's Day dawned bright and clear . . . We all went home and made roses in our hats – made out of red flags and white bandages. Everyone appeared to have a sparkle in their eyes. This morning at 10.45 I left the sick parade and formed a background to the General who addressed the men lined up in a square in front. He made a very sensible speech and said that a decoration will be awarded to Col. Thomas for saving the *Felix Roussel*. He praised the men for their part in that action [and] hoped that we would soon show our true worth. Our coming to the island was a political and not a military fault. He then went to a special church service, followed by taking a salute as the troops marched past. It all went off very well.[54]

Relating the same events in his diary, Charles Wilkinson agreed that the day had been a notable success and that 'Major-General Beckwith-Smith's address was excellent and inspiring'.[55] A week later, Merton returned on more routine business, Wilkinson noting that: 'The General (Beckwith-Smith) made an inspection [and] this went off fairly well. All hands on deck during the morning to put on a good show.'[56] In a further indication of his interaction with his units, Wilkinson recorded how, as the first of five drafts assembled for their journey to Thailand on 18 June:

> They paraded on the Gun Park at 17.00 hrs. The G.O.C. addressed them and wished them 'Good luck!' Major Sykes R.A.S.C. is in command of 'B [Battalion]' which is the one our men are in. They all went away in lorries and as they did so they all cheered the G.O.C. as they passed.[57]

Evidently, there is little reason to doubt that, by July 1942, Merton had acquired genuine popularity in a situation in which many other officers signally failed to shine, let alone inspire. Harry Silman, for example, a not ungenerous judge, deemed Percival 'not very impressive' when he encountered him in Changi a month after the surrender.[58] This affection was clear long before Merton's departure in August 1942, especially around his birthday on 11 July. The previous day, 'on the occasion of his birthday', the Northumberland Fusiliers 'sent a message of congratulation to the G.O.C.', one among 'many gifts and congratulatory messages' to which he replied with a special message of his own.[59] When he arrived at the 'New Windmill Theatre' for the debut of *The Dover Road*, Francis Dillon testified how 'the "by invitation" audience gave him a tremendous reception'.[60] However, this was not merely the acclaim of a select few. Writing in his journal on 12 July 1942, Silman reflected:

Further to yesterday's remarks about Becky – the general opinion of him has gone up by leaps and bounds. He has certainly done everything he could to make our stay here as pleasant as possible and he has actively identified himself with all the educational and university faculties. Given a fair opportunity in war, I am sure he would come out very well.[61]

And a sense of collective achievement was clearly widely diffused, even though its driving force was not immediately obvious. As Captain John Barratt, another officer of the 4th Norfolks, reflected: 'No doubt at 18th Division H.Q. there were those who visualised what our P.O.W. activities might be at Changi under [the] Geneva Convention. A university was started, much use was made of the playing fields and dramatic societies were formed.'[62] Although Idris Barwick of the RASC was among those who had misgivings about the standards of discipline imposed in 18th Division Area, and resented the RMP who enforced them, he was very much aware of the benign aspects of these months in Changi (which, for him, even included membership of a Welsh Society):

As the months rolled by, we settled down to a daily routine and much was achieved to ameliorate the misery of our situation. The areas were being efficiently run and we were like a lost legion, making our own little world and starting a new life.[63]

Much, he apprehended, was due to Merton, of whom he wrote:

> Unlike so many of his subordinate officers, General Beckwith-Smith
> was admired and respected by us all. He seemed to have quite a bit of
> influence with the Nips and had got us many little things which we
> would otherwise never have had.[64]

His message at the end of the battle for Singapore (which Barwick confused with his message of farewell in August 1942) seemed to show 'just
what a fine man he was and how much the Division meant to him'.[65]

However, if personal popularity was a by-product of Merton's efforts, it
was certainly not their goal, for his measures had a much deeper professional significance. In a shrewd dissection of Merton's policy written many
years later, Sir Richard Sharp, in Changi a subaltern of the Northumberland Fusiliers attached to Divisional Headquarters, described how:

> The G.O.C. [did] his utmost to keep alive and spread a corporate
> spirit within the Divisional Area, by encouragement of good
> administration, of games, education and entertainment. He insisted
> we were still part of the army, and everything should be done army
> wise.[66]

This meant that all units were still responsible for their own administration, and that the supporting services – the RE, the RASC – functioned
much as they did under normal conditions. However, realizing that these
continuities could only go so far, 'he forced education and outside interests down the throats of Commanding officers who thought they had no
value'. In turn, this produced a divisional university and even a secondary
school, as well as 'The new Windmill Theatre'.[67] Furthermore, Merton
asserted a very personal presence. As Sharp put it:

> He'd go round the hospital, encouraging the sick, seeing that they
> were not neglected by either the Hospital or their own units; take a
> look in at the University, listen to the lectures that were being given,
> and on his way past St. George's Church, have a word with the padre
> about the services. Watch any games that were being played, and

185

sometimes play himself . . . When he paid an official visit to a unit, it was usually not so much of a bugbear as most General Inspections are to the troops themselves; for although they still had a bit of polishing up to do, the inspection was always in the early morning, before breakfast, and he'd stay to see what sort of food they were getting. So, of course the [Quartermaster] had to dig into whatever reserves he held, to put up a good show. And that the troops loved. Naturally. Due to him it was generally recognised that the morale and discipline within the Division were better than elsewhere.[68]

The significance of these accomplishments should not be underestimated, nor their origins. Writing under the shadow of the Cold War, and the prospect of facing enemies who likewise had no regard for 'international agreements in relation to the treatment of prisoners of war', Francis Dillon drew 'special attention to the lack of official guidance to men and officers who find themselves placed as we were'.[69] Apart from Percival's intentions and the terms of the Geneva Convention, there had been nothing to guide Merton in his remarkable regeneration, even resurrection, of the 18th Division – apart from his own professionalism, personality and fundamental grasp of the situation.

However, what was also key to Merton's rebuilding of the division was the role of religious faith. Amidst the desolation and isolation that came with defeat and captivity, this often supplied a vital source of strength and solace. This was a natural function of the fact that, as reflected in wartime social surveys, the great majority of Britons (and, for that matter, Australians, Canadians and New Zealanders) still identified as believing Christians, a situation that underpinned the appeal and recurrence of wartime Days of Prayer across Great Britain and the 'white' Dominions.[70] John Foster Haigh, the Congregationalist chaplain of the 4th Suffolks, claimed that the religious pulse of the 18th Division had already quickened during its long voyage to the Far East, noting that:

Religion played an all important part in the life of this floating civilisation. It has been a source of encouragement that I found men interested in the deep things of the spirit. In Officers' cabins and Men's quarters, I have had the most astonishing discussions on life and religion, and despite our British tradition for reticence in matters of religious faith, I have discovered men ready and eager to express their religious convictions . . .'[71]

While this phenomenon may have reflected the stronger religiosity of rural East Anglia, it was not uncharacteristic of soldiers sailing into harm's way, being noted, for example, in the Task Force that sailed to the Falklands as late as 1982.[72] It also came to the fore in moments of obvious crisis. As widely noted in accounts of the fall of Singapore, the grim business of Sunday 15 February began with a service of Holy Communion at Percival's headquarters in Fort Canning.[73] What consolation Percival may have garnered from the Prayer Book's 'Order for the Administration of the Lord's Supper' can only be guessed at, though one can readily appreciate the pertinence of such petitions as, 'And we most humbly beseech thee of thy goodness, O Lord, to comfort and succour all them, who in this transitory life are in trouble, sorrow, need, sickness, or any other adversity.' However, this was a mood widely felt across Singapore that day, for as Noel Barber wrote:

All over the city people, as though sensing the moment of destiny was at hand, joined in Sunday-morning prayer. In the General Hospital . . . nurses gathered in a bleak ante-room for a brief service. In the [Anglican] cathedral, which was still filled with wounded, 'The Rev.' had put back as many pews as possible in the choir. Every one was filled, and every inch of space was crowded with standing worshippers. Those who could not get inside stood in the green compound. They could not hear the service but, as if impelled by some primitive instinct, they stayed there silent and devout, until it was over and those inside filed out.[74]

And nor did this heightened sense of dependence on God dissipate on entry into captivity. Harry Silman, the Jewish medical officer of the 9th Northumberland Fusiliers, averred that a 'trend towards religion' was manifest among his fellow POWs (who were overwhelmingly Christian) by July 1942.[75] This susceptibility was widely attested by Silman's contemporaries in Changi. As one RAOC private of the 18th Division put it: 'We had our full complement of churches of all denominations . . . and had we been left to our own devices we should have filled them to capacity at every service.'[76] The same point was made by C. F. Blackater of the Indian Army, who wrote in 1948:

[E]ach Sunday evening, upon the broad terrace overlooking the Straits, we would gather to sing, to pray, to hear the padre: 'He set His face steadfastly to go up to Jerusalem' [Luke 9.51] because 'only by suffering could he draw all men unto Him.' Then the National Anthem as evening closed round us. Communion service in the great hall at Easter, packed to overflowing, the padres in khaki and stoles. Or later, in a strange place, a miniature range converted to a chapel. A service on the veranda, whipped by rain; a sermon on the Crucifixion, 'The greatest moment in God's revelation of love, the lowest moment in the story of man.'[77]

Even those who did not regard themselves as conventionally religious admitted to turning to God for help. As Ernest Gordon of the 2nd Battalion of the Argyll and Sutherland Highlanders (part of the pre-invasion garrison of Malaya) recalled:

One noticeable change from ordinary barrack life was the obvious interest in religion on the part of so many. As disease spread, as spirits became depressed, as hope flourished and died and men had nothing to which they could look forward, they sought aid from beyond themselves . . . Church services were allowed by the Japanese. They were held in the open and were generally well attended. Several men whom I knew to have no religious ties went regularly, listened attentively, sang hymns lustily, prayed fervently and read their bibles . . . It seemed to me that for a good number of them, at least, religion was an attempt to find a quick and easy answer, a release from their fears.[78]

A case in point was John Coast, who remembered a time when one of his platoon lay dying of dysentery: 'That night, the first and last time for years, I went out on to the padang, and prayed a queer sort of agnostic prayer to any benevolent Deity who might exist.'[79] More positively, Alistair Urquhart of the 2nd Battalion of the Gordon Highlanders, part of the Fortress Garrison of Singapore, recalled how an impromptu church service proved a welcome addition to a successful open-air concert:

Eventually the Japanese guards present got bored and left. When they had gone an altar was set up and an interdenominational church service held. It proved a welcome morale-booster. Even people like me, not especially religious, found it comforting. It was to be my one and only church service during three and a half years of captivity but it struck a real chord and made me think seriously about Christianity for the first time. When the padre finished his sermon on our mount in Changi . . . thousands of miles from home, hundreds of voices joined in a moving rendition of 'The Old Rugged Cross'. The first verse seemed so appropriate to all of us caught up in the fall of Singapore:

On a hill far away stood an old rugged cross,
The emblem of suffering and shame;
And I love that old cross where the dearest and best
For a world of lost sinners was slain.[80]

This palpable turn to religion (or 'spiritual uplift', as one of Toosey's biographers called it)[81] was fed by a variety of factors. Besides the personal solace that could be found under the impact of defeat and the hardships of captivity, religious *activities* had a natural appeal. They were a means of recreation; they were permitted – *mutatis mutandis* – under Article 16 of the Geneva Convention (subject, significantly, to 'the routine and police regulations prescribed by the military authorities');[82] they represented, for many, continuity with an earlier life; they underlined a defiant sense of religious and cultural difference from the Japanese; and they had a deep resonance in the Judeo-Christian culture that was the inheritance of the vast majority of British and Dominion POWs, evoking a sense of Israel's captivity in Egypt and Babylon, the imprisonment of St Paul and the sufferings of countless Christian martyrs.[83] And, though most evident in the months that followed the fall of Singapore, and before tens of thousands of

POWs were thrown into much harsher conditions across the Co-Prosperity Sphere, this religiosity could prove highly resilient.[84] Contemporary statistics indicate that, from July to September 1942, around one-third of the British occupants of Changi were regular Anglican communicants – a proportion that remained remarkably stable until the end of the war and was far higher than in civilian life, especially among younger adult males.[85] Amidst all the misery of the Burma Railway, Len Gibson of the 125th Anti-Tank Regiment noted that its crudely improvised chapel became 'a vital part of the camp' at South Tonchan, and he credited his own survival to the prayers of his mother.[86] For Eric Cordingly, the former chaplain of the 9th Northumberland Fusiliers, who ministered in Changi and on the Burma Railway, his years of captivity were very far from being a spiritual wilderness:

> There is no doubt that those three and a half years were a wonderful opportunity for a parish priest, and I suppose in fact the most wonderful time in my life, in spite of the grim and hungry times . . . We were down to bedrock. One saw people as they really were. There was no reason for humbug or cant; many men had no use at all for religion, but great numbers had – and these men were no longer shy about the faith which they had found.[87]

Still, and as Cordingly acknowledged, individual responses varied, and could be quite complex and even contradictory. In *The Naked Island* (1952), for example, the Australian Russell Braddon wrote that he read the Bible twice from beginning to end while in captivity, before turning 'with relief . . . from the high-flown Hebraic imagery of the world's best seller to the cynicism of the complete works of George Bernard Shaw'.[88] However, one of the two dedicatees of Braddon's famous memoir was the celebrated chaplain of the 2nd Cambridgeshire Regiment, Padre Noel Duckworth. Peter Hartley, on the other hand, of the 5th Beds and Herts, who escaped from Singapore only to be captured in Sumatra, described his memoir *Escape to Captivity* (also published in 1952) as, in part, 'a spiritual autobiography' which witnessed to 'the triumph of faith over tribulation'.[89] Accordingly, each chapter was prefaced by a biblical text, a practice repeated in L. L. Baynes' memoir, *Kept – The Other Side of Tenko* (1984). While even Massy-Beresford penned reflections on faith, prayer and morality during his captivity in Formosa,[90] the experience of indefinite imprisonment could have more negative effects. Reflected in the wildly credulous responses to the self-appointed medium in the 5th Beds and Herts, such effects also took the form of an unhealthy type of biblical divination. As Ernest Gordon noted:

> The Bible they viewed as having magical properties; to the man who could find the right key all would be revealed. One group assured me with absolute certainty that they knew that the end of the war was at hand. When I asked them for proof they told me that they had found it in the books of Daniel and Revelation. They went on to demonstrate mathematically how they had arrived at this conclusion. They had manipulated numbers and words from these two books in a way that seemed convincing enough to them . . .[91]

Religion, therefore, was very much in vogue in Changi and its satellite camps from February to August 1942 (and, indeed, beyond). And it could, depending on its expressions, either reinforce or jeopardize order and morale. Given the strength and simplicity of Merton's personal faith, his professional sense of the utility of religion and his overarching task of rebuilding the discipline and spirits of the 18th Division, this was not a factor he was inclined to overlook. Consequently, he made a sustained effort to promote a healthy and orthodox church life, properly led and supervised by commissioned army chaplains. The centrepiece of these efforts in 18th Division Area – and, indeed, in Changi itself – was St George's Church, a former Indian Army mosque located in Changi's old 'India Lines'. According to J. N. Lewis Bryan, the senior British chaplain in Malaya Command:

> Of the 17 churches which we were able to establish, equip and operate, I regarded St. George's as the 'Cathedral Church' (so to speak) of the area. Its beauty of architecture and design and the dignity of its setting and its services, together with the faithful ministry of word and sacrament, combined to attract enormous numbers of men to all its services. It was always an inspiration to be present and preach when I had the opportunity.[92]

As Geoffrey Burton saw it, St George's – which served as a place of learning for 18th Division's University as well as a place of worship – was emblematic of the renaissance of divisional life in Changi:

> The university had its headquarters in the 18th Division Area Church. This church was originally a small mosque, but shortly after the beginning of our captivity, it was taken over, and converted for Church of England use. An organ was installed, and an altar, lectern and pulpit built by P.O.W.s. It is this church which always stands out in my memory as an instance of the triumph of ingenuity over adverse conditions.[93]

The origins of St George's Church lay in the early hours of 18th Division's occupation of India Barracks. According to Eric Cordingly, he chanced upon the mosque – 'a delightful building', partly concealed among the well-tended gardens of the barracks – the day after his arrival. A 'fairly large white building', domed and with verandas on three sides, its tiled and whitewashed interior was deemed 'admirably suited for a Church', being 'both light and pleasantly cool' and with a configuration that corresponded to a nave and chancel.[94] It was, he remembered, 'not difficult to get permission to use the building' and a number of volunteers, officers and men, 'spent their first Saturday in captivity in making a Church'.[95] While the mosque's 'religious books were safely stored away', the conversion of the mosque proceeded with remarkable speed: rough altar rails were installed, an altar was fashioned from an old sideboard, seating was transferred 'from the open-air cinema in the village of Changi', a blue marquee carpet was laid in the sanctuary, and an altar frontal and dorsal curtain was cut 'from a piece of an Indian tent'.[96]

Although the results were impressive 'even on that first Sunday in Captivity', over subsequent weeks and months the church was further adorned.[97] Helped by the fact that it largely served divisional troops, with their high proportion of skilled tradesmen, the church was named 'St George's' in honour of the Northumberland Fusiliers, its reredos 'a painted and carved plaque of St. George and the Dragon'.[98] According to Lewis Bryan, St George's could seat 600 worshippers and was 'soon lavishly furnished',[99] a point borne out by an RAOC private:

192

The form of the mosque made adaptation to a church easy enough for it had nave, chancel, vestry, churchyard and lychgate. Four units worshipped at St. George's – the Fusiliers and units of the Royal Engineers, the [Royal Army] Ordnance Corps and the [Royal Army] Service Corps – the last named being three units admirably fitted to carry out the necessary alterations as they comprised mechanics of all kinds . . . The Engineers made the Communion Table, altar rails, pulpit, lectern and wardens' staves while the Ordnance Corps fashioned an altar cross out of a brass shell case and inscribed it with the badges of the four units. They also arranged the lighting, made two candles for the altar and repaired a small harmonium to accompany the choir while the Service Corps undertook to provide every week the bread and wine for the Communion.[100]

Besides its fixtures and fittings, St George's had its full complement of church 'officials', including two churchwardens, 'a band of keen "sidesmen"', a sacristan, altar servers, a choir and choirmaster, and a verger – the latter Cordingly's batman, who kept St George's 'spotless' (and, as 'an artist at flowers', the sanctuary 'looking beautiful').[101]

Together with the 'New Windmill Theatre' and 18th Division's University, St George's 'Mark I', as it came to be known, was the project most associated with Merton's regeneration of the division. Opened just a week after the capitulation, it was 'closed down in April 1943 when [the] area was evacuated'. However, 'all furniture not taken to Thailand [was] removed and used in Churches built later in other areas'.[102] It also prompted emulation in other parts of Changi and in camps across Singapore Island. For example, St Luke's Chapel, Roberts Barracks Hospital, was opened on 12 July 1942 (and demolished in August 1943 to make way for a Japanese aircraft hangar). In keeping with precedents at St George's, it was 'designed by an officer of 18th Division and the Altar rail built by 18th Division R.E.';[103] a font was crafted by a captain of the 5th Suffolks, and a Toc H group used it to produce 'a Church Magazine for the wards'.[104] However, and as Lewis Bryan stated:

The great feature of this Chapel was the collection of mural paintings, the work of Bombardier Stanley Warren, 135 Field Regiment, R.A., who did these magnificent paintings as his thanksgiving for

193

recovery from [dysentery]. They consisted of [a] Nativity Scene; The Institution of the Last Supper; The Descent from the Cross; Christ's Commission, 'Go ye into all the World', and St. Paul dictating to the beloved physician, St. Luke.[105]

While all of this spoke of the remarkable success of Anglican church life in 18th Division ('No priest could wish for a happier "parish" or sphere of work,' Cordingly claimed),[106] its high point came on 20 July 1942 when, after an earlier no-show, the Bishop of Singapore, Leonard Wilson, came to St George's to confirm 179 officers and men, bringing with him 'a small quantity of Bibles and Altar wine and wafers'. This was accompanied by an ordination to the priesthood of one POW who 'had been ordained Deacon in Singapore cathedral during the battle', and by a Communion Service which saw 'a Christian Japanese officer, an Indian Canon from the Cathedral, a Dutch General from Java, as well as British officers and men' all receive – not to mention a Jamaican prisoner as well.[107] (Remarkably, Bishop Wilson, described by Stephen Alexander as 'amusing and spiritual' and a 'striking preacher', was at liberty to visit POW camps on the island, and was not interned until March 1943.)[108] As Cordingly put it, this was probably 'the first time in the history of Christendom a Confirmation and Ordination have been held in a mosque',[109] and the occasion was marked (despite the short notice) by the attendance of Merton and of some of Changi's most senior officers.

Although the churchmanship in evidence at St George's was rather at odds with Merton's preferred Low Church style, he lent his full support to Cordingly and his remarkable venture in church-building (in both senses of that term). On 1 March 1942, Merton resumed his longstanding practice of reading the lesson at public worship.[110] In addition, as the brief entries in his pocket diary show, he attended church with different units on different Sundays, joining the Royal Artillery (for example) on 22 March, and the 1st Cambridgeshires the following week.[111] As Cordingly wrote at the time, Merton's demonstrative support was indispensable to the promotion of religious life in general:

The work of St. George's Church is made so much easier by the help given them by the officers, both senior and junior, and one feels so very grateful to them . . . In the General commanding our Division we have a really fine Christian gentleman. Never have I met a layman who has been so keen on the work of a padre. He supports everything that is done and is often to be seen at the weekday Celebrations [of Holy Communion]. His encouragement and interest helps so tremendously, because one knows his religion is a big essential in his life. Time after time in discussion with him I have felt how really and truly the facts of Christianity are a part of his life. No man can have done more in this part of the camp for the spiritual, mental and physical welfare of those under his command.[112]

Significantly, Merton's complementary interests in 18th Division's University and St George's Church converged in his suggestion that Cordingly's embryonic 'theological college' (essentially his regular meeting of 'men who want[ed] to take Orders') should be 'affiliated to the Divisional University', then in its planning stage.[113] Subsequently, 'and at the request of the G.O.C.', Lewis Bryan asked Cordingly to take responsibility for 'the Theological Faculty of our University'. Conscious of his 'great limitations, not being a scholar, and having no books',[114] pressure on Cordingly was 'brought to bear from all directions' and so the reluctant padre compiled 'a syllabus and a list of lectures' and recruited 'an Officer who recently got a first at Cambridge' to teach Latin and New Testament Greek. Other elements of his deceptively 'simple course' included 'New and Old Testament Theology and Dogmatics and Church History under two padres who got good degrees', while Cordingly himself contributed 'some talks on Prayer Book and Worship'. As the incumbent of St George's acknowledged, the whole venture was modelled on B. K. Cunningham's approach at Westcott House, and chaplains were asked to propose men who wanted to test their vocation.[115] Eventually, the Theological Faculty numbered around 30 students, including 18 '"embryo" Ordinands', among whom were 'some first-rate future parish priests'.[116] Significantly, the breadth of the Theological Faculty was such that it also had a Free Church department under the Welsh-born Congregationalist chaplain John Foster Haigh, chaplain of the 4th Suffolks and founder, in September 1942, of the pan-denominational Changi Free Church.[117]

However, Merton's channelling and promotion of the religious energies of the 18th Division was not without its controversies. In particular, and in keeping with his larger aim of restoring divisional life to a semblance of normality, Sunday mornings saw the return of the ever-controversial church parade. A perennial source of complaint since the Victorian era, and an issue he had had to navigate while in Lahore, weekly church parades were the focus of much discontent in the British Army during both World Wars and were finally abolished in 1946 – one of the lesser-known achievements of the post-war Labour government. Apart from the compulsory nature of religious observance, which many citizen soldiers found infantilizing and improper, especially when their officers often opted out, these parades (with their inevitable inspections) also required a good deal of preparation, with plenty of spit-and-polish blighting the traditional day of rest.[118] Though they were widely perceived as the epitome of army 'bull', and reminiscent of public school and even prison,[119] Merton was not in sympathy with such opinions. As a professional soldier, a Guards officer and a general who put a strong premium on the importance of religion, Merton fully supported this convention, appearing (for instance) at church parades of Cordingly's Northumberland Fusiliers, where he took the salute, on 28 June and 26 July 1942.[120] For one private of the RAOC, who was otherwise favourable to the cause of religion in Changi:

[To] the higher-ups churches meant one thing – despite the protests of many of the padres – church parades. Compulsory church parades. With, as far as possible, all the spit and polish of such a parade at home. They became in fact excuses for full dress commanding officers' parade. And were, accordingly, disliked as heartily as any compulsory church parade in England . . .[121]

Idris Barwick of the RASC, a genuinely pious soldier, recalled that, in his unit, the restored regime of compulsory church parade foundered on the resistance of chaplains themselves: 'Our RSM [Regimental Sergeant Major] started compulsory Church parades. However, after one or two Padres had stated that they preferred volunteers, the parades ceased.'[122]

However, even this bone of contention failed to dent Merton's standing, as instanced by the division's response to his departure from Changi on

16 August 1942. The removal from Changi of all POWs above the rank of lieutenant-colonel – which effectively represented the 'decapitation of the POW body'[123] – was the culmination of a Japanese policy of eroding the authority of captured officers and weakening the command structures of their POWs. While it was convenient to harness an existing military hierarchy for the purposes of prisoner administration, from the Japanese perspective it was also important to put captured officers in their proper place. Accordingly, on 4 March an instruction was issued which required officer POWs to replace their insignia of rank with a single star worn over their left breast pockets. (As Charles Wilkinson put it: 'All "pips" ordered by Japanese to be removed from shoulders. Allowed one "pip" only on left breast pocket.')[124] While the slight was understood, what does not seem to have been widely recognized was that this insignia was that of a private second class in the IJA, the equivalent of a British lance corporal.[125] A more obvious provocation was the introduction of Sikh soldiers of the INA as guards in Changi, together with the requirement that *all* prisoners salute them, as they would their Japanese captors.[126] As Major D. M. Shean, an outraged staff officer of Malaya Command, fulminated in his diary: 'We salute Japs as our legitimate captors but the last straw is to have to salute traitors. I'm buggarized [*sic*] if I'm going to and hope I won't be shot.'[127]

Ultimately, the removal of Merton, his fellow officers, and senior civilian administrators (including Sir Shenton Thomas, Governor of the Straits Settlements) was a function of the growing mobilization of Japan's captive workforce. In early July, Tojo directed its overseers in Tokyo that it be driven relentlessly in the interests of the war effort. According to Sibylla Jane Flower:

Tojo's address to them insisted that the POWs should not remain idle 'even for a single day, so as to utilize most effectively their manpower and technical ability for the expansion of our industries and to contribute to the execution of the great East Asia War'.[128]

Hence, 'in removing these men the Japanese both eliminated the need to negotiate with any officers other than those in direct command of labour, and nullified possible threats to security in the way of organized resistance'.[129] What caused real confusion, however, were the destinations of the two overseas parties which sailed from Singapore on 16 August. The first, denominated the 'Special Party', of which Merton was a part, comprised 378 Britons and 22 Australians, whose destination transpired to be Formosa. However, Francis Dillon remembered that, at the time, it was understood only that it was heading 'to an unknown destination by sea'.[130] The other party, dubbed 'Japan "B"', sailed for Korea and included a large proportion of technicians and engineers.[131]

Still, the implications of this development were immediately obvious to the inmates of Changi. Firstly, there was the administrative confusion it left in its wake. After the departure of the 'Special Party', the senior British officer left at Changi was Lieutenant-Colonel E. B. Holmes of the 1st Battalion of the Manchester Regiment, part of Malaya's pre-war garrison, whose hasty promotion to colonel, by Percival, went unrecognized by the Japanese, and who held no authority over the Australians.[132] Thus, as Blackater grimly put it, 'the reign of Lt.-Cols. came into being'.[133] Secondly, there was the effect of their departure on what little leverage the POWs possessed, a fact evident even to those in the ranks. Writing worriedly in the light of this news, Charles Steel of the 135th Field Regiment noted that: 'A bad thing has happened. All senior officers over the rank of Colonel, i.e. Brigadiers and Generals are to go to Japan. Bad for us, because the higher the rank the better bargaining powers we have with the Nips.'[134] And, as Idris Barwick stated:

We had taken it for granted that our officers would remain with us. Despite the hatred we often felt towards them for their selfish ways and their failure to make the least effort to share the hardships of prison life with us, they dealt on the black market for decent food, for which, unlike us, they had the money to pay and which was so desperately needed by so many sick men ... Their selfishness and seeming indifference to our suffering and hardships made us pretty sore. Nevertheless, there was a certain feeling of security whilst they were there. Consequently, when the news came that all officers above the rank of Lieutenant Colonel were to go to Japan [sic], it came as a bit of a blow.[135]

In the event, such unease proved well-founded, for an almost immediate sequel to the departure of the Special Party was the notorious 'Selarang Incident' of September 1942. Prompted by the advent of a new Japanese commander of POW camps in Malaya and Sumatra, Major-General Shimpei Fukuye, and by the attempted escape (and consequent execution) of four POWs from Changi, this was sparked by Japanese demands that all prisoners sign a printed personal pledge that they would not, 'under any circumstances, attempt escape'. Faced with near-universal refusal, the Japanese marched more than 15,000 POWs from Changi to Selarang Barracks where, after a three-day stand-off, and coerced by the growing threat of hunger, thirst and disease, 'Colonel' Holmes finally ordered all ranks to sign it.[136]

While Idris Barwick, as we have seen, excluded Merton from his blanket condemnation of senior officers,[137] Merton's leadership continued to show itself amidst his preparations for departure. After obtaining 'special permission' to visit the smaller POW camp at Bukit Timah, Merton spoke for the last time with Philip Toosey of the 135th Field Regiment, always a kindred spirit and even, by now, a protégé. Shaking Toosey warmly by the hand, Merton told him, 'I've seen what you are doing, Phil, just carry on like that until the end of the war and God bless you.'[138] And the sadness at Merton's departure was widespread, with Charles Wilkinson writing in his diary on Sunday 16 August:

A very sad day indeed! The General (Beckwith-Smith) together with all the other Generals, all the Brigadiers and some of their staffs left for Japan today. All the 18th Division lined the roads and gave Gen. Beckwith-Smith ('Beckie' [sic] to all of us) a great send-off. He was obviously moved and so were we. He will be a great loss to us all! Archie Bevan went too. I went on to the Gun Park with Padre Cordingly and said goodbye to them. I wonder if we shall ever see them again? It looks very much like the end of the 18th Div.![139]

In a similar vein, Harry Silman wrote:

This morning . . . the first Japanese party left. It included from 18 Div colonels and upwards. All the troops lined the roads and gave the departing brass hats three rousing cheers. I went along also to bid my adieu to the chief who was obviously affected – tears were in his eyes as he leant out of his car to respond to the cheers of his men. It was a touching scene – a general saying goodbye to his Division – whom he may never see again and whom he had such a raw deal with.[140]

As for Ronald Horner of the RASC:

All Generals, Brigadiers, and full Colonels together with sundry staff officers and about 2,000 [other ranks] left today for either Formosa or Japan. We lined the route and cheered 'Becky' and our Brigadiers on their way. Poor 'Becky' was terribly affected; he was a grand man and I think blames himself quite unnecessarily for our being brought here when the general consensus of opinion was that the chances of holding the Island were pretty remote.[141]

Horner went on:

I think he had a very rough break, two-and-a-half years training a division and then not only see it put into front line action straight from landing and fighting a type of warfare in which they were completely untrained, but also seeing the various brigades and battalions under his command taken away by Malaya Command so that he hardly could be aware who he still had left under his command.[142]

Even John Coast was sympathetic, despite their differences, and especially given what followed:

We had our last Lining of the Route [when] all the officers over the rank of Lieut.-Colonel left for Japan. From then on a Lieut.-Col. was the highest British rank left in Singapore. We learned within a month or two that our General, whom everybody respected as a soldier, and of whom everyone was fond as a man, had died of diphtheria on the voyage. This was a blow felt by everyone in the Division. We knew his courageous record in France, and we sympathised because he had never even had the chance to command his own division in Singapore. It was a very sad business, and it rather filled us with alarm that travelling conditions under the Nips should be so bad that a British General could die in such a manner. It seemed such blatantly bad propaganda for themselves.[143]

The exchange of farewell messages that passed between Merton and his units prior to his departure testified to the strong bond of mutual affection that had formed in captivity. On behalf of the 135th Field Regiment, a message was sent from Bukit Timah Camp which read:

Dear General Beckwith-Smith,

I, with many others here, would have liked to wish you good luck goodbye and God speed on your journey . . . May I wish you that now and hope that one day in the not too distant future my Regiment may have the honour to serve under your leadership once more or perhaps march our final March Past past you back [in] civilian life when this war is won and over. Our esteem for you is not a thing which it is really ever possible to show but it is very much a real thing. Once more good luck and a safe return.

Yours very sincerely, Granville Keane. Capt. R.A.[144]

From Lieutenant-Colonel Rhys Thomas of the 5th Beds and Herts came the following:

My dear General,

I had hopes of getting up to see you before you were taken away from us, but it doesn't now seem possible.

May I therefore attempt to express in writing the blow it is both to me and all in my Battalion at being parted. We had begun to take it almost for granted that the separation from you which we most feared was not to be, but the blow has fallen. We shall all miss you more than you can possibly guess. You have always, if I may be allowed to say so, been such a grand example to us all, that I, as a commanding officer, feel that in your absence, we may not be good enough to carry on your traditions but I promise that we will all do our damnest [*sic*] not to let you down.

May I thank you with my deepest thanks for all your help and guidance, in all affairs, both to me personally and all under my command.

If at any time I or my Battalion have in any way disappointed you, will you please accept my humble apologies. I had hoped we were still to be given a chance, in the future, of showing you that your efforts to train us had not been wasted.

I and all my officers and men send you our very best wishes and hopes that it will not be long before we are again united.
May I ask you to pass on to those going with you our best wishes to them . . .[145]

For his part, in a 'Special Order of the Day' to his Division, Merton declared that:

On my departure for Japan I wish to take what may be my last chance to thank all ranks for their cheerful serious and loyal support on many shores and seas during the two years in which I have had the honour to command the Division.

I regret that I have been unable to lead you to the success in battle to which your cause and your sacrifice is entitled and although I leave you with a heavy heart I carry with me many precious memories and a sense of real comradeship such as could only have been inspired by the trials and disappointments which we have shared in the last few months. Difficult days may still be ahead but I know that the spirit which today animates all ranks of the Division will prevail and form the corner stone on which day a just and lasting peace will be founded. God grant that that day may not be long delayed and that we may soon meet again.

Meanwhile GOOD LUCK, HEADS UP – KEEP SMILING.

Signed M Beckwith Smith
Major General
16th August 1942[146]

This mutual regard and emotional farewell stood in striking contrast to the feelings of Major Shean at the departure of the senior officers of Malaya Command, of whom he wrote:

Well – the Special and A Japan party [sic] left yesterday. It is probably a day unparalleled in British military history that so many senior officers have left their troops and staff and left so few regrets behind. We all naturally went and said goodbye but it was pretty insincere on both sides. It's not so much that we do not like our commander [Percival] and senior staff officers for anything they did or did not do during operations, but is due to (a) what we think was their weak and vacillating policy with the Japs once we've been their prisoners and more especially (b) their complete lack of personal and friendly interest in their subordinates and their selfishness in ensuring that they lived at such a high standard here that they were completely blinded to the needs of all the rest . . . it's very sad and never before have I seen so many senior officers thoroughly despised . . .[147]

E. C. Dickson put the matter more succinctly, though with damning indifference: 'Generals go to Japan. Generals in one truck with their baggage.'[148]

9

Letters from captivity

If Merton's revival of the 18th Division was regarded as something of a triumph (one whose progress was marked by short, staccato entries in his small 1942 pocket diary), his hidden thoughts and struggles in Changi (and, later, in Formosa) were recorded in a series of 37 letters written to Honor from February to November 1942. Highly personal in nature, they remained, of necessity, unposted at the time but were carefully preserved after Merton's death. All of this was divulged in a letter written to Honor in December 1945 by Major-General Keith Simmons, the former commander of Singapore's Southern Area and Merton's roommate on Formosa, which was sent by diplomatic bag via Rear Admiral Leighton Bracegirdle, the Official Secretary to the Governor-General of Australia.[1] Here, Simmons wrote:

Dear Mrs Beckwith-Smith

I have received and answered your telegram and also heard from the Governor General's secretary – and here at last are the letters for which you have waited so long. I sewed them up in February four [*sic*] years ago in some mackintosh silk – and no one has laid eyes on them . . . so I feel that they are at last something which you have been spared of his. It is so maddening that none of his other treasures have got through. I fear there is little hope now that anything from Formosa will be collected – but one never knows.

I hope to see you when I get back early next year and may be able to tell you some things you may want to know.

I am so sorry that these have been so long in coming – but I know you understand that I did not want to risk losing them.[2]

Written every week, usually on a Sunday (as much to conserve paper as anything else),[3] these letters reflected the loneliness of command and the inner turmoil that Merton felt throughout his captivity, however imperceptible these feelings may have been to those under his command. Indeed, as Merton wrote in his pocket diary, apparently for his own benefit: 'Being alone without feeling alone is one of the great experiences of life and he who practices it has acquired an infinitely valuable possession.'[4] In his first letter, written on 22 February, barely a week after the surrender, he reflected on the circumstances leading to the capitulation:

It became obvious when I last wrote that the end could not be much longer delayed and it was really only a question of whether the end would be a disorganised mixture of massacre and surrender, or an organised surrender as it was. The former, if permitted, might have delayed the issue here for perhaps 48 hours but most of my men were so tired that I don't think it would have made 24 hours difference. I want to emphasise that it was bodily fatigue and disorganisation – the latter due to being thrown into the battle piecemeal and to the fact that for the majority it was their first experience of battle – which made any further prolonged resistance on my bit of the front impossible. Our battle casualties have not been heavy but I never had any reserve other than R.A.S.C. armed as infantry and, at the end, not even them and one can't fight a battle without some reserve and without a reserve it was impossible to give any relief to the units in front . . . But enough of excuses – we were up against a well-trained enemy properly equipped for the task and right on the crest of the wave.[5]

Despite dogged resistance, there was no disguising the fact that the position of the 18th Division was deteriorating rapidly:

I was fighting battles to [North] & [West] and until the last day had more or less held my front though on the last day they made a penetration to within 1000' of my H.Q. which we were preparing to defend to the end.[6]

A pleasant surprise, however, was that conditions in Changi were proving to be fair, with Merton describing his accommodation as:

[A warrant officer's] quarter with lovely view to the [east] with my troops concentrated in a small area all round me. We have really been treated v. well so far and are living on our own rations but this cannot go on for long. The situation must be unprecedented – for we are still running our own show – officers and men have not been separated – [and] we are wiring ourselves in . . . The problem will be how to keep the troops occupied . . .[7]

The following Sunday, St David's Day, brought with it fond recollections of the Welsh Guards – of 'Windsor, Aldershot, The Tower', and of a Sunday service at the latter in 1937 ('about the only time David [King Edward VIII] went to church during his short reign', he noted ruefully). In personal terms, Merton had the consolation of some keepsakes (a Prayer Book, a copy of the Apocrypha and a clock) and food was fairly plentiful.[8] By 8 March, however, matters were looking bleaker, with the lack of contact with home proving ever more disquieting:

[M]y great prayer for the time being still is that somehow you may get news of me to confirm your faith that I am alive and well. They say that arrangements are being made for us to communicate with each other and for parcels to be sent us.[9]

Besides its isolation, the division (which Merton persisted in calling his 'family') was short of space and accommodation and, in consequence, there was the growing threat of disease:

My family has to close into a much smaller space [and] it looks as if many will be without any cover . . . I am frightened of the consequences of crowding so many into such a small space. The sanitary arrangements are so difficult, especially as much of the ground is only 8 inches above sea level at high water. There have been a good many cases of dysentery already and flies, which were unknown here before, have begun to appear. The conditions in our main hospital are a scandal . . .[10]

Japanese interrogations had also begun in earnest, and (as an obvious subject) he related that:

> I . . . have been for interrogation twice, the first by a junior officer for two hours – the second by the chief Colonel with whom we have to deal. They seem most anxious to know about the [number] of [divisions] in England, especially Northern Ireland. Luckily, one knows little or nothing. In my second go the talk ranged wide as to the causes [of the war] and he kept on saying we had made economic war [on Japan] first.[11]

Despite such coercion, a small victory could be claimed in that the Japanese directive on the wearing of rank insignia had failed to have its desired effect:

> We received an order early in the week for all officers to take down their badges of rank and to wear only one star on the left breast. This may be due to the difficulty our captors have in recognising officers as, being small, they can't see our shoulders and their officers are only distinguished by badges worn on the left breast. This is not the reason given by our command. However, it hasn't made any difference to our authority. I think the men resent the order even more than we do.[12]

Despite his limited supply of notepaper, Merton's twenty-fourth wedding anniversary occasioned an exceptional letter on Saturday 14 March. Here, Merton expressed what he saw as the indissoluble links between his marriage, his family and his faith in God:

> Twenty-four years ago today just about this time you had become my wife. I went to communion at 8.30 am in the little Mohammedan mosque which one of my chaplains has converted into St George's church to say thank you . . . for all the happiness you have brought me in those years, happiness which has increased in the strength and depth of our love almost daily [and] which is present with me now both as a memory of the past and [as] hope and faith in the future . . . And now at this moment I picture you perhaps going to church to do the same thing.[13]

This letter also coloured his customary weekly letter, written the next day, in which he dwelt on their sex life (a new but marked tendency in this phase of his correspondence) before recounting a visit from Percival, whom he wearily described as 'not a great talker or very strong character'.[14]

The following week, Sunday 22 March, Merton reflected on the prosaic details of captivity, with much of life 'made up of thinking about how to cook rice' – an unfamiliar subject, as we have seen, and on which there seemed to be much disagreement. Furthermore, in a reflection of the rural East Anglian background of so many of his 'family', Merton reported that:

Everyone is very busy gardening and two of the Brigadiers are mad keen. Massy-Beresford and Duke, the latter very knowledgeable. It is difficult to produce vegetables for 16,000 men from the ground available and with few tools and little seed. I begin to know what sweet potato – Kang Kong, aubergine, Chinese Radish etc. etc. look like. Luckily, a Division like this can produce experts in any trade. Nurserymen gardeners and thatchers have been in great demand, especially the latter as we have had some very heavy rain again and the shacks in which a large number of men are living have no proper material for roofs.[15]

Amidst all this, moreover, the wounded from the battle for Singapore continued to die, with Merton making special mention of one of his chaplains, Richard Cradocke Chalk of the Reconnaissance Battalion:

I have just heard that CHALK who was a curate at Buckingham and who was with the Loyals, one of my units, has died of wounds. I went to see him in hospital two days ago. He was a nice little man and did well in the battle. The M.O. of the [battalion] was killed beside him.[16]

As a mark of respect, Merton attended Chalk's funeral later that day.[17]

Even as the mood of the division seemed to revive as March progressed, the terrible shadow of defeat seemed inescapable. On 29 March, Palm Sunday, Merton compared his division's fate to the sinking of the troopship *Birkenhead* off the South African coast in 1852, an episode famed for soldierly fortitude in the face of hopeless adversity:

In many ways this has been a gala week for General Heath has been inspecting and lecturing my units and I think has been favourably impressed. He has told us the story of the campaign out here and one sees now the reasons why things went wrong . . . someday the true story will out but I shall never believe we ought to have been sent here as and when we were. After reading the story of the last of my family to arrive (which when published will rank with that of 'The Birkenhead') I realise more and more how lucky I have been and so, hard though it may be, it does help to make it a bit easier to wait for you, my beloved.[18]

However, Easter brought spiritual encouragement too, with Merton writing on Easter Sunday, 5 April:

We were up at 7.15 this morning before it was light to go to Early Service in the converted Mohammedan mosque . . . When we got to the church we found it full – but as it's open at the sides and back that did not matter and someone brought us a chair and we were able to sit at the back with the Prayer Book Sarah gave us after Dunkirk and look at the card you sent me last year – 'Christ be with me' etc. I must say I prefer going to church with you in our own dear homes – or somewhere we can have it almost to ourselves (as in Lincolnshire) or else where we feel we are alone – just you and I – amongst a host of strangers. Still, it is nice to feel like this morning one is amongst one's own men and saying thank you as one of them – not as their commander all teed up in the front seat. Since we have been here that church – and indeed all that we have been able to set up – have had a wonderful response. I only trust that the gratitude that these men must feel will last through whatever trials may still be to come.[19]

Merton's letters for the rest of April were notably upbeat, no doubt reflecting his fulfilling involvement in the initiatives that were helping the lot of his men in Changi. On 19 April he reported:

The University has been a success beyond all my dreams and I myself have attended the most interesting and polished lectures in Economics,

History (French Revolution, Queen Anne and early English). [Also] The Prayer Book. We have besides Faculties in Maths, Geography and English and next month we will add others in Agriculture, Music, and Military History. Most of it has to be done without any books. That boy [Ken] Tomkinson on my staff gave a most excellent lecture on Queen Anne and I hope to attend him regularly twice a week. I really am thrilled and hope soon to start a miniature Sandhurst for the young regular or would be regular officers.[20]

If, as we have noted, Merton's 'miniature Sandhurst' did not necessarily land well, in a talk with Percival later that week Merton urged his superior to be more assertive with the Japanese 'in regard to food, clothing and the housing of the Division', an admonition that appeared to meet with 'a certain amount of success'.[21] As in India four years before, wretched conditions in the hospital also aroused Merton's instinctive paternalism:

The food in the hospital has been a disgrace and I was so upset about it that I sent my own catering adviser (Kingston late of Mayfair Catering) in to try and put things right. He has done much in a fortnight but, oh, the apathy of the doctors to anything but the medical side and their lack of power of organisation. (The Hospital is really nothing to do with me but is next door).[22]

(Although he did not mention this to Honor, by an order issued on 2 April, Merton had sent an additional 30 orderlies from 18th Division to help in Roberts Hospital.)[23] On the spiritual side, Merton also had to deal with a younger chaplain (V. S. Robertson, apparently)[24] over the vexed issue of church parades:

My other excitement this week has been with one of the chaplains who, when he heard from Young [the division's senior chaplain] that I had said I did not think present conditions suitable for mixing church parades with voluntary attendance, went up in smoke. Young brought him to see me and, as so often, he had got hold of the wrong end of the stick and all was well. I gather, however, he spoke in anything but a Christian spirit in front of his brother chaplains and so I have, I think, said to you before . . . it is dangerous for a [commander] ever to touch on the subject of Church Parades if he can help it. I only did so in full consultation with Young and we agreed. He was even more upset than I was by his padre's conduct.[25]

Lastly, clearly underestimating his impact on the Northumberland Fusiliers on their regimental day, he wrote three days later: 'I had to address the Northumberland Fusiliers on St George's Day – seemed to go all right though I had nothing very original to say to them.'[26]

By May, as we have seen, 18th Division's University was in full swing. Although Merton evinced great interest in military history and biblical studies (as some of his jottings indicate),[27] above all the Theology faculty gave him the opportunity to deepen his understanding of the Book of Common Prayer, to which (by dint of frequent services and university lectures) he was becoming ever more attached. On Sunday 10 May, Merton noted of the Communion service earlier that morning:

Young took the service. He is most sincere and says the Prayers as if they really meant something – or rather – the beautiful thoughts which they are meant to express. I still attend a lecture every week on the Prayer Book given by [Cordingly]. We are studying the origin of the Communion Service and it is admitted that probably at first it was held in the evenings or any hour of the day – and I personally think it is a pity the Church now lays such emphasis on going to it fasting. No doubt there are reasons for doing so which we shall be told later but up to the present the main one seems to be that when it was held in the evenings or late in the day too many of those attending had already had enough wine. I tackled [Cordingly] as to why when he gave the communion in [St George's] (which I know I have already told you about) he always left out the words that mean Do this in remembrance of me. He had no reason to offer except that it saved time – and asked me if I thought them important. I said that as an ordinary layman they seemed to me just as important as the first half of the sentence. Young too left them out this morning. I shall have to tackle him too sometime and must go to the other man's church again and see if he has mended his ways.[28]

Staying with eucharistic matters, Merton also noted that:

> Of course, there is no proper wine left now, except the Catholics have
> a little. (They are not allowed to use anything but wine from the
> grape. They had several bottles stolen from their sanctuary when we
> first came here. Awful to think what so-called civilised man can do
> when discipline is relaxed.) Our wine is made of raisins and Young
> dips the wafer (a few still left) and gives the bread and wine in one,
> as it were.[29]

However absorbed in his divisional initiatives, or intrigued by the unfamiliar practice of intinction, Merton continued to model his familiar
and approachable style, emphasizing in the same letter that: 'I always try
to impress on my subordinate commanders and heads of services that
they have direct access to me at any time and that I am not just an image
on a pedestal.'[30]

By the end of May, Merton was resigned to 'a minimum of two years
in captivity', but was not unduly daunted by the prospect – especially,
as he noted on Whitsunday, 'if the weeks slip by as quickly as they are
doing now'.[31] However, he made a remarkable admission (notwithstanding his successful restoration of discipline, his promotion of a 'miniature
Sandhurst', and the overarching assumption that the 18th Division might
still be required for active service) that his personal appetite for fighting
was ebbing away. As he confessed to Honor on 17 May, in sentiments that
echoed his mood on the eve of war:

> I know we here must be prepared to take a further part in this awful
> contest, though what form it will take it is hard to see – and one
> knows that the majority like myself are only longing for the day
> when they can get home to their dear ones. Still there are some
> [who] feel that having come all this way and taken such a small
> and inglorious part in the campaign [they] would like to contribute
> something more to the final victory. I suppose if I was worthy of
> my position, I should feel like that, but I can't hide from you, my
> own, whatever I may try and do to the others, what my real feelings
> are.[32]

As May slipped into June, the rigours of captivity were ameliorated further by the opening of a divisional golf course on 24 May, on which Merton displayed his golfing prowess,[33] and by a gathering of Old Etonians to celebrate the Fourth of June. This major College festivity, which had been routinely celebrated on the Western Front a generation earlier,[34] marked the birthday of King George III (and in 1942, as Merton also noted, in an indication of his deepening interest in the Eucharist, was the Catholic feast of Corpus Christi).[35] Instigated by Merton, who had spotted around 30 Old Etonians in the 18th Division and adjoining units, the event was orchestrated by Massy-Beresford and featured a jungle picnic, toasts to the alma mater and an emotional rendering of the 'Eton Boating Song'.[36] As Merton put it: 'A wonderful setting – one could hardly believe it to be real.'[37]

Nevertheless, by this time there was a growing cloud on the horizon, for on Sunday 7 June Merton confided that:

[I]t will be sad if we are moved and have to leave it all as we have had notice a day or two ago that we may have to do [that] in the not far distant future. That notice has been the only upset of the week. I try always to remember the closing words of that prayer you wrote in your mother's prayer book which I lost at Dunkirk. 'Teach me to accept loss or disappointment as but straws upon the tide of life.' But sometimes it is hard when one has so few straws to cling to.[38]

Meanwhile, though this notification of an impending move had left Merton with 'a sort of hand to mouth feeling',[39] there was ample scope for further religious enquiry and reflection. On Sunday 14 June, Merton ruminated:

I feel we all ought to be quite clear on the differences between Christianity, Mohammedanism and Buddhism, but no one has ever taught me anything about the last two and about the first I feel like [H. G. Wells] that the Church has hidden the real meaning of Jesus's message behind a camouflage net of dogma and ritual. By all means let us have whatever tapestries different peoples find necessary and beautiful behind the cross but don't let them hide it behind them. I hope my own, my angel, [that] you won't think from this that I am becoming a religious maniac but as I see it the fundamental message of all these three religions is the brotherhood – not the equality – of man and the possibility (certainly if this is recognised and put into practice) of a Kingdom of Heaven on earth. Anyhow darling, I think we in our lives have tasted of such a Kingdom and I just live for when I may enter into it again and hope that such happiness and peace as we have known may be granted to the millions who have not tasted of it.[40]

As to its practical corollaries, Merton went on:

The only practical step I can think of taking towards doing anything about it under these conditions is to get a small committee of kindred spirits to think out how, when this is all over, we would make a better peace than was made at Versailles. At least we have the lesson of that peace and the years that followed, as well as the Congress of Vienna 120 years ago, to guide us. It will be interesting to see if it comes off [and] if we come to the same conclusion as our leaders who I am told . . . are giving some consideration to this problem as well as to winning the war.[41]

If the spirit of 1942 – with the momentous Beveridge Report and the publication of Archbishop William Temple's *Christianity and Social Order* – was evident even in Changi, within a week there were (illusory) signs that links with home were about to get stronger. On Midsummer's Day, Merton wrote:

I am very well as I tried to convey to you in a [postcard] which I was allowed to send you yesterday. That postcard has been the big event of the week – in fact the biggest event in all our lives since we became prisoners. It has given great happiness to every man each one of whom has been allowed to send one. As you will realise, if it ever gets to you, we are only allowed to send a very simple message and God knows when, if ever, it will get to you. Still, [it] made me feel much nearer to you and almost as if I am going to get a reply from you tomorrow![42]

214

As his next letter of 28 June testified, by now conditions in Changi seemed to be as good as one could expect:

Just back from attending a church parade . . . A very good show in all its aspects: the men all clean and shaved and quite well turned out, the service simple and sincere and everyone taking part and enjoying it. I think they even enjoyed marching past me after! We are indeed fortunate to be allowed to run things like this. I believe some of the Japs wonder why we – or so many of us – seem so cheerful and carry our heads high. I am really proud of the way in which my family behaves itself. It gives one great encouragement for the future.[43]

By this stage, Merton's interest in ecclesiastical matters had grown deeper still, his favourite interlocutor being Padre Cordingly:

The Padre (Cordingly) preached a sermon which I had more or less put into his head. He is the one who lectures on the Prayer Book [and] so I have had a chance to talk to him about what one feels with regard to religion and life. He preached another sermon about a fortnight ago of which he sent me a copy as he said I had inspired it. My main theme in my talks with him has been 'let's get back to the fundamentals of Jesus' teaching and then for the likes of very ordinary people like myself let the church translate them into modern terms so that they can help us in our everyday life'. I also said that I thought our bishops ought to get about more . . . I pointed out that I do not command my Division by direct dealings with the men – though of course I mingle with and talk to them – but by continuous contact and orders to my senior subordinates as well as by visits and inspections to their units. However, perhaps it's very wrong to try and compare the Church and the army. Still, he was impressed and it has produced two sermons which I think have impressed their hearers.[44]

He went on:

I have also had a talk or two with Young, but he is a much harder man and seems to me to have the typical sort of parson mind. That we are all frightful sinners and our only hope is to keep on going to church to ask for forgiveness – an attitude which I simply can't understand. I refuse to believe that the majority of us are wilfully sinning all the time. We all sin and make mistakes, some more frequently than others, and we are usually pretty conscious of them even if we aren't punished for them. What seems to me to matter is that we shouldn't go on making the same mistakes, and that is where we want Christ and the church to help us. But, darling one, you'll think there is something very wrong with me for talking to you again like this – but I assure you I am very well and quite normal only perhaps one has a little more time for reading and thought . . .[45]

As Merton's fifty-second birthday approached, and his university's inaugural term drew to a close, his correspondence illustrated the depth of his engagement with an institution which he tellingly called 'my university' and explained why his religious reflections were increasingly tinged by social and economic concerns. On 5 July he described how he had chaired a 'debate in my university on Friday – the subject being that further co-operation and control with the ultimate aim of nationalisation of the land is essential to agriculture'.[46] While he declined to sum up the debate 'because my positions might carry too much weight with their consciences under these circumstances', the occasion had been rather spoiled by a querulous subordinate who was clearly not pleased by Merton's 'miniature Sandhurst':

There had been one or two caustic but good humoured references to army life and discipline – though one young officer who is altogether a nasty piece of work had got up and made a most irrelevant speech (I had to call him to order) and made reference too to 'unpopular courses which are being run in this Division'. (He has been ordered to attend a course which I have organised for young officers to ensure that their military knowledge is kept oiled just in case it may be wanted again . . . I addressed the class yesterday and told them how dangerous it is to think that when our captivity is ended we are going to get straight on a luxury liner for home. That's what we may all want but if not required to fight again we will very likely be required

216

to do garrison duty in some corner of our Empire. People were rather horrified by this remark . . .)[47]

Still, and after nationalization of the land had been rejected by a gratifying margin of 81 votes to 17, Merton was treated to a display of affection that was clearly generally felt:

Ailwyn de Ramsey [of the 135th Field Regiment] got up and made a very charming little speech in which he paid tribute to my initiative and determination in getting the university going – and then presented me with a parcel as a token of their esteem, provided I promised not to open it until next Saturday. The applause which greeted his speech was, I felt, as genuine as his words and I was deeply moved as I told them when I got up and tried to say thank you. I cannot express even to you, my angel one, the great depth of gratitude I feel within me that one's humble efforts to do something – so little – for all these splendid men should have met with so much appreciation and as I said it was sufficient without any gift to see the interest which people had taken in both the Agricultural and Economic faculties.[48]

In a further reflection of a major issue in British public life, and of a question that had been close to Merton's heart since February 1940, Merton was getting to grips with the question of Religious Education in the 18th Division's secondary school, a modest endeavour undertaken with the less academically accomplished in mind. As Merton explained to Honor:

I forget if I told you that I have also started what I call my public school – a slightly lower standard than university – and going well with a good number of N.C.O.s attending. Subjects [include] English, History, Maths, Geography, French and German and this last week I have had the idea of including some religious instruction, which has of course delighted Young and his subordinates. We have our Theology in the University – are we here to make the same mistake as at home of divorcing all elementary education from any religious instruction? It's a difficult problem as one would like the instruction to include all denominations but of course the R.C.s won't look at it even if the Presbyterians would – and even if they all agreed on some general course the result might be wishy-washy.[49]

Resuming his correspondence on 12 July by reflecting on his 'Wonderful Birthday' the day before,[50] Merton admitted to being deeply moved by the marks of affection which the occasion had elicited. At the 'early service' at St George's, Cordingly had announced that 'our prayers were specially required for the Divisional Commander which always makes one feel a bit awkward when one is present oneself', and this had been followed by a birthday breakfast, a cricket match, a garden party, and by the premiere of *The Dover Road*. As Merton affirmed:

They gave me the most wonderful birthday yesterday. I wish you could have been with me in body as I know you were in spirit to share it with me. I think you would have been as deeply moved as I was by the many messages and tokens of real affection which I received from all ranks and classes. I think I spoke last Sunday of the great gratitude I felt within me for the many mercies which have been vouchsafed to me in this camp and now I feel almost overwhelmed by it all.[51]

Still, the ominous shadow of his prospective departure from Changi had not been lifted, and on 19 July he noted how 'this week the whole outlook has been altered as now I and all the senior officers have been ordered off to Japan and are due to start on Wednesday next'. Perhaps simply out of bravado, he claimed that 'now that it has come I am almost looking forward to seeing this new far off land'.[52] Though the move was confirmed on 16 July,[53] owing to 'shipping difficulties'[54] his departure was delayed for another three weeks, an interval in which he toured Changi's satellite camps in the company of Percival (17 July); Bishop Wilson finally arrived to administer Confirmation (20 July); and medical checks were undertaken prior to embarkation (21 July).[55] Amidst this period of transition, he made a series of final inspections in Changi (the 5th Beds and Herts were 'bad', the 5th Suffolks 'fair' and the RAOC 'satisfactory')[56] and his interest in religious questions remained undimmed. By 2 August, Merton was doubting the adequacy of the religious instruction he had received at Eton and acclaiming the usefulness of modern editions of scripture which aimed to relate scriptural injunctions to the conditions of ordinary life. Some intriguing specimens of this kind had been brought to the camp by Bishop Wilson, while:

One of my padres (Cordingly) has a lovely big Bible which translates much of the Bible into modern parallels. This is what I have been telling my padres it is their job to do. It's no good their going on day after day telling us we must lead a Christian life if they don't tell what sort of life they visualise that to be in these days – or, again, telling us what sinners we are unless they tell us what sort of sins we are committing. Young preached a sermon this morning in which he said the Empire had been built up by men who were Christians. I wonder – no doubt they read their Bibles more than we do. They hadn't much else to read, but did they understand it any better – and, if you think of some of the things that Drake or even Warren Hastings did, were they living a more Christian life than we?[57]

By Sunday 9 August, his departure from Changi had taken centre stage, especially with the arrival of ships loaded with repatriated Japanese nationals en route for their homeland. As Merton recorded:

We have not been moved . . . but the latest idea seems to be that all we senior officers will be off within the next 48 hours – and if that is so it may be that we shall be put on board these repatriation ships . . . The ships are due in Singapore today . . . and the passengers are to be given a chance to look round. We should not be too badly off, I daresay, if we were moved in these ships even if we were all crowded into steerage accommodation. Anyhow, I feel we should be better off and safer than in some old transport. It is very unsettling not knowing. I am certain we will go sometime soon . . .[58]

However, it was six days later that the order to embark finally came. Consequently, on Sunday 16 August 'most of the morning [was] spent in affecting goodbyes with all sorts of people'. When Merton left 18th

Division Area in Percival's car (not, it should be stressed, in the lorry occupied by most of their peers), their route, as we have seen, was lined by those of its men who remained in Changi. Greatly underestimating the affection in which he had come to be held, Merton observed that 'though the cheering was by order I think much of it from all ranks came from the heart. Anyhow, it was a grand send off and you can imagine how moved I was. Even [Percival] said [it was] a good show.'[59]

Events, however, were about to take a dramatic turn for the worse.

10

Karenko

In the wake of his gratifying send-off, Merton's first stop was the commandant's office. As he had remarked from time to time, his firm handling of his division had met with the approval of their captors (by the end of June, for example, he was convinced that the Japanese regarded them as 'a well disciplined lot').[1] Perhaps for this reason, the commandant's farewell was an affable one:

At the [commandant's] office a newly arrived Major General addressed the 40 or so senior officers, wished us bon voyage and told us we were going to a good camp where we should be well looked after by an officer whom he knew.

This fed a mood of optimism. In his next letter, written on 11 September after a month-long hiatus, Merton admitted that:

Most of us had visions of, if not a luxury liner, a passenger ship with cabin accommodation and bungalows by the seaside after perhaps a week or 10 days voyage. Having said goodbye to little [Lieutenant] Okasaki, who had really run our camp, our visions were soon to be shattered for on arrival at the quay side [there were] no signs of anything but dirty old cargo ships.[2]

Though not quite 'Hellships' (nor, at this stage, greatly threatened by Allied air or submarine attack) the squalid conditions on these vessels were much worse than in Changi. Before embarkation at Keppel Harbour, there was the novel experience of the 'disinfecting bath on board a specially equipped old ship'. There, together with the most senior military and civilian officers of the Special Party, Merton 'had to strip and get into a big tank where I found myself next to the Governor of Singapore [Sir Shenton Thomas] to whom I was introduced – surely a novel scene for an introduction to such an august personage'. After a 'cup of sweet tea' in lieu of a meal, the 400 members of the Special Party were put on board the *Fukai Maru*, 'an old cargo steam vessel built in England about 1900', before being transferred to 'a more modern looking cargo diesel engine boat', the *Kanjong Maru*. Apparently, this followed an objection raised by Percival, but the accommodation in the hold of the *Kanjong Maru* proved no better than that on the *Fukai Maru*. As Merton elaborated:

[S]he turned out to be our home for the next fortnight – and a nightmare of a home too, for I don't think any pen could convey even an impression of the atmosphere in that hold at mealtimes or at nights. Only 25% of our party was allowed on deck at a time – luckily, generals were exempt from this rule and there was only a very limited deck space on which we were allowed by day to sit and walk [and] by night to sleep . . . The cookhouse consisted of a wooden lean-to similar [to] the W.C.s which were exactly the same as on our first ship.[3]

In terms of diet:

[A]ll the cooking was done for us and the Jap privates by about 4 Chinese . . . Our meals were 3 a day [at] 9 am, 1 pm and 5 pm, boiled rice (no barley), vegetable or fish soup with an occasional tiny bit of meat in the soup and some very weak tea at odd times. Twice in the fortnight some attempt was made to give us a small roll each . . . Most of my neighbours had brought considerable stores of tinned food with them and so with the little I had brought I did not fare too badly but, by the end of the voyage, there were few whose tummies were not affected and 25% had dysentery.[4]

As for living conditions:

Only dimmed lights were allowed in the hold after dark, and sometimes not even those when our captors were in a bad temper, so you can imagine the difficulty of getting off one's bench and finding one's way up over prostrate bodies. Luckily, my pitch was on the outside of the upper tier not far from the stairs and I had next [to] me Keith Simmons who was at the Staff College (junior team) while I was there and has been and is being a good friend to me. My pitch was also at Percival's feet but, after considerable pressure on the Japanese Second Lieutenant who was in charge of us, as a great concession he was allowed to share a cabin with the First Officer. But all the rest of us including the Governor, the Dutch Governor of Java, two chief justices (the civilians were as dirt in our guards' eyes) had to sleep on the bench like the Bicester dog hounds – all mixed up with the troops whose language is inclined to become a bit tiring unless checked . . .[5]

The *Kanjong Maru* weighed anchor on 20 August, the Special Party having boarded three days earlier. On the dockside, under the impression that their departure was the start of an accelerated exodus of POWs from Singapore, Merton spoke to some of his soldiers labouring in Keppel Harbour, telling them that 'there would be no British troops left on the island in thirty days' time'.[6] Though this did not prove to be the case, the subsequent days, spent languishing in the roadstead, saw 'yet another medical inspection – (rods up our backsides)'.[7] Bearing north across the South China Sea, in cloudy weather 'reminiscent of our departure from the Clyde' almost a year earlier, by 22 August the *Kanjong Maru* was anchored off Saigon. There the Special Party learned more about their voyage: 'we learned our destination was Takao in Formosa where we understood we would be disembarked – travel by train to the North end of that island – thence by sea again . . . to the island of Shikoku in Japan.'[8] The next day, the *Kanjong Maru* joined an unescorted convoy of six ships bound for Formosa, reaching Takao a week later. Besides his reading matter (Dickens and Galsworthy), the scurrying of rats in the ship's hold at night, and Massy-Beresford accidentally throwing his false teeth overboard, the most notable features of the voyage were the services held on the only Sunday at sea, 23 August, when, as Merton noted:

I listened in while washing in my cup of tea to an early service being conducted on deck. At 11 am I attended matins and read the lesson 1. Peter 5.5. We had brought one of my nice Padres with us.[9]

The Special Party disembarked at Takao on Monday 31 August. Ceded by China to Japan after the First Sino-Japanese War of 1894–5, Formosa had a population of around five million and was one of the more established parts of Japan's Greater East Asia Co-Prosperity Sphere.[10] (See Figure 5.) Eager to parade their high-level prisoners before the inhabitants of Takao, the Japanese then marched them through the port to a 'very modern' railway station, where they entrained in Third Class coaches for the town of Heito, roughly ten miles away. There, after another 'short march to entertain the populace', they were transported on a narrow-gauge railway to 'Branch Camp No. 3'.[11] On arrival, in a local version of the 'Selarang Incident' which would soon play out in Singapore, the prisoners were paraded to sign certificates to the effect that they would obey orders and would not attempt to escape.[12] As Merton described it, with a candour characteristic of these letters:

After much numbering and counting … by a lot of Second Lieutenants and a fat interpreter we were marched inside the camp and formed up facing some tables and told the signing ceremony would begin after a speech by the Commander. The Commander turned out to be a Lieutenant but before he began his speech a Colonel from the army staff got up on the bench and we all had to salute him. The Commander then made his speech (prepared) in Japanese which was then translated into English, also prepared by a bad interpreter. He did commiserate with us as prisoners but told us we must now obey all orders issued without hesitation – that the British and US navies had been swept from the Indian and Pacific oceans – that Australia was about to be invaded – but above all that we had looked down on the Japanese in the past and they were determined, in other words, to get their own back. Percival was then called to the table and told to sign . . . a document which had printed in English at its head an undertaking to obey all orders and a promise not to destroy Japanese property or attempt to escape. Percival pointed out that he was not allowed by regulations to give his parole and anyhow that he was not prepared to sign a blank cheque. But they would not listen [and] began to get cross and marched him off to the Guard room. His chief of staff (Lucas) then stepped up to the table (I was terrified they would call on me as next senior) and began to argue and explain. They got crosser and crosser – our sticks were seized from us and we were shouted at and made to stand to attention but eventually Percival was brought out again and allowed to confer with us. Some were for, others against signing. A U.S. officer who had been in the camp for some time was produced and said he had done a month in solitary confinement but had to sign in the end. The fat little interpreter came running round saying, 'Hurry up, sign it means nothing'. In the end the majority agreed and I advised Percival to sign on the grounds that we should . . . all be made to sign in the end and that a signature obtained under these conditions meant nothing – moreover the chances of escape were almost nil. So, in turn we all signed (N.C.O.'s and men as well) and were then about 8 pm marched to our huts and eventually got a meal of rice and soup.[13]

For Merton and his companions in the Special Party, conditions at Heito were once again much worse than at Changi. As Merton described it, the camp was 'in the bed of a stream in the middle of nowhere'. Furthermore, its huts were

only coolie ones, bamboo and thatch. Long, with a hound bench down each side and tables and benches down the centre – about 100 of us in our hut. Luckily, they were cool and airy and, though full of rats, they were less disturbing as we slept inside mosquito nets.[14]

A post-war source was more forthcoming about these conditions:

Heito Camp, described as being similar to 'a low-class coolie camp', was sited in what had been the bed of a river, and the whole place was a breeding place for mosquitos. The huts, measuring 10 feet by 24 feet, were made of mud plaster, with earth floors and cane-thatched roofs, and each was divided by bamboo rails into twenty bays holding from five to seven men. The prisoners slept on rough planking benches. The huts were overrun with rats and other vermin, and the whole camp swarmed with flies. In 1944 the huts, which disintegrated in the rains, were replaced by ones with thatched bamboo latticed walls and tiled roofs.[15]

Indeed, so dismal were their surroundings that Merton wondered if 'taking us off that original boat [i.e. the *Fukai Maru*] may have upset all their plans – anyhow, it was evident we were not expected in this camp in the desert near Haito [*sic*]'. As if to prove this, on Saturday 5 September orders came through 'that Generals and Colonels were to move to another camp on Monday'. Petitions to take adjutants and personal servants were rejected, with one servant being allotted to each pair of transferees. Furthermore, and as Merton noted glumly, 'the request to take the chaplain with us was also turned down'.[16] Consequently, the last chaplain-led services Merton attended were on the morning and evening of Sunday 6 September, when he was present at Holy Communion and Evensong.[17] The next day, Merton joined the most senior members of the Special Party for their next journey to 'Branch Camp No. 4' at Karenko.[18]

Taking their leave of Heito amidst 'the most terrific thunderstorm', Merton and his party of around 90 other prisoners then travelled by train, bus and (from Suo) 'a small coastal vessel' to the port of Karenko on the island's east coast, 'the whole journey lasting about 28 hours'.[19] From there, further divided into three squads of generals, colonels, and other ranks, they were taken by train to Karenko proper, where it seemed that 'all the population [was] assembled to greet us and see us into our final prison'.[20] 'Branch Camp No. 4', already home to 'senior American officers captured in the Philippines', had originally been 'a Japanese army barracks designed to accommodate 120', but was now home to around 400 POWs.[21] Remarkably, Merton's first impressions of the camp in which he was to spend the last nine weeks of his life were not unduly negative:

Inside the camp we were marched to a hut where we were first made to take off and hand in our boots – then addressed by the Commandant, a Captain who seemed a gentleman, and whose speech was quite reasonable and translated sentence by sentence instead of all in one go as at the other camp. After that we were made to strip stark naked and told to take out of our kits just the washing and shaving things, but not cutthroat razors, and other things for one night. These things and our clothing were then closely examined – the rest we were told to leave and we'd get back after examination next day. And then like little schoolboys we were marched off to our dormitories – given a kettle of tea and told to get into bed quick and get up at 7 am next day.[22]

In his subsequent letter, penned on Sunday 20 September, Merton expanded on his boarding school analogy:

We have now been in this camp nearly a fortnight and are settling down to the routine life of a private school – for our life is ordered and we live, and we are treated exactly, as I was at Warren Hill forty-two years ago. The bugle calls us at 6 am and the order is that we wash faces and make up our beds and roll up mosquito nets and be on parade for roll call by 6.30 am.[23]

However, and apart from mosquito nets, a glaring difference from the daily routine at Warren Hill was the nature of that morning ritual:

At 6.30 am we parade when the 2nd bugle goes, by squads and hang about until the Japanese orderly officer arrives, when we all have to salute him by turning our eyes towards him. He then visits each squad and we number off in Japanese and, when all squads have been so reported present, the orderly officer returns to the front of the parade and we all make a most polite bow (sai kay-ray) towards the Imperial Palace and I take the chance of saying 'God Bless my Beloved Honor' . . . That ceremony over, we do a few minutes P.T. (callisthenics according to our U.S. friends) until 7 am when breakfast appears from the [cookhouse] – carried by members of each squad in turn for their own squad.[24]

After breakfast, and now quartered with Percival and Simmons as one of 'the three senior British officers', there was cleaning to be done, followed by a shave and (in contrast to the intellectual riches of 18th Division's University) a German lesson with Percival and Backhouse under the tutelage of an Indian Army brigadier. The rest of the day was occupied by reading, playing bridge and supper, with lights out at 9 p.m.[25]

Besides the drastic contraction in opportunities for education and leisure, the diet at Karenko was more meagre than at Changi, especially in comparison with the standards Merton and his companions had come to expect. All meals were '(un)substantially the same – a small bowl of rice and barley and a small bowl of soup with vegetables – mostly roots – in it'.[26] As Merton testified on 20 September, acute weight loss was evident among the camp's existing American residents and he had lost at least a stone in only a month. And, unlike the situation at Singapore, there was no local currency with which to buy additional supplies.[27] With hunger a growing problem, the captive officers 'were eventually told that they would have to work if they wished more'.[28] Technically, these terms were in breach of the Geneva Convention but, given the prevailing hunger at Karenko, and as Gavan Daws has remarked, 'just about all of them voted with their stomachs and swapped their convictions for a hoe'.[29] As a result:

Farm work began at a slow pace towards the end of October, but soon increased to six hours of digging for those under the rank of Governor and Lieutenant-General and under the age of 60; those above these ranks and age herded goats.[30]

Besides hunger, there was also the threat of disease. On 20 September, Merton wrote that there had been a confirmed case of diphtheria and that 'for the last week we have all gone about with linen masks over our noses and mouths'. Inoculations had also been administered for dysentery, and sanitary arrangements had been tightened as a precaution.[31]

In addition to the heightened dangers of malnutrition and disease, there was also a marked increase in the beating of prisoners. With the most senior high-level Allied prisoners now concentrated in one place, these were the objects of a concerted campaign of intimidation and humiliation which commenced on 22 September (and which the prisoners came to term 'The Hate').[32] As Mark Felton has written in *Coolie Generals*:

To state that the regime at Karenko was appalling would be an understatement, and was deliberately made so by the Japanese who seemed to take a childish delight in bullying and assaulting the members of the Senior Officers Party at every opportunity. Discipline in the camp was enforced with the utmost brutality, and stemmed directly from the Commandant's orders.[33]

That commandant was a Captain Iwamura, who was later executed for war crimes owing to his subsequent record at Formosa's 'Branch Camp No. 1' which served the infamous Kinkaseki copper mine.[34] As a British investigation said of Karenko: 'Discipline was very strict and the prisoners were never free from the attention of the guards, "who displayed great ingenuity in inventing new reasons for exercising their apparently unlimited powers".' Significantly, it noted, within six months 'most of the officers had been struck'.[35] As at Changi, such assaults ostensibly arose from questions of military etiquette, with an order being issued which required 'all prisoners, regardless of rank . . . to salute *all* the Japanese staff and civilian employees of the camp'.[36] There was also an expectation that prisoners bow to their captors.[37] As was no doubt intended, this gave ample scope for the summary beating of prisoners caught unawares by their guards, or those who were deemed insufficiently deferential.[38]

And Merton was an early victim, being struck on the very first day of 'The Hate' by a Formosan guard who was fondly known as 'Scarface' or 'Satan'. On 27 September, and with his supply of writing paper now dwindling to the point where he had to 'limit' himself 'to these 2 pages weekly', Merton wrote: 'I had the indignity of having my face slapped on Tuesday past by a Japanese [*sic*] private soldier for alleged failure to salute him. There have been many other incidents but of these another time.'[39] According to the American Lieutenant-General Jonathan M. Wainwright, who mistakenly dated the incident to October:

Beckwith-Smith passed a Jap private near the parade ground . . . The British general gave the sneering man a good British salute, but the Jap did not like it . . . He chased after the general, wheeled him around roughly, and hit him twice in the face with clenched fists. It was so outrageously unfair that it made all of us boil with anger. Beckwith-Smith staggered back but did not fall. And, as furious as he was, he had the presence of mind not to strike back – or he most certainly would have been killed.[40]

When Percival and Wainwright (a cavalryman by background, who shared equestrian interests with Merton)[41] later wrote a letter of complaint and demanded to see the commandant, they were rebuffed by a subordinate, Lieutenant Nakashima, who

> glanced through the letter rapidly and flew into a rage. He shouted that we would not see the camp commander and that if we ever wrote another such letter of protest he would personally see to it that we were severely dealt with.[42]

Still, their temerity may have had some effect, for Merton wrote in his weekly epistle of Sunday 4 October:

> [I]t has been very noticeable that incidents have decreased . . . other than finding some wretched officer or man kneeling on the concrete floor in the [latrine] at 1 am because he has failed to bow to a sentry hidden in the dark outside. There has been no striking recently except for Keith [Simmons] who got a body blow with his own stick which had been tied as a clothesline to our veranda balcony by the same little devil who struck me – mad with rage because the stick looked like a machine gun pointing at a sentry down below.[43]

Amidst the ambient hunger, disease and brutality of Karenko, Merton drew ever more solace from public worship and the Book of Common Prayer, his old copy having been replaced by his younger daughter. On 27 September he wrote to Honor:

> We have just had our little service in the open. Each squad takes it in turn to run it as we have no Padre. It is our squad's turn next Sunday and Percival has warned me to take charge. I wish I had you to help me work it out, but your loving spirit is ever with me and I have the Prayer Book that Sarah gave me to replace the old family one of yours which I stupidly left behind on the mole at Dunkirk.[44]

On 4 October, after the service in question, he went on:

> And now my own I must tell you a little about the service I conducted this A.M. A lot have come to me since and said nice things but the

nicest I've heard was from a U.S. Private who said he reckoned they ought to make that little red headed Britisher the camp chaplain. We had 4 hymns, choice very limited. Love Divine, Holy, Holy, Holy, Guide me O thou Great Redeemer. I read Holy Father, in thy mercy as a prayer which I think moved them. I said the Benediction and thought of Mum's tune. How I wish I could sing or even hum . . . My own I know you helped me in that service as you do in all things and are ever nearer to me and dearer.[45]

Later, Wainwright recounted this service in his memoir, *General Wainwright's Story*, which was first published in 1945. Describing Merton as 'a first-class gentleman and soldier', who had been 'badly used' but kept his spirits up and proved 'a comfort to us all', Wainwright recalled that:

[O]ne Sunday morning we saw his fine reserve break up. We had been holding a religious service each Sunday since our arrival at the camp, though we had no chaplain. Two or three officers had copies of the Episcopal prayer book with them, and they would alternate in conducting services. We held such meetings near the parade grounds.

After General Beckwith-Smith joined us, and we learned that he was more than familiar with the prayer book, we asked him to conduct a service.

It rained hard that October morning, and after some deliberation the Japs permitted us to hold our service in the barracks, in a room which apparently had been used for classroom work for the Jap military.

General Beckwith-Smith used a Church of England prayer book that morning . . . All went well for a time, but then he began to read a prayer asking God's blessing on our loved ones and friends.

In the middle of the prayer, with all its unbearable visions of home, his voice suddenly broke and softly, helplessly, he began to cry. He could not stop it, nor could we. He turned his back to us for a long time, and when he could control himself he turned again and continued.[46]

Merton, significantly, made no mention of this incident in his letters to Honor – another sign, along with his boarding school trope, of his intention to shield her from the realities of Karenko (where, to add to its miseries, there were even earth tremors that autumn).[47] Instead, in his letter of 11 October, while their 'special relationship' matured in secular terms, he dwelt on the religious and liturgical differences between Britons and Americans:

Just back again from our little Sunday morning service which, I think I told you, each squad of officers takes [in] turn. They wanted me to do it again but I said, though willing, I thought it a mistake as by having someone from a different squad each Sunday gets variety and caters for all the different tastes whereas I can only stick to our own Prayer Book which, however, in my opinion, grows more sound and splendid each time I open it. I have had many more compliments on last Sunday and I have just lent my Prayer Book to an American who wants to copy out that hymn for our absent Loved ones. I gather [that] the majority of the Americans who go to church at all are Wesleyans [n.b. Methodists – the Wesleyan Methodists were a British, rather than American, denomination] or Baptists. Such Hymns as we have in common vary considerably in the wording and very few of the tunes are the same. There is even a slight variation in their wording of the Lord's Prayer ...[48]

Still, despite the prisoners' successful expedients, the lack of ordained clergy at Karenko was keenly felt, with Merton continuing:

I only wish we had the chaplain with us who started with us when we left Singapore. The authorities here have turned down the request of the R.C.'s in the camp for a Priest from the town to visit them but I propose to put in a request all the same for that chaplain to be allowed to come and give us Communion here about Xmas.[49]

As the autumn passed, Merton's correspondence also dwelt on more secular matters. The commencement of work meant that a small sum of pay was issued on 30 September.[50] Lieutenant-General Ando, the Japanese Commander-in-Chief in Formosa, visited Karenko in early October, presenting the prisoners with a pig which, when added to the camp staple of vegetable soup, 'lasted us for 3 meals'.[51] An assurance was also given that, starting with Percival, all prisoners would be able to write a letter home, a fabled letter that soon became just a postcard.[52] The prisoners' 'heavy baggage' also arrived – late and, in Merton's case, minus razor blades, scissors and all 'tobacco and eatables'.[53] Japanese intelligence-gathering continued with the distribution of a personal questionnaire, in which Merton declared that 'my only wish was to live peacefully at home with my family'. On 18 October he also mentioned that:

> We are in the midst of what we are told is the Japanese Harvest Festival. It appears to last 3 days though one doesn't see much outward signs of it except the non-arrival of stores etc. We were all made to parade yesterday and the Commandant explained to us how the good crops were due to God the Sun and so we must all salute him which we proceeded to do by bowing in the direction of the [Imperial] Palace. As yet the bountiful crops have not reached us . . .[54]

There was, furthermore, a trickle of often partial or garbled news about the wider war. In the same letter, Merton reported how news of the sinking of an unnamed Japanese ship had come through – one with, it was said, '1500 British Prisoners of War on board and only 300 saved'. Fearful that these might be the members of the Japan Party who had left Changi in mid-August, who included officers and men of the 18th Division, Merton confessed to 'feeling weak' and wrote to Honor:

> We are terribly afraid that Hutch and Andy and all my friends may have been on board. I have often wondered if my decision to move them to Japan was the right one – but I don't really think I had much alternative – still I did not sleep much the night I heard about it. One prays it may not be true and anyhow not them – but I'm afraid . . .[55]

In fact, the ship in question was the *Lisbon Maru*, which was torpedoed by an American submarine in the South China Sea on 1 October. Sailing from Hong Kong to Japan, the prisoners on board – hundreds of whom were either drowned or shot by the Japanese – had been captured at the fall of Hong Kong.[56] It was, therefore, with a measure of guilty relief that Merton noted in his pocket diary on 17 October, 'Papers show not our lot on Torpedoed ship.'[57]

In global terms, a Japanese officer had told Merton and Percival earlier that month that:

[T]he Japanese fleet was in the Atlantic and had suffered very little since the start. He also said that Stalingrad was only 1/3 in German hands – we had been told it had fallen weeks ago – and that the Russian army was fighting very well. Alex was in command in Egypt. Auchinleck, like all other British Generals, had been defeated and resigned![58]

Remarkably, and possibly even because of his trials at Karenko and the huge divergence in their wartime careers, Merton could still feel a pang of jealousy for his glamorous contemporary, whom he mistakenly believed had now taken command in Egypt. Consequently, he wrote in his final letter to Honor on Sunday 8 November (by which time Montgomery had already defeated Rommel at El Alamein):

It is hard to imagine Alex in that position and one tries hard not to be jealous – but grateful as one is for life and many other blessings it is hard not to feel sometimes one has had a bit of a rough deal. However, as you know my own – my only ambition ever has been to be allowed to live in peace with you – and please God that prayer may soon be answered. Meanwhile I promise you ... I don't mope and only really regret the increasing numbers of grey hairs in the moustache.[59]

However, by this point Merton was already feeling the symptoms of the disease that would lead to his death. Still sharing quarters with Percival and Simmons, on 18 October Merton had noted that 'both Percival and K.S. have been sick and I've had all the housework. K.S. has gone to Hospital now, sore throat – not diphtheria as far as we know, though there is a case and we have all been wearing masks again.'[60] On 6 November, Merton wrote in his pocket diary how he had developed a 'sore throat and a bit of a cold'.[61] Two days later, besides recounting the descent of 'a whole party of pressmen with cameras ... under a Japanese colonel', Merton was growing puzzled and apprehensive, writing to Honor:

Never have I wanted your love and attention more for I have a filthy sore throat and cold which came on the day before yesterday ... I am talking to you now ... sitting in Keith's ... armchair in the sun and warm breeze which is probably better for my throat than anything they have to offer me here, which isn't much, just what we and the U.S. people brought with them – nothing given by the Japanese. Of course, I have caught this throat from Keith and am terrified they may put me into isolation as they did him – why it has taken so long to come out I don't know. I am trying to avoid the doctors. Fred [Merton's soldier servant] had one a couple of days ago but it cleared up at once. I think Percival had a cold too a short time ago but would not admit it. I hope I don't pass this on to him or he'll be more gloomy than ever! I don't believe I've had a vestige of a cold or any illness since January '41.[62]

After penning these nervous lines, Merton's decline proved swift and dramatic. In an affidavit on the treatment of prisoners of war on Formosa dated February 1946, Brigadier C. H. Stringer, an inmate of Karenko and previously the Deputy Director of Medical Services in Malaya, testified that:

Attempts to get the advice and assistance of the Japanese doctor and to get supplies of anti-diphtheria serum failed. At 4 A.M. [on 11 November], when he was practically moribund, [Beckwith-Smith] was taken to a nearby Japanese hospital where a tracheotomy was done and he died shortly afterwards. No prisoner of war doctor was allowed to see him after his removal.[63]

Clearly, if Merton was stricken with diphtheria, there was more than an element of neglect in his treatment and, chronically weakened by a near-starvation diet, he could not survive the belated operation intended to clear his airways. As Wainwright later testified:

Major General Beckwith-Smith died on the morning of Armistice Day, 1942, of diphtheria and heart failure – and starvation. The American officers had become very fond of this plucky Englishman, but while we were grieved to see him go some of us felt in our hearts that he was better off than the rest of us.[64]

Because Merton had died with an infectious and potentially fatal disease, the disposal of his body was prompt and unsentimental. With no chaplain in attendance, 'Beckwith-Smith's body was cremated and the senior British, American, and Dutch officers attended the burial of the urn'.[65] This occurred outside the camp and, as Massy-Beresford noted, the small body of mourners in attendance was 'heavily escorted'.[66]

Merton Beckwith-Smith was the most senior British officer to die in captivity in the Second World War. And, for all their neglect and indifference, his captors could not ignore his demise. Consequently, Japan's official news service in Tokyo belatedly announced Merton's death on 19 November 1942, the London *Times* carrying a Reuters report the following day:

> The official Japanese news agency reported yesterday that Major-General Merton Beckwith-Smith died in a prison camp on Armistice Day of a heart attack while suffering from acute diphtheria.
>
> Colonel Robert Hoffman, of the United States Army, was at the bedside, together with other British generals. Brigadier Edward H. W. Backhouse (British Army) conducted a memorial service, at which 'Abide with me' was sung.
>
> Lieutenant-General A.E. Percival, Commander-in-Chief, Malaya, General Jonathan Wainwright, Commander-in-Chief American Forces in the Philippines, who was taken prisoner on Corregidor, and Major-General R. Overakker, of the Dutch Army, were present at the funeral. Major-General Beckwith-Smith commanded the 18th Division in Malaya.[67]

Hoffman, it should be noted, was the American interpreter at Karenko. According to Gavan Daws:

> He was the only American officer on Formosa with enough Japanese to qualify for the assignment. He was an intelligent, capable, useful man, a good camp diplomat. His reward was to have the Japanese shouting after him day and night, *HOH-MAN! HOH-MAN!* They hectored him, beat him, and finally drove him to a nervous breakdown.[68]

In addition to this announcement, Backhouse was permitted to write a short letter or postcard to Honor with the details of Merton's death. This was the first letter she had received from any of the prisoners taken at

Singapore, though Tufton Beamish (of Merton's staff) and L. C. Thomas (of the 9th Northumberland Fusiliers) had been in touch from India the previous March.[69] Backhouse reported that Merton, having taken to his bed two days earlier, had died just after 8.00 a.m. on 11 November. He had been well looked after by a medical orderly and by his soldier servant, Fred Peto, but, in Backhouse's words: 'the last few months had told on his general health, and when this serious illness overtook him, I am afraid it was too much for his heart.' That afternoon, at 3.30 p.m., and after observing the customary two-minute silence at 11.00 a.m. (not least because, as Wainwright explained, Merton 'would have been party to that plan'),[70] the prisoners at Karenko assembled to hear Backhouse read the Prayer Book's burial service (less the committal), to recite the 23rd Psalm and to sing 'Abide with me'. It was, Backhouse reported, 'a simple service such as he would have liked'. Merton's coffin was carried to a motor hearse by 'a small party of senior and 18 Division officers [who] went with it to the Crematorium'. Next day, Merton's ashes were returned to the camp for interment outside the wire.

In contrast to Merton's treatment when alive, or perhaps to ensure that his letter was passed by the censors, Backhouse insisted that: 'Throughout, the Japanese officers have been most helpful. The arrangements were dignified and simple.' While Merton's personal effects had been carefully preserved, his clothing had been 'distributed among those who need it most' (with Massy-Beresford inheriting Merton's 'peaked cap' complete with its 'red band)'.[71] In a more personal vein, Backhouse wrote of their mutual friendship, of their shared belief in God and desire 'to further His Kingdom', and of how 'all who had the honour of serving under him in 18 Division recognised what a fine commander he was'. More specifically, while Backhouse recognized that Merton had 'felt the surrender dreadfully; it was a heart-breaking end to all the work which he had done', he stressed that his late commander had risen magnificently to the challenges of captivity:

He said little to most people and carried on in the most amazing way to demonstrate to every officer and man how to bear the misfortune which had overtaken us all. These are no empty words . . . I know that every officer and man in the Division would wish me to express to you their sympathy and to tell you how they will always remember with pride that they served under a great leader whom they loved as well as respected.[72]

At Changi, where much of 18th Division still languished, news of Merton's death was met with outrage, sorrow and incredulity. A divisional memorial service was held on Sunday 22 November followed by another, more intimate service at Merton's 'home' church of St George's. As Padre Cordingly wrote soon afterwards:

It was a tremendous shock when we heard from the I.J.A. that he had died of diphtheria and heart failure in another prison camp overseas . . . To us it was a personal loss whose magnitude we cannot assess. Not only have we lost a man whose command we respected and whom to know was to love, but the Church on earth has lost a loyal and true son. He died on Armistice Day, and on the Sunday ten days later we, the remnants of the division, met for a memorial service. At Evensong in St George's we [later] paid to his memory that respect which we felt here as an intimate loss. He was an almost daily worshipper. May God rest his soul, he with 400 others have died in captivity, [and] we remember them and those who will mourn them.[73]

In the sermon he preached on that occasion, which later appeared in print, Cordingly described Merton as 'a constant visitor to India Lines, a cheery and a friendly man, [and] a man who loved St. George's'. Stressing his constancy as a communicant, their many discussions and his evident love for his family, Cordingly stated that 'never in my life as layman and priest has any person so influenced my life, and I suspect yours too, as did that great little man'.[74] Recalling 'the farewell Evensong' which Merton had attended before his departure, Cordingly repeated the sermon he had given on that occasion, a homily based on the words of Jesus in Luke 9.62: 'No man, having put his hand to the plough, and looking back, is fit for the kingdom of God.' In other words, Merton had been a model of Christian perseverance:

The example that was his must be ours, the faith that he showed and lived must be ours, even when it is hard to understand. He put his hand to the plough and he did not look back. The words of Saint Paul are words for our beloved friend 'Becky' – 'I have fought a good fight. I have finished my course. I have kept the faith – henceforth there is laid up for me a crown of righteousness' [2 Tim. 4.7–8]. May God bless him and his, and may God rest his soul.[75]

The same note was sounded by Padre John Foster Haigh, now minister of the newly formed Changi Free Church. In another memorial sermon to find its way into print, he dwelt more on the specifics of Merton's achievements and on their wider significance. While acknowledging Merton's 'charm, deep convictions, and large sympathies', his professional shrewdness and his capacity for friendship, Foster Haigh also stressed that 'Circumstances make men and nations.'[76] It was, for instance, in the harshness of the wilderness that 'the Israelites discovered God and Destiny' and that John the Baptist 'found his life's work'. Similarly, Merton 'reached his finest hour . . . when captivity settled upon his men', in 'a dark hour – full of tragedy and pain and bitterness'. In fact, he averred:

I shudder to think how deeply that hour would have affected us spiritually and morally, if the steady hand, and the clear shining of Christian idealism of the General, had not led us out of the wilderness of despair into the green pastures of an abiding hope.[77]

Rather than be broken by the calamity of surrender, Merton had chosen a very different course:

Slowly but surely, he organised his forces for his greatest campaign. His enemies were legion – not armed forces this time – but the soul destroying enemies of lost idealism, indifference, disillusion, spiritual and moral deadness. How thorough-going was his victory against all these foes, the blessings we now enjoy in this Camp are a glowing tribute.[78]

Foster Haigh went on:

His was the hand that brought order out of chaos in our medical services, breathing healing and comfort to our sick and wounded.

His was the hand that stopped the sickness of the morbid mind, by organising our splendid educational programmes, calculated to equip us men to meet the tasks that lie ahead in the brave new world. His was the hand that drove men to realise that they must keep their bodies fit by taking physical exercises daily. And his was the hand that re-called men to think more deeply about spiritual things. And as a result men have found a new lease of life – a new worthwhileness . . . When the history of this campaign comes to be written and the historian gathers all his facts together, the work done here and the leadership given by our beloved General, will shine out as the stars in the firmament.[79]

The 'secret of his greatness' was, he claimed, threefold: it lay in Merton's patriotism and love of 'all that was lovely and of good report, in this fair land of ours'; in his 'great love for his fellowmen', making him very much 'the "Tommy's friend"'; and in his 'great love for God', his faith being 'the master light of all his vision, the exhaustless spring from which he drew the living waters of guidance and inspiration . . . It shone out in his character. It inspired his patriotism. It dominated his love for his fellowmen.'[80]

However, though its impact was felt among British (and American) POWs in Singapore and Formosa, Merton's death made little impression at home, where, at last, the fortunes of war seemed to be swinging decisively in the Allies' favour. With Montgomery's triumph over Rommel at El Alamein (23 October – 4 November), the Anglo-American TORCH landings in Morocco (8 November) and Stalingrad still holding against the German onslaught, there was a great deal else to absorb the interest of the British public. Though reported in local newspapers in England and Scotland,[81] it was a relatively minor news item in the nation's newspaper of note. The Times' announcement of Merton's death on 20 November was made on page 4, sandwiched between a report on Pétain's exhortation to Vichy forces to continue their resistance to 'Anglo-Saxon aggression' in North Africa and an item on the sudden illness of Lord Londonderry.[82] A modest obituary followed on page 7, with the newspaper's daily list of 'Fallen Officers'. In professional terms, this noted the salient qualities and patent misfortunes of the late 'Commander of the 18th Division'. Quite aptly, it noted that:

His career was one of unbroken success, from the day when he joined the Coldstream Guards in 1912 [*sic*] to the moment when, with most of the division of which he was so proud, he was made a prisoner of war in Singapore in circumstances which made any other fate inescapable.[83]

Reviewing the course of Merton's career from commissioning to the outbreak of the present war, it noted especially his cool-headedness amidst the crises of Dunkirk and Singapore. Of his command of the 1st Division at Dunkirk, it claimed that:

Nobody better suited for such a role could have been chosen, and only recently a letter from a younger officer to whom warfare was then a novelty described how his own extreme apprehension at developments which seemed to him the last word in hazard were dispelled by the brigadier who continued to perform his task with complete unconcern.[84]

Subsequently:

An eleventh hour arrival in Singapore, in circumstances of unpreparedness for which he could have no shade of responsibility, brought active service to an end, and the last report of him was from a Malay planter who left him just before his division was overrun. He said, as all those who knew him would suppose, that to the end he remained quite undisturbed by calamity, continuing his duties even when the roof of his headquarters was burning over his head.[85]

Inevitably, the tidings of Merton's death raised public questions over the uncertain – even unknown – fate of tens of thousands of his fellow POWs in the Far East. As Eileen Backhouse, though the wife of a brigadier, had written despairingly in April 1942: 'One feels so helpless, as if the earth had swallowed them all up.'[86] Two days after reporting Merton's death as a front-page item, Dundee's *Evening Telegraph and Post* noted its wider reverberations:

The death of General Beckwith Smith, well known in Scotland, will bring memories in thousands of homes in this country. He was the first British general whose capture in Singapore was announced over the Japanese wireless. This was the first news to parents of soldiers of the 118th [sic] Division that their sons were probably in captivity. Beckwith Smith was essentially a fighter, and the fact that he was sent to a concentration camp to die from diphtheria is a double tragedy.[87]

That the fate of those captured at Singapore was now a political matter was made very clear by the paper's London correspondent:

Although Sir [James] Grigg [the Secretary of State for War] was unable to throw much light in the House of Commons on the recent statements that Malayan prisoners of war have been removed from the territory and are being well treated, confirmation is to some extent reaching London. Letters and postcards are being received in small numbers from the men themselves. One I saw, from an officer, informed his parents that the camps are well run, food adequate, and special facilities are being given for games, recreation and education.[88]

While this was not a grave distortion of the lot of officers in Changi, a few days later the highly uneven flow of news and information from the Far East prompted further questions in the Commons. On 26 November 1942, the *Derby Evening Telegraph* reported that:

Sir James Grigg . . . stated in a reply to Major S.F. Markham, M.P. for South Nottingham: 'The [1/5th] Sherwood Foresters were captured at the surrender of Singapore on February 15 1942. They formed part of the 18th Division, commanded by the late Maj.-Gen. M.B. Beckwith-Smith, D.S.O., M.C. No information is available with regard to the unit after the surrender of Singapore.'[89]

Furthermore, given the rancorous class-based jealousies and tensions that roiled in British society and the British Army in the war years, the fact that Merton's death was known and widely reported posed some awkward questions around the advantages of birth, wealth and privilege.

For instance, a marked interest was evinced (not least by one Scottish newspaper) in the value of Merton's estate, which in August 1943 was put at a tidy £106,000.[90]

In more personal terms, tributes flowed into Stratton Audley on the news of Merton's death, with others following in 1945 after the defeat of Japan and the liberation of its POW camps. On 20 November 1942, Colonel A. M. Bankier wrote to Honor on behalf of the Coldstream Guards, stating that 'Becky's death is a tragedy for the Coldstream, *for we always regarded him as really belonging to us* [my italics].' He also remembered visiting the 1st Guards Brigade in France in May 1940: 'It was at the time when the German advance began and the general situation was somewhat disturbing. "Becky" was completely unperturbed, in tremendous spirits and full of consideration for everyone else.'[91] Significantly, it was the Coldstream rather than the Welsh Guards who took the lead in organizing the memorial service for Merton at the Guards Chapel on 30 November 1942 – a service attended by Merton's family, by a representative of the Prime Minister and by a long list of aristocratic mourners including the Duchess of Marlborough. The suffragan Bishop of Hull, Henry Vodden, and the Chaplain to the Brigade of Guards, H. R. Norton, presided.[92] Three months later, in a reflection of the fondness which King George and Queen Elizabeth felt for the Beckwith-Smiths, and notwithstanding their closeness to the Duke of Windsor, the Queen wrote to Honor enclosing a photograph of Merton and her husband taken during his visit to the 18th Division in East Anglia in 1940. She also wrote, in recognition of Honor's ongoing work with the St John Ambulance Brigade, 'We felt so deeply for you over your terrible loss, and think it so brave and wonderful of you to carry on so nobly with all your splendid work – I do hope to see something of it on some future occasion.'[93]

The following year, in May 1944, amidst yet another reorganization of the camp at Changi, Colonel C. T. Hutchinson (or 'Hutch'), one of Merton's former staff officers, wrote to Honor recounting 'a little ceremony we had to-day'. Remarkably, even after the horrendous ordeal of the Burma Railway ('We certainly have been through many experiences and alas very unhappy ones too'), memories of Merton were still warm among the survivors of his old division. Written more in hope rather than expectation of delivery, Hutchinson's letter reported that:

A small wooden plaque – made of a fine piece of teak wood and carved – In Memoriam – Major General M.B. Beckwith-Smith, D.S.O., M.C., Commander 18th Division (and the [divisional] sign) who died at Formosa 11th November 1942, aged 52 years has been set up in the centre of [the] cemetery. Padre Cordingly took a dedication service which was beautiful in its simplicity. I was very glad Cordingly took the service as Becky had a special regard for him as a Padre. The Service was attended by a number of officers and men and each unit was represented. Unfortunately, under the conditions in which we find ourselves it was not possible to have the big number I would have liked to have attended and perforce many who would have liked to have come were not available.[94]

It went on:

Mrs. Becky we often think of you all and wonder how you are getting on. Becky's name lives amongst us all and it's amazing the number of private soldiers that still talk to me about 'the General'. He has indeed left us a very high standard to which to live.[95]

The lasting value of Merton's example was further attested in September 1945, when John Phillips, one of the 18th's first returnees (who 'flew all the way' back from the Far East), wrote to Honor on the abiding influence of Merton's leadership:

I cannot adequately describe to you what a blow Becky's death was to us . . . He was a very great gentleman and we all loved him . . . The work he did at Changi in looking after the welfare of the Division in maintaining morale and spirits was magnificent – we can never forget him and the debt we owe him for all his kindness and care.[96]

And this, it should be re-emphasized, had paid dividends on the 'railway of death', for as Phillips continued: 'I don't think I am exaggerating or biased when I say that the 18th Division as a group maintained easily the highest standards of morale and behaviour throughout their imprisonment, [and] they did not let Becky down.'[97]

In another mark of the enduring respect in which Merton was held, the post-war 18th Division Association (a group of officers formed in the early weeks at Changi)[98] featured his portrait in all its post-war publications, while his widow served as one of its three patrons, together with two of Merton's predecessors, Major-General T. G. Dalby and General Sir Bernard Paget.[99] Significantly, when H. E. I. Phillips called for a public inquiry into the fall of Singapore in October 1947, he did so because 'so much at least is due to the memory of those who died, and particularly of our gallant commander, General Beckwith-Smith'.[100] It was, therefore, a fitting reflection of Merton's standing in his old division that Honor, representing the British Red Cross, was part of the official reception party for the first contingent of 18th Division survivors who disembarked at Liverpool on 8 October 1945.[101] And the Red Cross was badly needed for, in a sign of the deplorable state of Merton's surviving 'family' after three and a half years of Japanese captivity, it was also reported that: 'Because of the condition of Service repatriates, special attention has been paid to diet, and on their six weeks' leave many will get priorities in shell-eggs and milk, with special vitamin preparations for those suffering from general malnutrition.'[102]

Despite these many consolations, the blow to Merton's family was a very heavy one. For the elderly Georgina in particular, the death of her only son, who had survived four years of fighting on the Western Front as well as the maelstrom of Dunkirk, was especially bitter. She died on Christmas Day 1942. In the wake of this double bereavement, Honor took comfort from a small group of 18th Division wives and widows known as the SOS Club, which gathered periodically in London from 30 January 1943.[103] Inspired by their long-term friendship and support, in 1949 she commenced a pilgrimage to the 'war cemeteries in the Far East', as 'photographs and details' were 'continually being sought by the relatives of those who lost their lives'.[104] Honor's journey was undertaken partly with the intention of visiting Merton's grave (which, like all British graves in Formosa, had been transferred to Hong Kong's Sai Wan Military Cemetery by the Imperial War Graves Commission in 1946), but a key incentive was her husband's own example for, as she confided to her friend and founder of the SOS Club, Mrs E. Horne: 'How often have I thought of all that my husband would do for those who served with him, and lost their lives, had he come home.'[105]

Although Honor was hoping that a memorial for Merton might be installed in the Guards Chapel from the autumn of 1943,[106] her plans were dashed the following June when a V-1 flying bomb destroyed the Guards Chapel on 'Waterloo Day' (Sunday 18 June), killing more than 120 people.[107] However, Merton's memorialization continued, albeit sporadically, over subsequent years. Twin memorial plaques were installed in St Paul's Church, Strathnairn and in St Mary and St Edburga's Church, Stratton Audley. Bearing the badges of the Welsh and Coldstream Guards, they commemorated their former parishioner in identical terms:

> To the Glory of God and in Proud and Loving Memory of
> Maj Gen Merton Beckwith-Smith, DSO, MC of Aberarder,
> Coldstream Guards 1910–1930
> Welsh Guards 1930–1938
> Commander Lahore Brigade Area 1938–1939
> Commander 1st Guards Brigade 1939–1940
> Commander 18th Division 1940
> Born 11 July 1890
> Died 11 November 1942 a prisoner of war in the Far East
> The Beloved Husband of Honor Beckwith-Smith
> 'And so it befell that when the hour of trial came, these men gave
> an example of courage and devotion the memory of which will
> never perish'.[108]

In February 1977, the white wooden cross that had marked Merton's grave at Karenko (and at Sai Wan, until it was replaced by a permanent headstone in 1950) was transferred from St Paul's Church, Strathnairn and laid up in the Guards Chapel at Pirbright.[109] In Sai Wan, Merton's headstone bears an epitaph appropriate for the dogged Christian warrior he undoubtedly was, and for the nature of the war in which he died:

FOR THE FAITH AND FOR THE FREEDOM OF MANKIND.[110]

Retrospect

Since his death in November 1942, the memory and achievements of Merton Beckwith-Smith have been buried under many layers of silence, distortion and amnesia. Even in victory, Britain's war against Japan took second place to its main effort against Germany, as the enduring moniker of Field Marshal Slim's 'Forgotten' Fourteenth Army serves to illustrate. In November 1942, despite being one of the very few British generals, and the most senior Guardsman, to die due to enemy action (or, in his case, inaction) during the Second World War, Merton's death was barely registered in Britain, especially in the wake of El Alamein. It was a legacy of much darker days amidst nationwide celebrations, for as Churchill famously (if erroneously) rejoiced: 'Before Alamein, we never had a victory. After Alamein, we never had a defeat.'[1] And what greater, unredeemed defeat than the fall of Singapore, a disaster of such magnitude that its potential reverberations – for the nation, the Empire and their war effort – precluded even a public inquiry? While it buried reputations (notably Percival's), its taint was such that there was little hope of redemption for those commanders caught up in its maw, however inadvertently.

And compounding the magnitude and ignominy of defeat was the scale and depth of the suffering that ensued, most infamously in the construction of the Burma Railway from June 1942 to October 1943, the hellishly voracious 'railway of death'. All told, one-quarter of their British Army POWs perished in Japanese hands, but the death rate among the 16,000 prisoners of the 18th Division – a large pool of prime labour – could have been as high as one-third.[2] Such was their suffering that a veil of silence was deliberately drawn over it after the war. As Sibylla Jane Flower has noted: 'The subject remained a painful topic as much to be avoided as confronted.'[3] The five-volume British official history of *The War against Japan*, completed in 1969, devoted only nine pages of an appendix to the experience of POWs, and a separate volume on the subject was quietly abandoned.[4] Though coloured in the 1960s by the need to cultivate Anglo-Japanese relations, after their liberation in 1945 returning POWs were issued with a written instruction – sternly entitled 'GUARD YOUR TONGUE' – to be discreet, to say the least, about their ordeal:

If you had not been lucky enough to have survived and had died an unpleasant death at the hands of the Japanese, you would not have wished your family and friends to have been harrowed by lurid details of your death. That is just what will happen to the families of your comrades who did die in that way if you start talking too freely about your experience. It is felt certain that now you know the reason for this order you will take pains to spare the feelings of others.[5]

Though tongues were loosened over time, especially after the egregious misrepresentations of prisoners' experiences in David Lean's Oscar-winning film, *The Bridge on the River Kwai* (1957), it appears that most former POWs obeyed this injunction, often suppressing their experiences at considerable (if hidden) cost to themselves and their families.[6]

If a prevailing silence enfolded the experience of former POWs, official recognition of Merton's remarkable role in Changi from February to August 1942 was equally unforthcoming – perhaps because it threw into question the conduct of other generals, among whom there was notably 'little appetite . . . to recall the captivity in any detail'.[7] Though medals are seldom won in captivity, it is ironic that, among his many honours and awards, Merton's greatest feat of military leadership – however widely acknowledged – went unrewarded after the war. In contrast, the outstanding leadership shown by Philip Toosey (which Merton had identified, endorsed and strongly encouraged) rightly earned him an OBE in 1946, and became a focus for some controversy after Alec Guinness's portrayal of the fictional Colonel Nicholson in *The Bridge on the River Kwai*.[8]

By virtue of his rank, of course, Merton was spared the degree of privation suffered by so many of his 18th Division 'family' – whether in Changi, on the Burma Railway, in Japan or elsewhere. Indeed, it stands as a perverse testimonial to the wretchedness of conditions in Japanese captivity that Merton (who was starved, beaten, deprived of communication with the outside world, and died through medical neglect) was counted, even in death, as among the more fortunate of British POWs. Though his sufferings were no less real, and his death no less avoidable, than those of the thousands of others who also died in captivity, as the decades passed his background and career also conspired to suppress his memory. As a man of considerable private wealth and personal privilege, a keen huntsman, a professional soldier, an imperial general, and even as a very public Christian, Merton seems less and less the stuff of an acceptable hero for the third decade of the twenty-first century.

However, while popular sensibilities have changed enormously since 1945, by the standards of his day the extent of Merton's accomplishments in Changi in 1942 – whether in establishing the 18th Division's University, driving the 'New Windmill Theatre' or channelling and promoting religious life amidst the physical and psychological wreckage of defeat – cannot be gainsaid. In 1941, General Sir Archibald Wavell, who played such a key role in determining the fate of the 18th Division, published his Lees Knowles Lectures, which were first delivered at Cambridge in 1939. Entitled *Generals and Generalship*, his volume presented the ideal attributes of the modern general. These included physical fitness; humanity and boldness; a strong grasp of logistics; and 'solid common sense, and a knowledge of humanity, on whose peculiarities, and not those of machines, the whole practice of warfare is ultimately based'. Summarizing the 'few principles that seem to me to embody the practice of successful commanders', Wavell went on:

A general must keep strict, though not necessarily stern, discipline. He should give praise where praise is due, ungrudgingly, by word of mouth or written order. He should show himself as frequently as possible to his troops, and as impressively as possible . . . He should never indulge in sarcasm . . . He should tell his soldiers the truth . . .[9]

As we have seen, and even in the desperate shadow of catastrophic defeat, Merton – uniquely, it would seem, among his peers – continued to fulfil these exacting desiderata. However much his work and legacy may have been obscured by the subsequent travails of a lengthy captivity, by a virtual post-war conspiracy of silence, by media obfuscation and by changing sensibilities in later decades, 80 years after his death it seems clear that he deserves much more than to have become a forgotten warrior.

Notes

Preface

1 IWM Documents, Brigadier Sir Philip Toosey, 93/14/1.
2 C. Smith, *Singapore Burning* (London: Penguin, 2006), p. 266.
3 P. Brune, *Descent into Hell: The fall of Singapore – Pudu and Changi – the Thai–Burma Railway* (Sydney: Allen and Unwin, 2014), p. 467.
4 M. Felton, *The Coolie Generals: Britain's Far Eastern military leaders in Japanese captivity* (Barnsley: Pen and Sword, 2008), p. 134; M. Gillies, *The Barbed-Wire University* (London: Aurum, 2012), pp. 198–201.
5 P. N. Davies, *The Man behind the Bridge: Colonel Toosey and the River Kwai* (London: Bloomsbury, 1991).
6 B. MacArthur, *Surviving the Sword: Prisoners of the Japanese 1942–45* (London: Time Warner, 2005), p. 46; S. Palmer (ed.), *Prisoners on the Kwai: Memoirs of Dr Harold Churchill* (Dereham: Larks Press, 2005), p. 92; J. Coast, *Railroad of Death* (London: Commodore Press, 1946), p. 54; I. Barwick, *In the Shadow of Death: The story of a medic on the Burma Railway 1942–1945* (Barnsley: Pen and Sword, 2005), p. 62.
7 Palmer, *Prisoners on the Kwai*, p. 92; J. Summers, *The Colonel of Tamarkan: Philip Toosey and the bridge on the River Kwai* (London: Simon and Schuster, 2005), p. 111.
8 R. Mead, *Churchill's Lions: A biographical guide to the key British generals of World War II* (London: Spellmount, 2007), p. 512.
9 Coldstream Guards Archives. Record of Service.
10 Coldstream Guards Archives. Record of Service.
11 IWM Documents, Brigadier Sir Philip Toosey, 93/14/1.
12 Smith, *Singapore Burning*, p. 266; Summers, *Colonel of Tamarkan*, p. 111.

1 'Second to none' – the Coldstream Guards

1 MBS/1 0401.

2 *Manchester Courier and Lancashire General Advertiser*, 6 November 1902, p. 10; *Western Gazette*, 10 August 1888, p. 7.

3 MBS/1 'The Fascinating Background of Georgina Butler Moore'; <http://places.galwaylibrary.ie/history/chapter136.html>, accessed 15 September 2022.

4 <https://www.chch.ox.ac.uk/fallen-alumni/major-general-merton-beckwith-smith>, accessed 15 September 2022.

5 *Aberdeen Journal*, 5 June 1921, p. 7; *Aberdeen Press and Journal*, 17 September 1926, p. 6.

6 MBS/1 0404.

7 M. Snape, 'Sir Douglas Haig, Religion, and the British Expeditionary Force on the Western Front' in P. McFarland and H. Pym (eds), *Scots in Great War London* (Warwick: Helion, 2018), p. 215.

8 <http://places.galwaylibrary.ie/history/chapter136.html>.

9 MBS/1 0001.

10 <http://www.whoisgeorgemills.com/2010/03/eastbourne-local-history-society-comes.html>, accessed 13 September 2022.

11 P. Parker, *The Old Lie: The Great War and the public school ethos* (London: Hambledon Continuum, 2007), p. 16.

12 A. Churchill, *Blood and Thunder: The boys of Eton College and the First World War* (Stroud: History Press, 2014), p. 13.

13 J. Lewis-Stempel, *Six Weeks: The short and gallant life of the British officer in the First World War* (London: Orion, 2010. Kindle edn), loc. 285–95.

14 Lewis-Stempel, *Six Weeks*, loc. 301.

15 M. Howard, *Captain Professor* (London: Continuum, 2006), p. 25.

16 A. Churchill, *Blood and Thunder*, p. 12.

17 A. Churchill, *Blood and Thunder*, p. 12.

18 Lewis-Stempel, *Six Weeks*, p. 20.

19 A. Seldon and D. Walsh, *Public Schools and the Great War: The generation lost* (Barnsley: Pen and Sword, 2013. Kindle edn), loc. 443.

20 Parker, *The Old Lie*, pp. 99–101.

21 MBS/1 0250.

22 MBS/1 0250.

23 MBS/1 0250.

24 MBS/1 0250.

25 MBS/1 0254.

26 MBS/1 0252.

27 MBS/1 0257.

28 MBS/1 0261.

29 <https://www.chch.ox.ac.uk/fallen-alumni/major-general-merton-beckwith-smith>, accessed 13 September 2022.

30 Welsh Guards Archives. Record of Service.

31 Coldstream Guards Archives. Record of Service; Welsh Guards Archives. Record of Service; I. Beckett, T. Bowman and M. Connelly, *The British Army and the First World War* (Cambridge: Cambridge University Press, 2017), p. 21.

32 T. Bowman and M. Connelly, *The Edwardian Army: Recruiting, training, and deploying the British Army 1902–1914* (Oxford: Oxford University Press, 2012), p. 13.

33 Bowman and Connelly, *The Edwardian Army*, p. 13.

34 Bowman and Connelly, *The Edwardian Army*, p. 10.

35 G. Sheffield, *Leadership in the Trenches: Officer–man relations, morale and discipline in the British Army in the era of the First World War* (Basingstoke: Macmillan, 1999), p. 2.

36 Beckett et al., *The British Army*, pp. 19–20.

37 Sheffield, *Leadership in the Trenches*, p. 2.

38 Apollo University Lodge register via Ancestry.co.uk, accessed 28 September 2022; householdbrigade2614.co.uk, accessed 28 September 2022; M. Chappell, *British Battle Insignia 1 1914–18* (London: Osprey, 1986), p. 9.

39 Coldstream Guards Archives. Record of Service.

40 *Coldstream Guards Notes on Regimental Customs and Traditions* (London, 1944), pp. 9–10.

41 *Coldstream Guards Notes on Regimental Customs and Traditions*, pp. 20–5.

42 Howard, *Captain Professor*, p. 57.

43 MBS/1 0005.

44 MBS/1 0008.

45 P. Hodgkinson, 'The Infantry Battalion Commanding Officers of the BEF' in S. Jones (ed.), *Stemming the Tide: Officers and leadership in the British Expeditionary Force 1914* (Solihull: Helion, 2013), p. 313.

46 A. F. Becke (ed.), *Order of Battle of Divisions. Part I: The regular British divisions* (London: HMSO, 1935), pp. 36–7.

47 MBS/1 0009.

48 TNA WO 95/1263/1.

49 Beckett et al., *The British Army*, pp. 220–1.

50 Beckett et al., *The British Army*, p. 221.

51 MBS/1 0014.

52 MBS/1 0024.

53 MBS/1 0029.

54 MBS/1 0012, 0029, 0039.

55 MBS/1 0031, 0035.

56 TNA WO 95/1263/1.

57 S. Jones, '"The Demon": Brigadier-General Charles FitzClarence V.C.' in S. Jones (ed.), *Stemming the Tide: Officers and leadership in the British Expeditionary Force 1914* (Solihull: Helion, 2013), pp. 243–8; TNA WO 95/1263/1.

58 TNA WO 95/1263/1.

59 J. Ross-of-Bladensburg, *The Coldstream Guards 1914–1918* (Oxford: Oxford University Press, 1928), I, p. 151; MBS/1 0432.

60 TNA WO 95/1263/1.

61 Jones, '"The Demon"', p. 247.

62 TNA WO 95/1263/1.

63 TNA WO 95/1263/1.

64 MBS/1 0036, 0037.

65 *Edinburgh Gazette*, 13 November 1914, p. 1335.

66 R. Holmes, *Tommy: The British soldier on the Western Front 1914–1918* (London: HarperCollins, 2004), pp. 582–3.

67 MBS/1 0047.

68 MBS/1 0073.

69 *Aberdeen Daily Journal*, 10 November 1914, p. 7; *Daily Mail*, 10 November 1914, p. 3; *Devon and Exeter Gazette*, 10 November 1914, p. 2; *Times of India*, 30 November 1914, p. 10.

70 Jones, '"The Demon"', p. 240; Beckett et al., *The British Army*, pp. 227–8.

71 Jones, '"The Demon"', p. 253; S. Doughty, *The Guards Came Through: An illustrated history of the Guards in the Great War* (London: Third Millennium, 2016), p. 49.

72 MBS/1 0067.

73 *List of Etonians Who Fought in the Great War MCMXIV–MCMXIX* (London: Eton College, 1921), pp. 60, 99.

74 MBS/1 0099.

75 MBS/1 0077.

76 MBS/1 0078.

77 MBS/1 0114.

78 MBS/1 0089.

79 C. Messenger, *Call-to-Arms: The British Army 1914–18* (London: Cassell, 2006), pp. 342–3.

80 P. Harris, *The Men Who Planned the War: A study of the staff of the British Army on the Western Front, 1914–1918* (London: Routledge, 2017), p. 194.

81 Harris, *The Men Who Planned the War*, p. 50.

82 Harris, *The Men Who Planned the War*, p. 173.

83 Harris, *The Men Who Planned the War*, p. 158.

84 Messenger, *Call-to-Arms*, pp. 342–6.

85 Ross, *Coldstream Guards 1914–1918*, I, pp. 434–5.

86 Messenger, *Call-to-Arms*, p. 348.

87 *Composition of Headquarters. British Armies in France* (January 1919), pp. 10–11.

88 MBS/1 0116.

89 Holmes, *Tommy*, pp. 238, 242.

90 Harris, *The Men Who Planned the War*, pp. 149–51; P. Ziegler, *King Edward VIII: The official biography* (London: Collins, 1990), pp. 67–8.

91 *London Gazette*, 4 June 1917, p. 5477; Harris, *The Men Who Planned the War*, p. 147.

92 *Supplement to the London Gazette*, 25 September 1917, p. 9946; Holmes, *Tommy*, p. 588.

93 Coldstream Guards Archives. Record of Service; MBS/1 0116.

94 MBS/1 0505.

95 *Daily Mirror*, 15 March 1918, p. 6.

96 *Sunday Pictorial*, 17 March 1918, p. 10.

97 <https://dorsetinthegreatwar.co.uk/war-memorials/moor-crichel-long-crichel-witchampton-war-memorial/>, accessed 7 September 2022; *Western Gazette*, 22 November 1918, p. 6.

98 MBS/1 0268.

99 MBS/1 0130.

100 MBS/1 0131.

101 Seldon and Walsh, *Public Schools*, p. 22.

102 *List of Etonians*, pp. viii, 279; Seldon and Walsh, *Public Schools*, pp. 282, 313.

103 Ross, *Coldstream Guards 1914–1918*, II, p. 400.

104 Ross, *Coldstream Guards 1914–1918*, II, p. 401.

105 Ross, *Coldstream Guards 1914–1918*, II, p. 405.

106 Welsh Guards Archives. Record of Service; <http://www.thepeerage.com/p16054.htm#i160532>, accessed 12 October 2022.

107 M. Snape, *A Church Militant: Anglicans and the armed forces from Queen Victoria to the Vietnam War* (Oxford: Oxford University Press, 2022), pp. 188–9.

108 MBS/1 0516.

109 MBS/1 0517.

110 *London Gazette*, 11 July 1930, p. 4362.

2 The Welsh Guards and Lahore

1 MBS/1 0508.

2 J. Retallack, *The Welsh Guards* (London: Warne, 1981), p. 3.

3 A. F. Becke (ed.), *Order of Battle of Divisions. Part I: The regular British divisions* (London: HMSO, 1935), p. 28.

4 T. Royle, *Bearskins, Bayonets and Body Armour: Welsh Guards 1915–2015* (Barnsley: Frontline Books, 2015), pp. 56–60.

5 Retallack, *The Welsh Guards*, p. 47.

6 Retallack, *The Welsh Guards*, p. 47; Royle, *Bearskins, Bayonets and Body Armour*, p. 63.

7 Royle, *Bearskins, Bayonets and Body Armour*, pp. 61–73; Retallack, *The Welsh Guards*, pp. 39–43.

8 Edward, Duke of Windsor, *A King's Story* (New York: G. P. Putnam's Sons, 1951), p. 123.

9 *Daily Mail*, 19 July 1923, p. 8; *Daily Mail*, 1 April 1926, p. 8; <http://www.pwsts.org.uk/limehouse.htm>, accessed 8 September 2022.

10 MBS/1 0511.

11 MBS/1 0517.

12 *Daily Mirror*, 16 March 1921, p. 1.

13 Royle, *Bearskins, Bayonets and Body Armour*, p. 27.

14 *Daily Telegraph*, 3 March 1933, p. 15.

15 Royle, *Bearskins, Bayonets and Body Armour*, p. 73; P. Ziegler, *King Edward VIII: The official biography* (London: Collins, 1990), p. 113.

16 Ziegler, *King Edward VIII*, p. 535.

17 Retallack, *The Welsh Guards*, p. 40.

18 MBS/1 0517.

19 C. Brown, *Religion and Society in Twentieth-Century Britain* (London: Routledge, 2006), p. 127.

20 MBS/1 0517.

21 Royal Archives, EDW/PRIV/MAIN/A/3247, 3371, 3387, 3417.

22 Ziegler, *King Edward VIII*, p. 346.

23 Royal Archives, EDW/PRIV/MAIN/A/3492, 3506.

24 *London Gazette*, 14 October 1930, p. 6247.

25 Royle, *Bearskins, Bayonets and Body Armour*, p. 73.

26 Coldstream Guards Archives. Record of Service.

27 Retallack, *The Welsh Guards*, p. 42.

28 Retallack, *The Welsh Guards*, p. 48.

29 MBS/1 0131.

30 MBS/1 0131.

31 MBS/1 0133.

32 MBS/1 0126.

33 MBS/1 0128.

34 MBS/1 0127.

35 MBS/1 0130.

36 *Daily Mirror*, 21 October 1937, p. 6; MBS/1 0134.

37 MBS/1 0129, 0133.

38 MBS/1 0131.

39 *Daily Mirror*, 25 September 1933, p. 5.

40 *London Gazette*, 5 October 1934, p. 6249.

41 MBS/1 0140–3, 0146.

42 MBS/1 0143.

43 MBS/1 0516.

44 MBS/1 0149.

45 IWM Sound, Arthur John Flint, 899, Reels 2–3.

46 MBS/1 0516.

47 Coldstream Guards Archives. Record of Service.

48 B. Holden Reid, 'Alexander' in J. Keegan (ed.), *Churchill's Generals* (London: Warner Books, 1992), p. 108.

49 P. Rose, 'Indian Army Command Culture and the North West Frontier, 1919–1939' in A. Jeffreys and P. Rose (eds), *The Indian Army, 1939–47* (Farnham: Ashgate, 2012); R. Johnson, 'Small Wars and Internal Security: The Army in India, 1936–1946' in A. Jeffreys and P. Rose (eds), *The Indian Army, 1939–47* (Farnham: Ashgate, 2012).

50 *Indian Army List*, April 1938, p. 12.

51 Coldstream Guards Archives. Record of Service.

52 MBS/1 0517, 0207, 0217; Coldstream Guards Archives. Record of Service.

53 MBS/1 0200.

54 MBS/1 0408.

55 MBS/1 0202.

56 MBS/1 0210.

57 MBS/1 0211–15.

58 MBS/1 0217.

59 *London Gazette*, 19 April 1938, p. 2594.

60 MBS/1 0202, 0207.

61 MBS/1 0203.

62 *Indian Army List*, April 1938, p. 24.

63 MBS/1 0411.

64 *Indian Army List*, April 1938, p. 24.

65 MBS/1 0205.

66 MBS/1 0207.

67 MBS/1 0205.

68 MBS/1 0205.

69 MBS/1 0235–7.

70 MBS/1 0218.

71 MBS/1 0219.

72 MBS/1 0206; *Welsh Guards Comrades' Association Annual Report*, 1938, pp. 26–9.

73 MBS/1 0209.

74 MBS/1 0411.

75 MBS/1 0217.

76 MBS/1 0220.

77 MBS/1 0220.

78 M. Snape, 'Twilight of the Padres: The end of British military chaplaincy in India' in T. Brekke and V. Tikhonov (eds), *Military Chaplaincy in an Era of Religious Pluralism: Military-religious nexus in Asia, Europe, and USA* (New Delhi: Oxford University Press, 2017).

79 MBS/1 0204.

80 MBS/1 0204.

81 MBS/1 0205.

82 MBS/1 0205.

83 MBS/1 0205.

84 MBS/1 0202.

85 MBS/1 0203.

86 MBS/1 0218.

87 MBS/1 0219.

88 MBS/1 0220.

89 MBS/1 0230.

90 MBS/1 0411.

91 MBS/1 0313.

92 MBS/1 0316.

93 *Times of India*, 18 February 1939, p. 14; 21 February 1939, p. 4.

94 MBS/1 0233.

95 *Times of India*, 23 June 1939, p. 4.

96 MBS/1 0412.

97 MBS/1 0233.

98 MBS/1 0234.

99 MBS/1 0312.

100 MBS/1 0313.

101 MBS/1 0316.

3 1st Guards Brigade

1 H. F. Jolsen (ed.), *Orders of Battle: Second World War 1939–1945* (London: HMSO, 1960), pp. 35–6.

2 B. Holden Reid, 'Alexander' in J. Keegan (ed.), *Churchill's Generals* (London: Warner Books, 1992), pp. 128–9.

3   Holden Reid, 'Alexander', pp. 109–10.

4   G. Blaxland, *Destination Dunkirk: The story of Gort's army* (Barnsley: Pen and Sword, 2018), pp. 12–13.

5   B. Bond, 'Gort' in J. Keegan (ed.), *Churchill's Generals* (London: Warner Books, 1992), p. 36.

6   B. L. Montgomery, *The Memoirs of Field-Marshal the Viscount Montgomery of Alamein* (London: Fontana, 1960), pp. 51–2.

7   D. French, *Raising Churchill's Army: The British Army and the war against Germany 1919–1945* (Oxford: Oxford University Press, 2000), p. 182.

8   R. Mead, *Churchill's Lions: A biographical guide to the key British generals of World War II* (London: Spellmount, 2007), p. 172; French, *Raising Churchill's Army*, p. 182.

9   French, *Raising Churchill's Army*, p. 157.

10 MBS/1 0332.

11 MBS/1 0332.

12 MBS/1 0317, 0333.

13 MBS/1 0413.

14 A. Allport, *Browned Off and Bloody-Minded: The British soldier goes to war 1939–1945* (New Haven, CT: Yale University Press, 2015), p. 37.

15 D. Fraser, *And We Shall Shock Them: The British Army in the Second World War* (London: Cassell, 1999), p. 26.

16 MBS/1 0322.

17 MBS/1 0326.

18 Montgomery, *Memoirs*, pp. 52–3.

19 Fraser, *And We Shall Shock Them*, pp. 27–8.

20 B. Bond, 'The British Field Force in France and Belgium, 1939–40' in P. Addison and A. Calder (eds), *Time to Kill: The soldier's experience of war in the West 1939–1945* (London: Pimlico, 1997), pp. 40–1.

21 B. Bond, 'The Army between the Two World Wars' in D. Chandler and I. F. W. Beckett (eds), *The Oxford Illustrated History of the British Army* (Oxford: Oxford University Press, 1994), p. 277.

22 B. Bond, 'Preparing the Field Force, February 1939 – May 1940' in B. Bond and M. D. Taylor (eds), *The Battle of France and Flanders 1940: Sixty Years On* (Barnsley: Leo Cooper, 2001), p. 6.

23 L. F. Ellis, *The War in France and Flanders 1939–1940* (London: HMSO, 1953), p. 249.

24 D. C. Quilter (ed.), *No Dishonourable Name* (London: William Clowes, 1947), pp. 16–18.

25 MBS/1 0343.

26 MBS/1 0325–6, 0338.

27 MBS/1 0329–30.

28 MBS/1 0325–6, 0330.

29 MBS/1 0332.

30 MBS/1 0338.

31 MBS/1 0349.

32 *London Gazette*, 4 July 1939, p. 4568.

33 T. Royle, *Bearskins, Bayonets and Body Armour: Welsh Guards 1915–2015* (Barnsley: Frontline Books, 2015), p. 91.

34 MBS/1 0330–1.

35 MBS/1 0342.

36 MBS/1 0342.

37 MBS/1 0332.

38 MBS/1 0342.

39 MBS/1 0345.

40 Blaxland, *Destination Dunkirk*, p. 15.

41 MBS/1 0344.

42 MBS/1 0335.

43 MBS/1 0336.

44 MBS/1 0330, 0335, 0342.

45 MBS/1 0322.

46 MBS/1 0340.

47 MBS/1 0344.

48 MBS/1 0345.

49 Allport, *Browned Off*, p. 44.

50 MBS/1 0342.

51 MBS/1 0326.

52 MBS/1 0415.

53 MBS/1 0317.

54 Allport, *Browned Off*, p. 44.

55 MBS/1 0326.

56 MBS/1 0335.

57 Allport, *Browned Off*, p. 19.

58 MBS/1 0338.

59 MBS/1 0320.

60 MBS/1 0320.

61 A. Adair, *A Guards' General: The memoirs of Major General Sir Allan Adair* (London: Hamish Hamilton, 1986), p. 105.

62 MBS/1 0321.

63 MBS/1 0332, 0413, 0344.

64 MBS/1 0414, 0348.

65 MBS/1 0414.

66 MBS/1 0332.

67 MBS/1 0324.

68 MBS/1 0414, 0338, 0334, 0347.

69 MBS/1 0415.

70 MBS/1 0348.

71 MBS/1 0348.

72 MBS/1 0349.

73 J. Thompson, *Dunkirk: Retreat to victory* (London: Pan, 2009. Kindle edn), loc. 490; Fraser, *And We Shall Shock Them*, p. 55; Quilter, *No Dishonourable Name*, p. 19.

74 Quilter, *No Dishonourable Name*, pp. 19–21.

75 D. Todman, *Britain's War, Volume I: Into battle, 1937–1941* (London: Allen Lane, 2016), p. 324.

76 I. Dear and M. R. D. Foot (eds), *The Oxford Companion to the Second World War* (Oxford: Oxford University Press, 1995), p. 414.

77 Todman, *Britain's War: Into battle*, p. 218.

78 Todman, *Britain's War: Into battle*, p. 334.

79 Quilter, *No Dishonourable Name*, p. 21.

80 Quilter, *No Dishonourable Name*, pp. 22–3.

81 Quilter, *No Dishonourable Name*, p. 23.

82 French, *Raising Churchill's Army*, pp. 175–6.

83 Quilter, *No Dishonourable Name*, p. 26.

84 Quilter, *No Dishonourable Name*, p. 26.

85 Quilter, *No Dishonourable Name*, p. 27.

86 Quilter, *No Dishonourable Name*, p. 27.

87 Quilter, *No Dishonourable Name*, p. 27.

88 Quilter, *No Dishonourable Name*, p. 27.

89 Quilter, *No Dishonourable Name*, p. 27.

90 Quilter, *No Dishonourable Name*, p. 28.

91 Quilter, *No Dishonourable Name*, p. 28.

92 French, *Raising Churchill's Army*, p. 182.

93 Todman, *Britain's War: Into battle*, pp. 64–5.

94 R. Atkin, *Pillar of Fire: Dunkirk 1940* (Edinburgh: Birlinn, 2000), p. 77.

95 Atkin, *Pillar of Fire*, p. 77.

96 W. Lord, *The Miracle of Dunkirk* (New York: Open Road Integrated Media, 2017), p. 36.

97 H. Sebag-Montefiore, *Dunkirk: Fight to the last man* (London: Penguin, 2007. Kindle edn), loc. 8753.

98 Atkin, *Pillar of Fire*, pp. 146–7.

99 J. M. Langley, *Fight Another Day* (London: Collins, 1974), p. 44.

100 Langley, *Fight Another Day*, pp. 44–5.

101 Langley, *Fight Another Day*, p. 45.

102 J. Crang, 'The Defence of the Dunkirk Perimeter' in B. Bond and M. D. Taylor (eds), *The Battle of France and Flanders 1940: Sixty Years On* (Barnsley: Leo Cooper, 2001), p. 73.

103 Quilter, *No Dishonourable Name*, pp. 28–30.

104 Fraser, *And We Shall Shock Them*, p. 71.

105 Fraser, *And We Shall Shock Them*, p. 70.

106 Crang, 'Defence of the Dunkirk Perimeter', p. 79; Ellis, *War in France and Flanders*, p. 234.

107 Thompson, *Dunkirk*, loc. 5247–60; Jolsen, *Orders of Battle*, p. 311.

108 Todman, *Britain's War: Into battle*, p. 336; Thompson, *Dunkirk*, loc. 2896–910.

109 J. Grehan, *Dunkirk: Nine days that saved an army* (Barnsley: Frontline Books, 2018), p. 221; Sebag-Montefiore, *Dunkirk*, loc. 8867.

110 Todman, *Britain's War: Into battle*, p. 336.

111 Ellis, *War in France and Flanders*, p. 242.

112 Ellis, *War in France and Flanders*, p. 242.

113 Crang, 'Defence of the Dunkirk Perimeter', pp. 80–1; Sebag-Montefiore, *Dunkirk*, loc. 8909–20.

114 Quilter, *No Dishonourable Name*, p. 33.

115 Thompson, *Dunkirk*, loc. 5233.

116 Quilter, *No Dishonourable Name*, p. 35.

117 P. Williamson, S. Taylor, A. Raffe and N. Mears (eds), *National Prayers: Special worship since the Reformation. Volume 3. Worship for National and Royal Occasions in the United Kingdom, 1871–2016*, Church of England Record Society, 26 (Woodbridge: Boydell Press, 2020), pp. 406–21.

118 MBS/1 0351.

119 MBS/1 0364.

120 MBS/1 0365.

4 18th Division

1 MBS/1 0352.

2 P. Williamson, S. Taylor, A. Raffe and N. Mears (eds), *National Prayers: Special worship since the Reformation. Volume 3. Worship for National and Royal Occasions in the United Kingdom, 1871–2016*, Church of England Record Society, 26 (Woodbridge: Boydell Press, 2020), pp. 419–25.

3 MBS/1 0352.

4 *The Times*, 17 February 1940, p. 7.

5 MBS/1 0352.

6 M. Snape, *God and the British Soldier: Religion and the British Army in the First and Second World Wars* (Abingdon: Routledge, 2005), p. 128.

7 MBS/1 0352.

8 I. Dear and M. R. D. Foot (eds), *The Oxford Companion to the Second World War* (Oxford: Oxford University Press, 1995), pp. 739–40.

9 MBS/1 0352.

10 TNA WO 373/89/78.

11 *Supplement to the London Gazette*, 20 December 1940, p. 7175; Coldstream Guards Archives. Record of Service.

12 MBS/1 0353.

13 MBS/1 0353.

14 *Supplement to the London Gazette*, 16 July 1940, p. 4345; 2 August 1940, p. 4729.

15 B. Bond, 'Ironside' in J. Keegan (ed.), *Churchill's Generals* (London: Warner Books, 1992), pp. 28–9.

16 Bond, 'Ironside', pp. 29–30.

17 MBS/1 0368.

18 MBS/1 0416.

19 MBS/1 0354.

20 TNA WO 166/466; D. Todman, *Britain's War, Volume I: Into battle, 1937–1941* (London: Allen Lane, 2016), pp. 350–1.

21 H. F. Jolsen (ed.), *Orders of Battle: Second World War 1939–1945* (London: HMSO, 1960), p. 60.

22 D. French, *Raising Churchill's Army: The British Army and the war against Germany 1919–1945* (Oxford: Oxford University Press, 2000), p. 53.

23 A. Allport, *Browned Off and Bloody-Minded: The British soldier goes to war 1939–1945* (New Haven, CT: Yale University Press, 2015), p. xviii.

24 J. Fennell, *Fighting the People's War: The British and Commonwealth Armies and the Second World War* (Cambridge: Cambridge University Press, 2019), pp. 63–4.

25 B. Bond, 'The Army between the Two World Wars' in D. Chandler and I. F. W. Beckett (eds), *The Oxford Illustrated History of the British Army* (Oxford: Oxford University Press, 1994), p. 275.

26 Bond, 'The Army', p. 275.

27 French, *Raising Churchill's Army*, pp. 53–4.

28 French, *Raising Churchill's Army*, pp. 53–4.

29 French, *Raising Churchill's Army*, p. 126.

30 Allport, *Browned Off*, pp. xxiii–xxiv.

31 P. Fussell, *Wartime: Understanding and behavior in the Second World War* (New York: Oxford University Press, 1990), p. 151.

32 D. Todman, *Britain's War, Volume II: A new world, 1942–1947* (London: Allen Lane, 2020. Kindle edn), loc. 3627.

33 D. Fraser, *And We Shall Shock Them: The British Army in the Second World War* (London: Cassell, 1999), p. 99.

34 C. Barnett, *Britain and Her Army: A military, political and social history of the British Army, 1509–1970* (London: Cassell, 2000), p. 474.

35 Fraser, *And We Shall Shock Them*, p. 100.

36 R. Mead, *Churchill's Lions: A biographical guide to the key British generals of World War II* (London: Spellmount, 2007), p. 49.

37 P. Elphick, *Singapore: The pregnable fortress* (London: Coronet, 1995), p. 236.

38 Fennell, *Fighting the People's War*, pp. 30–1.

39 Fennell, *Fighting the People's War*, p. 31.

40 I. Beckett, T. Bowman and M. Connelly, *The British Army and the First World War* (Cambridge: Cambridge University Press, 2017), pp. 297–8, 382–3.

41 Sir (Frederick) Ivor Maxse, *ODNB*; Beckett et al., *The British Army*, pp. 297–8.

42 Sir (Frederick) Ivor Maxse, *ODNB*; Beckett et al., *The British Army*, p. 382.

43 D. Fraser, 'Alanbrooke' in J. Keegan (ed.), *Churchill's Generals* (London: Warner Books, 1992), p. 102.

44 Alan Francis Brooke, *ODNB*.

45 Arthur Ernest Percival, *ODNB*.

46 Sir (Frederick) Ivor Maxse, *ODNB*.

47 C. Kinvig, *Scapegoat: General Percival of Singapore* (London: Brassey's, 1996), p. 20.

48 N. Storey, *To Singapore and Beyond: A brief history of the 4th, 5th and 6th Battalions, Royal Norfolk Regiment, from 1939 to 1945* (Norwich: Holyboy Publications, 1992), p. 7; K. Bailey, *Face of Adversity: Life as a prisoner of war* (privately published, 2009), pp. 7–8.

49 Jolsen, *Orders of Battle*, p. 60; TNA CAB 106/70.

50 Jolsen, *Orders of Battle*, pp. 293–5.

51 French, *Raising Churchill's Army*, pp. 186–7.

52 French, *Raising Churchill's Army*, p. 191.

53 Jolsen, *Orders of Battle*, p. 62.

54 Ronald William Fordham Searle, *ODNB*.

55 C. Smith, *Singapore Burning* (London: Penguin, 2006), p. 434.

56 IWM Documents, Sir Richard Sharp, 84/29/1.

57 Allport, *Browned Off*, p. 24.

58 Allport, *Browned Off*, p. 24.

59 S. Alexander, *Sweet Kwai Run Softly* (Bristol: Merriotts Press, 1995), p. 1.

60 Alexander, *Sweet Kwai Run Softly*, p. 18.

61 Alexander, *Sweet Kwai Run Softly*, p. 9.

62 MBS/1 0356.

63 D. Todman (ed.), *War Diaries: Field Marshal Lord Alanbrooke* (London: Weidenfeld and Nicolson, 2001), p. 96.

64 TNA WO 166/466.

65 MBS/1 0355.

66 MBS/1 0355.

67 MBS/1 0355.

68 MBS/1 0416.

69 TNA WO 166/466.

70 MBS/1 0416.

71 MBS/1 0416.

72 TNA WO 166/466.

73 TNA WO 166/467.

74 Jolsen, *Orders of Battle*, p. 60.

75 TNA WO 166/467, WO 166/471.

76 TNA WO 166/471, WO 166/473.

77 TNA WO 166/466; Todman, *War Diaries*, p. 105.

78 TNA WO 166/466.

79 TNA WO 166/466.

80 G. Forty, *British Army Handbook 1939–1945* (Stroud: Sutton, 2002), p. 335.

81 Todman, *War Diaries*, p. 120.

82 TNA WO 166/466.

83 TNA WO 166/466.

84 TNA WO 166/466.

85 TNA WO 166/466.

86 TNA WO 166/466.

87 TNA WO 166/466.

88 TNA WO 166/466.

89 TNA WO 166/466.

90 TNA WO 166/466.

91 TNA WO 166/466.

92 French, *Raising Churchill's Army*, p. 207.

93 French, *Raising Churchill's Army*, pp. 185–6.

94 French, *Raising Churchill's Army*, pp. 191, 197–8.

95 French, *Raising Churchill's Army*, pp. 196–7.

96 French, *Raising Churchill's Army*, p. 197.

97 French, *Raising Churchill's Army*, p. 199.

98 French, *Raising Churchill's Army*, p. 199.

99 French, *Raising Churchill's Army*, pp. 199–201.

100 French, *Raising Churchill's Army*, pp. 203–4.

101 French, *Raising Churchill's Army*, pp. 205–6.

102 French, *Raising Churchill's Army*, pp. 207–8.

103 French, *Raising Churchill's Army*, p. 202.

104 French, *Raising Churchill's Army*, pp. 202–3.

105 MBS/1 0317, 0417.

106 TNA WO 166/465.

107 TNA WO 166/465.

108 IWM Documents, Brigadier T. H. Massy-Beresford, 67/131/1.

109 IWM Documents, Brigadier T. H. Massy-Beresford, 67/131/1.

110 IWM Documents, Brigadier T. H. Massy-Beresford, 67/131/1.

111 IWM Documents, Brigadier T. H. Massy-Beresford, 67/131/1.

112 IWM Documents, Brigadier T. H. Massy-Beresford, 67/131/1.

113 TNA WO 166/466.

114 IWM Documents, Brigadier T. H. Massy-Beresford, 67/131/1.

115 IWM Documents, Brigadier T. H. Massy-Beresford, 67/131/1.

116 IWM Documents, Brigadier T. H. Massy-Beresford, 67/131/1.

117 IWM Documents, Brigadier T. H. Massy-Beresford, 67/131/1.

118 IWM Documents, Brigadier T. H. Massy-Beresford, 67/131/1.

119 Storey, *To Singapore and Beyond*, p. 8.

120 TNA WO 166/473.

121 TNA WO 166/470.

122 TNA WO 166/470.

123 TNA WO 166/473.

124 TNA WO 166/473.

125 Alexander, *Sweet Kwai Run Softly*, p. 22.

126 TNA WO 166/467.

127 Alexander, *Sweet Kwai Run Softly*, p. 27.

128 TNA WO 166/467.

129 Alexander, *Sweet Kwai Run Softly*, p. 27.

130 P. N. Davies, *The Man behind the Bridge: Colonel Toosey and the River Kwai* (London: Bloomsbury, 1991), pp. 29–30.

131 J. Summers, *The Colonel of Tamarkan: Philip Toosey and the bridge on the River Kwai* (London: Simon and Schuster, 2005), pp. 59–61.

132 Summers, *Colonel of Tamarkan*, p. 73.

133 IWM Documents, Brigadier Sir Philip Toosey, 93/14/1.

134 Alexander, *Sweet Kwai Run Softly*, p. 27.

135 Summers, *Colonel of Tamarkan*, p. 75.

136 Bailey, *Face of Adversity*, p. 8.

137 Bailey, *Face of Adversity*, p. 8.

138 Bailey, *Face of Adversity*, p. 8.

139 TNA WO 166/470.

140 J. Beach, 'Soldier Education in the British Army, 1920–2007', *History of Education*, 37 (2008), p. 680.

141 A. Danchev, 'The Army and the Home Front, 1939–1945' in D. Chandler and I. F. W. Beckett (eds), *The Oxford Illustrated History of the British Army* (Oxford: Oxford University Press, 1994), pp. 315–16.

142 Beach, 'Soldier Education', pp. 691–2.

143 TNA WO 166/465.

144 TNA WO 166/473.

145 TNA WO 166/470.

146 TNA WO 166/466.

147 TNA WO 166/466.

148 IWM Documents, Brigadier T. H. Massy-Beresford, 67/131/1.

149 TNA WO 166/466.

150 Alexander, *Sweet Kwai Run Softly*, p. 22.

151 TNA WO 166/473, WO 166/470, WO 166/477.

152 IWM Documents, Brigadier T. H. Massy-Beresford, 67/131/1.

153 IWM Documents, Brigadier T. H. Massy-Beresford, 67/131/1.

154 IWM Documents, Brigadier Sir Philip Toosey, 93/14/1.

155 TNA WO 166/470.

156 IWM Documents, Brigadier T. H. Massy-Beresford, 67/131/1.

157 TNA WO 166/465, WO 166/466.

158 TNA WO 166/465.

159 TNA WO 166/465.

160 TNA WO 166/466.

161 TNA WO 166/466.

162 TNA WO 166/466.

163 Bailey, *Face of Adversity*, p. 9.

164 TNA WO 166/465.

165 R. Burton, *Railway of Hell* (Barnsley: Pen and Sword, 2010), pp. 2–3.

5 The great misadventure

1 TNA WO 166/465.

2 MBS/1 0382.

3 TNA WO 166/465.

4 TNA WO 166/470.

5 TNA WO 166/465.

6 TNA WO 166/470.

7 TNA WO 166/465.

8 TNA WO 166/465.

9 TNA WO 166/465.

10 K. Bailey, *Face of Adversity: Life as a prisoner of war* (privately published, 2009), p. 11.

11 TNA WO 166/465.

12 IWM Documents, Brigadier T. H. Massy-Beresford, 67/131/1.

13 J. Summers, *The Colonel of Tamarkan: Philip Toosey and the bridge on the River Kwai* (London: Simon and Schuster, 2005), pp. 75–6; S. Alexander, *Sweet Kwai Run Softly* (Bristol: Merriotts Press, 1995), pp. 33–4.

14 IWM Documents, Brigadier T. H. Massy-Beresford, 67/131/1; TNA WO 166/465; MBS/1 0382.

15 P. Elphick, *Singapore: The pregnable fortress* (London: Coronet, 1995), pp. 281–2.

16 MBS/1 0382.

17 TNA WO 166/465; IWM Documents, Brigadier T. H. Massy-Beresford, 67/131/1; Bailey, *Face of Adversity*, p. 12.

18 TNA WO 166/465; MBS/1 0382.

19 TNA WO 166/465.

20 C. Smith, *Singapore Burning* (London: Penguin, 2006), p. 291.

21 Elphick, *Singapore*, p. 282.

22 TNA WO 166/465.

23 TNA WO 166/465.

24 TNA WO 166/465.

25 Bailey, *Face of Adversity*, p. 12.

26 Elphick, *Singapore*, pp. 282–3.

27 TNA WO 166/465.

28 MBS/1 0382.

29 TNA WO 166/465.

30 IWM Documents, Brigadier T. H. Massy-Beresford, 67/131/1.

31 TNA WO 166/465.

32 TNA WO 166/465.

33 IWM Documents, Brigadier T. H. Massy-Beresford, 67/131/1.

34 TNA WO 166/465.

35 MBS/1 0382.

36 TNA WO 166/465.

37 IWM Documents, Brigadier T. H. Massy-Beresford, 67/131/1.

38 Bailey, *Face of Adversity*, p. 13.

39 J. Keegan, *The Second World War* (London: Hutchinson, 1989), p. 256.

40 TNA WO 166/465.

41 Elphick, *Singapore*, pp. 267–70.

42 TNA WO 166/465.

43 TNA WO 166/465.

44 TNA CAB 79/15.

45 TNA CAB 79/55.

46 TNA CAB 106/70.

47 TNA WO 166/465.

48 TNA WO 166/465.

49 TNA CAB 106/70.

50 TNA CAB 106/70; TNA WO 166/465.

51 TNA CAB 106/70.

52 TNA CAB 106/70.

53 TNA WO 166/465.

54 TNA WO 166/465.

55 J. Nixon and B. A. Smith, *Mother's Apple Pie* (Stockport: A. Lane Publications, 2006), pp. 18–24.

56 R. Searle, *To the Kwai and Back* (London: Collins, 1986), pp. 25–7.

57 Searle, *To the Kwai*, p. 27.

58 Nixon and Smith, *Mother's Apple Pie*, p. 24.

59 IWM Documents, Brigadier T. H. Massy-Beresford, 67/131/1.

60 IWM Documents, Brigadier Sir Philip Toosey, 93/14/2.

61 Searle, *To the Kwai*, p. 28.

62 Searle, *To the Kwai*, p. 43.

63 Searle, *To the Kwai*, p. 43.

64 IWM Documents, Brigadier Sir Philip Toosey, 93/14/2.

65 MBS/1 0382.

66 IWM Documents, Brigadier Sir Philip Toosey, 93/14/2; M. Connelly, 'The Issue of Surrender in the Malayan Campaign' in H. Afflerbach and H. Strachan (eds), *How Fighting Ends: A history of surrender* (Oxford: Oxford University Press, 2012), p. 343.

67 IWM Documents, Brigadier T. H. Massy-Beresford, 67/131/1.

68 TNA WO 166/465.

69 TNA WO 166/465.

70 TNA WO 166/465.

71 Bailey, *Face of Adversity*, p. 14.

72 IWM Documents, Brigadier T. H. Massy-Beresford, 67/131/1.

73 TNA CAB 106/70.

74 Bailey, *Face of Adversity*, p. 18.

75 J. B. Chalker, *Burma Railway Artist* (London: Leo Cooper, 1994), pp. 13–14.

76 TNA CAB 106/70.

77 MBS/1 0382.

78 IWM Documents, Brigadier T. H. Massy-Beresford, 67/131/1.

79 Summers, *Colonel of Tamarkan*, p. 79.

80 Alexander, *Sweet Kwai Run Softly*, p. 42.

81 I. Kiyoshi, 'Anglo-Japanese Relations, 1941–45' in I. Nish and Y. Kibata (eds), *The History of Anglo-Japanese Relations, 1600–2000* (Basingstoke: Macmillan, 2000), pp. 116–17.

82 Keegan, *The Second World War*, pp. 256–7; A. Beevor, *The Second World War* (London: Weidenfeld and Nicolson, 2012), pp. 259–62.

83 Beevor, *The Second World War*, pp. 253–5.

84 I. Dear and M. R. D. Foot (eds), *The Oxford Companion to the Second World War* (Oxford: Oxford University Press, 1995), p. 712.

85 Keegan, *The Second World War*, p. 257.

86 L. Allen, *Singapore 1941–1942* (London: Frank Cass, 1993), p. 155; Elphick, *Singapore*, p. 541.

87 S. Woodburn Kirby, *The War against Japan. Volume I. The Loss of Singapore* (London: HMSO, 1957), p. 287; TNA CAB 106/70.

88 Summers, *Colonel of Tamarkan*, pp. 80–2.

89 *Second Supplement to the London Gazette*, 26 February 1948, p. 1296, para. 332.

90 Elphick, *Singapore*, p. 287.

91 Elphick, *Singapore*, pp. 287–8.

92 TNA CAB 106/70.

93 Allen, *Singapore 1941–1942*, p. 159; F. Owen, *The Fall of Singapore* (London: Michael Joseph, 1960), pp. 133–4.

94 Owen, *Fall of Singapore*, p. 133; Summers, *Colonel of Tamarkan*, p. 83.

95 S. L. Falk, *Seventy Days to Singapore: The Malayan Campaign, 1941–1942* (London: Robert Hale, 1975), p. 175.

96 Falk, *Seventy Days to Singapore*, p. 177.

97 Allen, *Singapore 1941–1942*, p. 155.

98 Summers, *Colonel of Tamarkan*, pp. 82–3; TNA CAB 106/70.

99 TNA CAB 106/70.

100 TNA CAB 106/70.

101 B. Farrell, *The Defence and Fall of Singapore* (Singapore: Monsoon Books, 2015), p. 355.

102 TNA CAB 106/70; Elphick, *Singapore*, p. 542; Smith, *Singapore Burning*, pp. 434–40.

103 Woodburn Kirby, *The Loss of Singapore*, p. 369.

104 Smith, *Singapore Burning*, pp. 434–40.

105 MBS/1 0418.

106 Woodburn Kirby, *The Loss of Singapore*, p. 261.

107 TNA CAB 106/70.

108 TNA CAB 106/70; Allen, *Singapore 1941–1942*, p. 152.

109 J. Smyth, *Leadership in War, 1939–1945* (Newton Abbot: David and Charles, 1975), p. 145.

110 *Second Supplement to the London Gazette*, 26 February 1948, p. 1300, para. 365.

111 Woodburn Kirby, *The Loss of Singapore*, pp. 324–5.

112 Farrell, *Defence and Fall*, p. 383.

113 Woodburn Kirby, *The Loss of Singapore*, p. 325; Farrell, *Defence and Fall*, pp. 383–4.

114 Farrell, *Defence and Fall*, pp. 203–4.

115 Farrell, *Defence and Fall*, p. 204.

116 Farrell, *Defence and Fall*, p. 355.

117 Elphick, *Singapore*, pp. 279–80.

118 D. Todman, *Britain's War, Volume II: A new world, 1942–1947* (London: Allen Lane, 2020. Kindle edn), loc. 3196–206.

119 A. Jackson, *The British Empire and the Second World War* (London: Continuum, 2006), p. 414.

120 Jackson, *The British Empire*, p. 416.

121 Owen, *Fall of Singapore*, p. 9.

122 Allen, *Singapore 1941–1942*, p. 276.

123 J. Fennell, *Fighting the People's War: The British and Commonwealth Armies and the Second World War* (Cambridge: Cambridge University Press, 2019), p. 185.

124 Allen, *Singapore 1941–1942*, p. 281.

125 Fennell, *Fighting the People's War*, p. 185.

126 Todman, *Britain's War: A new world*, loc. 1598–617; Allen, *Singapore 1941–1942*, pp. 272–87; Owen, *Fall of Singapore*, p. 9.

127 Farrell, *Defence and Fall*, p. 203.

128 W. S. Churchill, *The Second World War. Volume 4. The Hinge of Fate* (London: Cassell, 1951), p. 44.

129 W. S. Churchill, *Hinge of Fate*, p. 43.

130 Allen, *Singapore 1941–1942*, p. 288.

131 Woodburn Kirby, *The Loss of Singapore*, p. 258.

132 Todman, *Britain's War: A new world*, loc. 3258–99.

133 Farrell, *Defence and Fall*, p. 370.

134 W. S. Churchill, *Hinge of Fate*, pp. 48–9.

135 Smyth, *Leadership in War*, pp. 148–9.

136 Owen, *Fall of Singapore*, pp. 138–9; Smith, *Singapore Burning*, pp. 430–1.

137 W. S. Churchill, *Hinge of Fate*, p. 49; Falk, *Seventy Days to Singapore*, p. 184.

138 MBS/1 0382.

6 The battle for Singapore

1 MBS/1 0418.

2 MBS/1 0418.

3 C. Smith, *Singapore Burning* (London: Penguin, 2006), p. 449.

4 K. Bailey, *Face of Adversity: Life as a prisoner of war* (privately published, 2009), p. 21.

5 A. E. Knights, *Singapore and the Thailand–Burma Railway* (Bury St Edmunds: Arena Books, 2013), p. 18.

6 IWM Documents, Brigadier Sir Philip Toosey, 93/14/7.

7 IWM Documents, Sir Richard Sharp, 84/29/1.

8 J. Smyth, *Leadership in War, 1939–1945* (Newton Abbot: David and Charles, 1975), pp. 144–5.

9 J. Summers, *The Colonel of Tamarkan: Philip Toosey and the bridge on the River Kwai* (London: Simon and Schuster, 2005), p. 84.

10 W. S. Churchill, *The Second World War. Volume 4. The Hinge of Fate* (London: Cassell, 1951), pp. 44–5.

11 TNA CAB 106/70.

12 TNA CAB 106/70; B. Farrell, *The Defence and Fall of Singapore* (Singapore: Monsoon Books, 2015), p. 374; S. Woodburn Kirby, *The War against Japan. Volume I. The Loss of Singapore* (London: HMSO, 1957), p. 364.

13 L. Allen, *Singapore 1941–1942* (London: Frank Cass, 1993), p. 161.

14 Allen, *Singapore 1941–1942*, p. 161; E. Drea, *Japan's Imperial Army* (Lawrence, KS: University Press of Kansas, 2009), p. 225.

15 W. S. Churchill, *Hinge of Fate*, pp. 82–3; Farrell, *Defence and Fall*, p. 400; Allen, *Singapore 1941–1942*, p. 161.

16 TNA CAB 106/70.

17 TNA CAB 106/70.

18 TNA CAB 106/70.

19 TNA CAB 106/70.

20 P. Elphick, *Singapore: The pregnable fortress* (London: Coronet, 1995), pp. 415–16.

21 Knights, *Singapore and the Thailand–Burma Railway*, pp. 17–18.

22 TNA CAB 106/70.

23 MBS/1 0382.

24 TNA CAB 106/70.

25 TNA CAB 106/70.

26 C. Kinvig, *Scapegoat: General Percival of Singapore* (London: Brassey's, 1996), p. 237.

27 Woodburn Kirby, *The Loss of Singapore*, p. 364; F. Owen, *The Fall of Singapore* (London: Michael Joseph, 1960), p. 166.

28 Woodburn Kirby, *The Loss of Singapore*, p. 365; MBS/1 0382.

29 C. Bayly and T. Harper, *Forgotten Armies: Britain's Asian empire and the war with Japan* (London: Penguin, 2005), pp. 6–7.

30 R. Burton, *Railway of Hell* (Barnsley: Pen and Sword, 2010), p. 20.

31 TNA CAB 106/70.
32 TNA CAB 106/70.
33 TNA CAB 106/70.
34 MBS/1 0418.
35 MBS/1 0418.
36 MBS/1 0418.
37 TNA CAB 106/70.
38 TNA CAB 106/70.
39 TNA CAB 106/70.
40 TNA CAB 106/70.
41 K. Hack and K. Blackburn, *Did Singapore Have to Fall? Churchill and the impregnable fortress* (London: Routledge, 2004), p. 80.
42 TNA CAB 106/70.
43 TNA CAB 106/70.
44 MBS/1 0418.
45 TNA CAB 106/70.
46 TNA CAB 106/70.
47 Owen, *Fall of Singapore*, p. 168.
48 TNA CAB 106/70.
49 Woodburn Kirby, *The Loss of Singapore*, p. 369; Owen, *Fall of Singapore*, p. 156.
50 Kinvig, *Scapegoat*, pp. 198–9; 'General Percival and the Fall of Singapore' in B. Farrell and S. Hunter (eds), *Sixty Years On: The fall of Singapore revisited* (Singapore: Eastern Universities Press, 2002), pp. 257–8.
51 Kinvig, 'General Percival', p. 258.
52 Owen, *Fall of Singapore*, p. 158.
53 J. Keegan, *The Second World War* (London: Hutchinson, 1989), p. 261.
54 Owen, *Fall of Singapore*, p. 172.
55 Owen, *Fall of Singapore*, p. 174; Hack and Blackburn, *Did Singapore Have to Fall?*, pp. 82–3.
56 Hack and Blackburn, *Did Singapore Have to Fall?*, pp. 82–3.
57 Kinvig, 'General Percival', p. 259.
58 TNA CAB 106/70.
59 TNA CAB 106/70.
60 W. S. Churchill, *Hinge of Fate*, pp. 87–8.

61 W. S. Churchill, *Hinge of Fate*, p. 88.
62 C. F. Blackater, *Gods without Reason* (London: Eyre and Spottiswoode, 1948), p. 7.
63 TNA CAB 106/70; Woodburn Kirby, *The Loss of Singapore*, p. 392; W. S. Churchill, *Hinge of Fate*, p. 87.
64 Farrell, *Defence and Fall*, pp. 403–4; Smith, *Singapore Burning*, pp. 510–11.
65 W. S. Churchill, *Hinge of Fate*, p. 88.
66 TNA CAB 106/70.
67 TNA CAB 106/70.
68 TNA CAB 106/70.
69 TNA CAB 106/70.
70 TNA CAB 106/70.
71 Knights, *Singapore and the Thailand–Burma Railway*, p. 37.
72 TNA CAB 106/70.
73 TNA CAB 106/70.
74 Farrell, *Defence and Fall*, p. 417.
75 TNA CAB 106/70.
76 Owen, *Fall of Singapore*, p. 188.
77 Owen, *Fall of Singapore*, p. 188; TNA CAB 106/70.
78 MBS/1 0382.
79 TNA CAB 106/70.
80 TNA CAB 106/70.
81 Owen, *Fall of Singapore*, p. 189; Hack and Blackburn, *Did Singapore Have to Fall?*, p. 84.
82 TNA CAB 106/70.
83 TNA CAB 106/70.
84 Farrell, *Defence and Fall*, pp. 423–4.
85 Blackater, *Gods without Reason*, pp. 15–16.
86 TNA CAB 106/70; Farrell, *Defence and Fall*, p. 424.
87 TNA CAB 106/70.
88 TNA CAB 106/70.
89 Farrell, *Defence and Fall*, p. 405; Hack and Blackburn, *Did Singapore Have to Fall?*, pp. 83–4.
90 Woodburn Kirby, *The Loss of Singapore*, p. 409; Farrell, *Defence and Fall*, p. 428.

91 Hack and Blackburn, *Did Singapore Have to Fall?*, p. 82.

92 Farrell, *Defence and Fall*, p. 428; Woodburn Kirby, *The Loss of Singapore*, p. 409.

93 W. S. Churchill, *Hinge of Fate*, p. 91.

94 Woodburn Kirby, *The Loss of Singapore*, pp. 409–10.

95 Farrell, *Defence and Fall*, p. 428.

96 TNA CAB 106/70.

97 W. S. Churchill, *Hinge of Fate*, p. 91.

98 W. S. Churchill, *Hinge of Fate*, p. 91.

99 Woodburn Kirby, *The Loss of Singapore*, p. 410.

100 W. S. Churchill, *Hinge of Fate*, pp. 91–2.

101 TNA CAB 106/70.

102 TNA CAB 106/70.

103 TNA CAB 106/70.

104 TNA CAB 106/70.

105 TNA CAB 106/70.

106 Owen, *Fall of Singapore*, p. 203.

107 Hack and Blackburn, *Did Singapore Have to Fall?*, p. 85.

108 Elphick, *Singapore*, p. 476.

109 Hack and Blackburn, *Did Singapore Have to Fall?*, p. 85; Elphick, *Singapore*, p. 499.

110 W. S. Churchill, *Hinge of Fate*, p. 92.

111 Owen, *Fall of Singapore*, p. 203.

112 Farrell, *Defence and Fall*, pp. 428–9; Owen, *Fall of Singapore*, pp. 200–1.

113 Elphick, *Singapore*, p. 324.

114 Farrell, *Defence and Fall*, pp. 428–9.

115 Woodburn Kirby, *The Loss of Singapore*, p. 413.

116 MBS/1 0382.

117 Smith, *Singapore Burning*, p. 546.

118 Woodburn Kirby, *The Loss of Singapore*, pp. 413–14; Farrell, *Defence and Fall*, p. 429; W. S. Churchill, *Hinge of Fate*, pp. 92–4.

119 W. S. Churchill, *Hinge of Fate*, p. 94.

120 TNA CAB 106/70.

121 TNA CAB 106/70.

122 TNA CAB 106/70.

123 MBS/1 0382.

124 TNA CAB 106/70.

125 TNA CAB 106/70.

126 TNA CAB 106/70.

127 TNA CAB 66/24/7; M. Hastings, *All Hell Let Loose: The world at war 1939–1945* (London: HarperCollins, 2011), p. 209.

128 Smith, *Singapore Burning*, p. 541.

129 H. Gordon Bennett, *The Fall of Singapore* (Dehradun: Natraj Publishers, 1990), p. 192.

130 Smith, *Singapore Burning*, p. 541.

131 Woodburn Kirby, *The Loss of Singapore*, p. 403.

132 Farrell, *Defence and Fall*, pp. 416–17; Hastings, *All Hell Let Loose*, p. 212; TNA CAB 106/71.

133 Smith, *Singapore Burning*, pp. 541–2.

134 M. Connelly, 'The Issue of Surrender in the Malayan Campaign' in H. Afflerbach and H. Strachan (eds), *How Fighting Ends: A history of surrender* (Oxford: Oxford University Press, 2012), p. 347.

135 IWM Documents, Brigadier F. J. Dillon, 15/17/1.

136 IWM Documents, Brigadier F. J. Dillon, 15/17/1.

137 IWM Documents, Brigadier F. J. Dillon, 15/17/1.

138 IWM Documents, Brigadier F. J. Dillon, 15/17/1.

139 MBS/1 0382.

140 TNA CAB 106/70.

141 P. Brune, *Descent into Hell: The fall of Singapore – Pudu and Changi – the Thai–Burma Railway* (Sydney: Allen and Unwin, 2014), p. 249.

142 C. Kinvig, *River Kwai Railway* (London: Brassey's, 1992), pp. 27–8.

143 Elphick, *Singapore*, pp. 273–6.

144 D. Todman, *Britain's War, Volume II: A new world, 1942–1947* (London: Allen Lane, 2020. Kindle edn), loc. 2844.

145 Kinvig, *River Kwai Railway*, p. 211.

146 IWM Documents, Mrs E. Horne, P463.

147 IWM Documents, Brigadier T. H. Massy-Beresford, 67/131/1.

148 IWM Documents, Sir Richard Sharp, 84/29/1.

149 I. Barwick, *In the Shadow of Death: The story of a medic on the Burma Railway 1942–1945* (Barnsley: Pen and Sword, 2005), pp. 31–2.

150 L. L. Baynes, *Kept – The Other Side of Tenko* (Lewes: Book Guild, 1984), pp. 14–15.

151 J. Coast, *Railroad of Death* (London: Commodore Press, 1946), p. 31.

152 *The Times*, 10 October 1947, p. 2.

153 Knights, *Singapore and the Thailand–Burma Railway*, p. 12.

154 Bailey, *Face of Adversity*, pp. 29, 125–6.

155 J. C. Sharp, 'Impregnable Fortress: A brief collection of orders, articles and verses on the fall of Singapore (1942)' (Birmingham, 1947), item 11; IWM Documents, Captain E. C. Dickson, 84/29/1.

156 IWM Documents, Captain E. C. Dickson, 84/29/1.

157 G. Burton, *In the Shadow* (Warrington: Mackie and Co., 1946), p. 22.

158 Hack and Blackburn, *Did Singapore Have to Fall?*, p. 151.

159 W. S. Churchill, *Hinge of Fate*, p. 81.

160 E. M. Glover, *In 70 Days: The story of the Japanese campaign in British Malaya* (London: Frederick Muller Ltd, 1946), pp. 221–2.

161 Farrell, *Defence and Fall*, pp. 469–72.

162 Hack and Blackburn, *Did Singapore Have to Fall?*, p. 187.

163 Todman, *Britain's War: A new world*, loc. 2856.

164 Hastings, *All Hell Let Loose*, pp. 213–14.

165 Elphick, *Singapore*, pp. 239–42; Kinvig, 'General Percival', p. 240.

166 Keegan, *The Second World War*, p. 261; Elphick, *Singapore*, p. 238.

167 Elphick, *Singapore*, p. 238; Owen, *Fall of Singapore*, pp. 9–11.

168 Elphick, *Singapore*, pp. 393–5.

169 C. Bridge, 'Crisis of Command: Major-General Gordon Bennett and British military effectiveness in the Malayan Campaign, 1941–42' in B. Bond and K. Tachikawa (eds), *British and Japanese Military Leadership in the Far Eastern War 1941–1945* (London: Frank Cass, 2004), p. 73.

7 Changi

1 J. F. Vance (ed.), *Encyclopedia of Prisoners of War and Internment* (Santa Barbara, CA: ABC-CLIO, 2000), p. 147.

2 Vance, *Encyclopedia of Prisoners of War*, p. 108.

3 Vance, *Encyclopedia of Prisoners of War*, p. 108; Y. Kibata, 'Japanese Treatment of British Prisoners: The historical context' in P. Towle, M. Kosuge and Y. Kibata (eds), *Japanese Prisoners of War* (London: Hambledon and London, 2000), pp. 140–1.

4 I. Hata, 'From Consideration to Contempt: The changing nature of Japanese military and popular perceptions of prisoners of war through

the ages' in B. Moore and K. Fedorowich (eds), *Prisoners of War and Their Captors in World War II* (Oxford: Berg, 1996), p. 264; Vance, *Encyclopedia of Prisoners of War*, p. 108.

5 S. J. Flower, 'British Prisoners of War of the Japanese' in I. Nish and Y. Kibata (eds), *The History of Anglo-Japanese Relations, 1600–2000* (Basingstoke: Macmillan, 2000), pp. 152–3; Hata, 'From Consideration to Contempt', p. 264; <https://ihl-databases.icrc.org/applic/ihl/ihl.nsf/Article.xsp?action=openDocument&documentId=8DFED95C1E653FDAC12563CD00519226#:~:text=Geneva%2C%20 27%20July%201929.%20Part%20VI%20%3A%20Bureaux,about%20 the%20prisoners%20of%20war%20in%20their%20territory>, accessed 26 May 2022.

6 Flower, 'British Prisoners', p. 170; C. Bayly and T. Harper, *Forgotten Armies: Britain's Asian empire and the war with Japan* (London: Penguin, 2005), p. 336.

7 D. Tett, *A Postal History of the Prisoners of War and Civilian Internees in East Asia during the Second World War. Volume 1: Singapore and Malaya 1942–1945. The Changi connection* (Bristol: Stuart Rossiter Trust Fund, 2002), pp. xix–xx.

8 Flower, 'British Prisoners', p. 170.

9 C. F. Blackater, *Gods without Reason* (London: Eyre and Spottiswoode, 1948), p. 31.

10 L. L. Baynes, *Kept – The other side of Tenko* (Lewes: Book Guild, 1984), p. 51; R. P. W. Havers, *Reassessing the Japanese Prisoner of War Experience: The Changi POW camp, Singapore, 1942–5* (London: Routledge, 2003), pp. 52–3.

11 Flower, 'British Prisoners', p. 153; G. Daws, *Prisoners of the Japanese* (London: Robson Books, 1995), pp. 96–9.

12 Hata, 'From Consideration to Contempt', p. 266.

13 M. Sturma, 'Japanese Treatment of Allied Prisoners during the Second World War: Evaluating the death toll', *Journal of Contemporary History*, 55 (2020), p. 522.

14 J. C. Sharp, 'Impregnable Fortress: A brief collection of orders, articles and verses on the fall of Singapore (1942)' (Birmingham, 1947), item 2.

15 M. Hastings, *All Hell Let Loose: The world at war 1939–1945* (London: HarperCollins, 2011), p. 216.

16 Hastings, *All Hell Let Loose*, p. 216; S. C. Townsend, 'Culture, Race and Power in Japan's Wartime Empire' in P. Towle, M. Kosuge and Y. Kibata (eds), *Japanese Prisoners of War* (London: Hambledon and London, 2000); H. Furuya, 'Japan's Racial Identity in the Second World War: The cultural context of Japanese treatment of POWs' in P. Towle, M. Kosuge and Y. Kibata (eds), *Japanese Prisoners of War* (London: Hambledon and London, 2000).

17 Furuya, 'Japan's Racial Identity', p. 122.

18 Kibata, 'Japanese Treatment of British Prisoners', p. 139.

19 Hata, 'From Consideration to Contempt', pp. 267–9.

20 M. Burleigh, *Moral Combat: A history of World War II* (London: HarperCollins, 2010), pp. 18–20.

21 Bayly and Harper, *Forgotten Armies*, pp. 210–13.

22 Hastings, *All Hell Let Loose*, p. 216.

23 E. Drea, *Japan's Imperial Army* (Lawrence, KS: University Press of Kansas, 2009), p. 238.

24 Vance, *Encyclopedia of Prisoners of War*, pp. 33–5; Sturma, 'Japanese Treatment of Allied Prisoners', pp. 514–15.

25 Sturma, 'Japanese Treatment of Allied Prisoners', p. 529.

26 Vance, *Encyclopedia of Prisoners of War*, p. 336.

27 K. Bailey, *Face of Adversity: Life as a prisoner of war* (privately published, 2009), pp. 30–1; N. Storey, *To Singapore and Beyond: A brief history of the 4th, 5th and 6th Battalions, Royal Norfolk Regiment, from 1939 to 1945* (Norwich: Holyboy Publications, 1992), pp. 16–17.

28 R. Searle, *To the Kwai and Back* (London: Collins, 1986), p. 120.

29 A. D. Coox, 'The Effectiveness of the Japanese Military Establishment in the Second World War' in W. Murray and A. R. Millett (eds), *Military Effectiveness. Volume 3. The Second World War* (Cambridge: Cambridge University Press, 2010), p. 23.

30 D. Nelson, *The Story of Changi* (Singapore: Changi Museum, 2001), p. 14; Havers, *Reassessing*, p. 54.

31 <https://www.cofepow.org.uk/armed-forces-stories-list/the-story-of-changi>, accessed 15 June 2022.

32 TNA CAB 109/199; Bailey, *Face of Adversity*, p. 30.

33 Todman, *Britain's War: A new world*, loc. 3332.

34 Vance, *Encyclopedia of Prisoners of War*, p. 44; Nelson, *Story of Changi*, pp. 10–11.

35 Nelson, *Story of Changi*, p. 11; TNA CAB 109/199.

36 TNA CAB 109/199.

37 Nelson, *Story of Changi*, p. 10; TNA CAB 109/199.

38 TNA CAB 109/199.

39 TNA CAB 109/199.

40 Blackater, *Gods without Reason*, p. 24.

41 Blackater, *Gods without Reason*, p. 25.

42 Bailey, *Face of Adversity*, p. 31.

43 TNA CAB 109/199, 14.

44 Havers, *Reassessing*, pp. 43–8.

45 TNA CAB 109/199.

46 TNA CAB 109/199.

47 G. Burton, *In the Shadow* (Warrington: Mackie and Co., 1946), p. 25; S. Alexander, *Sweet Kwai Run Softly* (Bristol: Merriotts Press, 1995), pp. 72–3.

48 IWM Documents, Sir Richard Sharp, 84/29/1.

49 TNA CAB 109/199.

50 TNA CAB 109/199.

51 TNA CAB 109/199.

52 TNA CAB 109/199.

53 TNA CAB 109/199.

54 TNA CAB 109/199.

55 TNA CAB 109/199.

56 TNA CAB 109/199.

57 TNA CAB 109/199.

58 TNA CAB 109/199.

59 TNA CAB 109/199.

60 TNA CAB 109/199.

61 TNA CAB 109/199.

62 TNA CAB 109/199.

63 TNA CAB 109/199.

64 MBS/1 0374.

65 TNA CAB 109/199.

66 TNA CAB 109/199; Nelson, *Story of Changi*, p. 202.

67 Bayly and Harper, *Forgotten Armies*, p. 338.

68 IWM Documents, Brigadier T. H. Massy-Beresford, 67/131/1.

69 IWM Documents, Brigadier T. H. Massy-Beresford, 67/131/1.

70 IWM Documents, Brigadier F. J. Dillon, 15/17/1.

71 R. M. Horner, *Singapore Diary: The hidden journal of Captain R.M. Horner* (Stroud: Spellmount, 2007), p. 24.

72 Flower, 'British Prisoners', pp. 156–7.

73 S. J. Flower, 'Captors and Captives on the Burma–Thailand Railway' in B. Moore and K. Fedorowich (eds), *Prisoners of War and Their Captors in World War II* (Oxford: Berg, 1996), p. 245.

74 Flower, 'Captors and Captives', p. 227.

75 H. Ion, 'Brass Hats behind Bamboo Palisades: Senior officer POWs in Singapore, Taiwan, and Manchukuo, 1942–45', *Canadian Journal of History*, 46 (2011), pp. 303–31.

76 TNA CAB 109/199.

77 MBS/1 0382.

78 IWM Documents, Sir Richard Sharp, 84/29/1.

79 IWM Documents, Sir Richard Sharp, 84/29/1.

80 IWM Documents, Sir Richard Sharp, 84/29/1.

81 G. Burton, *In the Shadow*, p. 25.

82 I. Watt, 'The Liberty of the Prison' in G. Moir (ed.), *Beyond Hatred* (London: Lutterworth Press, 1969), p. 140.

83 Watt, 'The Liberty of the Prison', p. 141.

84 IWM Documents, Captain H. Silman, 15/18/1.

85 G. Burton, *In the Shadow*, p. 28.

86 Baynes, *Kept*, p. 27.

87 B. Best, *Secret Letters from the Railway: The remarkable record of Charles Steel – a Japanese POW* (Barnsley: Pen and Sword, 2004), p. 33.

88 IWM Documents, Captain H. Silman, 15/18/1.

89 Alexander, *Sweet Kwai Run Softly*, p. 74.

90 J. B. Chalker, *Burma Railway Artist* (London: Leo Cooper, 1994), p. 19.

91 IWM Documents, Brigadier F. J. Dillon, 15/17/1.

92 IWM Documents, Captain H. Silman, 15/18/1.

93 IWM Documents, Captain H. Silman, 15/18/1.

8 Reconstruction and renewal

1 G. Burton, *In the Shadow* (Warrington: Mackie and Co., 1946), pp. 28–9.

2 IWM Documents, Captain H. Silman, 15/18/1.

3 IWM Documents, Captain E. C. Dickson, 84/29/1.

4 IWM Documents, Captain E. C. Dickson, 84/29/1.

5 S. Alexander, *Sweet Kwai Run Softly* (Bristol: Merriotts Press, 1995), p. 63.

6 IWM Documents, Brigadier Sir Philip Toosey, 93/14/1.

7 J. Coast, *Railroad of Death* (London: Commodore Press, 1946), p. 13.

8 IWM Documents, Brigadier F. J. Dillon, 15/17/1.

9 IWM Documents, Brigadier F. J. Dillon, 15/17/1.

10 Coast, *Railroad of Death*, pp. 53–4.

11 I. Watt, 'The Liberty of the Prison' in G. Moir (ed.), *Beyond Hatred* (London: Lutterworth Press, 1969), p. 143.

12 Alexander, *Sweet Kwai Run Softly*, p. 72.

13 L. L. Baynes, *Kept – The other side of Tenko* (Lewes: Book Guild, 1984), p. 27.

14 Baynes, *Kept*, p. 27.

15 B. Best, *Secret Letters from the Railway: The remarkable record of Charles Steel – a Japanese POW* (Barnsley: Pen and Sword, 2004), p. 32.

16 IWM Documents, Lieutenant Colonel C. Wilkinson, 81/7/1.

17 IWM Documents, Lieutenant Colonel C. Wilkinson, 81/7/1.

18 IWM Documents, Lieutenant Colonel C. Wilkinson, 81/7/1.

19 MBS/1 0374.

20 IWM Documents, Lieutenant Colonel C. Wilkinson, 81/7/1; MBS/4, 'The Optimists present "Rice and Shine"'.

21 IWM Documents, Lieutenant Colonel C. Wilkinson, 81/7/1; IWM Documents, Captain J. A. L. Barratt, 92/14/1.

22 IWM Documents, Lieutenant Colonel C. Wilkinson, 81/7/1.

23 IWM Documents, Brigadier F. J. Dillon, 15/17/1.

24 IWM Documents, Lieutenant Colonel C. Wilkinson, 81/7/1.

25 IWM Documents, Lieutenant Colonel C. Wilkinson, 81/7/1.

26 IWM Documents, Lieutenant Colonel C. Wilkinson, 81/7/1.

27 IWM Documents, Lieutenant Colonel C. Wilkinson, 81/7/1.

28 IWM Documents, Lieutenant Colonel C. Wilkinson, 81/7/1.

29 IWM Documents, Brigadier F. J. Dillon, 15/17/1.

30 IWM Documents, Lieutenant Colonel C. Wilkinson, 81/7/1.

31 IWM Documents, Brigadier F. J. Dillon, 15/17/1.

32 IWM Documents, Lieutenant Colonel C. Wilkinson, 81/7/1.

33 IWM Documents, Lieutenant Colonel C. Wilkinson, 81/7/1.

34 IWM Documents, Lieutenant Colonel C. Wilkinson, 81/7/1.

35 IWM Documents, Lieutenant Colonel C. Wilkinson, 81/7/1.

36 IWM Documents, Captain H. Silman, 15/18/1.

37 R. M. Horner, *Singapore Diary: The hidden journal of Captain R.M. Horner* (Stroud: Spellmount, 2007), p. 36.

38 Horner, *Singapore Diary*, p. 32.

39 IWM Documents, Captain H. Silman, 15/18/1; D. Nelson, *The Story of Changi* (Singapore: Changi Museum, 2001), pp. 51–2.

40 M. Gillies, *The Barbed-Wire University* (London: Aurum, 2012), pp. 198–201.

41 IWM Documents, Captain E. C. Dickson, 84/29/1.

42 IWM Documents, Lieutenant Colonel C. Wilkinson, 81/7/1.

43 G. Burton, *In the Shadow*, p. 29.

44 IWM Documents, Lieutenant Colonel C. Wilkinson, 81/7/1.

45 Coast, *Railroad of Death*, p. 46.

46 E. Cordingly, *Down to Bedrock* (privately published, 2013), p. 52.

47 Coast, *Railroad of Death*, p. 15.

48 Coast, *Railroad of Death*, p. 8.

49 Coast, *Railroad of Death*, p. 22.

50 MBS/1 0382.

51 Horner, *Singapore Diary*, p. 25.

52 MBS/2, Unnamed correspondent to Honor Beckwith-Smith.

53 MBS/2, Unnamed correspondent to Honor Beckwith-Smith.

54 IWM Documents, Captain H. Silman, 15/18/1.

55 IWM Documents, Lieutenant Colonel C. Wilkinson, 81/7/1.

56 IWM Documents, Lieutenant Colonel C. Wilkinson, 81/7/1.

57 IWM Documents, Lieutenant Colonel C. Wilkinson, 81/7/1; MBS/1 0374.

58 IWM Documents, Captain H. Silman, 15/18/1.

59 IWM Documents, Lieutenant Colonel C. Wilkinson, 81/7/1; Captain H. Silman, 15/18/1.

60 IWM Documents, Brigadier F. J. Dillon, 15/17/1.
61 IWM Documents, Captain H. Silman, 15/18/1.
62 IWM Documents, Captain J. A. L. Barratt, 92/14/1.
63 I. Barwick, *In the Shadow of Death: The story of a medic on the Burma Railway 1942-1945* (Barnsley: Pen and Sword, 2005), pp. 46–8.
64 Barwick, *In the Shadow of Death*, p. 62.
65 Barwick, *In the Shadow of Death*, p. 62.
66 IWM Documents, Sir Richard Sharp, 84/29/1.
67 IWM Documents, Sir Richard Sharp, 84/29/1.
68 IWM Documents, Sir Richard Sharp, 84/29/1.
69 IWM Documents, Brigadier F. J. Dillon, 15/17/1.
70 M. Snape, *A Church Militant: Anglicans and the armed forces from Queen Victoria to the Vietnam War* (Oxford: Oxford University Press, 2022), pp. 243–50.
71 IWM Documents, Brigadier F. J. Dillon, 15/17/1.
72 K. Lukowiak, *A Soldier's Song* (London: Secker and Warburg, 1993), p. 174.
73 C. Kinvig, *Scapegoat: General Percival of Singapore* (London: Brassey's, 1996), p. 216; F. Owen, *The Fall of Singapore* (London: Michael Joseph, 1960), p. 204; A. Lane, *70 Days to Hell: A day by day account of the fall of Malaya and Singapore* (Stockport: A. Lane Publishing, 2011), p. 1006; N. Barber, *Sinister Twilight: The fall of Singapore* (London: Fontana, 1973), p. 222.
74 Barber, *Sinister Twilight*, p. 222.
75 IWM Documents, Captain H. Silman, 15/18/1.
76 IWM Documents, 95/9/1 [identity withheld].
77 C. F. Blackater, *Gods without Reason* (London: Eyre and Spottiswoode, 1948), pp. 30–1.
78 E. Gordon, *Miracle on the River Kwai* (London: Collins, 1972), pp. 68–9.
79 Coast, *Railroad of Death*, p. 148.
80 A. Urquhart, *The Forgotten Highlander* (London: Abacus, 2011), p. 103.
81 P. N. Davies, *The Man behind the Bridge: Colonel Toosey and the River Kwai* (London: Bloomsbury, 1991), p. 76.
82 <https://ihl-databases.icrc.org/applic/ihl/ihl.nsf/Article.xsp?action=openDocument&documentId=8DFED95C1E653FDAC12563CD00519226#:~:text=Geneva%2C%2027%20July%201929.%20

Part%20VI%20%3A%20Bureaux,about%20the%20prisoners%20of%20
war%20in%20their%20territory>, accessed 13 June 2022.

83 M. Snape, *God and the British Soldier: Religion and the British Army in the First and Second World Wars* (Abingdon: Routledge, 2005), pp. 173–4.

84 B. MacArthur, *Surviving the Sword: Prisoners of the Japanese 1942–45* (London: Time Warner, 2005), pp. 208–17.

85 J. N. Lewis Bryan, *Churches of the Captivity in Malaya*, (London: SPCK, 1946), p. 18.

86 L. Gibson, *A Wearside Lad in World War II* (privately published, 2005), pp. 47, 100.

87 Cordingly, *Down to Bedrock*, p. 151; 'Captive Christians' in G. Moir (ed.), *Beyond Hatred* (London: Lutterworth Press, 1969), p. 135.

88 R. Braddon, *The Naked Island* (London: Werner Laurie, 1952), p. 130.

89 P. Hartley, *Escape to Captivity* (London: J. M. Dent, 1952), p. vii.

90 IWM Documents, Brigadier T. H. Massy-Beresford, 67/131/1.

91 Gordon, *Miracle on the River Kwai*, p. 69.

92 Cordingly, *Down to Bedrock*, p. 18.

93 G. Burton, *In the Shadow*, p. 29.

94 Cordingly, *Down to Bedrock*, p. 29.

95 Cordingly, *Down to Bedrock*, p. 30.

96 Cordingly, *Down to Bedrock*, p. 30.

97 Cordingly, *Down to Bedrock*, p. 31.

98 Lewis Bryan, *Churches of the Captivity*, p. 24.

99 Lewis Bryan, *Churches of the Captivity*, p. 24.

100 IWM Documents, 95/9/1 [identity withheld].

101 Cordingly, *Down to Bedrock*, p. 33.

102 Lewis Bryan, *Churches of the Captivity*, p. 24.

103 Lewis Bryan, *Churches of the Captivity*, p. 42.

104 Lewis Bryan, *Churches of the Captivity*, p. 42.

105 Lewis Bryan, *Churches of the Captivity*, p. 42.

106 Cordingly, *Down to Bedrock*, p. 36.

107 Lewis Bryan, *Churches of the Captivity*, p. 24; Cordingly, *Down to Bedrock*, pp. 75–6.

108 Alexander, *Sweet Kwai Run Softly*, p. 88; C. Bayly and T. Harper, *Forgotten Armies: Britain's Asian empire and the war with Japan* (London: Penguin, 2005), p. 336.

109 Cordingly, *Down to Bedrock*, p. 76.

110 IWM Documents, Lieutenant Colonel C. Wilkinson, 81/7/1.

111 MBS/1 0374.

112 Cordingly, *Down to Bedrock*, p. 44.

113 Cordingly, *Down to Bedrock*, p. 34.

114 Cordingly, *Down to Bedrock*, p. 35.

115 Cordingly, *Down to Bedrock*, p. 35.

116 Cordingly, *Down to Bedrock*, p. 52.

117 IWM Documents, Brigadier F. J. Dillon, 15/17/1 and 15/17/3.

118 J. Crang, 'The Abolition of Compulsory Church Parades in the British Army', *Journal of Ecclesiastical History*, 56 (2005), pp. 92–106; Snape, *God and the British Soldier*, pp. 139–42; *The Royal Army Chaplains' Department 1796–1953: Clergy under fire* (Woodbridge: Boydell, 2008), pp. 338–9.

119 A. Allport, *Browned Off and Bloody-Minded: The British soldier goes to war 1939–1945* (New Haven, CT: Yale University Press, 2015), pp. 84–5.

120 IWM Documents, Lieutenant Colonel C. Wilkinson, 81/7/1.

121 IWM Documents, 95/9/1 [identity withheld].

122 Barwick, *In the Shadow of Death*, p. 50.

123 R. P. W. Havers, *Reassessing the Japanese Prisoner of War Experience: The Changi POW camp, Singapore, 1942–5* (London: Routledge, 2003), p. 62.

124 Havers, *Reassessing*, p. 55; IWM Documents, Lieutenant Colonel C. Wilkinson, 81/7/1.

125 P. Jowett, *The Japanese Army 1931–45* (Oxford: Osprey, 2002), II, pp. 26, 44.

126 Havers, *Reassessing*, pp. 58–9; TNA CAB 109/199.

127 Havers, *Reassessing*, p. 58.

128 S. J. Flower, 'Captors and Captives on the Burma–Thailand Railway' in B. Moore and K. Fedorowich (eds), *Prisoners of War and Their Captors in World War II* (Oxford: Berg, 1996), p. 153.

129 S. J. Flower, 'British Prisoners of War of the Japanese' in I. Nish and Y. Kibata (eds), *The History of Anglo-Japanese Relations, 1600–2000* (Basingstoke: Macmillan, 2000), p. 139.

130 IWM Documents, Brigadier F. J. Dillon, 15/17/1.

131 Nelson, *Story of Changi*, p. 202; TNA CAB 109/199.

132 TNA CAB 109/199; Nelson, *Story of Changi*, p. 39; IWM Documents, Brigadier F. J. Dillon, 15/17/1.

133 Blackater, *Gods without Reason*, p. 41.

134 Best, *Secret Letters*, p. 41.

135 Barwick, *In the Shadow of Death*, pp. 61–2.

136 TNA CAB 109/199; Nelson, *Story of Changi*, pp. 40–4.

137 Barwick, *In the Shadow of Death*, p. 62.

138 J. Summers, *The Colonel of Tamarkan: Philip Toosey and the bridge on the River Kwai* (London: Simon and Schuster, 2005), pp. 110–11; IWM Documents, Brigadier Sir Philip Toosey, 93/14/1.

139 IWM Documents, Lieutenant Colonel C. Wilkinson, 81/7/1.

140 IWM Documents, Captain H. Silman, 15/18/1.

141 Horner, *Singapore Diary*, p. 37.

142 Horner, *Singapore Diary*, p. 37.

143 Coast, *Railroad of Death*, p. 54.

144 MBS/4, Granville Keane to MBS, 17 July 1942.

145 MBS/4, Rhys Thomas to MBS, 20 July 1942.

146 IWM Documents, Captain H. Silman, 15/18/1; <https://www.chch.ox.ac.uk/fallen-alumni/major-general-merton-beckwith-smith>, accessed 15 June 2022.

147 Havers, *Reassessing*, p. 62.

148 IWM Documents, Captain E. C. Dickson, 84/29/1.

9 Letters from captivity

1 Information provided by Lucy Woodd.

2 MBS/4, Keith Simmons to Honor Beckwith-Smith, 15 December 1945.

3 MBS/3, 22 March 1942.

4 MBS/1 0374.

5 MBS/3, 22 February.

6 MBS/3, 22 February.

7 MBS/3, 22 February.

8 MBS/3, 1 March.

9 MBS/3, 8 March.

10 MBS/3, 8 March.

11 MBS/3, 8 March.

12 MBS/3, 8 March.

13 MBS/3, 14 March.

14 MBS/3, 15 March.

15 MBS/3, 22 March.

16 MBS/3, 22 March.

17 MBS/1 0374, 22 March 1942.

18 MBS/3, 29 March.

19 MBS/3, 5 April.

20 MBS/3, 19 April; MBS/1 0382.

21 MBS/3, 26 April.

22 MBS/3, 26 April.

23 IWM Documents, Captain E. C. Dickson, 84/29/1.

24 MBS/1 0374, 24 April 1942.

25 MBS/3, 26 April.

26 MBS/3, 26 April.

27 MBS/2, Military History Class; MBS/1 0374, 12 May 1942.

28 MBS/3, 10 May.

29 MBS/3, 10 May.

30 MBS/3, 10 May.

31 MBS/3, 24 May.

32 MBS/3, 17 May.

33 MBS/1 0374, 24 May 1942; MBS/3, 31 May.

34 J. Lewis-Stempel, *Six Weeks: The short and gallant life of the British officer in the First World War* (London: Orion, 2010. Kindle edn), loc. 346–56.

35 MBS/1 0374, 4 June 1942.

36 MBS/1 0386.

37 MBS/3, 7 June 1942.

38 MBS/3, 7 June 1942.

39 MBS/3, 14 June.

40 MBS/3, 14 June.

41 MBS/3, 14 June.

42 MBS/3, 21 June.

43 MBS/3, 28 June.

44 MBS/3, 28 June.

45 MBS/3, 28 June.

46 MBS/3, 5 July.

47 MBS/3, 5 July.

48 MBS/3, 5 July.

49 MBS/3, 5 July.

50 MBS/1 0374, 11 July 1942.

51 MBS/3, 12 July.

52 MBS/3, 19 July.

53 MBS/1 0374, 16 July 1942.

54 MBS/3, 26 July.

55 MBS/3, 26 July; MBS/1 0374, 17, 20–21 July 1942.

56 MBS/1 0374, 29 July, 5, 7 August 1942.

57 MBS/3, 2 August.

58 MBS/3, 9 August.

59 MBS/3, 11 September.

10 Karenko

1 MBS/3, 21 June, 9 August.

2 MBS/3, 11 September. For Okasaki, see R. P. W. Havers, *Reassessing the Japanese Prisoner of War Experience: The Changi POW camp, Singapore, 1942–5* (London: Routledge, 2003), pp. 51, 52, 66.

3 MBS/3, 11 September; TNA CAB 109/199.

4 MBS/3, 11 September.

5 MBS/3, 11 September.

6 E. Taylor, *A Cruel Captivity: Prisoners of the Japanese: Their ordeal and the legacy* (Barnsley: Pen and Sword, 2018. Kindle edn), loc. 2169.

7 MBS/3, 11 September; MBS/1 0374, 17–20 August 1942.

8 MBS/3, 11 September.

9 MBS/3, 11 September.

10 I. Dear and M. R. D. Foot (eds), *The Oxford Companion to the Second World War* (Oxford: Oxford University Press, 1995), p. 390.

11 MBS/3, 11 September; TNA CAB 109/199.

12 TNA CAB 109/199.

13 MBS/3, 11 September; TNA CAB 109/199.

14 MBS/3, 11 September.

15 TNA CAB 109/199.

16 MBS/3, 11 September.

17 MBS/3, 11 September; MBS/1 0374, 6 September 1942.

18 TNA CAB 109/199.

19 MBS/3, 11 September; TNA CAB 109/199.

20 MBS/3, 11 September.

21 TNA CAB 109/199.

22 MBS/3, 11 September.

23 MBS/3, 20 September.

24 MBS/3, 20 September.

25 MBS/3, 20 September.

26 MBS/3, 20 September.

27 MBS/3, 20 September.

28 TNA CAB 109/199.

29 G. Daws, *Prisoners of the Japanese* (London: Robson Books, 1995), p. 105.

30 TNA CAB 109/199.

31 MBS/3, 20 September.

32 M. Felton, *The Coolie Generals: Britain's Far Eastern military leaders in Japanese captivity* (Barnsley: Pen and Sword, 2008), p. 132.

33 Felton, *Coolie Generals*, p. 129.

34 Felton, *Coolie Generals*, p. 129; B. MacArthur, *Surviving the Sword: Prisoners of the Japanese 1942–45* (London: Time Warner, 2005), p. 351; Daws, *Prisoners of the Japanese*, p. 107.

35 TNA CAB 109/199.

36 Felton, *Coolie Generals*, p. 130.

37 Daws, *Prisoners of the Japanese*, p. 105.

38 IWM Documents, Brigadier T. H. Massy-Beresford, 67/131/1.

39 Felton, *Coolie Generals*, p. 132; MBS/3, 27 September; MBS/1 0374, 22 September 1942.

40 J. Wainwright, *General Wainwright's Story* (Westport, CT: Greenwood Press, 1970), pp. 183–4.

41 MBS/1 0374, 19 September 1942.

42 Wainwright, *General Wainwright's Story*, p. 184.

43 MBS/3, 4 October.

44 MBS/3, 27 September.

45 MBS/3, 4 October.

46 Wainwright, *General Wainwright's Story*, pp. 182–3.

47 MBS/1 0374, 24 September, 2 October 1942.

48 MBS/3, 11 October.

49 MBS/3, 11 October.

50 MBS/3, 4 October.

51 MBS/3, 11 October; TNA CAB 109/199.

52 MBS/3, 11 October, 18 October.

53 MBS/3, 11 October; MBS/1 0374, 10 October 1942.

54 MBS/3, 18 October.

55 MBS/3, 18 October; MBS/1 0374, 14 October 1942; D. Nelson, *The Story of Changi* (Singapore: Changi Museum, 2001), p. 38.

56 <https://www.forces.net/heritage/history/hell-ships-disastrous-sinking-killed-828-british-prisoners-war>, accessed 25 July 2022.

57 MBS/1 0374, 17 October 1942.

58 MBS/3, 4 October.

59 MBS/3, 8 November.

60 MBS/3, 18 October.

61 MBS/1 0374, 6 November 1942.

62 MBS/3, 8 November.

63 Felton, *Coolie Generals*, pp. 134, 188.

64 Wainwright, *General Wainwright's Story*, p. 188.

65 Wainwright, *General Wainwright's Story*, p. 188.

66 IWM Documents, Brigadier T. H. Massy-Beresford, 67/131/1.

67 *The Times*, 20 November 1942, p. 4.

68 Daws, *Prisoners of the Japanese*, p. 107.

69 MBS/1 0135.

70 Wainwright, *General Wainwright's Story*, p. 188.

71 MBS/1 0397; IWM Documents, Brigadier T. H. Massy-Beresford, 67/131/1.

72 MBS/1 0397.

73 E. Cordingly, *Down to Bedrock* (privately published, 2013), p. 85.

74 MBS/1 0361.

75 MBS/1 0361.

76 IWM Documents, The Revd John Foster Haigh CF, 15/16/1.

77 IWM Documents, The Revd John Foster Haigh CF, 15/16/1.

78 IWM Documents, The Revd John Foster Haigh CF, 15/16/1.

79 IWM Documents, The Revd John Foster Haigh CF, 15/16/1.

80 IWM Documents, The Revd John Foster Haigh CF, 15/16/1.

81 *Gloucestershire Echo*, 19 November 1942, p. 4; *Evening Telegraph and Post*, 19 November 1942, p. 1.

82 *The Times*, 20 November 1942, p. 4.

83 *The Times*, 20 November 1942, p. 7.

84 *The Times*, 20 November 1942, p. 7.

85 *The Times*, 20 November 1942, p. 7.

86 MBS/1 0135.

87 *Evening Telegraph*, 21 November 1942, p. 4.

88 *Evening Telegraph*, 21 November 1942, p. 4.

89 *Derby Evening Telegraph*, 26 November, 1942, p. 2.

90 *Evening Telegraph*, 9 August 1943, p. 8.

91 MBS/1 0421.

92 *The Times*, 1 December 1942, p. 6; Coldstream Guards Archives. Record of Service.

93 MBS/1 0502.

94 MBS/1 0435.

95 MBS/1 0435.

96 MBS/1 0436.

97 MBS/1 0436.

98 IWM Documents, Captain E. C. Dickson, 84/29/1.

99 IWM Documents, P463 Mrs E. Horne, 'The 18th Division Association', May 1948.

100 *The Times*, 10 October 1947, p. 2.

101 *Western Daily Press*, 9 October 1945, p. 1.

102 *Gloucestershire Echo*, 8 October 1945, p. 1.

103 IWM Documents, P463 Mrs E. Horne, SOS Club notebook.

104 *Illustrated London News*, 26 March 1949, pp. 394–5.

105 IWM Documents, P463 Mrs E. Horne, Honor Beckwith-Smith to E. Horne, 9 January 1949.

106 Coldstream Guards Archives. Record of Service.

107 M. Snape, *A Church Militant: Anglicans and the armed forces from Queen Victoria to the Vietnam War* (Oxford: Oxford University Press, 2022), p. 401.

108 <https://www.iwm.org.uk/memorials/item/memorial/75937>; <https://www.iwm.org.uk/memorials/item/memorial/31427>, accessed 19 September 2022.

109 <http://thereturned.co.uk/crosses/pirbright/>, accessed 19 September 2022; Coldstream Guards Archives. Record of Service.

110 <https://www.cwgc.org/find-records/find-war-dead/casualty-details/2220776/merton-beckwith-smith/>, accessed 19 September 2022.

Retrospect

1 <https://www.bbc.co.uk/news/uk-20107903>, accessed 22 September 2022.

2 <https://www.cofepow.org.uk/pow-casualties>, accessed 22 September 2022; *The Times*, 10 October 1947, p. 2.

3 S. J. Flower, 'Memory and the Prisoner of War Experience: The United Kingdom' in K. Hack and K. Blackburn (eds), *Forgotten Captives in Japanese-Occupied Asia* (London: Routledge, 2008), p. 64.

4 Flower, 'Memory', pp. 64–5.

5 E. Taylor, *A Cruel Captivity: Prisoners of the Japanese: Their ordeal and the legacy* (Barnsley: Pen and Sword, 2018. Kindle edn), loc. 186.

6 Taylor, *A Cruel Captivity*, loc. 3195–205; J. Summers, *The Colonel of Tamarkan: Philip Toosey and the bridge on the River Kwai* (London: Simon and Schuster, 2005), pp. 324–5.

7 Flower, 'Memory', p. 64.

8 K. Hack and K. Blackburn, '*The Bridge on the River Kwai* and *King Rat*: Protest and ex-prisoner of war memory in Britain and Australia' in K. Hack and K. Blackburn (eds), *Forgotten Captives in Japanese-Occupied Asia* (London: Routledge, 2008), pp. 152–62; Summers, *Colonel of Tamarkan*, p. 375; P. N. Davies, *The Man behind the Bridge: Colonel Toosey and the River Kwai* (London: Bloomsbury, 1991), p. 205.

9 A. Wavell, *Generals and Generalship* (London: The Times, 1941), pp. 1–19.

Bibliography

Archival sources

Coldstream Guards Archives, Wellington Barracks
Record of Service

Imperial War Museum Department of Documents
Captain J. A. L. Barratt, 92/14/1
Captain E. C. Dickson, 84/29/1
Brigadier F. J. Dillon, 15/17/1, 3
The Revd John Foster Haigh CF, 15/16/1
Mrs E. Horne, P463
Brigadier T. H. Massy-Beresford, 67/131/1
Sir Richard Sharp, 84/29/1
Captain H. Silman, 15/18/1
Brigadier Sir Philip Toosey, 93/14/1–2, 4–5, 7
Lieutenant Colonel C. Wilkinson, 81/7/1
Identity withheld, 95/9/1

Imperial War Museum, Sound Archive
Arthur John Flint, 899

Merton Beckwith-Smith papers
MBS/1 – Main series 0001–0517
MBS/2 – Supplementary series
MBS/3 – Unposted letters to HBS (1942)
MBS/4 – Lucy Woodd papers

The National Archives
CAB 66/24/7

CAB 79/15, 55
CAB 106/70–1
CAB 109/199
WO 166/465–7, 470–1, 473, 477
WO 95/1263/1
WO 373/89/78

Royal Archives, Windsor Castle
EDW/PRIV/MAIN/A/3247, 3371, 3387, 3417, 3492, 3506

Welsh Guards Archives, Wellington Barracks
Record of Service

Newspapers and periodicals
Aberdeen Journal
Aberdeen Press and Journal
Daily Mail
Daily Mirror
Daily Telegraph
Derby Evening Telegraph
Devon and Exeter Gazette
Edinburgh Gazette
[Dundee] Evening Telegraph
[Dundee] Evening Telegraph and Post
Gloucestershire Echo
Illustrated London News
Indian Army List
London Gazette
Manchester Courier and Lancashire General Advertiser
Sunday Pictorial
The Times
The Times of India
Welsh Guards Comrades' Association Annual Report
Western Daily Press
Western Gazette

Published primary sources

Adair, A., *A Guards' General: The memoirs of Major General Sir Allan Adair* (London: Hamish Hamilton, 1986)

Alexander, S., *Sweet Kwai Run Softly* (Bristol: Merriotts Press, 1995)

Bailey, K., *Face of Adversity: Life as a prisoner of war* (Privately published, 2009)

Barwick, I., *In the Shadow of Death: The story of a medic on the Burma Railway 1942–945* (Barnsley: Pen and Sword, 2005)

Best, B. (ed.), *Secret Letters from the Railway: The remarkable record of Charles Steel – a Japanese POW* (Barnsley: Pen and Sword, 2004)

Blackater, C. F., *Gods without Reason* (London: Eyre and Spottiswoode, 1948)

Braddon, R., *The Naked Island* (London: Werner Laurie, 1952)

Burton, G., *In the Shadow* (Warrington: Mackie and Co., 1946)

Burton, R., *Railway of Hell* (Barnsley: Pen and Sword, 2010)

Chalker, J. B., *Burma Railway Artist* (London: Leo Cooper, 1994)

Coast, J., *Railroad of Death* (London: Commodore Press, 1946)

Composition of Headquarters. British Armies in France (January 1919)

Cordingly, E., 'Captive Christians' in G. Moir (ed.), *Beyond Hatred* (London: Lutterworth Press, 1969)

——*Down to Bedrock* (privately published, 2013)

Edward, Duke of Windsor, *A King's Story* (New York: G. P. Putnam's Sons, 1951)

Gordon, E., *Miracle on the River Kwai* (London: Collins, 1972)

Gordon Bennett, H., *The Fall of Singapore* (Dehradun: Natraj Publishers, 1990)

Hartley, P., *Escape to Captivity* (London: J. M. Dent, 1952)

Horner, R. M., *Singapore Diary: The hidden journal of Captain R.M. Horner* (Stroud: Spellmount, 2007)

Howard, M., *Captain Professor* (London: Continuum, 2006)

Knights, A. E., *Singapore and the Thailand–Burma Railway* (Bury St Edmunds: Arena Books, 2013)

Lewis Bryan, J. N., *Churches of the Captivity in Malaya* (London: SPCK, 1946)

List of Etonians Who Fought in the Great War MCMXIV–MCMXIX (London: Eton College, 1921)

Lukowiak, K., *A Soldier's Song* (London: Secker and Warburg, 1993)

Montgomery, B. L., *The Memoirs of Field-Marshal the Viscount Montgomery of Alamein* (London: Fontana, 1960)

Nixon, J. and Smith, B. A., *Mother's Apple Pie* (Stockport: A. Lane Publications, 2006)

Palmer, S. (ed.), *Prisoners on the Kwai: Memoirs of Dr Harold Churchill* (Dereham: Larks Press, 2005)

Quilter, D. C. (ed.), *No Dishonourable Name* (London: William Clowes, 1947)

Searle, R., *To the Kwai and Back* (London: Collins, 1986)

Todman, D. (ed.), *War Diaries: Field Marshal Lord Alanbrooke* (London: Weidenfeld and Nicolson, 2001)

Urquhart, A., *The Forgotten Highlander* (London: Abacus, 2011)

Wainwright, J., *General Wainwright's Story* (Westport, CT: Greenwood Press, 1970)

Watt, I., 'The Liberty of the Prison' in G. Moir (ed.), *Beyond Hatred* (London: Lutterworth Press, 1969)

Wavell, A., *Generals and Generalship* (London: The Times, 1941)

Williamson, P., Taylor, S., Raffe, A. and Mears, N. (eds), *National Prayers: Special worship since the Reformation. Volume 3. Worship for National and Royal Occasions in the United Kingdom, 1871–2016*, Church of England Record Society, 26 (Woodbridge: Boydell Press, 2020)

Secondary sources

Allen, L., *Singapore 1941–1942* (London: Frank Cass, 1993)

Allport, A., *Browned Off and Bloody-Minded: The British soldier goes to war 1939–1945* (New Haven, CT: Yale University Press, 2015)

Atkin, R., *Pillar of Fire: Dunkirk 1940* (Edinburgh: Birlinn, 2000)

Barber, N., *Sinister Twilight: The fall of Singapore* (London: Fontana, 1973)

Barnett, C., *Britain and Her Army: A military, political and social history of the British Army, 1509–1970* (London: Cassell, 2000)

Bayly, C. and Harper, T., *Forgotten Armies: Britain's Asian empire and the war with Japan* (London: Penguin, 2005)

Baynes, L. L., *Kept – The Other Side of Tenko* (Lewes: Book Guild, 1984)

Beach, J., 'Soldier Education in the British Army, 1920–2007', *History of Education*, 37 (2008), 679–99

Beckett, I., Bowman, T. and Connelly, M., *The British Army and the First World War* (Cambridge: Cambridge University Press, 2017)

Beevor, A., *The Second World War* (London: Weidenfeld and Nicolson, 2012)

Blaxland, G., *Destination Dunkirk: The story of Gort's army* (Barnsley: Pen and Sword, 2018)

Bond, B., 'The Army between the Two World Wars' in D. Chandler and I. F. W. Beckett (eds), *The Oxford Illustrated History of the British Army* (Oxford: Oxford University Press, 1994)

—— 'The British Field Force in France and Belgium, 1939–40' in P. Addison and A. Calder (eds), *Time to Kill: The soldier's experience of war in the West 1939–1945* (London: Pimlico, 1997)

—— 'Gort' in J. Keegan (ed.), *Churchill's Generals* (London: Warner Books, 1992)

—— 'Ironside' in J. Keegan (ed.), *Churchill's Generals* (London: Warner Books, 1992)

—— 'Preparing the Field Force, February 1939 – May 1940' in B. Bond and M. D. Taylor (eds), *The Battle of France and Flanders 1940: Sixty Years On* (Barnsley: Leo Cooper, 2001)

Bowman, T. and Connelly, M., *The Edwardian Army: Recruiting, training, and deploying the British Army 1902–1914* (Oxford: Oxford University Press, 2012)

Bridge, C., 'Crisis of Command: Major-General Gordon Bennett and British military effectiveness in the Malayan Campaign, 1941–42' in B. Bond and K. Tachikawa (eds), *British and Japanese Military Leadership in the Far Eastern War 1941–1945* (London: Frank Cass, 2004)

Brown, C., *Religion and Society in Twentieth-Century Britain* (London: Routledge, 2006)

Brune, P., *Descent into Hell: The fall of Singapore – Pudu and Changi – the Thai–Burma Railway* (Sydney: Allen and Unwin, 2014)

Burleigh, M., *Moral Combat: A history of World War II* (London: HarperCollins, 2010)

Chappell, M., *British Battle Insignia 1 1914–18* (London: Osprey, 1986)

Churchill, A., *Blood and Thunder: The boys of Eton College and the First World War* (Stroud: History Press, 2014)

Churchill, W. S., *The Second World War. Volume 4. The Hinge of Fate* (London: Cassell, 1951)

Coldstream Guards Notes on Regimental Customs and Traditions (London, 1944)

Connelly, M., 'The Issue of Surrender in the Malayan Campaign' in H. Afflerbach and H. Strachan (eds), *How Fighting Ends: A history of surrender* (Oxford: Oxford University Press, 2012)

Coox, A. D., 'The Effectiveness of the Japanese Military Establishment in the Second World War' in W. Murray and A. R. Millett (eds), *Military Effectiveness. Volume 3. The Second World War* (Cambridge: Cambridge University Press, 2010)

Crang, J., 'The Abolition of Compulsory Church Parades in the British Army', *Journal of Ecclesiastical History*, 56 (2005), 92–106

—— 'The Defence of the Dunkirk Perimeter' in B. Bond and M. D. Taylor (eds), *The Battle of France and Flanders 1940: Sixty Years On* (Barnsley: Leo Cooper, 2001)

Danchev, A., 'The Army and the Home Front, 1939–1945' in D. Chandler and I. F. W. Beckett (eds), *The Oxford Illustrated History of the British Army* (Oxford: Oxford University Press, 1994)

Davies, P. N., *The Man behind the Bridge: Colonel Toosey and the River Kwai* (London: Bloomsbury, 1991)

Daws, G., *Prisoners of the Japanese* (London: Robson Books, 1995)

Doughty, S., *The Guards Came Through: An illustrated history of the Guards in the Great War* (London: Third Millennium, 2016)

Drea, E., *Japan's Imperial Army* (Lawrence, KS: University Press of Kansas, 2009)

Ellis, L. F., *The War in France and Flanders 1939–1940* (London: HMSO, 1953)

Elphick, P., *Singapore: The pregnable fortress* (London: Coronet, 1995)

Falk, S. L., *Seventy Days to Singapore: The Malayan Campaign, 1941–1942* (London: Robert Hale, 1975)

Farrell, B., *The Defence and Fall of Singapore* (Singapore: Monsoon Books, 2015)

Felton, M., *The Coolie Generals: Britain's Far Eastern military leaders in Japanese captivity* (Barnsley: Pen and Sword, 2008)

Fennell, J., *Fighting the People's War: The British and Commonwealth Armies and the Second World War* (Cambridge: Cambridge University Press, 2019)

Flower, S. J., 'British Prisoners of War of the Japanese' in I. Nish and Y. Kibata (eds), *The History of Anglo-Japanese Relations, 1600–2000* (Basingstoke: Macmillan, 2000)

—— 'Captors and Captives on the Burma–Thailand Railway' in B. Moore and K. Fedorowich (eds), *Prisoners of War and Their Captors in World War II* (Oxford: Berg, 1996)

—— 'Memory and the Prisoner of War Experience: The United Kingdom' in K. Hack and K. Blackburn (eds), *Forgotten Captives in Japanese-Occupied Asia* (London: Routledge, 2008)

Forty, G., *British Army Handbook 1939–1945* (Stroud: Sutton, 2002)

Fraser, D., 'Alanbrooke' in J. Keegan (ed.), *Churchill's Generals* (London: Warner Books, 1992)

—— *And We Shall Shock Them: The British Army in the Second World War* (London: Cassell, 1999)

French, D., *Raising Churchill's Army: The British Army and the war against Germany 1919–1945* (Oxford: Oxford University Press, 2000)

Furuya, H., 'Japan's Racial Identity in the Second World War: The cultural context of Japanese treatment of POWs' in P. Towle, M. Kosuge and Y. Kibata (eds), *Japanese Prisoners of War* (London: Hambledon and London, 2000)

Fussell, P., *Wartime: Understanding and behavior in the Second World War* (New York: Oxford University Press, 1990)

Gibson, L., *A Wearside Lad in World War II* (privately published, 2005)

Gillies, M., *The Barbed-Wire University* (London: Aurum, 2012)

Glover, E. M., *In 70 Days: The story of the Japanese campaign in British Malaya* (London: Frederick Muller Ltd, 1946)

Grehan, J., *Dunkirk: Nine days that saved an army* (Barnsley: Frontline Books, 2018)

Hack, K. and Blackburn, K., 'The Bridge on the River Kwai and King Rat: Protest and ex-prisoner of war memory in Britain and Australia' in K. Hack and K. Blackburn (eds), *Forgotten Captives in Japanese-Occupied Asia* (London: Routledge, 2008)

—— *Did Singapore Have to Fall? Churchill and the impregnable fortress* (London: Routledge, 2004) Harris, P., *The Men Who Planned the War: A study of the staff of the British Army on the Western Front, 1914–1918* (London: Routledge, 2017)

Hastings, M., *All Hell Let Loose: The world at war 1939–1945* (London: HarperCollins, 2011)

Hata, I., 'From Consideration to Contempt: The changing nature of Japanese military and popular perceptions of prisoners of war through the ages' in B. Moore and K. Fedorowich (eds), *Prisoners of War and Their Captors in World War II* (Oxford: Berg, 1996)

Havers, R. P. W., *Reassessing the Japanese Prisoner of War Experience: The Changi POW camp, Singapore, 1942–5* (London: Routledge, 2003)

Hodgkinson, P., 'The Infantry Battalion Commanding Officers of the BEF' in S. Jones (ed.), *Stemming the Tide: Officers and leadership in the British Expeditionary Force 1914* (Solihull: Helion, 2013)

Holden Reid, B., 'Alexander' in J. Keegan (ed.), *Churchill's Generals* (London: Warner Books, 1992)

Holmes, R., *Tommy: The British soldier on the Western Front 1914–1918* (London: HarperCollins, 2004)

Ion, H., 'Brass Hats behind Bamboo Palisades: Senior officer POWs in Singapore, Taiwan, and Manchukuo, 1942–45', *Canadian Journal of History*, 46 (2011), 303–31

Jackson, A., *The British Empire and the Second World War* (London: Continuum, 2006)

Johnson, R., 'Small Wars and Internal Security: The Army in India, 1936–1946' in A. Jeffreys and P. Rose (eds), *The Indian Army, 1939–47* (Farnham: Ashgate, 2012)

Jones, S., '"The Demon": Brigadier-General Charles FitzClarence V.C.' in S. Jones (ed.), *Stemming the Tide: Officers and leadership in the British Expeditionary Force 1914* (Solihull: Helion, 2013)

Jowett, P., *The Japanese Army 1931–45* (Oxford: Osprey, 2002), 2 vols

Keegan, J., *The Second World War* (London: Hutchinson, 1989)

Kibata, Y., 'Japanese Treatment of British Prisoners: The historical context' in P. Towle, M. Kosuge and Y. Kibata (eds), *Japanese Prisoners of War* (London: Hambledon and London, 2000)

Kinvig, C., 'General Percival and the Fall of Singapore' in B. Farrell and S. Hunter (eds), *Sixty Years On: The fall of Singapore revisited* (Singapore: Eastern Universities Press, 2002)

——*River Kwai Railway* (London: Brassey's, 1992)

——*Scapegoat: General Percival of Singapore* (London: Brassey's, 1996)

Kiyoshi, I., 'Anglo-Japanese Relations, 1941–45' in I. Nish and Y. Kibata (eds), *The History of Anglo-Japanese Relations, 1600–2000* (Basingstoke: Macmillan, 2000)

Lane, A., *70 Days to Hell: A day by day account of the fall of Malaya and Singapore* (Stockport: A. Lane Publishing, 2011)

Langley, J. M., *Fight Another Day* (London: Collins, 1974)

Lewis-Stempel, J., *Six Weeks: The short and gallant life of the British officer in the First World War* (London: Orion, 2010. Kindle edn)

Lord, W., *The Miracle of Dunkirk* (New York: Open Road Integrated Media, 2017)

MacArthur, B., *Surviving the Sword: Prisoners of the Japanese 1942–45* (London: Time Warner, 2005)

Messenger, C., *Call-to-Arms: The British Army 1914–18* (London: Cassell, 2006)

Nelson, D., *The Story of Changi* (Singapore: Changi Museum, 2001)

Owen, F., *The Fall of Singapore* (London: Michael Joseph, 1960)

Parker, P., *The Old Lie: The Great War and the public school ethos* (London: Hambledon Continuum, 2007)

Retallack, J., *The Welsh Guards* (London: Warne, 1981)

Rose, P., 'Indian Army Command Culture and the North West Frontier, 1919–1939' in A. Jeffreys and P. Rose (eds), *The Indian Army, 1939–47* (Farnham: Ashgate, 2012)

Ross-of-Bladensburg, J., *The Coldstream Guards 1914–1918* (Oxford: Oxford University Press, 1928), 2 vols

Royle, T., *Bearskins, Bayonets and Body Armour: Welsh Guards 1915–2015* (Barnsley: Frontline Books, 2015)

Sebag-Montefiore, H., *Dunkirk: Fight to the last man* (London: Penguin, 2007. Kindle edn)

Seldon, A. and Walsh, D., *Public Schools and the Great War: The generation lost* (Barnsley: Pen and Sword, 2013. Kindle edn)

Sharp, J. C., 'Impregnable Fortress: A brief collection of orders, articles and verses on the fall of Singapore (1942)' (Birmingham, 1947)

Sheffield, G., *Leadership in the Trenches: Officer–man relations, morale and discipline in the British Army in the era of the First World War* (Basingstoke: Macmillan, 1999)

Smith, C., *Singapore Burning* (London: Penguin, 2006)

Smyth, J., *Leadership in War, 1939–1945* (Newton Abbot: David and Charles, 1975)

Snape, M., *A Church Militant: Anglicans and the armed forces from Queen Victoria to the Vietnam War* (Oxford: Oxford University Press, 2022)

——*God and the British Soldier: Religion and the British Army in the First and Second World Wars* (Abingdon: Routledge, 2005)

——*The Royal Army Chaplains' Department 1796–1953: Clergy under fire* (Woodbridge: Boydell, 2008)

——'Sir Douglas Haig, Religion, and the British Expeditionary Force on the Western Front' in P. McFarland and H. Pym (eds), *Scots in Great War London* (Warwick: Helion, 2018)

——'Twilight of the Padres: The end of British military chaplaincy in India' in T. Brekke and V. Tikhonov (eds), *Military Chaplaincy in an Era of Religious Pluralism: Military–religious nexus in Asia, Europe, and USA* (New Delhi: Oxford University Press, 2017)

Storey, N., *To Singapore and Beyond: A brief history of the 4th, 5th and 6th Battalions, Royal Norfolk Regiment, from 1939 to 1945* (Norwich: Holyboy Publications, 1992)

Sturma, M., 'Japanese Treatment of Allied Prisoners during the Second World War: Evaluating the death toll', *Journal of Contemporary History*, 55 (2020), 514–34.

Summers, J., *The Colonel of Tamarkan: Philip Toosey and the bridge on the River Kwai* (London: Simon and Schuster, 2005)

Taylor, E., *A Cruel Captivity: Prisoners of the Japanese: Their ordeal and the legacy* (Barnsley: Pen and Sword, 2018. Kindle edn)

Tett, D., *A Postal History of the Prisoners of War and Civilian Internees in East Asia during the Second World War. Volume 1: Singapore and Malaya 1942–1945. The Changi connection* (Bristol: Stuart Rossiter Trust Fund, 2002)

Thompson, J., *Dunkirk: Retreat to victory* (London: Pan, 2009. Kindle edn)

Todman, D., *Britain's War, Volume I: Into battle, 1937–1941* (London: Allen Lane, 2016)

——*Britain's War, Volume II: A new world, 1942–1947* (London: Allen Lane, 2020. Kindle edn)

Townsend, S. C., 'Culture, Race and Power in Japan's Wartime Empire' in P. Towle, M. Kosuge and Y. Kibata (eds), *Japanese Prisoners of War* (London: Hambledon and London, 2000)

Woodburn Kirby, S., *The War against Japan. Volume I. The Loss of Singapore* (London: HMSO, 1957)

Ziegler, P., *King Edward VIII: The official biography* (London: Collins, 1990)

Reference works

Becke, A. F. (ed.), *Order of Battle of Divisions. Part I: The regular British divisions* (London: HMSO, 1935)

Dear, I. and Foot, M. R. D. (eds), *The Oxford Companion to the Second World War* (Oxford: Oxford University Press, 1995)

Jolsen, H. F. (ed.), *Orders of Battle: Second World War 1939–1945* (London: HMSO, 1960)

Mead, R., *Churchill's Lions: A biographical guide to the key British generals of World War II* (London: Spellmount, 2007)

Oxford Dictionary of National Biography

Vance, J. F. (ed.), *Encyclopedia of Prisoners of War and Internment* (Santa Barbara, CA: ABC-CLIO, 2000)

Websites

<https://www.bbc.co.uk/news/uk-20107903>

<https://www.chch.ox.ac.uk/fallen-alumni/major-general-merton-beckwith-smith>

<https://www.cofepow.org.uk/armed-forces-stories-list/the-story-of-changi>

<https://www.cwgc.org>

<https://dorsetinthegreatwar.co.uk/war-memorials/moor-crichel-long-crichel-witchampton-war-memorial/>

<https://www.forces.net/heritage/history/hell-ships-disastrous-sinking-killed-828-british-prisoners-war>

<householdbrigade2614.co.uk>

<https://ihl-databases.icrc.org/applic/ihl/ihl.nsf/Article.xsp?action=openDocument&documentId=8DFED95C1E653FDAC12563CD00519226#:~:text=Geneva%2C%2027%20July%201929.%20Part%20VI%20%3A%20Bureaux,about%20the%20prisoners%20of%20war%20in%20their%20territory>

<https://www.iwm.org.uk/memorials/>

<http://places.galwaylibrary.ie/history/chapter136.html>

<http://www.pwsts.org.uk/limehouse.htm>

<http://www.thepeerage.com/p16054.htm#i160532>

<http://thereturned.co.uk/>

<http://www.whoisgeorgemills.com/2010/03/eastbourne-local-history-society-comes.html>

Acknowledgements

This book is the product of the generosity and enthusiasm of many individuals. It would never have been possible without the help of Harry Henderson, John Beckwith-Smith, Anne Beckwith-Smith, Josie Reed, Lucy Woodd and Sir Ralph Waller. I extend to them my sincere thanks for their encouragement, support and collaboration. At SPCK, Philip Law, Joy Tibbs and Drew Stanley have been most kind and helpful, and Kay Webb of the Farmington Trust has been very efficient in administering the generous grant that enabled the completion of this project.

I also owe a debt of gratitude to Christopher Enraght-Moody, the regimental archivist of the Welsh Guards, to Colonel Simon Vandeleur, the regimental adjutant of the Coldstream Guards, and to Colonel Tom Bonas, the regimental adjutant of the Welsh Guards, for their generous help with my research and their kind permission to use material in their respective regimental archives. Likewise, I am indebted to Sarah Paterson of the Imperial War Museum, who facilitated access to its Department of Documents during the latter stages of the COVID-19 pandemic.

My warm thanks are also due to those who gave permission to use and cite material in their possession, or material for which they are the copyright holders, especially Harry Henderson, John Beckwith-Smith, Anne Beckwith-Smith, Lucy Woodd, Christopher Massy-Beresford and Lucinda Fraser. Every effort has been made to trace copyright holders, and I offer my apologies in advance for any omissions. The author and publishers will be pleased to add any necessary acknowledgements to subsequent editions of this book.

In broader professional terms, I am very fortunate to be a member of the Department of Theology and Religion at Durham University, and honoured to be an ecumenical lay canon of Durham Cathedral. I extend my thanks and appreciation to my colleagues at both institutions. For much academic stimulus over the years, I would also like to thank the many participants at the annual Amport (now Beckett House) Conference on war and religion in the modern world, and my postgraduate research students who have worked (and are working) in this expanding field. The Revd Andrew Totten and David Blake of the Royal Army Chaplains' Museum, the Revd Canon Paul Wright, Professor Bill Jacob, Professor Hugh McLeod, the Venerable Stephen Robbins and Dr Victoria Henshaw have, as ever, proved interested, patient and supportive interlocutors.

Last but by no means least, my thanks are due to Rachel, Katy, Helena (and Megsy), and to my brothers, John and Andrew, for always being there.

Index

ABDA (American-British-Dutch-Australian)
    Command 123–4
Aberarder, Invernesshire 2
Aldridge, Canon 1
Alexander, Major-General Harold 28
    career of 40
    commands 1st Division 40–1
    commends Merton for Dunkirk leadership
        67–8
    distant news of 234
    Dunkirk and 60, 62
    Merton's comments on 52
    nickname 73–4
Alexander, Stephen
    on artillery performance 91, 92
    on Bishop Wilson 194
    Merton in Changi 175
    prison camp and army 176
    'service in the field' 97
    training for jungle 114
Allen, Louis 117
Allport, Alan
    on BEF return to France 43
    volunteers and conscripts 71, 72
Anderson, Major-General Kenneth 66, 74
Ando, Lt-General 232
Anglo-Irish War 20
Arms and the Man (Shaw) 177
Army Bureau of Current Affairs (ABCA) 94
Arnold, Thomas 4
Auchinleck, Sir Claude 73, 234
Australia
    Battle of Singapore 135, 137, 140, 141, 147
    fear of Japanese invasion 123
    Selarang area POW camp 163
    Singapore and 122
Austria, *Anschluss* 35

Backhouse, Brigadier Edward H. W.

on Merton's death 237
    tributes to Merton 236–8
Backhouse, Eileen 241
Bailey, Kenneth
    on fall of Singapore 155
    rumours about Alexandra Hospital 162
    on training 93, 99
    on US Navy ships 103
    on voyage to Singapore 113, 126
Bankier, Colonel A. M. 243
Barber, Noel 187
Barker, Lt.-General Michael 56–7
Barne, George, Bishop of Lahore 32
Barnett, Correlli 73
Barratt, Captain John 184
Barstow, Major-General A. E. 157
Barwick, Idris
    on Changi routine 184–5
    on fall of Singapore 154
    on Merton's departure 199
    resistance to church parades 196
Battye, Major P. L. M. 20
Bayly, Christopher 167
Baynes, L. L.
    on discipline in camp 176
    fall of Singapore 154
    Kept - The Other Side of Tenko 190
    rumours in Changi 172
    writing home as POW 159
Beamish, Captain Tufton
    on Australian resistance 147
    in India 237
    Singapore's coastal defences 130
    size of 18th Division in Singapore 153
Beckwith-Smith, Beckwith (father) 1
Beckwith-Smith, Georgina (nèe Butler Moore,
    aka Persse, mother)
    character of 2–3
    death of 2, 245

Index